The Panoramic Language of God

THE COMPLETE SEER SERIES

Fred Raynaud

Dream Weaver Publication

ANNA MARIA, FLORIDA

Copyright © 2015 by Fred L. Raynaud.

All rights reserved. This book is protected by the copyright laws of the United States of America. This book may not be copied or reprinted for commercial gain or profit. The use of short quotations or occasional page copying for personal or group study is permitted and encouraged. Permission will be granted upon request. Unless otherwise identified, Scripture quotations taken from the New King James Version. Scripture taken from the New King James Version®. Copyright © 1982 by Thomas Nelson, Inc. Used by permission. All rights reserved. Emphasis within Scripture quotations are the author's own. Please note that the author capitalizes certain pronouns in Scripture that refer to the Father, Son, and Holy Spirit, and may differ from some authors and publishers' styles. Take note that the name satan and related names are not capitalized. The author chooses not to acknowledge him, even to the point of violating grammatical rules.

F. L. Raynaud/Dream Weaver Publications
P.O. Box 503
Anna Maria, FL, 34216

www.DreamWeaverBooks.com
www.SeersGift.com

Book Layout ©2015 Dream Weaver Books
Quantity sales. Special discounts are available on quantity purchases by corporations, associations, and others. For details, contact the "Special Sales Department" at our website.

The Panoramic Language of God, The Complete Seer Series/Fred Raynaud. —1st ed.
ISBN 978-0-9905959-5-3

Contents

The Panoramic Language of God 1
Acknowledgement 13
   Preface 19
      The Populist Perspective 22
      Why this Book 23
      The Days in Which We Live 23
      Who is this Book For? 25
      The Seer Gift is for You 27
Part 1: The Seer's Gift 31
   Seeing Cross-eyed 33
      Understanding the Power of Rest 39
What is a Seer? 45
      Modalities 45
      The Seer 48
How the Seer Operates 49
Metaphorical Language 53
      To Illustrate 54
      Similitudes and Symbolism 56
Types of Seeing 61
      Seeing 61
Dream Camps 62
External Seeing 62
Angelic and Visions 63
Trances 65
      Illustrative Example of Visions in a Trance 67
Preparing a Banquet Table 67

Tears of Healing	69
Temple Worship	72
Can I See?	81
How can I tell if someone operates as a seer?	81
How can I activate my seer senses?	82
What if I can't see?	85
The Language of Visions and Dreams	89
Redeemed Imagination	94
God Speaks	101
Revelatory Gifts	105
The Spirit of Revelation	108
Testing and Interpreting Visionary Language	111
System Check	113
Listening	114
Sources of Revelation	115
The Holy Spirit	116
demonic Realm	120
Mixture	123
Testing revelation	125
Interpreting	127
Application	128
The Seer and the Gifts	129
Tri-unity of Gifting	131
Gifts of the Father	131
Gifts of the Holy Spirit	132
Gifts of the Son – The Office Gifts	134
Aurora	139

Let me illustrate.. 146
The Bride 149
Part 2: The Seer & Healing 159
  Thy Kingdom Come 161
    The Kingdom 161
    The Model for Team Prayer 170
  Healing and the Kingdom 173
    Healing is Part of the Kingdom 174
    How did Jesus Heal? 180
  Compassion and Mercy 182
  Jesus is our model 183
  Authority and Power 187
  He uses us 189
  Healing & Seeing 195
    Illustrative Example 201
  Say unto that Mountain, Flee, ... 201
  Directional Seeing 207
    Seeing What to Do 207
    Illustrative Examples 211
  Cradle in the wind 211
  An extension of My hands 214
  Healing in General 217
    The Seer and Healing 217
    Illustrative Example 218
  X-Ray 218
  Inner Healing 223
  Sozo 233
    Visions, Dreams, and the Ministry of Sozo 235

Illustrative Examples	236
Francis and Judith MacNutt	236
School Days	239
Sozo, My Love encounter with the Godhead	245
Healing of the Demonized	257
Foundational Truths	260
It's not just the lost!	263
Heaven, Angels, and the Demonic	267
Angels	269
Holy Angels	272
Evil Angels	273
Confined Fallen Angels	273
Free evil angels	275
Shifting Atmospheres	277
What are Demons?	281
demons and Necromancy	284
Revelatory Insight	287
Dealing with demons	303
Deliverance	306
The effect of demonic oppression	307
Personal Preparation and the Deliverance Process	308
My Story	313
Part 3: The Seer & Prophecy	**335**
The Seer & Prophecy	337
Prophecy Defined	338
The Prophetic Person	342
How to deal with and nurture prophetic people	346
Types of Prophetic People	347

In the Old Testament 347
In the New Testament 351
Prophetic Layers 355
Simple Prophecy 357
Prophetic Gifting 357
Prophetic Ministry 358
Office of Prophet 358
Growing as a prophet 358
    Forms of Prophecy 360
The Prophetic Oracle 360
Prophetic Exhortation 362
The Prophetic Prayer 363
The Prophetic Song 363
Personal Prophecy 364
Prophetic Action 366
Prophetic Dreams & Visions 369
    Prophetic Seeing 370
    Illustrative Examples 372
Illustration One: Personal Prophecy 372
Illustration Two: Personal Prophecy 373
Illustration Three: Personal Prophecy 375
    Prophecy and Directional Seeing 376
Illustration One – Directional Seeing 376
    Prophecy and the Gathered Assembly 378
Illustration One – Prophecy and the Gathered Assembly 379
Illustration Two – Prophecy and the Gathered Assembly 380

Gifts and Callings 383
Illustration One 384
   Summary 385
It takes faith 386
Guidelines for Prophetic Ministry 389
   Convergence Council's Principles, Ethics, and Protocols 391
The Preamble 392
Biblical Principles Concerning Ethics and Protocols Relating to New Testament Prophetic Ministry 393

Part 4: Words to the Church 403
Section Introduction 405
   Introduction 405
Season of the Corn 407
Let it Rain 415
   The Call of Jesus in this Hour 423
God's strategy: You 426
Mercy Drops are Falling 433
The House of Bread 447
The Vision of the Bread of Life 456
Coffeehouse of Hope 461
   The Parable... Given in a Dream 462
The story and its interpretation, ... 465
The Shaking 469
The Anointing 477
Thick Oil for a Chosen Generation 483
Drink, My Bride 495
Verily, Verily 511
Last Thought 525

Part 5: The Seer's Guide to Symbolism 535
Similitudes, Metaphors, & Symbolism 537

A 541
- Angels 541
- Animals 544
- Aroma 546
- Art 547
- Authority Figures 547

B 551
- Birth, Pregnancy, Babies, and Children 551
- Beverages, Drinking 553
- Birds 554
- Blood 556
- Body Parts 556
- Books, Scrolls, Letters, Writing 560
- Being Bound 561
- Bugs, Insects 561
- Buildings & Houses 562

C 565
- Celebration 565
- Cleaning & Cleaning Agents 565
- Colors 565
- Communication 567
- Confinement 567
- Construction, Building Something 568
- Containers (all kinds) 568
- Cooking 570
- Covering and Mantles 571
- Crime 571

- Crushed, Carried, Trapped, Stuck, Smothered 572

D 575
- Digging 575
- Direction 575
- Doors, Gates, Windows 576

E-F 579
- Education 579
- Emotions, Feelings, Reactions 580
- Farming, Planting, Plowing, Harvest 580
- Finance and Provision 581
- Fire 581
- Fish and Fishing 582
- Flying 583
- Food 583

G 587
- Garments and Clothing 587
- The importance of clothing type: 587
- Gems, Jewels, Jewelry 589
- Geographic, Nations, and Cities 590
- Glory of God 590

H-K 593
- Hell 593
- Homelessness 593
- Hygiene 594
- Intersession, Watching 594
- Keys 595

L 597
- Ladders, Steps, and Stairs 597

- Land, Soil, Deserts, Valleys 598
- Light, Electricity, Lightning 600

M 603
- Medical, Sickness, Healing 603
- Metal 604
- Mirrors, Pictures 604
- Music and Worship 605

N 607
- Numbers 607
- Numeric perfection 611

O-P 615
- Occult and Witchcraft 615
- Oil 615
- Plant Life 616

Q-R 621
- Roads, Trails & Potholes 621
- Rocks, Walls 622
- Royalty 622
- Running 623

S 625
- Seas, Lakes, Rivers, and Streams 625
- Seasons 628
- Sight, Eyes, and Lens 629
- Signs, Banners, and Billboards 630
- Sounds 631
- Space 632
- Speaking 632
- Sports & Games 632

  Stage, Platforms 635
 T-Z 637
  Tickets 637
  Time 638
  Tools 639
  Transportation 641
  Trees 643
Bibliography 651
About the Author 653

In Memoriam

To John Wimber: Founder of the Vineyard movement.

May Vineyard always stay fresh with the beauty and presence of Christ!

Acknowledgement

There are several people I would like to acknowledge in the preparation of this book. Foremost I want to thank my wife Jan for putting up with my crazy schedule and supporting me while I got up in wee hours of the morning to take on this task.

Of course no writing effort would be complete without the diligence of a good Godly copyeditor, and Christy Jones, in spite of her tight schedule raising kids and preparing for various triathlons, heeded that call and helped me to hone my writing and stay focused on the subject at hand. Thank you Christy, your work was a true blessing! I also want to thank my friend Leo Griego for his insight and editorial assistance. Finely, I want to thank my sister Jean, whose fine eye caught what we all missed, simple spelling and phraseology. Her attention to detail is incredible!

Other Books by Fred Raynaud

Healing Rain: The Rain King
A Novel, book one of the Sons of Thunder series

The Seers Gift
A Look at the Language of Visions & Dreams

The Seer & Healing
The Seer Gift and the Ministry of Healing

The Seer & Prophecy
The Gift & Office of the Seer Prophet

The Seer's Guide to Symbolism
Similitudes, Metaphors, & Symbolism

The Eyes of a Chef
Kitchen Tales on Food & Faith

The Chef Architect
Concept Development & Design

"For there is nothing hidden which will not be revealed, nor has anything been kept secret but that it should come to light. If anyone has ears to hear, let him hear. Then He said to them, 'Take heed what you hear. With the same measure you use, it will be measured to you; and to you who hear, more will be given. For whoever has, to him more will be given; but whoever does not have, even what he has will be taken away from him.'"

- Mark 4:22-25, NKJV

PREFACE

"Now the Lord spoke to Paul in the night by a vision, 'Do not be afraid, but speak, and do not keep silent;"

- Acts 18:9

"But when He was alone, those around Him with the twelve asked Him about the parable. And He said to them, 'To you it has been given to know the mystery of the kingdom of God; but to those who are outside, all things come in parables, so that "Seeing they may see and not perceive, and hearing they may hear and not understand; Lest they should turn, and their sins be forgiven them." And He said to them, 'Do you not understand this parable? How then will you understand all the parables?'"

- Mark 4:10-13

This is the complete Seer Series in a single volume. This book explores the incredible pictorial language of God in the life of the believer. Dedicated to His bride—the Church, it is a call to press in and experience the presence of Christ and the amazing panoramic language of heaven. In part one of this volume we explore the language of visions and dreams and dive into the depths of the Seer's Gift. In part two we move into "how" the Holy Spirit uses this panoramic language while ministering healing to those in need. In part three we look at the Seer Prophet and glen understanding on the gift and office of the Seer Prophet. In part four I share practical examples of pectoral language in various forms. Finely, in part five I layout examples (in glossary form) of symbolism and metaphors often experienced in the body of Christ.

It's a timely work. We live in exciting times! Everywhere you turn God is pouring out the Spirit of prophecy and revelation upon his people, often through the language of dreams and visions. Dreams and visions are one of those mysterious things that always seem to intrigue people. Everyone, at one level or another, is interested in dreams and visions. We all have dreamt.

Nevertheless, for some in the church community, dreams from God are fantasy, something too uncomfortable to consider; and visions... forget about it, you're written off as a loon or one being deceived by the devil. There is a tendency to dismiss visions and dreams as a flight of the imagination. Some people get spooked when you talk about having a dream or seeing a vision. They view these phenomena as emotionalism, extreme fantasy, or even worse occultism. There are segments within the body of Christ that view such happenings through a lens of fear and disbelief. Fear often stems from a lack of understanding which fogs the ability to see God move in this way; lacking the ability to believe it is easy to judge and cast off all who move in revelatory gifting.

The truth is: God always has, does, and will continue to speak to His children. Whether through that small still voice, an inspired sermon, a dream, a vision, a prophetic word, a word of knowledge, a word of wisdom, circumstance, or even through nature, Jesus speaks loud and clear—He has given us His Holy Spirit to be that conduit. Get this; it's important, He does it all through the consistent truth of His revealed Word—the Bible.

God has not changed. His desire to speak is no different today than it was in the garden, the days of Samuel, John the Baptist, or the entirety of the New Testament era. The bible speaks of dreams and visions 171 times, 96 of which deal with visions. Virtually every major turning point in scripture was proclaimed, accompanied by, or foretold through the language of visions and dreams. Dreams and visions are one of the tools that God uses to communicate to His children.

James Goll, founder of the Encounter Network (www.jamesgoll.com) and a leading authority on the prophetic, dreams, and visions states:

> *"What God did then, God does today, and God will continue to always do. Dream language is the language of the ages. It is this mysterious way that God comes into our lives, invades our uncomfortable zones, and simply comes to speak to us."*

In a recent article entitled, "The Master Dream Weaver Is Downloading His Dreams Within Us," James Goll, references several historical facts regarding church history and belief in God's ability to speak through dreams.

Great portions of the church father's writings record dreams and visions, and have only recently been translated into English. Consider the following:

- Thomas of India, received instruction from his dreams
- Polycarp was given a vision of his martyrdom
- Irenaeus had wise understanding of dreams
- Clement believed that dreams come from the depth of a soul
- Tertullian devoted eight chapters of his writings to dreams
- Gregory of Nyssa spoke of the meaning and the place of the dream.

- John Chrysostom, called "golden mouthed" because he had such oratorical grace upon him, called dreams the source of revelation.
- Constantine was directed in a dream regarding the Heavenly sign that he was to carry into battle.
- Thérèse de Lisieux life was changed through a dream.
- John Newton, an early slave trader, was stopped in his tracks in his lifestyle and his vocation by a dream from God. This became the man, who so turned around his life; he eventually became chaplain to the King of England. He went on to write the hymn that is possibly one of the greatest Protestant hymns of all ages: "Amazing Grace."

By understanding this type of communication, you will be better equipped to fulfill your destiny and walk with God in new and exciting ways.

The Populist Perspective

The general populace, on the other hand, dives into anything and everything that appears to offer a way to hear from God. Today's interest in spirit guides, eastern mysticism, psychic reading, horoscopes, new age spirituality, and other practices are evident of humanities desire to seek God. It is built into their DNA. What they don't know is, that the "who" they are seeking, is seeking them. Jesus is on the move and His heart is to seek and save that which is lost. That God shaped hole in the heart of humanity is seeking a relationship with the Lord of Glory.

Now here's the rub; if the Church doesn't come to grips with its fear and place revelatory language in its proper perspective they will miss the opportunity to proclaim Jesus to the lost while the world continues to run to anyone that claims to have a connection to deity—even if it is false. We must be like Daniel in Babylon, who was surrounded by astrologers and false revelators, yet he rose to the top like cream in a sea of nonfat milk, proclaiming the truth and exposing the falsehoods of the spirit of antichrist. We must move out in power within the marketplace and take our rightful place as messengers of righteousness for the Kingdom and for our God.

Why this Book

This book is for the everyday Christian, the average Joe, the layperson. With this book I want to stir your heart to go deeper in Christ. I want to ignite your desire to pursue your destiny. This book is written as a training manual. It offers insight into practical ways of "how" to listen to God and move out in effective ministry.

The Lord does speak to His people. He speaks to them through His Word. He speaks to them with that small still voice. He speaks to them through circumstance, and He speaks through the panoramic language of visions and dreams. This book will help you listen in a new way as you operate to fulfill God's will in your life. You will learn to understand how visions and dreams operate through gifting—whither it's a word of knowledge, prophecy, healing, or discerning of spirits.

The Days in Which We Live

We have been living in the fulfillment of Joel's prophecy for about 2,000 years and as the "*signs of the times*" increase in magnitude and scope, we should anticipate the outpouring of the Holy Spirit would come in the same manner. Many recognize the times we are living. There is not a segment in the church, or in the world for that matter, that questions wither we are living in the last days.

The truth is, we are just a little bit farther down the timeline than the New Testament church was. I am troubled about modern teachings on eschatology is the emphases on an escape plan. Too many evangelicals have hanged-their-hat on a rapture mindset. The high watermark of their theology is to be "caught-up" before the going gets tough, instead of moving out in power to bring in a harvest in this final hour. This series is about being the gospel. It is about doing the gospel.

The hardest thing for me growing up as a Christian in a church community in the midst of change was the lack of information and teaching, on the practical side of dreams and visions. To understand this pictorial communication as a type of language is important. We need to know how dreams and visions function when we are conducting ministry. No matter what the manifestation of God's Spirit is operating within your ministry, dreams and visions often become an active part of the process.

We have many books on the gifts of the Holy Spirit and its operation within the body of Christ. We have seen a flood of books on the prophetic in the church today. Even several study bibles are available that take a charismatic theme. I am not here to take up the cause of defending the place of spiritual gifts in the church today. There are many solid works out there from writers more competent than I that have taken up that cause. My assumption is that the gifts of God are alive and well, and if you're reading this book, chances are you do too. If you are one of those folks, this book is for you.

Who is this Book For?

This book, for the most part, is for those who are presently moving in the operations of the Holy Spirit and seeing the pictorial language of God operating in their lives. I have written this book to illuminate the realm of visions and dreams. I have written it to show that often times, the Seer (1 Samuel 9:9-19; 2 Samuel 15:27, 24:11), moves in more arenas than that of classic prophecy. This book was written to show the relationship of "*seeing*" and the other revelatory gifts. Frequently people who "*see*," see while operating in words of knowledge, discerning of spirits, prophecy, revelation, healing, and words of wisdom.

The challenge arises when the Seer, after seeing, has to listen, interpret, and then with Godly wisdom, obey and implement, what God has commanded. It has been my experience that the Seer's ability to listen is twofold: First, the Seer listens with his eyes, or the eyes of his mind, while God speaks to him through visions or dreams. Second, he must listen with his ears and his spirit, sifting that experience through the truth of scripture and prayer to gain understanding on what he has seen, thus, getting a fuller understanding of what God is saying in a given situation.

For the Seer, an understanding of how various gifts function is necessary in applying the Lord's will in a given situation. It is helpful for a Seer to know what gift is operating while ministering so that he may move in the appropriate stance. In this book, I hope to give incisive information on the operation of "seeing" in most applications. However, the main areas that I plan to cover involve healing, inner healing, healing the demonized, and the prophetic, it must be understood that the language of visions and dreams, function alike within all the gifts.

Throughout this book, I will share many personal stories. Stories are important. Remembering what God has done can become seeds for you in your own life. They are invitations for Jesus to do again what He did in the past. Set your hearts to find the seeds of blessing in these stories, for yourself. Sharing stories can ignite a future generation. Stories are testimonies that push and propel us forward. In Joel 1:1-3, it says:

> *"The word of the Lord that came to Joel the son of Pethuel. Hear this, you elders, and give ear, all you inhabitants of the land! Has anything like this happened in your days, or even in the days of your fathers? Tell your children about it, let your children tell their children, and their children another generation."*

Moses understood the power of remembering and proclaiming when he said in Deuteronomy 4:7-10:

> *"For what great nation is there that has God so near to it, as the Lord our God is to us, for whatever reason we may call upon Him? And what great nation is there that has such statutes and righteous judgments as are in all this law which I set before you this day? Only take heed to yourself, and diligently keep yourself, lest you forget the things your eyes have seen, and lest they depart from your heart all the days of your life. And teach them to your children and your grandchildren,"*

In 2 Timothy 1:3-7, Paul says to Timothy:

> *"I thank God, whom I serve with a pure conscience, as my forefathers did, as without ceasing I remember you in my prayers night and day, greatly desiring to see you, being mindful of your tears, that I may be filled with joy, when I call to remembrance the genuine faith that is in you, which dwelt first in your grandmother Lois and your mother Eunice, and I am persuaded is in you also. There-*

fore I remind you to stir up the gift of God which is in you through the laying on of my hands. For God has not given us a spirit of fear, but of power and of love and of a sound mind."

Sharing stories and reminding people of the wonderful things Jesus has done is our testimony. In the book of Revelation, it says that the testimony of Jesus is the Spirit of Prophecy.

Read the words John in Revelation 19:6-10:

> *"And I heard, as it were, the voice of a great multitude, as the sound of many waters and as the sound of mighty thunderings, saying, "Alleluia! For the Lord God Omnipotent reigns! Let us be glad and rejoice and give Him glory, for the marriage of the Lamb has come, and His wife has made herself ready." And to her it was granted to be arrayed in fine linen, clean and bright, for the fine linen is the righteous acts of the saints. Then he said to me, "Write: 'Blessed are those who are called to the marriage supper of the Lamb!'" And he said to me, "These are the true sayings of God." And I fell at his feet to worship him. But he said to me, "See that you do not do that! I am your fellow servant, and of your brethren who have the testimony of Jesus. Worship God! For the testimony of Jesus is the spirit of prophecy."*

What that means to you – is YOU can hear the word of testimony, and say, "That word is for me, for my life, for my house, for my generation."

The Seer Gift is for You

I believe that every Christian can receive the Seer's Gift and see into the heavenly realms.

Paul says in Ephesians 1:15-18:

> "Therefore I also, after I heard of your faith in the Lord Jesus and your love for all the saints, do not cease to give thanks for you, making mention of you in my prayers: that the God of our Lord Jesus Christ, the Father of glory, may give to you the spirit of wisdom and revelation in the knowledge of Him, the eyes of your understanding being enlightened; that you may know what is the hope of His calling, what are the riches of the glory of His inheritance in the saints,"

Paul is praying that the eyes of your spirit would be opened. Every believer has two sets of eyes. Obviously, we have our physical eyes to view the world around us. However, we also have our spiritual eyes, or the eyes of our heart, to perceive the spiritual realms around us. We are first spirit beings housed in a body of flesh. When we trust the heart of Jesus and what He did on the cross, we move to that place of hearing God more clearly. As our minds are renewed the clarity of the Hearing Ear and the Seeing Eye becomes sharpened. In essence, the Holy Spirit flips the switch of our imagination giving God another access point for the Him to speak to us. To make this happen it takes childlike faith. Notice the words of Jesus in Mark 10:14-15:

> "But when Jesus saw it, He was greatly displeased and said to them, "Let the little children come to Me, and do not forbid them; for of such is the kingdom of God. Assuredly, I say to you, whoever does not receive the kingdom of God as a little child will by no means enter it."

The kingdom of God is here and now. As you read this volume, let your heart be stirred to press into His kingdom as a little child and be transformed!

This book is divided into the following parts:

- Part One—The Seer's Gift: a look at the Language of Visions and Dreams.
- Part Two—The Seer and Healing, How visions and dreams operate in the ministry of healing.
- Part Three—The Seer & Prophecy, The Gift and Office of the Seer Prophet.
- Part Four—Words to the Church.
- Part Five—The Seer's Guide to Symbolism.

Part 1: The Seer's Gift

CHAPTER 1

SEEING CROSS-EYED

"For in Him dwells all the fullness of the Godhead bodily; and you are complete in Him, who is the head of all principality and power."

– Colossians 2:9-10, NKJV

What an amazing gift we have in Christ Jesus! As believers in the saving grace of Calvary we have been given something the world longs to see and know. We have been grafted into the bosom of Christ Himself, born again, and seated at the right hand of majesty. This incredible gift cannot be earned. It is not something that we strive for as if the works of our hands can somehow bring us to that place of reconciliation with God. It is a gift of grace for all that call Him Lord.

The problem is that the same church that understands the nature of saving-grace struggles when it comes to believing that they are filled with fullness of the Godhead. That somehow, after receiving salvation, we have to work at, or struggle even, to receive all that the Holy Spirit has to offer. We pray for an open Heaven. We strive to be filled with His presence. We work with all that we can muster, to try to obtain what we already have. What we fail to understand is that this striving is often based on a works mindset. Now that does not mean that we should not hunger and thirst for more. We should we do for His presence is drawn to the thirst and hunger of His children. Our souls crave for more of Him. However, that kind of hungering is birthed out of relationship and longing, like a bride for her groom.

Works, on the other hand, is performance driven. We call out wanting what Christ has already given us. What we fail to understand is in Christ, all the fullness of the Godhead dwells. The promise of Jesus is that the believer would be filled to the full with Christ, Poppa, and the Holy Spirit, for all the Godhead is in Him. Consider the following Scriptures:

> *"Jesus answered and said to him, "If anyone loves Me, he will keep My word; and My Father will love him, and We will come to him and make Our home with him."*

– John 14:23

> *"And of His fullness we have all received, and grace for grace."*

– John 1:16

Paul reinforces this truth when he tells us:

> *"Do you not know that you are the temple of God and that the Spirit of God dwells in you?"*

- 1 Corinthians 3:16

So, I can think of no better place to start this volume than with a very foundational truth. You have been redeemed and all the fullness of God dwells in you. You are the temple of the Holy Spirit, bought and paid for. It was the Father's good pleasure to fill you even as Christ is full (Colossians 1:19[OB]). When you were born again, you were crucified with Christ, raised from the dead with Christ, and are now seated with Him in Heavenly places.

> *"I have been crucified with Christ; it is no longer I who live, but Christ lives in me; and the life which I now live in the flesh I live by faith in the Son of God, who loved me and gave Himself for me."*
>
> – Galatians 2:20

> *"And raised us up together, and made us sit together in the heavenly places in Christ Jesus,"*
>
> – Ephesians 2:6

You have a completely new nature. You have a dual citizenship. You are a child of the King with residency in Heaven, seated at His right hand, and you are an ambassador of Heaven on Earth, created to bring the Kingdom of God to the rest of humanity. You have more of God in you than you can imagine.

> *"But if the Spirit of Him who raised Jesus from the dead dwells in you, He who raised Christ from the dead will also give life to your mortal bodies through His Spirit who dwells in you."*
>
> – Romans 8:11

You did not earn your Poppa's DNA. You do not "press in" for it. It is who you are. There is nothing you can do to gain the Holy Spirit. Christianity is not a lifelong course of moral activities and performance. You are a new creature in Christ. It is not about doing, it about being. You have the same power living in you that raised Christ from the dead. You just have to believe it.

> *"Most assuredly, I say to you, he who believes in Me, the works that I do he will do also; and greater works than these he will do, because I go to My Father. And whatever you ask in My name, that I will do, that the Father may be glorified in the Son. If you ask anything in My name, I will do it."*

– John 14:12-14

Belief is the catalyst for all that is in Christ. No longer do you have lack. At that very first moment of faith in Christ, you became a source of Kingdom blessing. Jesus was very clear, "*The Kingdom of God is within you*" (Luke 17:21). You are much larger on the inside than you are on the outside; you just have to believe it. You were meant to be a spring overflowing with living water.

> *"On the last day, that great day of the feast, Jesus stood and cried out, saying, "If anyone thirsts, let him come to Me and drink. He who believes in Me, as the Scripture has said, out of his heart will flow rivers of living water."*

– John 7:38-39

You are not alone. He has sent His Spirit to dwell in you in fullness.

> *"And I will pray the Father, and He will give you another Helper, that He may abide with you forever—the Spirit of truth, whom the world cannot receive, because it neither sees Him nor knows Him; but you know Him, for He dwells with you and will be in you. I will not leave you orphans; I will come to you."*

– John 14:16-18

Everywhere you go your life should spill over with God's abundance. I don't know why it is easier for us to believe that someday Jesus is going to do a work in us, instead of believing that the work was finished at the cross of Calvary. On the cross, your old sinful nature was abolished and you were given access to a glorious new world. All of your problems were solved on that cross. It may seem hard to believe but it's true. That's why they call it *"good news."*

Jesus died to give you what you could never gain on your own. Religion wants to give you formulas, keys, and tasks to perform, when you already have the ultimate gift in you. The problem for us is that so often we are not outwardly manifesting the fullness of God so we lower our theology to meet the standard of our experience, or lack thereof.

The truth is the perfect sacrifice of Christ was, in truth, good enough to get the job done. If you are not manifesting the fullness of God it is simply because you don't believe. I know that this sounds harsh, but it is the truth. Stop striving and rest in the fact that you have it (Hebrews 4). As you rest and trust in His finished work on Calvary, you will begin to act and live like a completely different person. A person always manifests what he believes.

The word "*believe*" in the Greek literally means "*reality*." Hebrews 11:1 tells us that faith is a tangible substance. True believing always involves demonstration. The Kingdom of God is not a matter of mere talk, but of demonstration of power.

> *"For the kingdom of God is not in word but in power."*
>
> - 1 Corinthians 4:20

Really, this is a process of changing the way we think. It is a call to have our minds renewed to believe the truth. I like the way John Crowder puts it.

> *"You have become an oasis in the desert. Your inner life bubbles up like pools of fresh water in a thirsty land. On the one side of the cross, you were a beggar, longing for a blessing. But on this side of the cross, you have truly become a source of blessing. You are provision for the hungry. You are drink for the thirsty. You are an endless supply of supernatural oil."*
>
> - John Crowder, Seven Spirits Burning

Remember the primary goal of salvation was not to empty you of evil, but rather to fill you with Himself. The work of the cross gave Him a Holy vessel to fill. Your purpose is "to be" the temple of the Holy Spirit! Calvary is our foundation and our capstone. It is the Spirit Filled life. It is the open door in Heaven. When we seek to move in the fullness of Christ, and understand the mysteries of the Kingdom, it takes faith.

Without faith, it is impossible to please God. It is faith that causes us to access the things of the Spirit. Faith is the magnet and the aroma that attracts the dancing hand of the Spirit (John 3:8).

> *"The wind blows where it wishes, and you hear the sound of it, but cannot tell where it comes from and where it goes. So is everyone who is born of the Spirit."*

Encounter with the Holy Spirit is not a onetime event. We should be receiving the Spirit fresh everyday! The cross put us into forever union with the Spirit. By abiding in Christ we can continually drink from His presence. We already have an open heaven and it is open because the veil of Christ's flesh was torn.

As you seek to understand how God communicates, please understand the depth of your relationship with Christ and know "*who*" you are in Him. The blood of Jesus is the anchor of our faith, it's the oil of our anointing, it's the fountainhead of our praise, and it is the lens to peer into the mysteries of the Kingdom. It is our stairway to Heaven.

When I speak of seeing cross-eyed, this is exactly what I am talking about, *peering through* the finished work of the **cross** and completely being submerged into this vat of His glorious wine and finished work. Revelation of this truth creates a true sense of peace and freedom to pursue the lover of our souls. It is the place of rest!

Understanding the Power of Rest

"*Rest*," boils down to understanding "*who*" you are in Him, but more importantly, who He is in you. Before we were saved, we were trapped in the cycle of performance. After we were saved, we found out that we are accepted in Christ, unconditionally. It is the revelation of "*acceptance*" that solidifies our identity. It is out of the reality of that identity that we move into rest.

Rest is that confidant reassurance of the Father's love-nature towards you. He is good all the time. He does not waver from His goodness or love towards you. When the revelation of your identity merges with the understanding of His incredible love and commitment to you and you receive a fresh understanding of the finished work of Christ on the cross, you have found the secret to the place of rest (Psalm 37:1-7).

> "*Do not fret because of evildoers, nor be envious of the workers of iniquity. For they shall soon be cut down like the grass, and wither as the green herb. Trust in the Lord, and do good; Dwell in the land, and feed on His faithfulness. Delight yourself also in the Lord, and He shall give you the desires of your heart. Commit your way to the Lord, trust also in Him, and He shall bring it to pass. He shall bring forth your righteousness as the light, and your justice as the noonday. Rest in the Lord, and wait patiently for Him; Do not fret because of him who prospers in his way, because of the man who brings wicked schemes to pass.*"

When you are at rest, you are no longer driven by the pressure to perform. You don't feel or have the need to strive to prove yourself worthy of His grace. You become comfortable in your own skin, in Him. Because He is good and He is for you and not against you, you can inter into His rest.

In Hebrew, the word "*rest*" has two definitions. The first is "*to stand still.*" The second meaning has the notion of "*going for a stroll or walk.*" The latter, I believe captures the essence of rest the best. I am reminded of God walking in the garden in the cool of the day with Adam, or what Jesus said in Mark 6:31 "Come away by yourselves to a secluded place and rest a while." He was asking them to go for a walk, a stroll with Him to a place of rest and solitude. The beauty and power of this is amazing.

Rest is that place in life where we learn to simply walk with Jesus in all circumstances. There is no striving or performance. In all things, we just want to be with Him. It really is that simple.

The process of abiding in Him is the process of adoration, worship, and love—resting in Him, no matter the circumstances. When you remember that peace is a person and that person is in love with you, rest is at your door. Listen to the words of Jesus in Matthew 11:28-30.

> "Come to Me, all you who labor and are heavy laden, and I will give you rest. Take My yoke upon you and learn from Me, for I am gentle and lowly in heart, and you will find rest for your souls. For My yoke is easy and My burden is light."

Again, Jesus says

> "Then He said to His disciples, "Therefore I say to you, do not worry about your life, what you will eat; nor about the body, what you will put on. Life is more than food, and the body is more than clothing. Consider the ravens, for they neither sow nor reap, which have neither storehouse nor barn; and God feeds them. Of how much more value are you than the birds? And which of you by worrying can add one cubit to his stature? If you then are not able to do the least, why are you anxious for the rest? Consider the lilies, how they grow: they neither toil nor

spin; and yet I say to you, even Solomon in all his glory was not arrayed like one of these. If then God so clothes the grass, which today is in the field and tomorrow is thrown into the oven, how much more will He clothe you, O you of little faith?"

- Luke 12:22-28

The closest example I can come up with is something that happened, just a short while ago. I was writing this very topic, when suddenly, my little baby granddaughter Anise (19 months old), came running over to me and grabbed a hold of my leg and began to just hold me. She looked up and lifted her arms with her fingers wiggling, saying in beautiful baby talk, "Hold me." Well, my response was like any grandpa in their right mind. I dropped everything, picked her up, and just held her. She snuggled in all the more, so I rocked her and cuddled her, and whispered to her a soft little song, kissing her on the cheek, as she cuddled, even more. I have to tell you, I could have stayed in that spot for hours. That is the whole point. If I, a frail human, treasures such a moments, how much more will our Father treasure us in His embrace. That is rest.

Get this—rest attracts rest. I am reminded of the story of Noah. In Genesis 8:8-9 we read:

> *"Also he sent forth a dove from him, to see if the waters were abated from off the face of the ground; But the dove found no rest for the sole of her foot, and she returned unto him into the ark, for the waters were on the face of the whole earth: then he put forth his hand, and took her, and pulled her in unto him into the ark."*

Here we see the symbolism of the Holy Spirit seeking a place to rest. The parallel verse to this is found in the gospels. Jesus is at the Jordan (the same place the people of Israel crossed to enter the Promised Land) getting ready to be baptized by John the Baptist. John records it this way:

> *"The next day John saw Jesus coming toward him, and said, 'Behold! The Lamb of God who takes away the sin of the world! This is He of whom I said, 'After me comes a Man who is preferred before me, for He was before me. I did not know Him; but that He should be revealed to Israel, therefore I came baptizing with water.' And John bore witness, saying, 'I saw the Spirit descending from heaven like a dove, and He remained upon Him. I did not know Him, but He who sent me to baptize with water said to me, 'Upon whom you see the Spirit descending, and remaining on Him, this is He who baptizes with the Holy Spirit.''"*

- John 1:29-33

Jesus knew who He was. He had no problem understanding His identity. Obviously, Jesus was already full of the Holy Spirit; after all, He is God incarnate. This was the place of public confirmation, the place where the Father and the Holy Spirit display their affirmation and joy for the mission that Jesus was about to fulfill. It is also interesting that the dove remained on Him. Jesus lived a life of true spiritual rest, totally dependent upon the Father. He walked with the Father everywhere He went and in everything, He did.

Jesus promised to give us the same Holy Spirit, as witnessed in Acts chapter two. The thing is, the Holy Spirit is drawn (in fullness) to people that have learned to abide in Christ and find their rest in Him. He, like the dove of Noah, is searching for that place of rest. He wants to live (in power) on a people that know their identity in Heaven and simple want to worship and walk with God in all they do. Through their ability to simply rest in Him, the Holy Spirit is more able to bring the Kingdom of Heaven in demonstration and power. Jesus is that model. My heart's cry for you is that you will seek to be at rest in your identity in Him, that you will know the power of His love towards you, and that your life will be lived in that state of rest.

Pray, Father, show me your love towards me. Teach me your ways. Teach me to walk with you in the comfort of your love. Let my mind be fixed on you and may my heart be as a child and know who I am in you. Let me be comfortable in my own skin, in you! Fill me to overflowing with the dove of your Holy Spirit. Amen!

CHAPTER 2

WHAT IS A SEER?

"Now the acts of David the king, first and last, behold, they are written in the book of Samuel the seer, and in the book of Nathan the prophet, and in the book of Gad the seer,"

- 2 Chronicles 29:29"

Modalities

A few years ago, I was speaking to our corporate head of training. During the Conversation, she looked over at me and said, "*You're a visual learner, aren't you?*" I asked her what she meant. She went on to explain to me how people process information through both the right and left-brain hemispheres. Most people, however, use one side more than the other, which makes learning some subjects far easier than others. She went on to say that everyone also has a preferred learning style, depending on the side of the brain and learning modality that is most developed. She explained to me that modes or styles of learning include kinesthetic (touching, feeling), audio (hearing) and visual (seeing).

Research has shown that visual, auditory, kinesthetic, gustatory, olfactory, and digital, are the six primary sensory modalities that we use to experience the world around us. These modalities are also known as representational systems. They are the primary ways we represent, code, store and give meaning or language to our experiences. The three main representational systems are visual, auditory, and kinesthetic, although digital, gustatory, and olfactory senses do not play a major role and are often included with kinesthetic.

We use all of our senses and depending on the circumstances may focus on one or more of them, when listening to a favorite piece of music, we may close our eyes to more fully listen and to experience certain feelings. As a chef, I work with aroma and fragrances and I use and rely on my gustatory and olfactory senses to a large degree in my profession. However, in general, my preferred representational system is visual.

Each of us has preferred representational systems. For example, when learning something new, some of us may prefer to see it or visualize it being performed, others need to hear how to do it, others need to get a feeling for it, and yet others have to make sense of it. One system is not better than any other. However, depending on the context, one or more of the representational systems may be more effective: artists, visual, musicians, auditory, athletes—kinesthetic, and mathematicians—digital. Typically, people at the top of their profession can use all of the representational systems and to choose the one most appropriate for the situation.

Annette Moser-Wellman in her book, "*The Five Faces of Genius,*" outlines five modalities that governed the greatest minds of history. The first modality is that of the Seer. She states:

> *"Seers see pictures in their mind's eye, and these pictures become the impetus for ingenious ideas. In the same way that someone can imagine his team's final jump shot at the buzzer or how his living room would look with a new color of paint, highly creative use the skill of the seer to imagine new ideas."*

Though Mrs. Moser-William is speaking of the natural creative nature and power of the mind to dream and envision, the idea is similar. God has given humanity the ability to create and envision, it is built into that incredible muscle called the brain.

What is powerful to me is the consistency of the world's scientific observations of learning and the creative process of innovation and the way that the Lord chooses to speak to His children. The Lord's method of communication spans the entire spectrum of sensory modalities and beyond. However, that should not be a surprise He created us that way. We were programmed in our very DNA to experience and communicate with God.

The Christian life should not be lived in silence, waiting for that final day in heaven when we can finely speak to Him. We are designed to speak and hear from Him today. We are His temple and He does live in us after all. We need to interact with Him. Our souls long to have vivid, two-way conversations with Him. We need to see what He is saying. We need to hear the sound of His voice, to feel His heartbeat and passion. We are driven with a desire to taste His goodness, and smell the aroma of His presence. We are incomplete in our life with Christ without interaction. Our senses were designed that way.

The Seer

When I speak about the *"Seer's Gift,"* I am talking about folks that operate in God's modality of *"seeing"* what He is saying. These folks operate through the gift of "seeing." Visions and dreams are normal for the Seer. They, often see first and hear second. However, it is my firm convection that the gift of seeing is available to every believer. Like all gifts of the Spirit they are grace endowed, given freely to the hungry. I also believe that they can be given through impartation (more on that later).

The *"Seer Prophet,"* on the other hand operates out of all modalities, however he is heavily weighted in the *"seeing"* arena. Bob Jones, a father of this last generation's prophetic movement, said it best.

> *",A seer is everything. Prophets are the eyes, but seers are the entire head: eyes, ears, smell, taste, and feelings. That is what Isaiah 29:10 says: 'He has shut your eyes, the prophets; and He has covered your heads, the seers.', As a seer you move in all five realms, and because of that, you are more discerning. The enemy is never really able to fully shut you down. The prophet can be momentarily blinded, but if the enemy blinds you, you will still be able to hear, smell, taste, and feel…. The prophet can speak the future, but the seer can see what the people need to let go of in the past, tell them what the Lord is saying to them today, and declare what the Lord is offering them tomorrow. A seer can feel the strongholds of a town…. You can smell what's happening. You can discern what's wrong with a church or a city or even a nation, because you can smell it."*

In Old Testament Hebrew the word "Seer," is found 34 times, 22 come from the Hebrew word "chozeh," a noun meaning: seer, a prophet who sees visions, a beholder in vision. Gad, Heman, and Iddo are good examples of the word Seer.

> *"For when David was up in the morning, the word of the Lord came unto the prophet Gad, David's seer, saying"*
>
> - 2 Samuel 24:11

> *"All these were the sons of Heman the king's seer in the words of God, to lift up the horn. And God gave to Heman fourteen sons and three daughters"*
>
> - 2 Chronicles 25:5

> *"Now the rest of the acts of Solomon, first and last, are they not written in the book of Nathan the prophet, and in the prophecy of Ahijah the Shilonite, and in the visions of Iddo the seer against Jeroboam the son of Nebat?"*
>
> - 2 Chronicles 29:29

The second Hebrew word for "*Seer*" is "*ra'ah*," meaning: to see, look at, inspect, perceive, consider; to cause to look intently at, behold, cause to gaze at. Samuel is a good example of this word.

> *"For when David was up in the morning, the word of the Lord came unto the prophet Gad, David's seer, saying"*
>
> - 2 Samuel 24:11

How the Seer Operates

Ra'ah takes the definition of the word seer and expands upon the way a seer operates. Unlike the word "*Nabi*," meaning "*prophet*," whose root means to "*bubble up*" as in spontaneous prophecy, the seer receives a word from the Lord as in a vision or dream, but then has to ponder, look at intently, inspect it, and consider it. I call this process "*marination*" or "*stewing*." So often, when the Lord shows me something, it is only during the process of letting that word "*stew*," sometimes for days or weeks, and in this process, the Lord expands His thoughts, and speaks to me regarding the depth and width of the vision. He will show me various visions in the same context. He will speak to me regarding the word repeatedly, expanding its meaning. He will drive me into the Scriptures and slather more marination on it.

Only after a season of listening and digging, will I find the richness of what He is saying. Usually, this takes place when he is speaking, what I call "*big words*," a word that is meant for the global body or group of people. Still, I find this process at work even when the context is personal prophecy, or spontaneous prophecy. I have learned that it is critical for me to stop in those moments, relax, dial down, and listen. I need to hear more from the Lord, to look for its interpretation and application, before sharing it.

This process applies to all folks moving in the prophetic, however, for the Seer, even more so. Every time I have been wrong in the interpretation, it was because I didn't wait for God to confirm the meaning in my spirit. Because I think metaphorically and God usually starts speaking to me metaphorically, I have a tendency to lean on my own experience in this arena.

This needs to be kept in check. If I don't listen, stew, and wait for that peace of God in confirmation with my spirit and rush into the interpretation, I can miss what God is really trying to say. Without the Holy Spirit's guidance we will find ourselves treading the waters of assumption. Jim Driscoll, author of "*the Modern Seer*," said it well.

> *"If we are overly optimistic in nature, we'll be prone to assume that everything we see is positive, when something might be corrective. If we're overly pessimistic, we'll tend to think everything is negative and therefore may have a hard time accu-*

rately revealing the Father's heart to those around us. There is a moment when we're looking for metaphorical understanding and we let go of all our preconceptions. At that moment, it feels like we have no idea what we are doing. We don't have a clue what God is going to tell us about what we're seeing, but based on our history with Him, we know He's going to tell us something. In that moment of being completely open, we experience great growth, because that is when we experience the spark."

CHAPTER 3

Metaphorical Language

"I have also spoken by the prophets, and I have multiplied visions, and used similitudes, by the ministry of the prophets."

- Hosea 12:10 (KJV)

Panoramic visionary language is a wonderful metaphorical language, but it is critical to be well grounded in the Word. The Word of God paired with your relationship and intimacy with the Lord is the plumb line for your discernment meter. Discernment is very important in sifting out the meaning of metaphorical speech. God loves speaking metaphorically. He can pack so much truth in a simple picture, its mind blowing.

Just a walk through the Scriptures and gleaning from all the ways God spoke to the prophets of old, or listening to the words of Jesus as He used simple stories and parables to illustrate powerful truths of the Kingdom, and you will come away with a wealth of insight and a love for "the way" God speaks.

It has been my experience that much of the metaphorical speech that the Lord uses is rooted in scripture; however, He also uses metaphors from our own life experiences. As a Chef by trade, the Lord has used the world of culinary to speak powerful truths to me in metaphorical language. He draws it out of my life like water from a well. The emulsification of a hollandaise sauce becomes a word of salvation, the simmering of a stew on a hot stove points to something rich and savory the Lord cooking up, breaking down the fleshly sinew, to create tenderness in the life of an individual. Both examples are types of metaphor.

To Illustrate

Several years ago, I saw a vision of the Lord seated by a river's edge. He was seated next to a flat rock. He had in His hand stalks of wheat. He took the wheat and beat it against the rock. As He beat it, the kernels of wheat were separated. The wind rose up and blew against the chaff, releasing the kernels. He then reached down and began to grind the wheat with His hands on the rock. As He was grinding, He reached into the river and pulled up some water. He drizzled the water into the floury substance, and then He started to work the mass into dough with His hands. As He was kneading the dough, He turned and looked at me and said, "*I knead you.*"

At that moment I was overcome with His Spirit and His love. I not only understood that He wanted me and needed me, but I understood the process of kneading, and the structure it produced in the dough. When water and flour are kneaded together, the proteins in the flour expand and form strands of gluten, which gives bread its texture. The kneading process warms and stretches these gluten strands, eventually creating springy and elastic dough, and thus giving it strength. If bread dough is not kneaded enough, it will not be able to hold the tiny pockets of gas (CO_2) created by the leavening agent (such as yeast or baking powder), and will collapse, leaving a heavy and dense loaf. The CO_2, like the breath and power of the Holy Spirit, needs a vessel "*kneaded*" to sustain it.

Jesus will take us to that place of kneading. He will massage us into a work of His hands. Like the master potter, He will keep at it until we are at a place to sustain what He pours into our lives. This is a powerful example of the Lord speaking a word that is not only rooted in my life experience, but also established in the Word of God.

Of course, God is not limited in the metaphors He uses. In my world, I see the Lord speaking virtually everywhere, through dreams, visions, aromas, nature, feelings, hearing, the whole gambit, and I wouldn't have it any other way. When I heard the sound of geese honking as they flew by, I also heard the voices of a platoon of angels declaring a season in transition. When I was surrounded by butterflies and a butterfly landed on my shoulder, I heard the Lord say, "*Metamorphoses, it's time to take flight and pollinate—stir up the next generation.*" When I tasted honey in my mouth, I knew there was a sweet prophetic word for someone. When I saw the wind rise up and blow leaves off a tree, I heard the Holy Spirit say, "*I am shacking the trees and releasing my servants into the streets and to the communities they influence.*" When I smelled the flowers of spring and saw flower petals falling from the wind, I knew that the Lord was ready to shower His bride with love and grace. When I heard the sound of dogs barking in the streets, I was caught up into a place of warfare prayer, knowing that the enemy was biting at the heels, of something or someone.

The key in this endeavor is to simple pay attention; always have Jesus on your mind; and listen to what the Holy Spirit is saying. He is speaking all the time.

Similitudes and Symbolism

> *"As I walked through a great wilderness I came to a certain place where there was a Den, and I laid myself down in that place to sleep: and as I slept I dreamed a dream.*
>
> *I dreamed; and I thought that I saw in my dream a man standing with his face turned away from his own house. He was clothed in rags, a book was in his hand, and a great burden was on his back.*
>
> *Then I saw him open the book and read; and as he read, he wept and cried out, 'What shall I do?'."*
>
> - John Bunyan, The Pilgrim's Progress

When I first started thinking about these similitudes and symbolism in the glorious language of God I was drawn to that incredible pilgrim and warrior in the faith, John Bunyan. He is best remembered for his book "*The Pilgrims Progress*" which he says, was "*Delivered under the similitude of a DREAM.*" He wrote it from a prison cell almost three hundred fifty years ago (1678). John Bunyan's dream story has become the most famous allegory in English literature. It has been read by more people than any other religious book in history, second only to the Bible, and it has been translated into more languages than any other book in the English tongue.

In the book of Hosea we read:

> *"I have also spoken by the prophets, and I have multiplied visions, and used similitudes, by the ministry of the prophets"*
>
> - Hosea 12:10, KJV

The Hebrew word for "*similitude*" in this verse is "*dama*" meaning to liken, to compare, to imagine, think, a symbol, or similitude. To that definition I would include the words, metaphor, allegory, simile, and parable. As you can see from this book the Lord loves to speak through stories. His language is so broad and wide it defies our linear mindset.

Moving in dreams and visions is available to every believer in some degree or another. While everyone is not called to the ministry of the seer-prophet, all can move to some extent in this realm.

In this book I have tried to show the value of metaphor and teach you how God uses the language of visions and dreams to speak to you. I want to encourage you to learn to think metaphorically. Consider the way God speaks. Much of the Old Testament is given to us veiled in allegory, shadows, types, and metaphor. From Genesis to Revelation we see the fundamental truths of the Gospel and the face of Jesus woven throughout the Scriptures like nuggets of revelation tucked away in the melody of the Word.

The main reason people miss interpretations is by thinking in literal rather than metaphorical terms. God uses symbolism that is familiar to your life. He knows every aspect of your being and will speak through your makeup and the things that have marked your life experience. He knows your life, your makeup, who you are, and what you do. He knows your passions, and interests, He is interested in you. If you are a mechanic, God may speak to you along those lines. If you are a Chef, God may show you an area that you can relate to. Jesus spoke to the people of His day in parables that they could relate to. As an agrarian society that worked the land and fished in the Sea of Galilee they understood when Jesus spoke of tilling the soil and casting out nets for a catch.

God may show you the same type of symbols and their meaning and be very consistent in their use, interpretation, and application. For instance, in the Word of God a lamb is a common symbol that has a consistent thread of meaning throughout Scripture.

Whenever certain symbols manifest pictorially to you, it will become fairly obvious what they mean.

On the other hand God does not want us to turn His creative voice into a formula. His desire is to stretch us and cause us to dig for truth through fellowship with Him. He wants us to be constantly dependent upon Him and His Word. When we think we have it down pat, He will show us a symbol that we thought we knew, and suddenly it made no sense at all. The Lord does this to keep our dependency on Him. Always seek Him and His Word to search out the meaning of His speech. John Paul Jackson put it this way regarding visionary interpretation:

> *"The closer we can maintain our intimacy with the Holy Spirit, the better we can begin to hear His voice in understanding what He is speaking to us. We can learn all the mechanics and they are immensely helpful, but after that we must depend upon His voice to lead us."*

Follow Daniel's lead. Daniel knew that "*Interpretations belong to God*" and He sought the Lord through prayer and the Lord revealed the meaning of the dream (Daniel 2). In the end, it is hearing His voice that brings the revelation.

Symbolism found in visions and dreams are often similar, however, the interpretation may be quite different. Often visions operate through the gifts of "*the word of knowledge*," "*discerning of spirits*," or "*prophecy*" and the interpretation and application may come quickly, as God speaks to your heart regarding the matter. Dreams on the other hand may need more digging and often revolve around your life destiny, mission, life, and God's desire for you personally. I will try to bring this to light as we discuss similitudes.

As you learn the metaphorical language of the Holy Spirit your ability to see will reach new heights.

Proverbs 25:2 says that:

> *"It is the glory of God to conceal a matter but the glory of kings (or man) is to search out a matter."*

God places great value on our seeking out the things that He conceals. Use this section of the book as a reference tool to spark your mind to think metaphorically. Press in and press on dear saints. The Lord desires to speak to you!

In part five of this book we explore various similitudes, metaphors, and symbols that are commonly found in the body of Christ.

As you move through this book embrace the beauty of God's panoramic pictorial language. Nothing compares to a relationship with God that overflows with communication, adoration, and love.

- A call to you, your church, or others to climb higher and press into the presence of the Lord.
- A word regarding promotion, that God is taking you to a higher place, spiritually or in your occupation.
- A word regarding progression, such as *"step out" "take the next step,"* or *"move forward."*

Chapter 4

Types of Seeing

"In a dream, in a vision of the night, when deep sleep falls upon men, while slumbering on their beds, then He opens the ears of men, and seals their instruction. In order to turn man from his deed, and conceal pride from man, He keeps back his soul from the Pit, and his life from perishing by the sword."

- Job 33:15-17

Seeing

A *"Seer"* sees three basic ways. The first is internal. A person receives images, pictures, or visions in his mind. This can happen any time but often happens during worship or while the person is in the mode of ministering to someone's need. They can be single frame pictures, but more often than not, they are more like a movie being played out. This type of activity can happen in a vision or a dream.

Dream Camps

Holy Spirit inspired dreams fall into three camps. In the first camp, you're the object of the dream. You are in the dream and are doing something, or a story is being played out and you're in it. This type of dream can be metaphorical or be direct communication from the Lord to you. When it is not a metaphor, it is very clear, and may even involve an angelic visitation.

The second dream camp is being shown something. You are watching the dream, as an outsider. It's as if a story is unfolding. This type of dream is often metaphorical, but can be more literal.

The third camp of Holy Spirit inspired dreams is the forgotten dream. This is the type of dream is where the Holy Spirit downloads something into your spirit. Your involvement is not necessary; He is simply dropping and sealing instructions into your spirit. Job 33:15-17 says:

> "In a dream, in a vision of the night, when deep sleep falls upon men, while slumbering on their beds, then He opens the ears of men, and seals their instruction. In order to turn man from his deed, and conceal pride from man,"

Have you ever had one of those moments where you walked into a place and felt as if you were there before, like déjà vu? This often is a result of the third dream camp. You were shown something for that moment. When this happens, pay attention, and ask the Lord how you should respond to that situation.

External Seeing

The second type of seeing is external. The person sees a vision in front of them. It may be translucent or solid. This type of vision can also come as written words over someone. The words can be a sign of a condition in someone's life such as a sin or sickness, example being the word "*adultery.*" They can be declarative or a word of destiny for a person's life, like the word "*Teacher*" or "*Prophet.*"

Angelic and Visions

This type of vision is also active in the areas of discernment, where you see the spirits behind a situation such as in the demonic. We read in Hebrews 5:14:

> *"But solid food belongs to those who are of full age, that is, those who by reason of use have their senses exercised to discern both good and evil."*

On the other hand, you may see the angelic in their ministry to the body of Christ. David says in Psalms 34:7:

> *"The angel of the Lord encamps all around those who fear Him, and delivers them."*

Moreover, in Psalm 91:11-12:

> *"For He shall give His angels charge over you, to keep you in all your ways. In their hands they shall bear you up, lest you dash your foot against a stone."*

The writer of Hebrews 13:1-2, tells us:

> *"Let brotherly love continue. Do not forget to entertain strangers, for by so doing some have unwittingly entertained angels."*

Angelic activity can be externally seen as translucent (most common), or an actual physical encounter. This type of seeing is not really seeing, as in visions, but peering, as in seeing into the Spirit realm.

An example of this is can be seen when Elisha prayed for the eyes of his servant to be opened so he could see the angelic forces around them.

> *"And Elisha prayed, and said, "Lord, I pray, open his eyes that he may see." Then the Lord opened the eyes of the young man, and he saw. And behold, the mountain was full of horses and chariots of fire all around Elisha.*
>
> - 2 Kings 6:17

Just recently, I had an angel encounter that brought me great comfort. I walked down into my study and felt the presence of the Holy Spirit in the room. As I looked across the room, I saw an angel. He was standing in the corner, wings, and all, about 6 feet tall, big, soft-spoken, and strong like confidence wrapped up in love. All I could do was walk over, stand in front, bow my head, and say thank you to the Father. I kept telling the Father, repeatedly, thank you. The angel wrapped his wings around me, caressed me, and said, "*Child, the Father is very pleased with you.*" I cried. Then he said, "*I am here to encourage you and help you fulfill your destiny. You are loved; the Father is so very pleased.*" I was blown away. Still am. The next day I was driving. I thought I felt his presence. So I spoke up, "*Are you still here?*"

I heard him say, "*Yes child, this is my assignment. The Father is very pleased.*" Then the Holy Spirit just flooded my heart. Since that encounter, I have had a new level of acceptance, love, and boldness fill my heart. That encounter was a blend of translucence and physical manifestation. To be honest, in the last thirty years, not counting the sensing of angelic presence during worship, I have had no more than seven encounters with the angelic that I am aware of, two in dreams, one physical encounter, three in visions, and this last event. God has sent his angelic forces to minister to the saints, to assist us in fulfilling our destiny, and to battle on our behalf.

However, like all things, decrement is your lifeblood. Test all things, hold fast to that which is good, for we know that Satan himself can transform into an angel of light, and his only goal is to deceive, lie, steal, and destroy.

Trances

The third type of "*seeing*" is what the Scriptures refer to as a "*Trance.*" A trance is not the vision itself but the mode the Holy Spirit puts you into to receive it. The Greek word for "*trance*" is "*ekstasis.*" According to Strong's it means a displacement of the mind, i.e. bewilderment, ecstasy: amazement, astonishment, or a trance. It is where the mind and emotion are transported, as it were, out of one's self, and into a raptured state.

One may be awake, but the mind is drawn off from all surrounding objects and wholly fixed on things divine. It is in this state that one sees nothing but the forms and images lying within. The event is so real that it feels as if you have been transported to heaven or wherever the Lord is taking you, or showing you. The root word means "*amazement*" a state of wonderment, a state of Holy drunken perception. It is a place where our hunger for the Lord becomes so rich we have to move into His realm. Peter had such an encounter in Acts 10:9-16. In Acts 11:4-5 he explains this vision:

> *"The next day, as they went on their journey and drew near the city, Peter went up on the housetop to pray, about the sixth hour. Then he became very hungry and wanted to eat; but while they made ready, he fell into a trance and saw heaven opened and an object like a great sheet bound at the four corners, descending to him and let down to the earth. In it were all kinds of four-footed animals of the earth, wild beasts, creeping things, and birds of*

> the air. And a voice came to him, "Rise, Peter; kill and eat." But Peter said, "Not so, Lord! For I have never eaten anything common or unclean." And a voice spoke to him again the second time, "What God has cleansed you must not call common." This was done three times. And the object was taken up into heaven again."

Paul had a similar experience in the book of:

> "I was in the city of Joppa praying; and in a trance I saw a vision, an object descending like a great sheet, let down from heaven by four corners; and it came to me. "Now it happened, when I returned to Jerusalem and was praying in the temple, that I was in a trance and saw Him saying to me, 'Make haste and get out of Jerusalem quickly, for they will not receive your testimony concerning Me.'"
>
> - Acts 22:17-18

John Crowder, in his book, the Ecstasy of Loving God, said it this way:

> "The word ecstasy refers to an intense, euphoric experience. It can be hard to define, as it refers both to a heightened state of spiritual contentiousness, as well as an intensely pleasant experience. As one's concentration comes into a divinely heightened state of focus, our awareness of exterior senses and intellectual thoughts are often diminished. It is often accompanied by a cessation of voluntary physical mobility. The resulting "spiritual drunkenness" is what the early apostles experienced on Pentecost-what the priests of Solomon's temple experienced as they were unable to stand up under the glory cloud. It is what the Christian mystics encountered in the deep throes of inner prayer, and it is the Charismatic Christian practice which we all call being "slain in the Spirit." It has accompanied the First and Second Great Awaken-

ing revivals in the Americas, and was present in the birthing of every significant new move of God or new denomination in church history."

Illustrative Example of Visions in a Trance

To illustrate this further I would like to share three other examples of visions I had while in a trancelike state.

Preparing a Banquet Table

A while back, the Lord gave me the following vision. I was in the midst of worship at church. All of a sudden, I was transported. I was standing in a carpenter's shop like you would see on a farm. It was so real I could smell the wood and feel the dust in the air. Jesus was standing there next to a carpenter's bench. The room was filled with particles of wood dust like a cloud. The sun was shining in the door to the wood shop so you could see the particles floating in the air, almost in slow motion. He was leaning over a large flat piece of wood like a door or a tabletop. He was working with a plane very meticulously; removing layer after layer until the top was perfectly smooth. I asked the Lord what He was making.

He said,

> *"Don't you know that when I want to take you higher, to take you to the next level, into that next season, that I need to take you deeper? I take the place where you are, right now, and I plane it, stripping away the last season in order to reveal the next. You see, what worked in the last season will not work in the next. What worked in the wilderness will not work in the Promised Land, the manna has ceased, and the fire and the cloud have disappeared. Go in and possess the Land."*

He went on to say,

> "I am bringing you from a place of personal protection; Where your shoes never wore out; Where I fed you daily with manna from heaven; Where I caused water to flow and quail to fall from the sky; Where I nourished you and cared for you throughout the last season, to a place of proclamation and position; Where you will become a feeder; Where you become a person – that stills the storm; Where you become the extension of my hands; This is a place where slaves become friends; Where paupers become Kings and Priests; and where the kingdoms of this world will see the Glory of the My Kingdom. The planning process creates a door into the next season of your life. And when the dust settles, and you allow Me to take you deeper, and you enter in – that door will become a banquet table prepared in the presence of your enemies, and waves of Mercy and Grace will fill the streets."

Then I saw the Lord standing at a lathe working a piece of wood. I asked the Lord what He was making and He said,

> "I'm creating a scepter out of trees of righteousness. I am creating a people that will walk in My authority and carryout My great commission."

Then He showed me a picture of a grand stallion, dressed and decked in blue and white, like it was leading a precession. The rider was dressed in like manner, with a silver trumpet in His hand and he had on a headdress that was made of long flowing feathers. I asked the Lord what it meant and He said,

> "I am about to enter the grand arena of Life, where My body, in My Glory, will parade the Kingdom of Heaven before men. They have been dressed for the occasion. They are covered in the Kingdom. Proclamation is in their hands, and they are called

to summon all to My banqueting table. Their head is covered with the nature of my Spirit and the world will see My glory."

Then He showed me a tall blue curtain that shot up to heaven, so high you couldn't see where it started. It was tied back like the drapes in a house. When I saw it, I understood it to be the veil of the temple that was torn from the top to the bottom. The veil was tied back inviting all to enter in, an invitation, to step into the throne of grace, to gaze into the windows of heaven, to watch as the Lord himself, with the hosts of heaven, step on stage, and take us into this next glorious season in the Kingdom.

The message was so full of hope and encouragement. It breathed life and promise. The beauty of how He spoke to me was just as altering as the words that He spoke. It is forever burned into my spirit. In fact, I can say that every word that the Lord has breathed in my spirit in this way is etched in like manner. I don't care if it was thirty years ago; it is as fresh today as the moment it happened.

Tears of Healing

During prayer and worship, the Lord brought me into his heart and I saw the heartstrings of God playing an incredible melody to my soul.

He met me at the bank of a river. It was cloudy and stillness covered the land. The base of the river was like a marshland—Reeds were growing up all around it everywhere, like passive stocks of wheat. They were blowing in the wind and the reeds were rich with substance, stalks full of the water of life—feeding off the water edge. A soft wind was blowing and moving upon the reeds. They almost danced as the breeze rustled the reeds of God. Then Jesus came up beside me and said, "Walk with me."

He touched me and my heart began to melt within me. I knew that this was going to be different, be deep. I knew in my spirit we were going into a deep place. Something inside me was struck with the heaviness of this moment. It was thick, like the clouds, before it rains. Something whaled up inside of me and I started to cry.

Instantly I was in this place. There were pillars like muscles, tendons, and they were vibrating to worship. I felt very unsure of myself. I did not know how to stand in this place. I moved around trying to find my footing. The worship continued and tears continued to come as I moved around, almost trying to hold on. There were many tendons, some wide, some narrow, each moving at different tones of melody. Finely, I reached out and grabbed hold of the biggest muscle next to me and I held on worshiping the Lord. *"God, what is this? What am I seeing?"* Instantly, I understood I was standing in the heartstrings of Jesus. I was struck with the reality that I did not know how to stand in this place.

There was this incredible melody of love vibrating from within His heart. I walked around in amazement and bewilderment not knowing what to do or how to be here. His heartstrings were playing in waves that overcame me and all I could do was cry. I asked the Lord "What's wrong with me?"

He said, *"You do not know how to rest in My Love."*

I knew that I did not know how to receive His love. I did not know the depth of His love for me. I did not know how to take-it-in. I was trying but I did not know how. I was trying hard to understand. I was walking around looking, trying to find that place in Him, when I ran into a very big muscle. I looked up and saw how high it went. I could not get around it. I was overtaken by the knowledge that I did not know what to do. I asked the Lord, "*I don't know how to receive Your love, how to love You like I should. What are we going to do? Now what do we do?"*

Then the Lord spoke, graciously, without hesitation, "*I am just going to have to Love you more, more love, more love.*" This time the tears began to flow like a river. My heart was breaking and melting, and throbbing for Him. I felt something changing on the inside.

Then I was gone. He brought me to a river at night. It was a glorious river, full of life. I looked at the river and the life around it, the foliage, and lily pads, flowers, and frogs, and fish. The night sky was incredibly clear with tones of dark blue that became the canvas to the most perfect full moon I had ever seen. The light of the moon glistened upon the waters. I was struck with the most incredible feeling of peace, just to be with Jesus, looking out at this incredible scene. The serenity, quietness, the cool night breeze, the sounds of stillness, with Him by my side, was breathtaking. Then He reached over and wrapped His arm around me and His very shadow (shadow at night – wow) caused my very nature to want to lean into Him.

Then He said, "*Have you ever walked upon the water under a clear moon light?*" And He embraced me.

That night the Lord did something inside of me that has changed my life forever. The Lord showed me His love nature towards me. For the first time, I saw Him as the LOVER of my soul—in a very deep way.

That was the start of a long love journey. I am still working and resting, learning to trust Him and let Him love me deeply. I am forever in love with my Lord.

The following Monday the Lord continued this dialog and it was incredible. I call it temple worship.

Temple Worship

I was in deep prayer and worship when the Lord took me away. He took me into His temple. I looked and I saw the Glory of His dwelling. There were large pillars of marble, majestic white marble laced with gold, everywhere. I saw myself standing behind a pillar. I was standing there, like a young servant or slave that wasn't sure if he really should be there. I was in the portico in front of the throne room. There was activity happening around the throne. The court of the King was active with His angels moving about as if they were on a mission, as if they were creating battle plans.

The angel that was standing next to Him was tall and slender, almost graceful, if you will. He had a scroll in his hand. There seemed to be a sense of urgency in their dialog. I watched from behind the pillar, as if I was eavesdropping, as if I was listening to things I shouldn't be, like I was in a place of Royalty – and I was but a pauper.

Suddenly, all eyes were fixed on me. It was as if I had knocked something over, and I was found out. I tried to hide behind the pillar but I was drawn to Him, I was drawn to peek from behind my hiding place. Everyone was looking—smiling at me. There was a joy present that is hard to describe. The place was thick with His joy. The Lord was dressed in a brilliant white robe with blue trimming. He was leaning forward, trying to see me. He had the most incredible smile upon His face. He was beckoning me with His hand to come closer. He was calling me with His smile, He was beckoning me with His eyes. He wanted me to step out from behind the pillar and come to Him.

As I stepped from behind the pillar and began walking towards Him, I was transformed into a child. Instantly, I was a boy cradled in His arms. I was not just a boy; I was like an autistic boy that did not know how to be held. I was squirming about, moving in all directions. In spite of my wiggling, He just kept holding me, until, slowing, I began to change, and His peace filled my being, and I rested in His arms.

And I heard the Lord say me...

> *"My people have not learned their abiding place in Me. My people do not know the place of My dwelling and the position I have called them into. They have a poverty mindset. They feel like paupers in the palace of the King. They do not see the depth of My love and the secret place in My Heart for them. Tell them I am calling them to a higher place. I am enlarging their footprint and their place in Me. Tell them I am calling them to a place of sweet comfort, to a place of dwelling—to be seated with Me in the Heavens. Tell them I desire to have them where I am. No longer shall they be called servants, but friends—friends of the Most High God. I am bringing them into My presence—I'm bringing them into the place of son-ship, that where I am they will be also.*
>
> *They are of the Royal line – They have access to My throne, not only access, but a dwelling place, a home set within the temple of My heart. Tell them there is a secret place in the temple of the King. There is a place in which I will abide in them and they will rest in the cradle of My arms. It is there, that I shall whisper. It is there, that I will share the deep desires of my heart."*
>
> *My children do not know how to rest in this place. They are standoffish, they are trapped with a spiritual autism, and they squirm and turn, losing their*

> *focus. They have not found that quiet place; they have not found the stillness of My presence. The world has imprinted them with preoccupation, hyperness has invaded their minds and fear, anxiousness, and impending disappointment has over taken them.*

Then the Lord said,

> *"But I am breaking down the walls of their minds – I am renewing their way of thinking, and I will fill them with My peace and My love. I am placing them in the cradle of My arms and speaking life into their hearts. I will hold them – and teach them the depth of My love. But they need to relax, to rest in Me, and to trust Me. I will be their trust. Tell them—it's ok. Tell them to go ahead, press into the door that is set before them. Permission has been granted, and they shall learn the place of Royalty and My joy, My unspeakable joy.*
>
> *They need to come to Me like a child would come. There are places in Me that they will not know how to stand, or how to settle into. But I shall cover them and I shall teach them, and I shall be their hiding place—for they shall learn to live and be in me. I know how to comfort My beloved – they can trust in Me."*

Most importantly, I also understood He was talking about me, and I could feel a deep healing in my heart and our love relationship.

Then the Lord stood up and took me by the hand. He walked with me to the most incredible patio. It was circular like an arch wrapped in marble with pillars on either side. It was so incredibly beautiful and peaceful. The balcony faced the darkness of the night skies of heaven and the heavens were illuminated with the glory and splendor of God.

I stood there overcome with His peace. It was a peace that is so very hard to explain, like you could almost breath it in. We leaned against the balcony staring out at the stars; it seemed like hours of just resting and staring out at the sky. Jesus pointed at various places in the heavens. *"Look there,"* He said, and a shooting star would fly by in utter brilliance. *"Look over there,"* and the swirling mass of stars were dancing in the galaxy.

Then the Lord said as he paned and pointed across the night sky:

> *"Behold my endless possibilities. Know the power of My presence for My hands have embraced the fire of the sun. My chest brushed against the heavens and the lights of Aurora were created."*

I was undone, overwhelmed by the depth and majesty of His desire, and my heart stirred within me.

Then the Lord pointed to a horizon. The sun was coming up in radiant brilliance. Surrounding the sun was a massive wave of clouds that stretched across the horizon and peeked at the center of the sun. He kept pointing at the clouds and the clouds were coming towards us. Like a massive wave of white, bordered in brilliant fiery orange, they kept rolling, faster and larger, and closer towards us—until I was caught up into the clouds.

The clouds were moving so fast and the Lord said: *"Fly away with Me."*

Suddenly, I was flying in the midst of the cloud. The cloud was moving incredibly fast. The cloud was wet with His presence and the wind against my face was incredible. It took my breath away, and the wetness washed me and refreshed me even down to my very pores. Then I heard the voice of the Lord say, *"Follow the cloud—and not the crowd. Follow the cloud, and not the crowd,"*

Suddenly, the cloud landed and I was standing in a desert place on a dirt path. In front of me was a mighty pillar of cloud, a la Moses. It turned with the intensity of a tornado. It was massive, big! I could see the power of the cloud digging into the dirt and the rocks, kicking up a path as it turned and moved.

Then the Lord said:

> *"When you enter the deep places of My heart, when you enter My temple, and embrace your place in Me, then you shall hear the whispers of My heart and you will call forth My desires.*
>
> *When you follow the cloud of My glory and taste the water of My presence, then you shall call that which is in My heart, to come and be on earth, in this place, even now, as it is in Heaven. The cloud of My glory shall be unto to you like a pillar of My glory and it shall carve out a path of My presence and make straight a highway in the desert. Every valley shall be exalted; every mountain and hill shall be brought low. The crooked places shall be made straight and the rough places shall be made smooth. My Glory shall be revealed and all flesh shall see it."*

As I looked down towards my feet—I saw the feet of Jesus. They were mighty and strong, bruised, worn, and dusty, calloused as if they had walked this path before. He had sandals on and His feet dug into the ground. I was amazed at the strength in his feet. Then I looked at my hands, and they too were the hands of Jesus, only strong, calloused, and rugged. I stood back in amazement, and I heard the Lord say:

Then I saw the Lord standing in front of the pillar of cloud and He was filled with incredible joy. He began to dance along the path in front of him. In His hands were doves. As He danced he released the doves, over, and over, one dove after another.

> *"This is abiding, this is abiding, When you abide in Me, you will truly be changed, for you will be in Me, and you will be captured by My desires and be thrust into the work of My hands. You will say, "I can't help it, I must, I have to, I need to be about the work His hands, for He has captured my heart, and I am undone...."*
>
> *Lift up your voice with strength; Lift it up, and be not afraid. Say to the cities, "Behold your God. Behold, the Lord God shall come with a strong hand. And His arm shall rule for Him; Behold, His reward is with Him, and His work before Him. He is calling you to a higher place."*

Then, suddenly, in a moment, His face was inches in front of mine—and my breath left me as I stared into His eyes. He was moving so close I thought he was going to move right through me. I was captivated by His look – His eyes. He got so close – like millimeters away and said, "***And I shall abide in YOU.***"

I was overtaken by His presence, and I could see Him envelope me like a translucent glove, and I was moving in Him and He in me, and I wondered, and I was amazed at how deep He was calling and yearning for our presence with Him. I was beginning to understand what it means to abide – but more so – for Him to abide in us.

Then I saw the profile of His eye, large massive, filling the sky – His eye lashes moved to the sound of worship, and I looked and I saw His hands, and I looked and saw His feet, and He said very slowly and very powerfully:

> "***My eyes***," then he paused
>
> "***My feet***," then he paused
>
> "***My hands***," then he paused

Pausing that seemed to fill the room with expectance between each proclamation. LOUDER this time…

"My Eyes,"

"My Feet,"

"My Hands,"

LOUDER STILL with deep passion…

"MY EYES,"

"MY FEET,"

"MY HANDS,"

I was blown away. I had to abide. I had to let Him abide in me.

Then I saw Jesus, with the same rugged look and attire as His feet hands, sitting against a well. He was so very strong, but peaceful and confidant, waiting. He had in His hand a cup. He looked at me, extended the cup, and said:

"**Drink**," pause….

My heart was racing.

He said it again, "**DRINK**,"

My heart was really pounding.

"**Drink**," a third time he said it with a smile"

Suddenly, I was right in front of Him with the cup to my mouth, and as I began to drink, I was suddenly drawn into the cup, swimming in the deep water of His presence. I was floating and swimming, and I looked up at the surface of the water from inside the cup and saw His reflection, and I was overcome.

Then He said:

> *"Let the water of My presence overwhelm you. Let the reflection of My presence burn deep within your soul. Let it soak you and fill you till water is coming out of your very pores and you can stretch out your hands and be the reflection of My Glory, For I desire to abide in YOU. He who has measured the waters in the hollow of His hands has come unto you, And He shall come again"*

Even so, Come Lord Jesus, come!

By sharing these last three encounters I hope to give you not only an understanding of the function of a seer and how visions work within a trance encounter, but also wish to stir your hearts to go deeper with the lover of your soul. I want to cause your hearts to burn for the revelation of His tender mercy and inexpressible love for you and offer the cup of His presence to you – so that you may drink deeply from the Master's hand.

CHAPTER 5

CAN I SEE?

"And when the servant of the man of God arose early and went out, there was an army, surrounding the city with horses and chariots. And his servant said to him, Alas, my master! What shall we do? So he answered, Do not fear, for those who are with us are more than those who are with them. And Elisha prayed, and said, Lord, I pray, open his eyes that he may see. Then the Lord opened the eyes of the young man, and he saw. And behold, the mountain was full of horses and chariots of fire all around Elisha."

- 2 Kings 6:15-17

How can I tell if someone operates as a seer?

The easy answer is this; Listen to how they introduce their message or word. If they begin by saying, "The Lord showed me" or "I saw" they, more than likely, operate from the seer modality. If they say, "The Lord would say" or "I believe I heard the Lord say," they are operating in the prophetic "hearing" modality. Remember the root word for prophet is "*Nabi*" meaning to "bubble up," a spontaneous impartation of a word from the Lord.

How can I activate my seer senses?

One of Apostle Paul's main desires in his letter to the Corinthians was that they would not be ignorant regarding spiritual gifts (1 Corinthians 12:1).

> *"Now concerning spiritual gifts, brethren, I do not want you to be ignorant:"*

Paul was interested in activation as well as order. He did not want to hinder their ability to function in the gifts. On the contrary, he encouraged them for he said that they could all prophecy (1 Corinthians 14:31):

> *"For you can all prophesy one by one, that all may learn and all may be encouraged."*

When speaking to Timothy regarding his gifting he encouraged him to activate the gift of God that was in him.

> *"When I call to remembrance the genuine faith that is in you, which dwelt first in your grandmother Lois and your mother Eunice, and I am persuaded is in you also. Therefore I remind you to stir up the gift of God which is in you through the laying on of my hands. For God has not given us a spirit of fear, but of power and of love and of a sound mind."*
>
> – 2 Timothy 1:5-7

The question arises: How do I know I have this gift? They simple answer is to start by asking for it. "*Holy Spirit, release in me the ability to "see" what you are seeing. Activate all my senses so that I may walk in the fullness of all your revelatory communication.*"

You see God's desire is for you to communicate with Him in all dimensions, as His is with you. In Ephesians 1:15-18, Paul prays that the Father of glory would give them the spirit of wisdom, and revelation in the knowledge of Him and that the eyes of their understanding would be enlightened.

> *"Therefore I also, after I heard of your faith in the Lord Jesus and your love for all the saints, do not cease to give thanks for you, making mention of you in my prayers; that the God of our Lord Jesus Christ, the Father of glory, may give to you the spirit of wisdom and revelation in the knowledge of Him, the eyes of your understanding being enlightened; that you may know what is the hope of His calling, what are the riches of the glory of His inheritance in the saints,"*
>
> – Ephesians 1:15-18

When Elisha prayed in 2 Kings 6 for his servants eyes to be open, he didn't pray, *"Lord, if he has the gift of seeing, open his eyes."* No, he simply prayed, *"Lord, I pray, open his eyes that he may see."*

> *"And when the servant of the man of God arose early and went out, there was an army, surrounding the city with horses and chariots. And his servant said to him, "Alas, my master! What shall we do?"*
>
> *So he answered, "Do not fear, for those who are with us are more than those who are with them." And Elisha prayed, and said, "Lord, I pray, open his eyes that he may see." Then the Lord opened the eyes of the young man, and he saw. And behold, the mountain was full of horses and chariots of fire all around Elisha."*

I find it interesting in the book of Revelation, when the Lord speaks to the church of Laodicea he says:

> *"Because you say, 'I am rich, have become wealthy, and have need of nothing'—and do not know that you are wretched, miserable, poor, blind, and naked—I counsel*

> *you to buy from Me gold refined in the fire, that you may be rich; and white garments, that you may be clothed, that the shame of your nakedness may not be revealed; and anoint your eyes with eye salve, that you may see."*
>
> - Revelation 3:17-18

In this verse, we see a description, not only of our state before the cross, i.e. wretched, miserable, poor, blind, and naked. We also see His desire for us after salvation. He wants to clothe us in His righteousness, give us spiritual riches beyond measure, and – now get this – trade our blindness by anointing our eyes with eye salve that that we might see. Paul teaches us that that we are to desire spiritual gifts, especially the prophetic, because it can equip and benefit the body of Christ.

> *"Pursue love, and desire spiritual gifts, but especially that you may prophesy."*
>
> - 1 Corinthians 14:1

The Greek word for "*desire*" is "*zeloo*" meaning to "*burn with zeal*" or "*to be zealous in the pursuit of something.*" In this case, that "*something*" is spiritual gifts. The Greek for "*especially*" is "*mallon*" meaning "*more, to a greater degree, rather.*" Ironically, it is the same word found in Luke 11:9-13 where Jesus is speaking about the gift of the Holy Spirit.

> *"So I say to you, ask, and it will be given to you; seek, and you will find; knock, and it will be opened to you. For everyone who asks receives, and he who seeks finds, and to him who knocks it will be opened. If a son asks for bread from any father among you, will he give him a stone? Or if he asks for a fish, will he give him a serpent instead of a fish? Or if he asks for an egg, will he offer him a scorpion? If you then, being evil, know how to give good gifts to your children, how much more [mal-*

lon] will your heavenly Father give the Holy Spirit to those who ask Him!"

This is the starting place, ask, seek, knock, desire, and be zealous for your eyes to be open. Clearly, this is the Lords will. All it takes is faith and an open heart.

Second, pay attention. It takes time to recognize God's voice. When you stop brushing aside that small still voice or ignoring that faint image that floats across your mind when you are in worship, and pay attention you will beginning to see and hear differently. One of the keys to seeing in the spiritual realm is relearning "how" to think, and "how" to process information. Learn to understand the metaphorical language of God. Ask the Lord to teach you His metaphorical speech. Devour the Scriptures and pay attention to "How" he speaks. Pay attention to the symbolism from your own life experiences.

Learn to rest, and be quiet before the Lord. Distraction is the worst enemy to hearing from God. We live in a society where we are inundated with voices and noise. When you learn to block out distraction you have taken the first step in listening. It takes time, but you can train yourself to dial down, focus, and listen or look at what the Lord is saying.

What if I can't see?

Jim Driscoll, founder of "Stir the Waters" and author of the "Modern Seer" (www.stirthewaters.com), answered this question very well:

"Potentially everyone can see. When we can't see, it could be for a few different reasons: Our gifting is dormant, we aren't ready to see yet, we don't realize we already seeing (that the pictures in our

> *heads are from God), something in our bloodline (like a spiritual curse) is keeping out gifts from functioning, or the enemy made us fearful of our giftings when we were young and we responded by shutting them down,"*

As we will discuss later in this volume, seeing is one of the many ways God communicates. It is open to all believers, as a tool to equip them for the work of ministry. It is not necessarily a prophetic gift as much as it is a language. You can see while operating with words of knowledge or wisdom. It can manifest while ministering healing or deliverance. Not everyone is called to be a Seer or Prophet at a highly public level, but everyone is free to embrace the seer gift and see. The Lord is simply speaking. Let's open up the dialog.

Keys to seeing, listening, and activating the seers gift in your life:

- Start by paying attention, even if what you see does not make sense at the time.
- Evaluate what God seems to be saying.
- Wait for God. Quiet your spirit. Learn to hit the pause button.
- Ask God for clarification. Talk back to God. Dialog is a two way street.
- Pray about it. Look for that inner peace that will resonate in you.
- Realize that God can speak through anything. All your senses are open to listening.
- Sharpen your discernment meter by staying in the Word and through prayer.
- Practice with the Holy Spirit. Jesus said the Holy Spirit would teach you all truth. It is ok to practice.

Doing the things of the Spirit is the surest way to hone your ability to hear. Sharing your experiences with your brothers and sisters in a home group or other safe setting will reinforce your growth in this area.

CHAPTER 6

THE LANGUAGE OF VISIONS AND DREAMS

"And the whole earth was of one language, and of one speech."

- Genesis 11:1

"The heavens declare the glory of God; and the firmament shows His handiwork. Day unto day utters speech, and night unto night reveals knowledge. There is no speech nor language where their voice is not heard."

- Psalms 19:1-3

"Then He said, 'Hear now My words: If there is a prophet among you, I, the LORD, make Myself known to him in a vision; I speak to him in a dream.'"

- Numbers 12:6

Henry Longfellow once wrote, "*Three silences there are: the first of speech, the second of desire, and the third of thought.*" From the very beginning, language has been a part of life, as we know it. It works together with all that we know or do. Desires, thoughts, passions, feelings, praise, worship, and prayer, all move in and out of this vehicle called language.

In the Scriptures, God's written language to the world, we see the inception of language for humanity and earthly creation. In the first book of the Bible, we have the story of creation. In this account, God not only speaks creation into existence but also gives names to that which He created. Man, in his attempt to elevate himself to new heights, concluded that developed language came through maturation from a primate to Homo sapiens.

Yet in Genesis, we see that language is part of the very nature of God and that He created man with that same ability to communicate through a symbolic system.

In Genesis we read:

> "Then God said, "Let Us make man in Our image, according to Our likeness; let them have dominion over the fish of the sea, over the birds of the air, and over the cattle, over all the earth and over every creeping thing that creeps on the earth." So God created man in His own image; in the image of God He created him; male and female He created them."

- Genesis 1:26-27

Here we have the impartation of or the reflection of God's image in man. Part of this attribute was the ability to communicate thoughts and ideas, to have emotions and feel love. In fact, the first act of man on this planet was the naming of the animals as seen in Genesis 2:19.

> "Out of the ground the Lord God formed every beast of the field and every bird of the air, and brought them to Adam to see what he would call

> them. And whatever Adam called each living creature, that was its name."

And about Eve he states:

> "Then the rib which the Lord God had taken from man He made into a woman, and He brought her to the man. And Adam said: "This is now bone of my bones and flesh of my flesh; She shall be called woman, because she was taken out of man."
>
> - Genesis 2:22-23

Language has under gone many definitions. Henry Sweet, an English phonetician and language scholar, stated:

> "Language is the expression of ideas by means of speech-sounds combined into words. Words are combined into sentences, this combination answering to that of ideas into thoughts."

Bernard Bloch and George L. Trager, both linguists, made this definition:

> "A language is a system of arbitrary vocal symbols by means of which a social group cooperates."

The key words in both definitions are "*ideas*," "*thoughts*," and "*social group cooperation*." The idea of social group cooperation is so powerful that in Genesis 11:1-9 we read the story of Nimrod the hunter. In this account we read:

> "Now the whole earth had one language and one speech. And it came to pass, as they journeyed from the east, that they found a plain in the land of Shinar, and they dwelt there. Then they said to one another, "Come, let us make bricks and bake them thoroughly." They had brick for stone, and they had asphalt for mortar. And they said, "Come, let us build ourselves a city, and a tower whose top is

> *in the heavens; let us make a name for ourselves, lest we be scattered abroad over the face of the whole earth. But the Lord came down to see the city and the tower which the sons of men had built. And the Lord said, "Indeed the people are one and they all have one language, and this is what they begin to do; now nothing that they propose to do will be withheld from them. Come, let Us go down and there confuse their language, that they may not understand one another's speech." So the Lord scattered them abroad from there over the face of all the earth, and they ceased building the city. Therefore its name is called Babel, because there the Lord confused the language of all the earth; and from there the Lord scattered them abroad over the face of all the earth."*

In this account, we find humanity in a unified force bound by their ability to communicate and imagine. This unity is so powerful that the Lord changes their language in order to scatter them across the face of the earth. We also see a link between the imagination and imagery and it's correlation to language. Creative powers to accomplish that which is envisioned, if they all think, speak, and desire the same thing, so all three linguistic scholars are right to some extent in there definition of language.

Nonetheless, they fall short in that they actually define speech, which is only one kind of language. Take for example sign language used by the deaf around the world. In sign language, we do not have vocal symbols to communicate. The symbols used are hand symbols representing the vocal language of a given culture. We have body language, instrumental language, the language of art, the language of creation, and yes even the dance of the bees.

Language can better be defined as a set of symbolic images, which conjure up ideas and thought patterns to communicate one to another.

In Leanne Payne's book "*The Healing Presence,*" chapter 9 entitled "*Imagery and Symbol: "The Imagery Really Matters*" she states:

> "*...We are mythic beings: we live by and in our symbols. Man is an animal who symbolizes, who talks. (To talk is to symbolize. Language itself is symbol.) Thus man is set apart from the rest of the natural creation. Symbols bind up reality for us.*"

When I speak of the language of visions and dreams, I am not talking about oneirmancy, occult divination by dreams brought on by the demonic world to confuse and twist the hearts of man. Nor am I speaking of Freud's dream analyses and Jung's archetypes, as helpful as they may be in the field of psychoanalyses.

What I am speaking about is the "*Rehma*" of God (God's spoken word to a person at a given moment regarding a specific situation, in contrast to the "*Logos,*" his eternal written Word to humanity) coming to man in pictorial language. As stated earlier, this spoken language from God may come through any of the senses including visionary dreams or visions.

In the crazy fast-paced world we live in, many times we are so preoccupied that it is hard for us to hear God. Yet, God is speaking and He desires to get or attention. If He cannot get our attention while we are awake, He will get our attention while we sleep and that through dreams. Our Heavenly Father often will use dreams and visions as a vehicle to identify the barricades that are hindering our path to His purpose in our life as illustrated in Job.

> "*In a dream, in a vision of the night, when deep sleep falls upon men, while slumbering on their beds, then He opens the ears of men, and seals their instruction.*"
>
> - Job 33:15-16

Dreams and visions are a major part of the outpouring of God's Spirit in the Last Days!

> *"And it shall come to pass afterward, That I will pour out My Spirit on all flesh; Your sons and your daughters shall prophesy, Your old men shall dream dreams, Your young men shall see visions. And also on My menservants and on My maidservants I will pour out My Spirit in those days."*
>
> - Joel 2:28-29

Redeemed Imagination

We regard the imagination as our ability to picture, pretend, or envision a given situation. A student sits in a classroom staring out the window, transfixed by thoughts a million miles away and we say he's daydreaming. A little girl playing with her dolls is actively engaged in a conversation with a friend nobody sees and we say she has an imaginary friend. The mysterious mind with all of its facets is truly a wonder.

Yet, what is the function of pizza dreams, nightmares, daydreams, visual thinking, imagery, dreaming, and alike? How do we rationalize all the workings that involve our imaginations? What was the creative purpose in the eyes of God for this kind of activity, before we fell from grace?

When God created man, he put within his mind, the mechanism, or ability to receive pictorially, communication from God. Much like a TV receiver man can see what God was speaking into his spirit. Then, at the fall of man, he lost this ability and the receiver became distorted, opening it to other signals. These signals may come from the emotional pain of one's past, pizza, fleshly pleasure, creative thought, or even the demonic realm.

Yet, it was not until the redemption of man through Christ that this operation of the mind began to function properly, though through a glass darkly (1 Corinthians 13:12), the healing process had begun. In the old covenant, it came through the forward look to the cross.

> *"For now we see in a mirror, dimly, but then face to face. Now I know in part, but then I shall know just as I also am known."*
>
> - 1 Corinthians 13:12

In the new covenant regeneration and the renewing of our minds by the Holy Spirit healed it.

This is the creative working of the living God in the life of the believer, the healing of our broken nature. The casting-down of worldly symbolic thoughts that have invaded our minds and restoring the channel to its intended purpose so that we can listen and receive from God that which He desires to breath into our lives.

A dear friend of mine Lyn Sorensen, a seer in her own right, put it this way:

> *"I see pictures and it's like He (the Lord) connects the dots ... pointing the way or an idea or something he's saying to the world... I call it connecting the dots ... some dots are very large, but some are very small..."*

That is how it works, the regenerative process of hearing what God is saying. All the communicative gifting of God, be it prophecy, the word of knowledge, the word or wisdom, distinguishing of spirits, or preaching as an oracle of God, are the out flow of this healing processes.

James Goll, referring to dreams and visions states:

> *"God is the Master Dream Weaver. Through dreams, God communicates directly with us concerning our destiny as well as the destinies of our families, our nation, and our world. Many people today, particularly in the Western culture, never recognize God speaking to them in this way, because they have been conditioned by a skeptical and sophisticated society to discount the language of dreams. Within our own generation, God is reconnecting us to a vital part of our spiritual heritage."*

There are two very similar Hebrew words used in the Old Testament to refer to *"dreams."* The first is *"chalam"* meaning *"to dream, or dreamer"* as in Genesis 37:19, where the brothers of Joseph call him a *"dreamer."*

> *"And they said one to another, Behold, this dreamer [chalam] cometh."*

The second word is *"chalom,"* meaning "a dream." Where either word is used, the Old Testament makes it clear that God is the one orchestrating the dream. He downloads His dreams within us and thereby transforms us into dreamers of His will.

There are three primary words for *"vision"* in Hebrew. The first is *"chazon,"* meaning vision, but carries with it of being in an ecstatic state or trance as seen in 1 Samuel 3:1 (KJV).

> *"And the child Samuel ministered unto the Lord before Eli. And the word of the Lord was precious in those days; there was no open vision.[chazon]"*

The second word is *"mar'eh"* meaning vision or sight, but the emphasis is on the phenomenon, spectacle, appearance, or vision – it is about *"what is seen,"* or the *"power of seeing,"* as seen in Exodus 24:17 (KJV).

> *"And the sight [mar'eh] of the glory of the Lord was like devouring fire on the top of the mount in the eyes of the children of Israel."*

The third word is *"chizayon,"* meaning *"ecstatic vision,"* vision (in the night), or vision, oracle, prophecy e.g. divine communication as seen in 2 Samuel 7:17 (NKJV).

> *"According to all these words, and according to all this vision [chizayon], so did Nathan speak unto David."*

"Onar" is the common word for dream in the New Testament. It is the kind of dreaming we all do when we sleep. God can and does use common dreams to communicate with ordinary people. Example is Joseph's dream to wed Mary, in Matthew 1:20.

> *"But while he thought on these things, behold, the angel of the Lord appeared unto him in a dream [onar], saying, Joseph, thou son of David, fear not to take unto thee Mary thy wife: for that which is conceived in her is of the Holy Ghost."*

The second word is *"enypnion,"* meaning a vision or a dream received while asleep. Enypnion stresses a surprise quality that is contained in that dream. It is the kind of dream that carries weight or has a surprising effect as seen in Acts 2:17 (KJV),

> *"And it shall come to pass in the last days, saith God, I will pour out of my Spirit upon all flesh: and your sons and your daughters shall prophesy, and your young men shall see visions, and your old men shall dream dreams [enypnion]."*

and Jude 1:8 (KJV):

> "Likewise also these filthy dreamers [enypniazomai] defile the flesh, despise dominion, and speak evil of dignities."

There are three primary words used in Greek for the word "*vision*." The first word is "*horama*," meaning that which is seen, spectacle, a sight divinely granted in an ecstasy or in sleep, or a vision as seen in Matthew 17:9 (KJV).

> "And as they came down from the mountain, Jesus charged them, saying, Tell the vision [horama] to no man, until the Son of man be risen again from the dead."

The second word is "*optasia*," meaning a vision, an appearance presented to one whether asleep or awake as seen in Luke 1:22 (KJV).

> "And when he came out, he could not speak unto them: and they perceived that he had seen a vision [optasia] in the temple: for he beckoned unto them, and remained speechless."

The third word is "*horasis*," meaning the act of seeing, a vision, an appearance in visible form, or an appearance divinely granted in an ecstasy or dream as seen in Revelation 4:3; 9:17 (KJV).

> "And he that sat was to look upon like a jasper and a sardine stone: and there was a rainbow round about the throne, in sight [horasis] like unto an emerald."

And Revelation 9:17 (KJV):

> "And thus I saw the horses in the vision [horasis], and them that sat on them, having breastplates of fire, and of jacinth, and brimstone: and the heads of the horses were as the heads of lions; and out of

their mouths issued fire and smoke and brimstone."

The Greek highlights the fact that visions can come within a dream, come in a state of ecstasy, or come in an open vision where the appearance is in visible form.

Wither its dreams or visions, God desires to invade our minds and open the doors of communication so that we my function with Him, by Him, and through Him, in all that we do, that we may be one even as He is one.

The purpose of visual communication is to awaken us to a new dimension in Christ, to quicken us to be alive in Him, and be used by Him, anytime and in any place. Jesus is calling us to put on the mind of Christ and to renew our minds, and be changed. He wants to transform our thought processes so we think in Heavenly mode. He wants us to operate out of a Kingdom mindset and not function in a fallen earthly mode.

As we begin to seek His face, and release the symbolic images of our fallen nature to Him, we can replace those images with the Word of God and the eternal truth of His Kingdom. That is where the healing process begins and our "*receivers*" are honed to tune in to Heaven's channel.

Only then will we hear the Word of God through all that we think and do. His Word will dance upon our minds when we sleep. It will leap upon the mountaintops when we walk through woods enjoying the work of His creative hands. It will move before us in mighty visions as we tread upon serpents in our missionary journeys. It will lead us beside the still waters and comfort us when we are alone. The Word will be active and sharper than any two edged sword and will pierce asunder the thoughts and intents of the hearts of man.

God desires to baste us in the presence of His Word. He desires to envelope us in the cloud of His Glory so that every dot and title of our life revolves around fellowship with Him. This is the language of visions and dreams, the expansion of a hearing ear through the renewing of a mind that was once fallen.

> *"That you put off, concerning your former conduct, the old man which grows corrupt according to the deceitful lusts, and be renewed in the spirit of your mind, and that you put on the new man which was created according to God, in true righteousness and holiness."*
>
> - Ephesians 4:22-24

Chapter 7

God Speaks

"But he who enters by the door is the shepherd of the sheep. To him the doorkeeper opens, and the sheep hear his voice; and he calls his own sheep by name and leads them out. And when he brings out his own sheep, he goes before them; and the sheep follow him, for they know his voice. Yet they will by no means follow a stranger, but will flee from him, for they do not know the voice of strangers."

- John 10:2-5

I find it very exciting to look at creation and examine how God has woven us together, every detail complete in His eternal design. For example, did you know that the nerves leading to the eye are much larger than those leading to the ear? Science tells us that we give twenty-five times as much attention to what we see as to what we hear.

Accordingly, a communication expert for the Army has stated that, *"If you want people to remember what you say, illustrate your talk."* Today we know, in educational circles, that the best way of increasing the retention rate of your students is to blend visual aids with verbalization. When relying on verbalization alone to communicate, an estimated 90% of a message is misinterpreted or forgotten entirely. We learn 10% of what we hear and 83% by what we see. By using both visual in conjunction with verbal, are retention rate is approximately 50%, and if we "*say*" what we "*see*," we retain 70%. However, if we "say" and "*do*," our retention rate climbs to 90%. The Lord has wired us to not only to be "*hearers*" of His Word, but to "*see*" His Word, and once we have "*seen*" to "*speak*" His Word, and finely, to be "*doers*" of His Word (John 1:22-25).

> *"But be doers of the word, and not hearers only, deceiving yourselves. For if anyone is a hearer of the word and not a doer, he is like a man observing his natural face in a mirror; for he observes himself, goes away, and immediately forgets what kind of man he was. But he who looks into the perfect law of liberty and continues in it, and is not a forgetful hearer but a doer of the work, this one will be blessed in what he does."*

It's easy then to understand why the Lord, in His desire to communicate to His children, has chosen a wide variety of creative mediums and has created us to listen from all the spectrums of His creative speech. The power of visionary language paired with the act of proclamation and action results in not only advancing the Kingdom, but also hard wiring the truth of His Word into our renewed minds.

A quick look at some of the resources that God has deposited in our lives causes us to remember the riches we have in communication with Him. One of the greatest of all the gifts that He has given us is the Comforter; that blessed Holy Spirit that descended on the Church, on the day of Pentecost. The Holy Spirit lives in you, and through you. Incredible as it sounds, when you stop and grasp this, it is a very powerful truth; not only this, but the Father Himself abides in you, as well as the blessed Son of the Most High God.

Yet, the Lord did not stop there in His desire to secure a living and breathing relationship with His children, He has given us the inspired Word of God. The entire Scripture is one inspired revelation of God's mind, will, and word communicated to man and bound within the cover of a book we call the Bible. Take a look at these Scriptures:

> *"All Scripture is given by inspiration of God, and is profitable for doctrine, for reproof, for correction, for instruction in righteousness, that the man of God may be complete, thoroughly equipped for every good work."*
>
> - 2 Timothy 3:16-17

> *"And so we have the prophetic word confirmed, which you do well to heed as a light that shines in a dark place, until the day dawns and the morning star rises in your hearts; knowing this first, that no prophecy of Scripture is of any private interpretation, for prophecy never came by the will of man, but holy men of God spoke as they were moved by the Holy Spirit."*
>
> - 2 Peter 1:19-21

We know from these Scriptures that this written revelation of sixty-six books, penned in three different languages, by forty different authors, over thousands of years, by men, of all walks of life, is God's complete revelation to humanity. The Bible is perfect and sufficient to bring all the revelation of God that we can comprehend in our present mortality. No further prophetic communication from God is required. Yet God did not stop there in His desire to communicate to His Church.

In the Greek there are two words used for the word "*word.*" The first is "*Logos,*" and the second is "*Rhema.*" Greek scholars and Biblical theologians have debated about whether these words are synonymous. Yet, many believe that the inspired writers chose each word to express the exact meaning that they were trying to get across. Thus we see two words to express God's communication to man. When we refer to the word "*Logos*," we are referring to the "*Word (Logos) of God*," the Scriptures, the Holy Bible. Logos also refers to Jesus Christ Himself as seen in John 1:1 and 14.

> *"In the beginning was the Word (Logos), and the Word (Logos) was with God, and the Word (Logos) was God... And the Word (Logos) became flesh and dwelt among us, and we beheld His glory, the glory as of the only begotten of the Father, full of grace and truth."*

The Logos of God is settled and complete, it shall never pass away; it is the same, yesterday, today, and forever and can never be added to. It is God's eternal standard, outlining His eternal plan, principles, doctrines, and decrees, by that we use to weigh all truth, in its light. However, what of "*rhema*," how is it used in scripture? What role does rhema play in the life of the Christian and how does it operate in God's communication to His Church?

To better understand rhema let's examine the word rhema as defined by W. E. Vine's Expository Dictionary of the New Testament Words.

> *"Rhema denotes that which is spoken, what is uttered in speech and writing: in the singular, a word. The significance of rhema (as distinct from LOGOS) is exemplified in the injunction to take the sword of the Spirit, which is the word (rhema) of God"*

- W. E. Vine

We see here that the reference is not to the whole Bible but to a single word or truth from scripture that the Holy Spirit brings to remembrance in a time of need. One needs to store the Word (*Logos*) within his spirit so there is something to draw from. So

Logos then is like a well of living water and rhema is like a cup of water drawn from that well; It is like that timely, Holy Spirit inspired word from the Logos that brings faith, life, and power to fulfill God's will in a given situation. Romans 10:17 states, *"So then faith cometh by hearing, and hearing by the word (rhema) of God."* Therefore, we see that the hearer must receive rhema with faith for it to fulfill its desired mission.

Revelatory Gifts

To understand rhema one needs to understand the various gifts that God has placed within His Church. The gifts of the Holy Spirit are referred to in several places in scripture, one of which is found in 1 Corinthians 12.

The Greek word used there for gifts is the word *"charismata,"* which means *"gifts of grace."* The whole purpose of giving these free-gifts of God to His people is to do the work of the Kingdom and to move in deeper fellowship with Christ. They are not given to exalt a believer or to be hidden in a closet. These gifts are given so that Christ, through His body, can buildup its members and equip the saints, for the work of ministry.

Let's look at a few of revelatory gifts that are considered rhema from God.

The Word of Knowledge: Is the speaking or uttering of a truth given to an individual, in a given moment, or a particular situation. This gift is divine illumination or insight from the Holy Spirit; it is a particular disclosure of knowledge and not formed through natural means. The gift is not knowledge but the declaration thereof, a gift of oracular utterance.

The Word of Wisdom: Is a manifestation of the Holy Spirit where the supernatural wisdom of God is declared or proclaimed. It is an impartation of depth and understanding regarding the truth of the gospel or a specific situation. This is neither a result of man's wisdom, human elegance, or the work of a great orator. It is an outflowing from the Holy Spirit concerning the depths of God's heart, a revelation of wisdom, in a given situation or moment.

Discerning of Spirits: It is the supernatural ability given to an individual to see through the outer-man and discern the spirit of the inner-man. It relates to "spirits" and can involve the distinguishing of the human spirit, demonic spirit activity, or angelic spirit activity. This insight into the spiritual realm can only be made possible through the workings of the Holy Spirit. The purpose is to discern the spirit at work in any activity within the body of Christ, in a region, a city, or within an individual.

Prophecy: It is a revelation, given by the Holy Spirit, as with all the gifts it is subordinate to the Word of God. It is communication from God, spoken in the common language, to an individual, to the corporate body at large, or to a nation. It is an expression of the mind and Spirit of Christ. Prophecy can be foretelling-to know the future (Acts 11:28),

> *"Then one of them, named Agabus, stood up and showed by the Spirit that there was going to be a great famine throughout all the world, which also happened in the days of Claudius Caesar."*

Or it can be forthtelling-to cause the future (Ezekiel 37:1-10).

Prophecy is for the edification, exhortation, and consolation (comfort) of the believer (1 Corinthians 14:3).

> *"But he who prophesies speaks edification and exhortation and comfort to men."*

Prophecy is for building up and not tearing down. Prophecy can speak to a present situation or future events. Prophecy is to always be weighed and judged (1 Corinthians 14:29).

> *"Let two or three prophets speak, and let the others judge."*

Weighed as to the depth of what God is saying, Judged as to testing the source, whether it be of the Lord, of the flesh, of the demonic realm, or a combination. In essence, it's the weighing of the significance and the source of what's been said. We know in part and prophesy in part.

Tongues and Interpretation of Tongues: A manifestation of the Holy Spirit where one has yielded the ability of speech to the Holy Spirit and is speaking in one of many languages, be it the language of men or of angels, as the Spirit gives utterance. The mind in essence is bypassed and the spirit is directly speaking through the depths of the Holy Spirit in a given moment.

The gift of tongues can be divided into two categories. The first being ministry tongues where the purpose is to speak the mysteries of God to the assembly of the church as a whole. The exercise of this gift, in this context, is for the edification of the body of Christ and is always accompanied by the gift of interpretation of tongues, the latter being the supernatural gift to translate in a given moment what is spoken by the Holy Spirit, to the gathered assembly.

In these situations, the gift operates very much like prophecy. The second category is that of devotional tongues. Used by an individual for either prayer or praise to God. There are no limitations on devotional tongues. When one prays in tongues ones spirit is praying making intercession, with the Holy Spirit who sees the hidden and unknown things of God and searches the heart of God making one's request known to God. Praise in tongues my happen in song or utterance and is used for personal edification or for intersession.

Along with these gifts, we can add to that list some methodology on how they could come to you:

- A small still voice of the Holy Spirit
- An inner witness of the Holy Spirit
- Revelatory Prayer
- Prophetic Song
- Vision or Dream
- Audible voice of God
- A surge of supernaturally knowing
- Angelic Utterance
- Prophetic Action or Event
- Natural Events or Events in Nature

The Spirit of Revelation

After examining the various ways that God speaks to us, it is imperative that we learn wisdom in handling revelation. We need to learn "how" to test and weigh all that comes in our direction, to move into what God desires to do in our lives. God is speaking today. God is a God of communication. His very name is the "*Word*" and he wants to speak to you today. Dive into the depths of God and listen to all the ways He is speaking to you. God is speaking today. He speaks through the tongues of men and of angels. He speaks through His Word of pin and quill. He speaks through His servants, both prophet and preacher. He speaks through His creation, great and small. He speaks in a wind, or a wee little whisper. He speaks through a child—with childlike faith. He's speaking today—if you listen, you can hear it. In the book of Ephesians 1:17-18, Paul prays the following:

> *"...that the God of our Lord Jesus Christ, the Father of glory, may give to you the spirit of wisdom and revelation in the knowledge of Him, the eyes of your understanding being enlightened; that you may know what is the hope of His calling, what are the riches of the glory of His inheritance in the saints,..."*

In this verse he is praying that they may receive the spirit of wisdom and revelation and that the eyes of their understanding being enlightened. The Greek word there for understanding is "*dianoia*" meaning, the exercise of deep thinking using ones imagination, mind, understanding.

Therefore, Paul is asking the Father to pour out the spirit of revelation upon them and with that revelation infuse them with divine wisdom. He is asking the Father to open their eyes, to let them see, light a spark and set a fire within their hearts igniting their imaginations and their minds with understanding.

This is my prayer for you, that the Father would pour out revelation upon you and you would be a seer filled with all wisdom and understanding, that your minds would be lubricated and your imaginations be released to see. That you, like Elijah, can infuse that ministry into the lives of those around you.

CHAPTER 8

TESTING AND INTERPRETING VISIONARY LANGUAGE

"For a good tree does not bear bad fruit, nor does a bad tree bear good fruit. For every tree is known by its own fruit. For men do not gather figs from thorns, nor do they gather grapes from a bramble bush. A good man out of the good treasure of his heart brings forth good; and an evil man out of the evil treasure of his heart brings forth evil. For out of the abundance of the heart his mouth speaks."

- Luke 6:43-45

"Do not quench the Spirit. Do not despise prophecies. Test all things; hold fast what is good."

- 1 Thessalonians 5:19-21

This book deals mainly with visionary language. The purpose of this chapter is to explain how to test and interpret dreams and visions, though the principles also apply to the testing of all the "*rhemas*" of God.

There are three core components to understanding and implementing a revelation from God. The first is the Revelation itself. The second is the Interpretation of that revelation. The third is the Application of that revelation. Before we dive into the details of these three areas, let's set some groundwork or foundational principles.

The first step in discerning revelation is taking a hard look at your own life, a spiritual survey if you will. You need to do a system check. You need to test your heart and character. Ask yourself various questions to get a spiritual measurement of your walk with the Lord. Take a spiritual pulse-check if you will. This is very important because your discernment is in direct relationship to your abiding in Christ. You were a "fallen" creature that has been saved by grace. Currently you are housed within a mortal fallen body, with all its flaws. It is only by abiding in Him that the spiritual filter of the Holy Spirit can function fully in you. We are in a war and the enemy of our souls will not stop in his efforts to delude and destroy all that God is trying to do in your life. Jesus said,

> *"I am the true vine, and My Father is the vinedresser. Every branch in Me that does not bear fruit He takes away; and every branch that bears fruit He prunes, that it may bear more fruit. You are already clean because of the word which I have spoken to you. Abide in Me, and I in you. As the branch cannot bear fruit of itself, unless it abides in the vine, neither can you, unless you abide in Me."*

> *"I am the vine, you are the branches. He who abides in Me, and I in him, bears much fruit; for without Me you can do nothing. If anyone does not abide in Me, he is cast out as a branch and is withered; and they gather them and throw them into the fire, and they are burned. If you abide in Me, and My words abide in you, you will ask what you desire, and it shall be done for you."*

- John 15:1-7

System Check

Here are some key questions to ask when doing a spiritual system check.

How is my devotional life? Am I regularly reading the Word of God along with studying the Scriptures? It is very important not to just study the Bible, but to devotionally read the Bible, slowly, and meditatively, giving the Holy Spirit an opportunity to breathe His truth into your spirit; Much like dining on the Word of God, savoring every bit, as opposed to studying the recipes, which though very important, do not compare to eating a solid diet of simple reading and extracting all its nutrients.

Check your prayer life. How is my prayer life? Do I spend quality quiet time with the Father? Is my prayer life more than corporate prayer or intersession? Do I have quiet fellowship with the Lord? Do I listen as much as I speak? Devotional prayer is just as important as any other kind of prayer. To learn to savor those moments with God on a regular basis will build a life style of abiding.

Am I having fellowship with other believers? You need to fellowship within the body of Christ. You need to be a part of a local fellowship. A branch set apart from the vine soon withers. A log removed from a burning fire soon smolders. Ask yourself, how is my fellowship?

Do I have un-confessed sin in my life? Jesus said, *"And whenever you stand praying, if you have anything against anyone, forgive him, that your Father in heaven may also forgive you your trespasses."* (Mark 11:25.) The ability to release the issues of life to the Father and confess your sins quickly and expediently unto the

Lord is the surest way to stay on the path of abiding. If we confess our sins, he is faithful and true to forgive us our sins, and to cleanse us from all unrighteousness.

What are my motives? Do I seek to edify the body of Christ? Am I others oriented? Do I have a humble and contrite spirit or am I filled with pride, religiosity, or one-up-man-ship? God is searching for humble hearts of simple devotion to Him. This trait is often honed in the fire of adversity, trial, and brokenness ... but is one that should be strived for.... The ability to seek His face and not just His hand is the surest posture to take when abiding.

Listening

Once you have done a system check, and find yourself in a place of abiding, then you are ready to discern, listen, and judge what God is breathing into your spirit. You must understand that it is important to judge and test revelation. In 1 Corinthians we read:

> *"Let two or three prophets speak, and let the others judge. But if anything is revealed to another who sits by, let the first keep silent. For you can all prophesy one by one, that all may learn and all may be encouraged. And the spirits of the prophets are subject to the prophets. For God is not the author of confusion but of peace, as in all the churches of the saints."*
>
> - 1 Corinthians 14:29-33

Testing and judging are the natural outcome of moving in revelatory knowledge. Too many times people want to throw out the baby with the bath water. Because of fear, they despise prophecy, deny the moving of God's Spirit, and turn from God to protect the church from error.

Yet, Paul tells us in 1 Thessalonians 5:19-21:

> *"Do not quench the Spirit. Do not despise prophecies. Test all things; hold fast what is good."*

The command here is proper balance, testing without grieving, judging without despising. One of the difficult problems believers face as they learn to move in revelatory knowledge is to discern what is accurate or inspired by the Holy Spirit or what is inaccurate or fleshly.

To help better understand this let's look at three sources of revelation that can come into your mind. It is critical to our understanding, for Peter tells us that:

> *"But there were also false prophets among the people, even as there will be false teachers among you, who will secretly bring in destructive heresies, even denying the Lord who bought them, and bring on themselves swift destruction.*
>
> *And many will follow their destructive ways, because of whom the way of truth will be blasphemed. By covetousness they will exploit you with deceptive words; for a long time their judgment has not been idle, and their destruction does not slumber."*
>
> — 2 Peter 2:1-3

The very fact that false teachers shall arise should move us even more into the direction of abiding, but abiding does not mean abandonment of the gifts that God has given us.

Sources of Revelation

Now let's look at a few sources of revelation that exist.

The Holy Spirit

The first and most important source of revelation comes from the Holy Spirit.

In 2 Peter 1:21, we are told:

> *"For prophecy never came by the will of man, but holy men of God spoke as they were moved by the Holy Spirit."*

The Greek word here for "*moved*" is "*Phero,*" meaning to bear, carry, or borne along. This word is also used in Acts 27:15-17, where Paul, on his way to Rome by ship, was caught in a fierce storm.

> *"So when the ship was caught, and could not head into the wind, we let her drive. And running under the shelter of an island called Clauda, we secured the skiff with difficulty. When they had taken it on board, they used cables to undergird the ship; and fearing lest they should run aground on the Syrtis Sands, they struck sail and so were **driven**."*

The winds drove (*Phero*) the ship into the island of Malta where it was shipwrecked. In this instance, we see the same word used for the ship being driven by the wind as was used previously.

This is reminiscent of the rushing wind we see in Acts 2:2:

> *"The winds drove (Phero) the ship into the island of Malta where it was shipwrecked. In this instance, we see the same word used for the ship being driven by the wind as was used previously."*

On several occasions Jesus, in the book of John speaks of the Holy Spirit and His relationship to the church, let's look at a few of them (See John 14:16-17):

> *"And I will pray the Father, and He will give you another Helper, that He may abide with you forever—the Spirit of truth, whom the world cannot receive, because it neither sees Him nor knows Him; but you know Him, for He dwells with you and will be in you."*

In this passage, we learn four things:

1. He is with us forever.
2. We will see and know Him.
3. He will dwell in us.
4. He is the Spirit of truth.

> *"But the Helper, the Holy Spirit, whom the Father will send in My name, He will teach you all things, and bring to your remembrance all things that I said to you."*
>
> - John 14:26

Two important keys come out of this verse:

First, He is our teacher. Second, He will cause us to remember. This is the activation of rhema, where the Holy Spirit makes the reservoir of the Logos, stored in our spirit, alive for us in a given situation.

> *"But when the Helper comes, whom I shall send to you from the Father, the Spirit of truth who proceeds from the Father, He will testify of Me."*
>
> - John 15:26

The scripture tells us that the testimony of Jesus is the Spirit of prophecy (Revelation 19:10).

> *"And I fell at his feet to worship him. But he said to me, See that you do not do that! I am your fellow servant, and of your brethren who have the testimony of Jesus. Wor-*

ship God! For the testimony of Jesus is the spirit of prophecy."

Here we see the Holy Spirit as the activating force behind the testimony of Jesus.

> "Nevertheless I tell you the truth. It is to your advantage that I go away; for if I do not go away, the Helper will not come to you; but if I depart, I will send Him to you."
>
> - John 16:7

We see in this verse the urgency, expediency, necessity, and the heartbeat of Jesus. It is as if He is saying:

I have to go away, if I don't I cannot pour into you my Spirit. You NEED me to pour into you My Spirit. He is your comforter.

> "However, when He, the Spirit of truth, has come, He will guide you into all truth; for He will not speak on His own authority, but whatever He hears He will speak; and He will tell you things to come. He will glorify Me, for He will take of what is Mine and declare it to you. All things that the Father has are Mine. Therefore I said that He will take of Mine and declare it to you."
>
> - John 16:13-15

This is very powerful. When He, the Holy Spirit, comes, He will get your marching orders from the King and speak those things into your life. He will show you what is to come. He will always glorify Jesus. What He receives from Jesus, He will show you.

Along with the Holy Spirit as a source for revelation, there are two other sources that can invade our minds. The Human Spirit or Soul and the demonic.

A second source for revelation is the human spirit or soul. This is illustrated for us in the book of Ezekiel we read:

> *"And the word of the Lord came to me, saying, "Son of man, prophesy against the prophets of Israel who prophesy, and say to those who prophesy out of their own heart, 'Hear the word of the Lord!'"*
>
> *Thus says the Lord GOD: "Woe to the foolish prophets, who follow their own spirit and have seen nothing! O Israel, your prophets are like foxes in the deserts. You have not gone up into the gaps to build a wall for the house of Israel to stand in battle on the day of the Lord. They have envisioned futility and false divination, saying, 'Thus says the Lord!' But the Lord has not sent them; yet they hope that the word may be confirmed. Have you not seen a futile vision, and have you not spoken false divination? You say, 'The Lord says,' "but I have not spoken."*
>
> *Therefore thus says the Lord GOD: "Because you have spoken nonsense and envisioned lies, therefore I am indeed against you," says the Lord GOD."*
>
> - Ezekiel 13:1-8

This is a perfect example for God's people falling into the delusion of false revelation brought on by their own sinful hearts. The Lord links their delusion with the vanity of their walk, the lack of abiding in Christ and resting in their own prideful ways. Jeremiah also expounds on:

> *"Thus says the Lord of hosts: "Do not listen to the words of the prophets who prophesy to you. They make you worthless; They speak a vision of their own heart, Not from the mouth of the Lord. They continually say to those who despise Me, 'The Lord has said, "You shall have peace"'; And to everyone who walks according to the dictates of his own heart, they say, 'No evil shall come upon you.'" For who has stood in the counsel of the Lord, And has perceived and heard His word? Who has marked His word and heard it?"*
>
> - Jeremiah 23:16-18

It is evident from these passages that the need to stay humble before God, to seek His face and not simply His Hand, and keeping our hearts pure before Him, is the only way to abide. This calls for the fruit of the Spirit in all its meekness, anything less, simply leads to strong delusion. In Colossians Paul tells us that we should:

> "Beware lest anyone cheat you through philosophy and empty deceit, according to the tradition of men, according to the basic principles of the world, and not according to Christ."
>
> - Colossians 2:8

Here again we see the role that vanity plays in deception and the pride of human philosophy in the web of deceit. We must be wise and humble in all our ways lest we fall into the pitfall of deception.

The wounded soul is also a source of false revelation. In book two of this series, "*The Seer and Healing*," we talk about the renewing of the mind and inner healing of the wounded soul. The whole process of healing the wounded soul will help guard against soulish delusion.

demonic Realm

The third source of revelation comes from the demonic realm. Paul makes it very clear in Ephesians 6, that our warfare is not waged against humanity but the spiritual forces of darkness. Paul further elaborates for us in Second Corinthians the craftiness of the enemy in his pursuit to destroy what God is doing (2 Corinthians 11:3-4; 13:15).

> "But I fear, lest somehow, as the serpent deceived Eve by his craftiness, so your minds may be corrupted from the simplicity that is in Christ. For if he who comes preaches another Jesus whom we have not p reached, or if you re-

ceive a different spirit which you have not received, or a different gospel which you have not accepted—you may well put up with it!"

- 2 Corinthians 11:3-4

"For such are false apostles, deceitful workers, transforming themselves into apostles of Christ. And no wonder! For Satan himself transforms himself into an angel of light. Therefore it is no great thing if his ministers also transform themselves into ministers of righteousness, whose end will be according to their works."

- 2 Corinthians 13:15

A good example of this kind of warfare encounter is found in the book of Acts 16:16-18 were read:

> "Now it happened, as we went to prayer, that a certain slave girl possessed with a spirit of divination met us, who brought her masters much profit by fortune-telling. This girl followed Paul and us, and cried out, saying, "These men are the servants of the Most High God, who proclaim to us the way of salvation." And this she did for many days."

In this account, we see a woman possessed by a demon of necromancy. The deception that she was using, to infiltrate the church, was not a lie, but a truth that was being proclaimed through a demonic spirit. No doubt, this was to give credence to her divination, and I presume, that her ultimate desire was to secure a position in the church that would ultimately lead to damnable heresies.

However, Paul grieved in his spirit, through the gift of discerning of spirits, saw through this false angle of light, and cast the demon out. Oh, how much more today do we need this gift? I pray that the Lord would richly pour out this gift upon us in these Last Days.

This whole process of judging revelation takes on major elements of warfare and that many times this takes place in our minds. That's why we are commanded to renew our minds, and put on the mind of Christ. Take up the helmet of salvation and the sword of the Spirit, which is the Rhema of God. Paul tells us in Second Corinthians that:

> *"For though we walk in the flesh, we do not war according to the flesh. For the weapons of our warfare are not carnal but mighty in God for pulling down strongholds, casting down arguments and every high thing that exalts itself against the knowledge of God, bringing every thought into captivity to the obedience of Christ,"*

- 2 Corinthians 10:3-5

The key here lies in taking every thought captive and sifting it through the Word of God. We must keep our hearts in check. For vain imaginations and thoughts that proceed, either from the flesh or the demonic realm, have only one purpose in mind and that is to kill the life of Christ in you, to rob you and the Church of the blessings of the Most High, and to destroy all that God desires to do in this dying world.

We must pray for a humble heart, and discern what is of God and what is not. Therefore, as Jesus has stated, we must take heed **how** we hear....

> *"Therefore take heed how you hear. For whoever has, to him more will be given; and whoever does not have, even what he seems to have will be taken from him."*

- Luke 8:18

This is truly a call to heart cleansing, for,

> *"With the pure You will show Yourself pure; And with the devious You will show Yourself shrewd."*

- Psalm 18:26

Mixture

Many times revelation will be a mixture of the above. Having a mixture does not necessarily label you as a false prophet, for we are in a fallen world with a fallen nature, not perfect, and must sift out what is good and beneficial and ignore the parts that are not. John Wimber once said, "*I always throw out the bones when I eat chicken.*" Sifting unmingled truth is simply tossing out the bones and eating the tender, juicy meat.

Remember Paul's words to Corinth:

> "*For now we see in a mirror, dimly, but then face to face. Now I know in part, but then I shall know just as I also am known.*"

- 1 Corinthians 13:12

Paul also tells us in 1 Thessalonians 5:19-21:

> "*Do not quench the Spirit. Do not despise prophecies. Test all things; hold fast what is good.*"

Peter is a perfect example of mixture in revelation. Look at these two events in the book of Matthew:

> "*Simon Peter answered and said, "You are the Christ, the Son of the living God."*
>
> *Jesus answered and said to him, "Blessed are you, Simon Bar-Jonah, for flesh and blood has not revealed this to you, but My Father who is in heaven."*

Then in just a few verses later, Peter was in a different mode.

> "*From that time Jesus began to show to His disciples that He must go to Jerusalem, and suffer many things from*

> *the elders and chief priests and scribes, and be killed, and be raised the third day.*
>
> *Then Peter took Him aside and began to rebuke Him, saying, "Far be it from You, Lord; this shall not happen to You!"*
>
> *But He turned and said to Peter, "Get behind Me, Satan! You are an offense to Me, for you are not mindful of the things of God, but the things of men."*

- Matthew 16:16-17, 21-24

At one moment Peter is receiving divine revelation regarding Jesus' identity, and at another moment the devil is speaking through him with lying revelation. Jesus response to all this is a call to self-denial, seeking the will of God and not selfish ambitions. I would guess that Peter felt proud after Jesus blessed him saying (Matthew 16:18-19):

> *"And I also say to you that you are Peter, and on this rock I will build My church, and the gates of Hades shall not prevail against it. And I will give you the keys of the kingdom of heaven, and whatever you bind on earth will be bound in heaven, and whatever you loose on earth will be loosed in heaven."*

This opened his heart to be deceived and give ungodly counsel. If Peter, can fall into this trap, how much more can we in the church today? The fruits of the flesh are not the only doors to false revelation. Fatigue, sickness, tiredness, stress, certain forms of medication, and depression can all add to the confusion found in receiving Godly revelation.

> *"The words of the Lord are pure words, Like silver tried in a furnace of earth, Purified seven times."*

- Psalms 12:6

Judas, being filled with greed and the need for power, opened up the door to the devil, which lead to the betrayal of our Lord.

> *"And supper being ended, the devil having already put it into the heart of Judas Iscariot, Simon's son, to betray Him,"*
>
> - John 13:2

Proverbs tells us that *"All the ways of a man are pure in his own eyes, but the Lord weighs the spirits."* (Proverbs 16:2). Knowing this we must *"Commit your works to the Lord, and your thoughts will be established."* (Proverbs 16:3).

This is why fellowship is so important. We must submit ourselves to one another (Ephesians 5:21 OB). For, *"Where there is no counsel, the people fall; But in the multitude of counselors there is safety."* (Proverbs 11:14).

Testing revelation

When testing revelation we must also look for evidences of influences other than the Spirit of God. Examine the heart or center core of your revelation. Do a system check of your spiritual walk.

Following is a list of eleven tests for judging revelation:

- Test your motivation and the purpose in giving the revelation. *"But he who prophesies speaks edification and exhortation and comfort to men."*, 1 Corinthians 14:3; Ephesians 4:11-12. If your motives are other than those outlined above, your heart is not pure in this regard and the revelation is probably not from the Holy Spirit. The result of all of God's work lies in redemption.

- What is the beneficial purpose? Does it bring conviction or condemnation, or does it strengthen and edify?
- Test it against the Scriptures. Does it agree with the Word of God? (2 Timothy. 3:16, 17; Revelation 22:18-19). Does it line up with the purpose of God's written revelation in the Word? (2 Corinthians 1:17-20)
- Test the content of the revelation (1 Thessalonians 5:19-22). Is the rhema confirming something that God is doing in your life or the life of the person it is for? Does it flow with the Scriptures, and is God speaking the something to many people in your fellowship.
- Does it seek to Glorify Jesus Christ? (John 16:14, 15; Revelation 19:10; Daniel 7:1-14.) All rhema from God will woo you to Jesus Christ and seek to lift Him up with praise and honor.
- What is the fruit of the revelation and the resulting fruit in your own life? (Matthew 7:15-18; Ephesians 5:9, 10; Galatians 5:19-26.)
- Does it come to pass? (Deuteronomy 18:20-22; 1 Corinthians 13:9-12)
- Does it draw you away from Jesus? (Deuteronomy 13:1-5)
- Does it produce liberty or bondage? (Romans 8:15; 1 Corinthians 14:33; 2 Timothy 1:7; 2 Corinthians 3:17)
- Does it produce life or death? (2 Corinthians 3:6)
- Does the Holy Spirit attest to the revelation? (1 John 2:27) Is it confirmed in your spirit or the spirits of others?

In conclusion, we must test every spirit, and test the spirit of every revelation (1 John 4:1-6). Testing not only involves discerning if the revelation is from God or not, but once discerned that it is of

God then, if a vision or dream, it must be interpreted by God before it can be applied.

Interpreting

The interpreting of visions and dreams starts with your investment in the Word of God. The richness of time you spend in the Word is in direct correlation to your understanding what God has shown you in pictorial form. Throughout the Word, God has illustrated His truth, and you need the truths of scripture to live deep within your being. When that happens the Holy Spirit is able to reach down into your spirit and pull the relevant truth to the surface and merge it with your revelation.

Secular bookstores, for years, have sold books on dream interpretation, linking various symbols with their interpretation. These books are carnal and often demonic in nature. There are a few Christian books on dream interpretation and they are useful to some degree. However, it must be remembered that God's visionary language is creative in nature, individual in purpose, and selective, designed for the one receiving the vision. It can't be mass-produced and handed out to the curious like candy.

The only consistency found in the symbolic language of God's visions and dreams is the richness of the truth it proclaims. We do see commonality at times throughout the body of Christ but these are not set in stone. Symbolism has its foundation in the Word of God! Many times God will use symbols found in the Scriptures. On the other hand, he often will use symbols that are relevant to your life experience. God is a creative God. His very nature causes the springing-forth of creative activity in every move. He will not be put into a box. When God speaks to you through visions or dreams, He speaks very personally.

In the back of this book I have placed a glossary of symbolism. However, it must be remembered that this list is very general and not fixed. Your best source for understanding metaphorical symbolism is the Word of God. It is so rich it will reach across all spectrums of life and communication. It is simply there as a guide on how to look at symbolic imagery.

Application

Application not only involves God's timing, place, and method, but also the motives of your heart in the deliverance of the revelation.

Ask God:

- **Who** is this revelation for? Is it for me, for someone else, or for the whole group?
- **How** should I give this word?
- **When** should I give this word? Timing is critical for the fruit of a word to be spoken in power and received by the intended audience.
- **What** should I do after giving this word? And so on.

Remember, when giving a rhema from God, your heart is always in focus. Abide in Him, stay humble, and seek His face. Dare to be a Daniel and strive for the deeper things in Him. Don't settle for revelation, for the sake of revelation. Seek His face in the midst of revelation and you will overflow with rivers of living water. Then, and only then, will your cup, be a cup of blessings to others around you.

CHAPTER 9

THE SEER AND THE GIFTS

"Now the boy Samuel ministered to the Lord before Eli. And the word of the Lord was rare in those days; there was no widespread revelation., So Samuel lay down until morning, and opened the doors of the house of the Lord. And Samuel was afraid to tell Eli the vision., So Samuel grew, and the Lord was with him and let none of his words fall to the ground. And all Israel from Dan to Beersheba knew that Samuel had been established as a prophet of the Lord."

- 1 Samuel 3:1, 15, 19-20

"As they went up the hill to the city, they met some young women going out to draw water, and said to them, "Is the seer here?,
Samuel answered Saul and said, "I am the seer. Go up before me to the high place, for you shall eat with me today; and tomorrow I will let you go and will tell you all that is in your heart."

- 1 Samuel 9:11, 19

There are many reasons why I have chosen the term *"Seer"* in describing the one who receives communication from God through visions and dreams. As stated earlier, the foremost reason for this lies in the Hebrew meaning of the word *"Seer."* In the Hebrew, the word *"Seer"* is *"ro'eh"* (roh-ay), meaning a visionary, a seer, or one who sees visions. Ro'eh comes from the root verb *"ra'ah,"* which means, *"to see."* In the Old Testament, the word "Seer," was used in interchangeably with *"Prophet."*

In the book of Samuel 9:9 we read:

> *"Formerly in Israel, when a man went to inquire of God, he spoke thus: "Come, let us go to the seer"; for he who is now called a prophet was formerly called a seer."*

I have chosen the word *"Seer"* in the title of this book, not in the narrow sense of being a prophet, but in the wider sense of one who sees visions and dreams. This may very well include the ministry and/or office of a prophet but it can also include many of the other new covenant ministries within the church.

In the Old Testament, there existed three types of ministries within the theocracy of the nation of Israel. These were the offices of Prophet, Priest, and King. When Jesus came, he fulfilled all those offices as Messiah. He was that Prophet like unto Moses; he is our Great High Priest; and most of all he is the King of Kings and Lord of Lords. Whereas in the Old Testament we saw three ministry offices at work for the people of God, in the New Testament we see three sets of gifts given by the Godhead to His church. This is hinted at in 1 Corinthians 12:4-7.

> *"There are diversities of gifts, but the same Spirit. There are differences of ministries, but the same Lord. And there are diversities of activities, but it is the same God who works all in all. But the manifes-*

> *tation of the Spirit is given to each one for the profit of all."*

From this verse, one could say that the Holy Spirit distributes the gifts; the Lord Jesus assigns the administrative positions; and God the Father lays out the foundational operations within the church. Yet, it is the Triune God that is at work in perfect unity (John 17) and in all the functions of the body. It also can be compared to our governmental system where we have the Administrative Branch, the Legislative Branch, and the Judicial Branch. I wonder where our founding fathers got that idea.

Tri-unity of Gifting

This tri-unity of gifting is broken down as follows:

Gifts of the Father

In Romans 12:3-8, we see the gifts of the Father, which speak of our place in God's created order. Their focus appears to be characterized by basic *"motivations,"* or *"inherent tendencies."* These *"gifts"* are foundational to our kingdom makeup and more than likely we are made up with a mixture of these things. Following is a list of the Fathers gifts:

Prophecy: Speaking of general prophecy, which belongs to all believers (Joel 2:28).

Ministry: Serving others (Matthew 20:26).

Teaching: Supernatural ability to expound the truths of God.

Exhortation: To entreat, comfort, or instruct (Acts 4:36; Hebrews 10:25).

Giving: Out of a spirit of generosity (2 Corinthians 8:2; 9:11-13).

Leadership: Being a model by example (Romans 12:8; 1 Corinthians 12:28; Acts 6:1-7; Titus 1:5; Numbers 27:18).

Mercy: The spirit of empathy and sympathy for another; related to a burden bearer (Romans 12:8; Matthew 5:7, 9:27, 1:16-24; Acts 9:36; Luke 10:33-35; 2 Timothy 1:15-18).

Gifts of the Holy Spirit

The gifts of the Holy Spirit are found in 1 Corinthians 12:7-11.

> *"But the manifestation of the Spirit is given to each one for the profit of all: for to one is given the word of wisdom through the Spirit, to another the word of knowledge through the same Spirit, to another faith by the same Spirit, to another gifts of healings by the same Spirit, to another the working of miracles, to another prophecy, to another discerning of spirits, to another different kinds of tongues, to another the interpretation of tongues. But one and the same Spirit works all these things, distributing to each one individually as He wills."*

Their purpose is to profit or bring together the body of the church. These gifts are available to every believer within the church. You can also view these gifts of the Spirit as the toolbox or arsenal of God.

When the church has a need to be met it is here in this toolbox that you will find a gift to meet the need. The manifestations of these gifts are to be expected within the life of a spiritual healthy church (1 Corinthians 13, 14:1).

> *"Pursue love, and desire spiritual gifts, but especially that you may prophesy."*

- I Corinthians 14:1

The nine gifts mentioned in 1 Corinthians are listed as follows (many of which we have defined previously):

Word of Wisdom: Supernatural perspective and/or plan to accomplish God's will.

Word of Knowledge: Supernatural revelation about a person in any of a multiplicity of situations.

Faith: Supernatural ability to believe God, without doubt.

Gifts of Healing: Supernatural healing without human aid.

Working of Miracles: Supernatural power to overcome earthly and/or demonic forces; Also applies to the creative regeneration of human body parts.

Prophecy: Divinely inspired message or utterance from God to His people, by way of the human element.

Discerning of Spirits: Supernatural revelation and insight into the spirit realm, whether human, Holy, or demonic.

Different Kinds of Tongues: Supernatural utterance in languages unknown; Can take the form of prayer, praise, song, prophecy, or intersession.

Interpretation of Tongues: Supernatural ability to reveal the meaning of a tongue; Works side by side with tongues as a form of prophecy; Could have been one of the any miracles that occurred in Acts 2.

The wisdom of Paul illustrated in Romans 12 highlights the momentum of the gifts in action and our responsibility to be fully engaged:

> "For I say, through the grace given to me, to everyone who is among you, not to think of himself more highly than he ought to think, but to think soberly, as God has dealt to each one a measure of faith. For as we have many members in one body, but all the members do not have the same function, so we, being many, are one body in Christ, and individually members of one another. Having then gifts differing according to the grace that is given to us, let us use them: if prophecy, let us prophesy in proportion to our faith; or ministry, let us use it in our ministering; he who teaches, in teaching; he who exhorts, in exhortation; he who gives, with liberality; he who leads, with diligence; he who shows mercy, with cheerfulness."
>
> - Romans 12:3-8

Gifts of the Son – The Office Gifts

Now we come to the gifts of the Son of God, which are found in Ephesians 4:7-16.

> "But to each one of us grace was given according to the measure of Christ's gift. Therefore He says:
>
> > "When He ascended on high,
> > He led captivity captive,
> > And gave gifts to men."
>
> (Now this, "He ascended" —what does it mean but that He also first descended into the lower parts of the earth? He who descended is also the One who ascended far above all the heavens, that He might fill all things.)

> *And He Himself gave some to be apostles, some prophets, some evangelists, and some pastors and teachers, for the equipping of the saints for the work of ministry, for the edifying of the body of Christ, till we all come to the unity of the faith and of the knowledge of the Son of God, to a perfect man, to the measure of the stature of the fullness of Christ; that we should no longer be children, tossed to and fro and carried about with every wind of doctrine, by the trickery of men, in the cunning craftiness of deceitful plotting, but, speaking the truth in love, may grow up in all things into Him who is the head—Christ—from whom the whole body, joined and knit together by what every joint supplies, according to the effective working by which every part does its share, causes growth of the body for the edifying of itself in love."*

- Ephesians 4:7-16

This section can be referred to as the administrative arm of the church. The purpose of these gifts is to insure that the other gifts are activated within the church. Their purpose is to place leaders within the church so to cause the body of Christ to grow into maturity. This is seen in Ephesians chapter four.

The office gifts of Christ are as follows:

Apostle: Refers to a select group of individuals in the church who have tremendous insight into extending the work of the church, opening new territories to the gospel, and administering over large bodies of believers

Prophet: A spiritually proven prophet to the larger body of Christ with a divinely focused message to the church and/or the world

Evangelist: A divinely inspired preacher whose main focus is to the lost

Pastor: A leader and shepherd to the flock of God. Capable of not only feeding and leading the church but also caring and protecting a body of believers

Teacher: A leader within the church with a special anointing to teach the larger body of Christ the truths of God.

It is due to this diversity of manifestations, gifts, and offices, that I use the word seer in lieu of prophet when speaking of people who receive dreams or visions from the Lord. There are many in the body of Christ who consistently receive revelations through the language of dreams and visions that may very well be budding prophets of the Lord.

Yet, there are many more who are simply functioning in the body through various gifts such as receiving words of wisdom, words of knowledge, discernment of spirits, ministry of healing, and intersession; let us not confuse the language of visions and dreams with the office of a Prophet.

All believers are to eagerly desire prophecy. It is called, the greater of the gifts, do to its edification attributes. Yet, not all believers hold the office of a prophet. There are various stages of growing in the prophetic that I discuss in Book three of this series, "*The Seer and Prophecy*," dealing specifically with the prophetic. Prophecy is not my intended focus of book one. The dynamics of receiving visions and dreams are open to almost all the manifestations of the spirit. This is true because visions and dreams are a kind of pictorial language and not the mission itself. By holding this view, I feel that far more people within the church will benefit from this teaching.

Therefore, to summarize, a "*seer*," in the context of this book, is a Christian who receives, on a regular bases, visions and dreams. They may function in any of the offices of the church, or may be a servant member of a local fellowship. Whichever the case, wither a prophet of the Lord or a servant in the fellowship, their desire is to serve Jesus with all their heart, and see His Kingdom fill the whole earth. It is to these individuals that this book is written.

I want to encourage you to embrace the Seer's Gift. Exercise all your senses. Fellowship with the Lord and Let him speak to you through all the wondrous ways of heavenly dialog. You were created to hear and communicate with your God. As you hone your senses and are cognizant of Him during every walking hour, He will flood your heart with His desires. The Seer's Gift is a gift of intimacy. Jesus craves an intimate relationship with you.

The Seer's Gift is given that you might hear clearly and run the race set before you. For the gifts and callings of God to be truly effective in your life you need to hear from your commander and chief, to need marching orders, clarity of vision, and the ability to dream and envision your destiny. The Seer's Gift will hone your hearing ear, and cause you to be effective in your journey with Him.

Chapter 10

Aurora

"Oh, that You would rend the heavens! That You would come down! That the mountains might shake at Your presence — As fire burns brushwood, as fire causes water to boil — To make Your name known to Your adversaries, that the nations may tremble at Your presence! When You did awesome things for which we did not look, You came down, the mountains shook at Your presence. For since the beginning of the world men have not heard nor perceived by the ear, nor has the eye seen any God besides You, who acts for the one who waits for Him.

- Isaiah 64:1-4

I can think of no better topic to end this section then with the topic of being embraced and filled with the Holy Spirit of promise. You see, deep in the heart of every person there is a yearning for God. For those that know Him, it is a heart cry for more of Him and it increases with every passing touch of His presence. Like estranged lovers, we ache to see His face, to hear His whisper, and to feel His breathe upon our lives. For those that don't, it is the hollow sound of searching, trying to fill a craving they don't understand. Like an ancient dry well scarred by the desert heat, their voice echoes in the wind, crying out for the source of living water.

This desire is not new; it is built into our DNA. We were created to know Him and seek after more of His presence in our lives. Expressions of that desire are seen in our passions, hunger, creative nature, need for love, and our ability to dream. Those traits are but a reflection of the One we are groaning for. We are after all, created in His image. When these innate abilities go unchecked by heaven's purpose they spin off into worldly desires, lusts, and the pursuit of false fulfillment. However, when they are ignited by Holy passion they become the catalyst in bringing the Kingdom of Heaven to earth, and the fulfillment of who we were created to be, and our identity blossoms.

Consider the words of Isaiah, "*Oh, that You would rend the heavens! That You would come down!*" In this verse Isaiah sums up the cry and desire of all creation. It is not only a cry for presence, but also a cry for influence, a call for God to invade earth and explode in the hearts of humanity. Yet, from the moment Adam and Eve sinned, the answer to that cry was put in motion, and from the seed of the women would come forth a redeemer, Jesus, who conclusively, would unite humanity back to his Creator.

Isaiah heard the whisper of this promise. You can hear it in many of his prophecies, Isaiah 9:6; 11:1; and 61, to name a few. Those that know Him hear that same whisper. For those that don't, Isaiah leaves them with the reality of their condition, and this promise (Isaiah 32:13-16):

> "*On the land of my people will come up thorns and briers, yes, on all the happy homes in the joyous city; Because the palaces will be forsaken, the bustling city will be deserted. The forts and towers will become lairs forever, a joy of wild donkeys, a pasture of flocks—*

> *Until the Spirit is poured upon us from on high, and the wilderness becomes a fruitful field, and the fruitful field is counted as a forest. Then justice will dwell in the wilderness, and righteousness remain in the fruitful field...."*

In this passage Isaiah acknowledges God's awareness of the pain and travail caused by sins invasion upon the planet. However, he also leaves all of us this promise, "*Until the Spirit is poured upon us from on high, and the wilderness becomes a fruitful field.*" That is what we all want. For those that have experienced God's touch through the kiss of the Holy Spirit, our yearning is for more of Him. For those that don't, their true craving is to be filled with the giver of life, the Holy Spirit of comfort.

John the Baptist echoed the same promise, not knowing that the answer to that promise was headed in his direction.

> *"I indeed baptize you with water unto repentance, but He who is coming after me is mightier than I, whose sandals I am not worthy to carry.* **He will baptize you with the Holy Spirit and fire.** *His winnowing fan is in His hand, and He will thoroughly clean out His threshing floor, and gather His wheat into the barn; but He will burn up the chaff with unquenchable fire."*
>
> *Then Jesus came from Galilee to John at the Jordan to be baptized by him. And John tried to prevent Him, saying, "I need to be baptized by You, and are You coming to me?"*
>
> *But Jesus answered and said to him, '**Permit it to be so now, for thus it is fitting for us to fulfill all righteousness.**'"*
>
> - Matthew 3:11-15

Suddenly, he saw the Lamb of God approaching. Struck by his own need, he pleads, "*I need to be baptized by You, and you are coming to me?*" In other words, I am not worthy to do such a thing, to be in your presence. Please baptize me with Holy fire!

Then Jesus responded, "**Permit it to be so....**" The answer to all the cries of history, past and present, was looking him in the eyes. A proclamation was made, Jesus was declaring to the entire universe, now is the time, and today is the day of your visitation.

At that, John baptized Him, and in doing so, a rift was torn in the universe and the Heavens opened, the Spirit of the living God had come.

> *"And immediately, coming up from the water, He saw **the heavens parting** and the Spirit descending upon Him like a dove. Then a voice came from heaven, "You are My beloved Son, in whom I am well pleased."*

- Mark 1:10-11

That was not just a quaint prophetic act; it was a violent act. One in which the Spirit of God tore through the heavens and forever changed the atmosphere and creation. The rending that Isaiah cried out for just took place and the Spirit of God filled the Son of God, in His humanity. It was the same power and rending that we saw at the cross when the veil of the temple was torn from top to bottom, and the earth quaked, and the rocks split (Matthew 27:51).

> *"Then, behold, the veil of the temple was torn in two from top to bottom; and the earth quaked, and the rocks were split,"*

At the Jordan we saw Heaven open and the Spirit descend upon the promised one. At the cross we saw Heaven open and the veil of the temple tore, giving all believers access to the throne room of God. Today, every believer is living under that same open Heaven. Without that access and your ability to abide in Christ and be filled with the Holy Spirit, you can do nothing (John 15:4). However, if you live desiring to want more, and you seek His face, you will be filled, for you **are** the temple of the Holy Spirit. You were created to house the thunderous presence of Almighty God. When you die to your old man, and seek the giver of life, you will see as Isaiah did (Isaiah 6:1):

> *"In the year that King Uzziah died, I saw the Lord sitting on a throne, high and lifted up, **and the train of His robe filled the temple.**"*

That word for "*filled*" in Hebrew has the essence of continual motion. In other words, His robe filled, and kept on filling, the temple. What a wondrous thing it is to know that God's desire to fill us is not a one-time event. He is looking to fill us to overflowing, and continue that process until we see Him face-to-face. However, filling is for the thirsty. God wants you so thirsty for Him that nothing else will satisfy. To be filled you not only have to thirst, but you have to go after Him and drink. No one can force you to thirst, seek, or drink. Those acts are yours alone. By them you will be filled or not, its really all up to you. You see faith mingled with thirst and seeking produces drinking. When you stir your hearts desire to press in, no matter the cost, a cup of blessing will await you.

> *"On the last day, that great day of the feast, Jesus stood and cried out, saying, **"If anyone thirsts, let him come to Me and drink. He who believes in Me, as the Scripture has said, out of his heart will flow rivers of living water."** But this He spoke concerning the Spirit, whom those believing in Him would receive; for the Holy Spirit was not yet given, because Jesus was not yet glorified."*
>
> - John 7:37-39

Jesus desires to fill you with the Spirit. Other than the kingdom of Heaven and doing the works of the Kingdom, it was the promise He talked about the most. He called it the promise of the Father. Consider the following Scriptures:

> *"And I will pray the Father, and He will give you another* **Helper,** *that He may* **abide with you forever**—*the* **Spirit of truth,** *whom the world cannot receive, because it neither sees Him nor knows Him; but you know Him, for* **He dwells with you and will be in you.**
>
> *But the Helper, the Holy Spirit, whom the Father will send in My name,* **He will teach you all things, and bring to your remembrance all things** *that I said to you."*

- John 14:16-18, 26

> *"But when the Helper comes, whom I shall send to you from the Father, the Spirit of truth who proceeds from the Father,* **He will testify of Me."**

- John 15:26

> *"I still have many things to say to you, but you cannot bear them now.* **However, when He, the Spirit of truth, has come, He will guide you into all truth;** *for He will not speak on His own authority, but* **whatever He hears He will speak; and He will tell you things to come. He will glorify Me, for He will take of what is Mine and declare it to you.** *All things that the Father has are Mine. Therefore I said that He will take of Mine and declare it to you."*

- John 16:12-15

One of the first acts of Jesus after He was resurrected was to commission and empower His disciples. His desire was that they would do just as He had done. Their mission was to follow the model of Jesus and heal the sick, cast out demons, and raise the dead. They were to be totally dependent upon the Father and to walk filled with the Holy Spirit. After He spoke to them about their mission, He breathed on them, and declared, "Receive the Holy Spirit."

> *"So Jesus said to them again, "Peace to you!* **As the Father has sent Me, I also send you."** *And when* **He had said this,**

> *He breathed on them, and said to them, "Receive the Holy Spirit."*
>
> - John 20:21-22

Then a little while later He lit the fire again, only this time the filling of the Spirit was coming in power, and it was not just for them, but for all who tarry for His promise.

> *"Behold, I send the Promise of My Father upon you;* **but tarry in the city of Jerusalem until you are endued with power from on high."**
>
> - Luke 24:49

His desire for them to be filled was unstoppable. He met with them again and proclaimed:

> *"And being assembled together with them, He commanded them not to depart from Jerusalem, but to wait for the Promise of the Father, "which," He said, "you have heard from Me; for John truly baptized with water, but you shall be baptized with the Holy Spirit not many days from now."*
>
> - Acts 1:4-5

Suddenly it happened!

> *"When the Day of Pentecost had fully come, they were all with one accord in one place.* **And suddenly there came a sound from heaven, as of a rushing mighty wind, and it filled the whole house where they were sitting.** *Then there appeared to them divided tongues, as of fire, and one sat upon each of them.* **And they were all filled with the Holy Spirit** *and began to speak with other tongues, as the Spirit gave them utterance."*
>
> - Acts 2:1-4

This filling was not a one-time event:

> *"For the promise is to you and to your children, and to all who are afar off, as many as the Lord our God will call."*
>
> - Acts 2:39

We are to seek Him with all our hearts and be filled with His glory and presence. This is our heart's pursuit, and when the Glory comes it will shake the very foundations of our lives. My desire for you, as you read this book, is to be filled to overflowing. My heart's cry is that you would be so ignited by the flame of His presence that you would set the world ablaze with the love of our Master. When we come together as believers we should expect no less than what the priests of the old covenant experienced.

> *"And it came to pass, when the priests came out of the holy place, that the cloud filled the house of the Lord, so that the priests could not continue ministering because of the cloud; for the glory of the Lord filled the house of the Lord."*
>
> - 1 Kings 8:10-11

That is church my friends. That is the heart cry of Him who sits upon the throne. He so desires to fill you that He will not relent until He has a bride so full of Him, that she glows with the glory of the lover of her soul.

Let me illustrate

To illustrate the Lord's desire to fill His house with His presence and purpose, let me share with you a vision the Lord gave me a while back at church on Father's Day.

I was caught up in worship and as I was worshiping I saw in space what looked like the lights of Aurora. They were brilliant, tall and streaming down in colors, shades of blue, green, red and white. They filled the heavens with such incredible brilliance I was awestruck.

I asked the Lord what it was and He said, "*It is the rain of Heaven.*" In an instant, I was watching the rain of Heaven come down in sheets of light. Then, all of a sudden, Jesus stepped through the light like He was opening a shower curtain. He was beaming with the same brilliant light, only more glorious, majestic, sparkly, incredible. His hands were cupped, and beaming out from the sides, and between His fingers were beams of more incredible, colorful, light. It was like He was holding a ball of brilliance. Suddenly, He opened His hands, and out shot the dove of promise, with His wings extended as if ready to fly. It too, was draped in incredible light. The colors were amazing.

Then Jesus said, "*This is the promise of the Father. It is the Father's gift on this Father's day.*"

I was blown away. How awesome it is that the Father would send His only begotten Son, to give us not only His precious Son, but also the Gift of promise, the Holy Spirit, to all that are thirsty and desire to be wrapped in the glorious light of His presence.

Dear ones, before you do anything. Before you read any further, stop what you are doing and praise the name of Jesus. Worship Him in His splendor. Don't settle for anything less than His sweet presence. Lay on the floor if you have to, but don't stop until the lover of your soul kisses you and fills you with the Spirit of promise. Praise Him, and seek to be filled, even at this moment. Call on the Holy Spirit, and cry out,

> "*Send me the Father's promise, Lord. Fill me Lord. Make me an instrument of your peace and alter my life course with your love and beauty. Come Holy Spirit, Come!*"

Chapter 11

The Bride

"My heart is overflowing with a good theme; I recite my composition concerning the King; my tongue is the pen of a ready writer.

You are fairer than the sons of men; Grace is poured upon your lips; Therefore God has blessed You forever. Gird Your sword upon Your thigh, O Mighty One, with Your glory and Your majesty. And in Your majesty ride prosperously because of truth, humility, and righteousness; And Your right hand shall teach You awesome things. Your arrows are sharp in the heart of the King's enemies; the peoples fall under You.

Your throne, O God, is forever and ever; A scepter of righteousness is the scepter of Your kingdom. You love righteousness and hate wickedness; Therefore God, Your God, has anointed You with the oil of gladness more than your companions. All Your garments are scented with myrrh and aloes and cassia, out of the ivory palaces, by which they have made you glad. Kings' daughters are among Your honorable women; at Your right hand stands the queen in gold from Ophir.

Listen, O daughter, Consider and incline your ear; Forget your own people also, and your father's house; so the King will greatly desire your beauty; because He is your Lord, worship Him. And the daughter of Tyre will come with a gift; the rich among the people will seek your fa-

vor. The royal daughter is all glorious within the palace; her clothing is woven with gold. She shall be brought to the King in robes of many colors; the virgins, her companions who follow her, shall be brought to you. With gladness and rejoicing they shall be brought; they shall enter the King's palace.

Instead of Your fathers shall be Your sons, whom You shall make princes in all the earth. I will make Your name to be remembered in all generations; therefore the people shall praise You forever and ever."

- Psalm 45

They call this Psalm "*The Glories of the Messiah and His Bride.*" A poetic prophet of the sons of Korah wrote it. It was set to the tune of the "*Lilies,*" pointing us to love writings of the Song of Solomon, and speaks of the passion of the King for His bride. In fact, the writer calls this psalm, "A song of love." It was a royal wedding song and was more than likely sung at the wedding of King David or Solomon and one of his princesses. Charles Wesley was so moved by this psalm he paraphrased it in his hymn, "*My heart is full of Christ, and longs its glorious matter to declare.*" Prophetically, it speaks of Christ and His love for the church.

The first nine verses speak to the glorious nature and splendor of the King and His might against all falsehood, pride, and injustice. The next five verses speak directly to the bride. The writer is calling her to the high place; he is exhorting her to forsake her old life and accept her new position as queen, with all its sacrifices, duties, rewards, and pleasures, but above all to yield herself fully to the King.

It is fitting to end this section on the Bride of Christ. In fact, I thought I was done with this section after completing the previous chapter. However the Lord had another idea. You see He woke me up out of an incredible dream the other day, and for the last two days I haven't been able to shake it.

In the dream I was taken to the throne room of God. I saw myself walking up to the throne to embrace my King. Above the throne was a banner with the word *"commission"* written across it. I saw myself walk between two pillars that lead to the throne. Then I saw myself exit the throne through two other pillars on the right. I was dressed in a white bridle gown with boots on. The time between entering the first two pillars and exiting the second set of pillars my mind was filled with incredible revelations regarding the Bride of Christ and her commission and destiny.

I understood that the foundation of her commission was found in the loving embrace of her King, and in that embrace, in her love fellowship with her husband, she would be endued with power and glory to fulfill her call.

Then, as I walked away, in my new bridal attire, instantly I was standing in the workplace, holding the elbow of a young lad. I looked down at his elbow and saw the residue of scar tissue from surgery, where they pieced together his elbow with metal pins. I began to pray and commanded the metal to leave his body.

As I was praying this young man jumped back with a startled look and said, *"What are you doing to my arm?"*

I watched as the Lord began to miraculously recreate his elbow and remove all the metal from his body. The boy was smiling era-to-ear, blown away at what was happening. Then I looked out to the crowd and said, *"Join with me loved ones, say the name of Jesus, and watch the Glory of the Lord."* Instantly, everybody began to say, *"Jesus"* in perfect harmony. Their voices filled the atmosphere like a Holy choir from heaven. As they spoke I saw the metal plate in the boy's head dissolve and eject from his body. Then I woke.

Taken back by the dream I began to pray, and my prayers continued throughout the day. At the time I didn't know what the dream meant ... whether it was literal, in the sense that I would see this boy and bring the King's healing gift to him, or whether it was something more.

By noon, as I was standing outside reflecting on the dreams meaning, the Lord spoke to me very load and clear. "Tell them..." He said,

> *"Tell them how much I love them, how much My heart burns for My bride. Tell them that My love for them is unshakeable, it is so deep that My heart beats with passion at the very thought of her. Tell My bride that I am head-over-heals for her, and in this hour, I shall take her into the wedding chamber and there she will know the tenderness of My touch. I shall wrap My arms around her and caress her with Holy love and with fire. In my embrace I will shower her with My desires. I shall cover her with My presence and trade her earthly garments with the wardrobe of heaven. I will put rings on her fingers and bells on her toes. I shall engrave her heart with My image and she shall see what I see. She shall feel as I feel. She shall touch others even as I have touched her. She shall be a queen in My kingdom, and her garments will radiate her beauty because she has looked upon the face of her lover. In this hour, this hour of the Bridal Shower, I shall wrap myself around her in My embrace, she shall see My heart for her and for humanity and in so doing, she will rise with a burning conviction, yes with a Holy commission, and return to the land that I send her, and there she shall reach out and bring the love touch to all she encounters.*

Yes, My love touch is amazing, for in that touch is wrapped up all the mysteries of creation. She shall speak and limbs will be created. She shall whisper and the ears of the deaf shall be restored. Where ears do not exist, they shall be created at the breath of My bride. For this is the hour of the Bridal Shower, and the rain she has so longed to see will come even as the wind blows upon the garment of my bride, as she walks amongst the hosts of heaven. Her aroma is like sweet raspberries. The very taste of her brings healing to the land, for she has been to the wedding chamber and felt My embrace. She has kissed the lips of her lover and has left changed into the beauty I saw the day I created her. This is how I feel about My bride, she is the lover of My soul. Prepare for the bridal shower, My bride, and come to me. Let me embrace you and give you My heart."

As He spoke those words to me I could feel His love flow over my like warm oil. Liquid love covered my heart and I, like the psalmist, took up the pen of a ready writer. As I began writing I was suddenly caught up in the Spirit to the worship song "*Dying to Return,*" by Vineyard. As the sounds of this song flooded my heart, I saw Jesus in this incredible montage. As I heard these words His love filled my heart.

"He walked with a smile...."

I saw Him as the Son of Man, strong and eloquent, walking along dusty roads, smiling and touching all along the side of the road. His features radiated with mission and purpose. With every touch His face beamed with the most incredible smile. Then He turned, looked into my eyes ... and smiled. The song continued.

"He walked with peace...."

I was overcome by His peaceful nature. Peace flowed out from Him like waves of light flooding the atmosphere. Then, it was as if he was looking around, but no one really understood the true meaning of His life mission. He was listening to the hearts of those around Him. The road was lined with people, some wanted food, others healing, others just desiring to see miracles, and there were others there, mocking Him in unbelief. Yet, in all, it seemed that no one understood. Then, like before, He turned and looked at me ... and smiled. It was a smile that said, "I know, and they will soon know ... when its finished." The song continued.

"But His heart cried out...."

When I heard those words I could see His heart pour out to the Father, the only one that knew the road He was on, the only one that truly understood. Then He bowed His head as if He heard the words from His Poppa respond back to Him, "*All is well My Son ... it is almost finished, you're almost there.*" Then He lifted His head in perfect peace and strength, and with Holy confidence He looked over at me again, and smiled, and His smile carried so much weight in it. It was like a smile of assurance in the outcome of His destiny. The song continued.

"He was alone...."

Instantly I saw Him in His loneliness on this planet. His heart was in perfect unity with His Father and the Holy Spirit, but He walked as a man alone. I could feel the ache in His heart, desiring the lover of His soul, to be united with her so that she would see and understand fully His love for her. The song continued.

"He broke the world, Made all things new...."

I saw Him on the road to the cross, as venomous words spewed out of the mouths of all around Him. His heart was torn at the blindness of the crowed. Yet, again, at that moment He turned and looked in My eyes, and smiled. My heart tore with His love and I was overtaken and undone. The lover of my soul was hurting, and in His hurt was the soul desire to embrace me. As the onlookers mocked Him, and tried to crush His spirit, He stood silent, and then turned again to me ... and smiled.

"And He tore my heart as He stood silent...."

I was overwhelmed by His beauty and His tenderness, His love and desire for me was killing me and I saw Him, in His sacrificial journey, to redeem me and bring me to Himself, and I was undone.

"So beautiful, So beautiful...."

I saw Him as His heart cried out in the garden, and I saw Him as they spit on Him, and the cat-of-nine-tails came ripping down, tearing open His flesh. With every scourge, I could see His eyes, His incredibly tender and loving eyes. I saw His the strength of His perseverance, as the whip ripped across His back... Then as before, He turned and looked again, and the whip came lashing down, and as His eyes met mine... He smiled. I was undone.

Then I saw them as they mocked Him and put that scarlet robe upon His back and pressed that crown of thorns into His skull. I saw blood begin to run down the sides of His face, and onto the ground, onto the earth that He created.

I saw Him as they nailed nine-inch spikes into His hands and feet and hung Him on the cross. I saw Him, as He cried out:

"Where are You?"

"Where are You?"

"My God why have You forsaken me?"

I was so moved, my body began to shake, and tears filled my heart at the sight of this perfect man hung between heaven and earth ... alone.

"Up there alone this perfect man...."

My heart was overcome at the sight of His sacrifice and I watched, as He turned, and again, looked at me in my eyes ... and smiled. Then He turned and said, "It is finished ... I'll be back," and He smiled again. I saw Him as He gave up His Spirit to the Father.

"Dying to return the Son was killed...."

I understood like never before, the words of the writer of Hebrews 12:1-2 when he wrote:

> *"Therefore we also, since we are surrounded by so great a cloud of witnesses, let us lay aside every weight, and the sin which so easily ensnares us, and let us run with endurance the race that is set before us, looking unto Jesus, the author and finisher of our faith, who **for the joy that was set before Him endured the cross, despising the shame, and has sat down at the right hand of the throne of God.**"*

The same passion and love for you that drove Him to the cross is the same passion and love that drives His desire for you today. It is that same unshakeable passions, that desires to embrace His bride, the lover of His soul. He will not stop until He can embrace you and wrap you in the wedding garments of His good pleasure. Consider the words of John.

> *"And I heard, as it were, the voice of a great multitude, as the sound of many waters and as the sound of mighty thunderings, saying, "Alleluia! For the Lord God Omnipotent reigns! Let us be glad and rejoice and give Him glory, for the marriage of the Lamb has come, **and His wife has***

> *made herself ready." And to her it was granted to be arrayed in fine linen, clean and bright, for the fine linen is the righteous acts of the saints.*
>
> *Then he said to me, "Write: 'Blessed are those who are called to the marriage supper of the Lamb!'"*
>
> - Revelation 19:6-9

Readiness happens in His presence. Readiness takes place in intimacy. Transformation takes place when we snuggle up to Him and open our hearts to receive the fullness of His love for us. The commission of this next season will be the commission of the bride, it will usher in the power of God like never seen before, and it will be birthed from a Lover, to the beloved, and will change humanity forever.

> *"Then I, John, saw the holy city, New Jerusalem, coming down out of heaven from God, prepared as a bride adorned for her husband. And I heard a loud voice from heaven saying, "Behold, the tabernacle of God is with men, and He will dwell with them, and they shall be His people. God Himself will be with them and be their God. And God will wipe away every tear from their eyes; there shall be no more death, nor sorrow, nor crying. There shall be no more pain, for the former things have passed away."*
>
> - Revelation 21:2-4

Your destiny is calling you...

> *"And the Spirit and the bride say, "Come!" And let him who hears say, "Come!" And let him who thirsts come. Whoever desires, let him take the water of life freely."*
>
> - Revelation 22:18

I look for the day the rains come down in sheets of liquid love. I am looking for the season of the saints where the bridal shower of the Bride shakes the very foundations of the earth. Where limbs are created where there were no limbs. Where eye sockets are filled with the creative love touch of Jesus. Where the deaf hear, for the first time, the voice of Jesus as He whispers in their newly created ears how much He loves them. I am looking for the day when average Joes step out in thunderous power and change the face of nations. I am looking for the day that the lover of our souls embraces us with His passion and pushes us into our destiny. I'm waiting for the rain of God! Let's move the heart of God and worship Him on His throne. It's time church. Get ready, get ready, get ready! So shake the dust off your feet and don't look back. This is the season of the bride. Rise up dear ones and embrace your King, for He is madly in love with you.

Part 2: The Seer & Healing

CHAPTER 12

THY KINGDOM COME

"Now it came to pass, as He was praying in a certain place, when He ceased, that one of His disciples said to Him, Lord, teach us to pray, as John also taught his disciples. So He said to them, When you pray, say: Our Father in heaven, Hallowed be Your name. Your kingdom come. Your will be done, on earth as it is in heaven.,"

- Luke 11:1-2"

"Then He called His twelve disciples together and gave them power and authority over all demons, and to cure diseases. He sent them to preach the kingdom of God and to heal the sick."

- Luke 9:1-2

The Kingdom

"After these things the Lord appointed seventy others also, and sent them two by two before His

> *face into every city and place where He Himself was about to go. Then He said to them, The harvest truly is great, but the laborers are few; therefore pray the Lord of the harvest to send out laborers into His harvest.*
>
> *Go your way; behold, I send you out as lambs among wolves. Carry neither money bag, knapsack, nor sandals; and greet no one along the road.*
>
> *But whatever house you enter, first say, Peace to this house. And if a son of peace is there, your peace will rest on it; if not, it will return to you.*
>
> *And remain in the same house, eating and drinking such things as they give, for the laborer is worthy of his wages. Do not go from house to house. Whatever city you enter, and they receive you, eat such things as are set before you.*
>
> *And heal the sick there, and say to them, 'The kingdom of God has come near to you.'"*
>
> *- Luke 10:1-9*

Before we dive into the operation of visionary language in the midst of the healing ministry, I thought it best to layout some fundamental truths regarding the King we serve and His Kingdom.

I was saved in 1979 at a time when the church was experiencing tremendous revival. There were basically two streams of revival flowing at that time. The first stream was, what I will call, the Last Days Rapture stream proclaimed by such folks as Chuck Smith of Calvary Chapel Costa Mesa and Hal Lindsey, author of the Late Great Planet Earth. The second stream was, for lack of a better term, the Power Encounter stream ushered in by John Wimber of the Vineyard Christian Fellowship. Both moves were sweeping across the land with incredible speed. To the former, the Kingdom of God referred to the sudden return of Jesus Christ, His kingdom, and the pre-tribulation rapture of the church. For the latter, the Kingdom of God referred to the Kingdom, in the gospel sense of the word, as taught by Jesus Christ. Now this is an over simplification of the times but for the sake of expedience, it works for my purpose.

I was fortunate in three ways. First, the hand of God saved me, without any historical ties to church doctrine or religion which freed me to believe all that the scriptures said regarding the Good News and helped me to personally build a one on one relationship with my King that was not watered down by tradition. Secondly, my first church was Calvary Chapel of Costa Mesa under Chuck Smith. I was immersed in the word. With teachers like Chuck Missler, in depth bible study and worship became my passion. Calvary was the perfect place for being grounded in the word.

I was plunged in the eschatology of Calvary Chapel. In fact, I remember the day I was baptized, I drove my motorcycle to the cove in Newport Beach and was baptized in the ocean with about 300 other young people. Norwegian TV was there, filming the revival. I had made a t-shirt that said, "See you at the Rapture." Now, soaking wet I road my bike back home to tell Jan what had happened. I love the ministry of Calvary. Yet, during that season in my life, as I studied the scriptures and church history, I became disillusioned with the pre-tribulation theory of the rapture. I could not reconcile the persecution of the church throughout church history and the special treatment the church of the western world was expecting (read "Fox's Book of Martyrs" and dc Talk's "Jesus Freaks and the Voice of the Martyrs.") I also had trouble with the over emphasis of the Kingdom in the by-and-by, as opposed to the words of Christ when He taught us to pray, "*Thy Kingdom come, thy will be done, on earth as it is in Heaven.*" This internal struggle lead me to the third reason I was I was fortunate, finding John Wimber and Vineyard Christian Fellowship.

It was 1981. That's when I discovered John Wimber at the Canyon High School in Yorba Linda. When I arrived it was shortly after that landmark day in Vineyard history – when on Mother's day, John Wimber asked Lonnie Frisbee to preach and at the end of his message he called all the kids under the age of 25 to come forward and hundreds came up – then he prayed "Come Holy Spirit" and the rest was history. God just fell on the place. That grace filled Mother's Day, was the beginning of the future Vineyard movement.

I found my home. I would spend half my time at Calvary Costa Mesa, learning the word, and half my time at John Wimber's church, just loving Jesus, worshiping, and soaking in the presence. They were meeting at the old Canyon High School in Anaheim Hills, worshiping on bleachers and seeking the face of Jesus. Then, in 1982, Calvary Chapel of Yorba Linda became the Anaheim Vineyard Christian Fellowship.

Vineyard was alive with the presence of God. You would simply walk in and the presence of the Holy Spirit was upon you

- Folks were getting healed left and right.
- The demonized were being set free everywhere.
- Miracles, signs and wonders were part of this new vibrant body of believers.
- The worship was alive with the breath of God.
- Kinship groups were training camps of fellowship were folks learned to practice the gifts of the Kingdom.

The non-pretentious, un-religious message and nature of John Wimber was refreshing for so many of us. We just wanted God to be God. John had a passion and a mission to train, equip, and deploy, and he had a vision to take the message of **"doing the stuff"** and **"everyone gets to play"** to the world. This naturally supernatural message was affecting denominations around the world.

Like Lonnie Frisbee before him, John was on fire for a personal relationship with the power and presence of Jesus Christ. John put into words everything I believed and was experiencing in my life. His passion for Jesus and his focus on Christians being authentic, filled, and "doing the stuff," was exactly what my DNA was crying out for. John Wimber developed a model of ministry that he had dubbed "naturally supernatural" and it reinforced in my heart the Lord's desire to live from a Kingdom mindset. His model took ministry off the platform and allowed all of us to participate in lending a hand to **"what the Father was doing."**

John Wimber was a professional musician who played the Las Vegas circuit for 5 years. John later signed with the Righteous Brothers. When God gripped John in 1963, he was a "beer-guzzling, drug abusing pop musician, who was converted at the age of 29 while chain-smoking his way through a Quaker-led Bible Study.

One of my favorite stories of John's was when he recalled his first years as a believer. He became a voracious Bible reader and after weeks of reading about life changing miracles in the Bible and attending, what he called "boring" church services. John asked a lay leader at that "boring" church:

> *"When do we get to do the stuff? You know, the stuff here in the Bible; the stuff Jesus did, like healing the sick, raising the dead, healing the blind – stuff like that?"*
>
> *He was told that they didn't do that anymore – only what they did in their weekly services. John replied, "You mean I gave up drugs for that?"*

- John Wimber

John used to always say, "Everyone gets to play," which meant that all of us could participate in "doin' the stuff." It wasn't just for the pastors and preachers; it was for folks in the pews, folks like you and me. We soon learned that the "real meat was in the street" and Jesus was about to send all out and spawn a church growth movement that was simply remarkable. Everyone being allowed to do the stuff, the emphases on worship, and fellowship through "kinship" groups became part of the guiding foundation, hallmark, and marching orders of the Vineyard Movement in the early years.

John taught me that the most important thing in my life was intimacy with Jesus. That single core value has been my guiding pursuit for most my Christian life. I can say with full conviction that John was my true father in the faith, thank you John! John put into words the conflict that I was experiencing and the simplicity of the truth. John recalls his thinking on the Kingdom when he said:

> *"For the first twelve years of my Christian life, I gave little thought to the kingdom of God. My pastors and Bible teachers had taught that the kingdom would come at the second coming of Christ and, therefore, had little significance in our lives today...I find my neglect of the kingdom remarkable because it is so clearly at the center of Jesus' teaching ... I [now realize] that at the very heart of the gospel lies the kingdom of God, and that power for effective evangelism and discipleship relates directly to our understanding and experiencing the kingdom today."*
>
> *- John Wimber*

I like what John Bright had to say regarding the Kingdom of God:

> *"The gospel according to Mark begins the story of Jesus' ministry with these significant words" 'Jesus came into Galilee, preaching the gospel of God, saying, "The time is fulfilled, and the kingdom of God is at hand; repent, and believe in the gospel" (1:14—15). Mark thus makes it plain that the burden of Jesus' preaching was to announce the Kingdom of God; that was the central thing with which he was concerned. A reading of the teachings of Je-*

> sus as they are found in the Gospels only serves to bear this statement out. Everywhere the Kingdom of God is on his lips, and it is always a matter of desperate importance."

Perhaps, you have given little thought to the Kingdom of God. Maybe you were taught that the Kingdom of God was only something to be experienced when you die and go to heaven, or you, like many others, have not really thought about it in regards to your daily life and walk with Christ.

Yet the truth is, the Kingdom was central to the teachings of Christ. In fact, the phrase "Kingdom of God" or the "Kingdom of Heaven" appears 84 times in the gospels alone. How does this compare with other core Christian terms in the Gospels? Consider this: the "cross" appears 17 times, and the words "gospel" and "Good News" appear only 23 times.

In Luke 8:1-3 we read how Jesus went through every city and village, preaching and bringing the good news of the Kingdom of God.

> "Now it came to pass, afterward, that He went through every city and village, preaching and bringing the glad tidings of the kingdom of God. And the twelve were with Him, and certain women who had been healed of evil spirits and infirmities—Mary called Magdalene, out of whom had come seven demons, and Joanna the wife of Chuza, Herod's steward, and Susanna, and many others who provided for Him from their substance."

In this passage we see not only the words of the Kingdom proclaimed through preaching and teaching the demonstration of the Kingdom through the healing of the demonized. This is no better seen than when Jesus passes the baton to the twelve in Luke 9:1-2:

> "Then He called His twelve disciples together and gave them power and authority over all demons, and to cure diseases. He sent them to preach the kingdom of God and to heal the sick."

In this passage there is a clear connection to the preaching of the Kingdom of God and the release of power and authority to heal the sick. Some believe that this was some special impartation just for the twelve however, in Luke 10:1-9 we see a different story unfold:

> "After these things the Lord appointed seventy others also, and sent them two by two before His face into every city and place where He Himself was about to go. Then He said to them, the harvest truly is great, but the laborers are few; therefore pray the Lord of the harvest to send out laborers into His harvest. Go your way; behold, I send you out as lambs among wolves.
>
> Carry neither money bag, knapsack, nor sandals; and greet no one along the road. But whatever house you enter, first say, Peace to this house. And if a son of peace is there, your peace will rest on it; if not, it will return to you. And remain in the same house, eating and drinking such things as they give, for the laborer is worthy of his wages. Do not go from house to house. Whatever city you enter, and they receive you, eat such things as are set before you.
>
> And heal the sick there, and say to them, The kingdom of God has come near to you"

John Wimber referred to Jesus as the "word worker" because he proclaimed the Kingdom of God and then demonstrated it through healing and deliverance. There is no better example of that than in Jesus' response to John the Baptist's question in Matthew 11, Jesus says:

> *"Go and tell John the things which you hear and see: The blind see and the lame walk; the lepers are cleansed and the deaf hear; the dead are raised up and the poor have the gospel preached to them."*
>
> - Matthew 11:4-5

These miracles, signs, and wonders were more than just a confirmation of Jesus' message. Healing and deliverance from demonic powers are tangible signs of the presence of the kingdom, just as much as salvation and the forgiveness of sins are the gifts God bestows upon us when we enter the Kingdom. We need to expect that these signs will follow those who believe when God's rule and reign is established in the here and now.

> *"And these signs will follow those who believe: In My name they will cast out demons; they will speak with new tongues; they will take up serpents; and if they drink anything deadly, it will by no means hurt them;* **they will lay hands on the sick, and they will recover."**
>
> - Mark 16:17-18

When His children release the Kingdom of God, folks get physically and spiritually better. Jesus "passed the baton" to His disciples: first to the twelve in Luke 9 and then to the seventy-two in Luke 10, now to all of the body of Christ. We are to do the things that Jesus did. In Acts 1:3 we read that that for forty days after the resurrection Jesus spoke to them all things pertaining to the Kingdom of God.

> *"He also presented Himself alive after His suffering by many infallible proofs, being seen by them during forty days and speaking of the things pertaining to the kingdom of God."*

In verses 4-8 we read:

> *"And being assembled together with them, He commanded them not to depart from Jerusalem, but to wait for the Promise of the Father, which, He said, you have heard from Me; for John truly baptized with water, but you shall be baptized with the Holy Spirit not many days from now.*
>
> *Therefore, when they had come together, they asked Him, saying, Lord, will You at this time restore the kingdom to Israel?*
>
> *And He said to them, It is not for you to know times or seasons which the Father has put in His own authority. But you shall receive power when the Holy Spirit has come upon you; and you shall be witnesses to Me in Jerusalem, and in all Judea and Samaria, and to the end of the earth"*

The Kingdom of God was central to the ministry of Jesus. His desire to fill His children with power and pass on His authority is part of the Kingdom culture. He came to proclaim that the rule of satan was over, and His Father's Kingdom was established and advancing. Once we get this, that Jesus came preaching the good news of the Kingdom of God, we will be able to grasp more fully everything He taught and did while He was on this earth. This is vital to understand. To be effective as ministers of the gospel we not only need to be hearers of the Word but doers of the Word, in power. The following model will help you and your team, become affective in ministering to those in need.

The Model for Team Prayer

John Wimber sets out one of the best models that I have seen for prayer-ministry in his book "Power Healing." John gives us a five-step process that the prayer team should go through while ministering to someone. I must point out that it is recommended that three to no more than four people be involved in team ministry.

One person should take the lead i.e. ask the questions, direct the prayer; this will cut back on any confusion. The others should pray silently in their prayer language and listen to the Spirit for God for direction.

The first step in this five-step model is what John calls the Interview. Here the person is asked, what do you need prayer for? Where does it hurt? This is not a medical interview but a very practical time of probing. John tells us that we should listen on two levels: the natural and the supernatural. On the natural level, we evaluate the answer through the filter of our biblical knowledge, what we know about the person, and our own experience in praying for similar problems. On the supernatural level, we listen to what the Spirit of God has to say about this hurt.

The second step is referred to as, making a diagnostic decision. It is here in this step that we identify and clarify the root of the person's problem. This is where we ask the Holy Spirit to give insight into the condition and root cause if any. This can come through words of knowledge or wisdom, prophetically, discernment of spirits. For the seer this information often comes through the vehicle of visions. This is also the time we learn what kind of prayer is needed to bring healing.

Step three, is referred to as, the prayer selection. At this point, we are agreeing with the perfect will of God. We are waiting for a green light, not only what to pray for but when the Lord is going to heal this person. There are many types of prayers. They include, according to John, the following:

- Prayers of petition
- Intercession
- Words of command
- Proclamation

- Prophecy

These prayers will take one of two roles. First, words directed towards God and secondly, words that we receive from God. These can be words such as commands spoken to a demon or the condition, a prophecy or proclamation, or pronouncement, or rebuke. At this point, you may also ask your team if they have anything to add.

John refers to step four as, the prayer of engagement. Here the question is answered, how are we doing? In this mode, we look for symptoms of the presence of the Holy Spirit upon the person being prayed for i.e. warmth or heat, tingling sensations, trembling or shaking, deeper breathing, eyes that flutter, laughing, sobbing, exuberant praise, and so forth. At this point, it is appropriate to ask questions. Do you feel anything right now? Has God shown you anything? This process will keep you in the flow of what God is doing. Questions will not disturb the ministry process.

The final step is post prayer direction. What does this person need to do to retain this healing? What should be done if the person is not healed? This is a very practical step and a time for you to ask God to solidify what he is doing in the person's heart. For a deeper understanding of team ministry healing, I recommend John's book highly.

To be effective in proclaiming the kingdom it is critical that we learn how to pray and the importance of team prayer ministry. Team is at the heart of being a member of the body of Christ. Only by engaging the enemy will we be able to the glory of His kingdom here on earth.

CHAPTER 13

HEALING AND THE KINGDOM

"Now when He was asked by the Pharisees when the kingdom of God would come, He answered them and said, the kingdom of God does not come with observation; nor will they say, See here! Or See there! For indeed, the kingdom of God is within you."

- Luke 17: 20-21

"Then Jesus answered and said to them, Most assuredly, I say to you, the Son can do nothing of Himself, but what He sees the Father do; for whatever He does, the Son also does in like manner. For the Father loves the Son, and shows Him all things that He Himself does; and He will show Him greater works than these, that you may marvel. For as the Father raises the dead and gives life to them, even so the Son gives life to whom He will"

- John 5:19-21

Healing is Part of the Kingdom

My first experience with healing happened in Canada shortly after Jan and I got married. We had moved from Huntington Beach and taken a trip to Vancouver, Canada, to open a restaurant at my cousin Jim's hotel in Whistler. Many incredible things happened up there on that mountain. I remember, during one snowstorm, a little boy came running into the hotel lobby, crying uncontrollably. Everyone in the bar came running out to see what was wrong. When I ran outside, I saw the boy standing over the body of a dead frozen dog, lying in the snow. A man, who also happened to be a doctor walked over and checked the dog's vitals – He confirmed it, the dog was dead. Now the boy was really weeping. I couldn't take it. My heart was breaking for that child – I ran over to the dog, placed my hands on it, and cried out to Jesus. Faith surged in my heart and I said, "**In the name of Jesus, get up!**"

Suddenly, the dog began to shiver, and then shake, and then it stood, shaking and running in circles. **God had raised it from the dead**. I was crying and laughing, the boy was crying and laughing, and the crowd just stood there amazed as this boy hugged his dog.

Now, here's the thing. Jesus intervened in a situation that many would think was too small or insignificant for His attention. After all, it's only a dog. However, that is not the case. Jesus was drawn by two elements, compassion and faith. These two elements were magnets for the Holy Spirit because they reflect the heart nature of the Father and glorify who He is.

The love nature of God is far greater than we can comprehend. What I love about this story is that the tears of a child, the faith of a young cook, and the frozen dead body of a boy's dog became a sign and a wonder to a crowd in a hotel bar. God is truly amazing, indeed (see Mark 16:17)!

I thank God I was a young Christian. The only model I had for such an event was what I read in scripture. I suspect that had I been around the church for a while and had been taught, like many others, that the wonders of Jesus were meant only for Him, in that time, and at that season, my faith would have fizzled out. On the contrary, the Jesus I read about, the Jesus I had come to know was the Jesus of the Gospels and His love heart spawned a fire in my heart that drove me to action, and to seek His faith. This event also set me on a path to understand God's heart towards healing. As a result, I found that I had many more questions than I had answers.

The biggest question was, is it God's will to always heal the sick? If healing is something God wants us to do and experience, then we ought to pray for the sick whenever we can. But if healing is not God's will, then praying for the sick is both pointless and wrong. It's pointless, because praying won't change what God decrees, and it's wrong because Jesus instructs us to pray according to the will of God.

As Christians, the primary way we determine the will of God is by the Scriptures. In the Bible, God reveals His plan for us and our actions and deeds to be accomplished here on earth. But some folks teach a radical view of God's sovereignty. The Bible clearly teaches that God is sovereign and in control of His creation. However, when one takes the doctrine of God's sovereignty to an extreme, they assume that everything that happens in this world is also the will of God. As this thought process progresses they conclude that since nothing can happen that is outside of His will, then all sickness must be God's will, because He is in control, He is sovereign.

It is interesting to note that at one time, Christians applied this same thought process to evangelism. They believed that if God wanted people saved, He would do it with or without the help of missionaries and evangelists. Most Christians today reject this reasoning and see both the need for and the value in missionary work and evangelism. Unfortunately, many are still applying this kind of thinking to healing.

Taking such a radical position concerning God's sovereignty and His will sounds reasonable, but it is actually inconsistent with the Bible. For example, the Bible clearly teaches that it is God's will for all humans to be saved (Matthew 18:14; 2 Pet. 3:9; I Timothy 2:4). At the same time, there are many people in the world who are not saved. It would contradict Scripture, though, for us to conclude that this is God's will. There are other factors involved besides the will of God that affect whether or not a person is saved. So, just because there are sick people in the world, we should not and cannot assume that this is God's will.

One of the most powerful teachings that I can remember from my early days at the Vineyard was the concept of "the now and the not yet." John Wimber taught us that we live between the first and second comings of Christ. At His first coming, Jesus inaugurated the kingdom of God (Matthew 4:17; 12:28), but it is not yet present in its fullest expression (Matthew 25:31—33, 46). Wimber wrote:

> *"His sovereignty, lordship and kingdom are what brings healing. Our part is to pray 'Thy kingdom come" and trust him for whatever healing comes from His gracious hand. And if in this age it does not come, then we still have assurance from the atonement that it will come in the age to come."*

- John Wimber

We know from the Scriptures that some things are a mystery to us (Deuteronomy 9:9), but as Christians we know that God is also willing to intervene in our lives as we engage Him through faith-filled prayer (Genesis 18:16—33; John 14:12—14).

To better understand God's will towards healing, the best place to look is at the life and ministry of Jesus. He perfectly personified the heart and will of the Father. He was the visible image of the invisible God (Colossians 1:15).

> *"He is the image of the invisible God, the firstborn over all creation."*

According to Jesus, He did only what the Father wanted Him to do:

> *"Then Jesus answered and said to them, Most assuredly, I say to you, the Son can do nothing of Himself, but what He sees the Father do; for whatever He does, the Son also does in like manner."*
>
> - John 5:19

> *"And He who sent Me is with Me. The Father has not left Me alone, for I always do those things that please Him."*
>
> - John 8:29

> *"If I do not do the works of My Father, do not believe Me; but if I do, though you do not believe Me, believe the works, that you may know and believe that the Father is in Me, and I in Him"*
>
> - John 10:37-38

> *"Then Jesus cried out and said, He who believes in Me, believes not in Me but in Him who sent Me. And he who sees Me sees Him who sent Me."*
>
> - John 12:44-45

> *"Jesus said to him, Have I been with you so long, and yet you have not known Me, Philip? He who has seen Me has seen the Father; so how can you say, Show us the Father? Do you not believe that I am in the Father, and the Father in Me? The words that I speak to you I do not speak on My own authority; but the Father who dwells in Me does the works. Believe Me that I am in the Father and the Father in Me, or else believe Me for the sake of the works themselves."*
>
> - John 14:9-11

Clearly, these Scriptures demonstrate what God wants regarding healing by what Jesus did. In the gospel accounts, Jesus healed a lot! In fact, He healed every person who came to Him for healing. He even healed some who never asked for healing but were brought to Him for help by others.

Let's look at one of the many healing stories that are found in the gospels and use Jesus as our model for what God really wants.

> *"When He had come down from the mountain, great multitudes followed Him. And behold, a leper came and worshiped Him, saying, Lord, if You are willing, You can make me clean. Then Jesus put out His hand and touched him, saying, I am willing; be cleansed. Immediately his leprosy was cleansed. And Jesus said to him, See that you tell no one; but go your way, show yourself to the priest, and offer the gift that Moses commanded, as a testimony to them."*
>
> - Matthew 8:1-4

In Leviticus 13 and 14 we read about the laws relating to "leprosy" or what we would call Hansen's disease. Leprosy is highly infectious, being transmitted from person to person with incubation periods as short as just a few weeks. Left untreated, leprosy can be progressive, causing permanent damage to the skin, nerves, limbs and eyes. Secondary infections can result in tissue loss causing fingers and toes to become shortened and deformed, as cartilage is absorbed into the body. The Levitical laws governing this disease are recorded in verses 13:45-46.

> *"Now the leper on whom the sore is, his clothes shall be torn and his head bare; and he shall cover his mustache, and cry, Unclean! Unclean! He shall be unclean. All the days he has the sore he shall be unclean. He is unclean, and he shall dwell alone; his dwelling shall be outside the camp."*

Skin ailments were probably common then in Israel, since Jesus mentions them in Matthew 10, when He sent out the twelve with authority to heal.

Like HIV today, there was tremendous social isolation and shame associated with leprosy. There was also the stigma that leprosy might be a curse sent from God (Numbers 12:10—12, Miriam afflicted with leprosy by God as judgment for her sin; Job 18:13).

In the Old Testament, healing from leprosy was rare and considered extremely difficult (2 Kings 5:7). Possibly this man and others believed God has deliberately cursed him with leprosy because of some sin he had committed.

Surprisingly, the man seemed to believe that Jesus could heal him. It wasn't that his disease was too difficult to heal or that Jesus lacked the power and ability. The real question for him was whether or not Jesus wanted to. It is clear that he wanted to be healed because he came out of the crowd and went right up to Jesus. Lepers were supposed to keep their distance from people, which the ten lepers in Luke 17:12—13 did. But this fellow came up close enough for Jesus to be able to reach out and touch him. He knew what he wanted; he just didn't know what Jesus had in mind. He believed in Jesus' power to heal, but was not sure about

Jesus' desire to heal. Nowhere else in all the gospels did anyone ever ask Jesus if He was willing to heal!

This man's dilemma is very similar to ones today when Christians pray for healing. Believers often pray, "Lord, if it's your will, please heal Joe's back problem." Most likely this comes from an attempt to imitate Jesus' prayer in the Garden in Gethsemane, "Father, if it is Your will, take this cup away from Me; nevertheless not My will, but Yours, be done" (Luke 22:42). However, it also reveals that we doubt God's willingness to heal.

Many Christians assert that God can do anything, and that nothing is too difficult for Him, including the healing of a particular illness. It's His intentions that they are unsure of. How does God feel about the sickness? Does He care? Does He want to teach a lesson through the sickness? Will He teach and then alleviate it? What is God's will?

How did Jesus Heal?

Jesus healed this man differently than He did the ten lepers in Luke 17.

> *"Then as He entered a certain village, there met Him ten men who were lepers, who stood afar off. And they lifted up their voices and said, Jesus, Master, have mercy on us! So when He saw them, He said to them, Go, show yourselves to the priests. And so it was that as they went, they were cleansed."*
>
> - Luke 17:12-14

In that instance, He simply spoke to them (Luke 17:14). But with this man, Jesus first reached out and touched him. The law forbade such an action since lepers were unclean and anyone touching them would become unclean as well. Jesus disregarded the regulations and touched the man first, to demonstrate His willingness to heal. He also told the man that He was willing, so that by word and deed, the man would be convinced of Jesus' desire to heal. He then spoke a command that resulted in the man's healing from the leprosy. A touch from Jesus made the man clean, rather than the leper making Jesus unclean! Nothing Jesus touches can remain defiled.

Note that Jesus did not rebuke or correct the man for asking Him if He was willing to heal. Jesus seemed only too happy to prove that He was willing. In contrast, Jesus corrected the father of the demonized boy in Mark 9:21—27 for questioning His ability to heal:

> *"So He asked his father, How long has this been happening to him? And he said, 'From childhood. And often he has thrown him both into the fire and into the water to destroy him. But if You can do anything, have compassion on us and help us.' Jesus said to him, 'If you can believe, all things are possible to him who believes.' Immediately the father of the child cried out and said with tears, 'Lord, I believe; help my unbelief!'*
>
> *When Jesus saw that the people came running together, He rebuked the unclean spirit, saying to it, Deaf and dumb spirit, I command you, come out of him and enter him no more! Then the spirit cried out, convulsed him greatly, and came out of him. And he became as one dead, so that many said, 'He is dead.' But Jesus took him by the hand and lifted him up, and he arose"*

For Jesus, to question or doubt God's ability and power was ridiculous!

> *"So Jesus said to them, Because of your unbelief; for assuredly, I say to you, if you have faith as a mustard seed,*

> *you will say to this mountain, Move from here to there, and it will move; and nothing will be impossible for you. However, this kind does not go out except by prayer and fasting."*
>
> - Matthew 17:20-21

Jesus forcefully confronted unbelief wherever He found it. However, He seemed to deal more gently with doubt in His willingness to heal (Matthew 12:20).

> *"A bruised reed He will not break,*
> *And smoking flax He will not quench,*
> *Till He sends forth justice to victory..."*

Jesus told the man to go show himself to the priest so that he may be declared "clean," in accordance with the law in Leviticus 14. Because this disease had social ramifications, the healing needed to be confirmed in a social situation. For the man to be completely healed, he had to be recognized as "clean" by the priests so that he could re-enter society and resume living as a healed person. Some people actively engaged in the healing ministry discourage the use of medicine and medical professionals. Yet, we see that Jesus instructed this man to follow the conventional course of his day and go to the priests to be declared healed by them. It wasn't that Jesus' word was inadequate. Confirmation from others can help solidify the miracle for the person who was healed. It's also clear that Jesus' motivation was not to further publicize Himself since He told the man to tell no one else about what had happened.

Compassion and Mercy

> *"Then Jesus, moved with compassion, stretched out His hand and touched him, and said to him, I am willing; be cleansed."*

- Mark 1:41

The compassion of Jesus is explicitly mentioned in several healing accounts in the Gospels and perhaps assumed in most.

> "And when Jesus went out He saw a great multitude; and He was moved with compassion for them, and healed their sick"
>
> - Mark 14:14

Compassion and mercy is key to understanding God's will or desire to heal. We know it is possible for a person to be able but unwilling to help in a situation because of stinginess, indifference, or just plain selfishness. The attitude of the heart is key to the will. The God of the universe is able to do anything He wants. But He has a choice. It is God's attitude—how he feels towards the sick—that determines His willingness to heal. When we look at Jesus, we find a person who was always willing to heal the sick. This should tell us volumes about God's will concerning healing.

Jesus is our model

Dr. Ken Blue, author, consultant, and conference speaker, pointed out the challenge of many healing models today.

> "In reading the New Testament, I was initially disturbed to see that Jesus healed the sick and cast out demons very differently from the way we do it today. Every healing ministry I am familiar with depends largely on prayer. Jesus healed primarily by command. Unlike His followers today, he did not petition for healing; he pronounced it."

Jesus commissioned the twelve and later seventy-two other disciples to go from town to town, preaching the kingdom and healing the sick:

> "Then He called His twelve disciples together and gave them power and authority over all demons, and to cure diseases. He sent them to preach the kingdom of God and to heal the sick."
>
> - Luke 9:1-2

> "After these things the Lord appointed seventy others also, and sent them two by two before His face into every city and place where He Himself was about to go. Then He said to them, The harvest truly is great, but the laborers are few; therefore pray the Lord of the harvest to send out laborers into His harvest ... And heal the sick there, and say to them, The kingdom of God has come near to you"
>
> - Luke 10:1-2; 9

In other words, He commissioned His followers to do His ministry. In Acts 1:1, Luke implied that the apostles were continuing to do what Jesus began in His earthly ministry.

> "The former account I made, O Theophilus, of all that Jesus began both to do and teach,"
>
> - Acts 1:1

Second, in John 14, Jesus tells His disciples that if they believe in Him, they will do what He had been doing! In fact, Jesus tells them that whatever they ask He will do it.

> "Most assuredly, I say to you, he who believes in Me, the works that I do he will do also; and greater works than these he will do, because I go to My Father. And whatever you ask in My name, that I will do, that the Father may be glorified in the Son. If you ask anything in My name, I will do it"
>
> - John 14:12-14

What had Jesus been doing? He ministered by preaching and teaching about the kingdom of God and healing the sick:

> *"And Jesus went about all Galilee, teaching in their synagogues, preaching the gospel of the kingdom, and healing all kinds of sickness and all kinds of disease among the people"*
>
> *- Matthew 4:23*

> *"When evening had come, they brought to Him many who were demon- possessed. And He cast out the spirits with a word, and healed all who were sick, Peter's Mother- in- Law Healed that it might be fulfilled which was spoken by Isaiah the prophet, saying: He Himself took our infirmities and bore our sicknesses."*
>
> *- Matthew 8:16-17*

> *"Then Jesus went about all the cities and villages, teaching in their synagogues, preaching the gospel of the kingdom, and healing every sickness and every disease among the people"*
>
> *- Matthew 9:35*

> *"Jesus answered and said to them, Go and tell John the things which you hear and see: The blind see and the lame walk; the lepers are cleansed and the deaf hear; the dead are raised up and the poor have the gospel preached to them."*
>
> *- Matthew 11:4-5*

> *"And when Jesus went out He saw a great multitude; and He was moved with compassion for them, and healed their sick."*
>
> *- Matthew 14:14*

"At evening, when the sun had set, they brought to Him all who were sick and those who were demon. And the whole city was gathered together at the door. Then He healed many who were sick with various diseases, and cast out many demons; and He did not allow the demons to speak, because they knew Him."

- Mark 1:32-34

"When the sun was setting, all those who had any that were sick with various diseases brought them to Him; and He laid His hands on every one of them and healed them. And demons also came out of many, crying out and saying, You are the Christ, the Son of God."

- Luke 4:40-41

"And He came down with them and stood on a level place with a crowd of His disciples and a great multitude of people from all Judea and Jerusalem, and from the seacoast of Tyre and Sidon, who came to hear Him and be healed of their diseases, as well as those who were tormented with unclean spirits. And they were healed. And the whole multitude sought to touch Him, for power went out from Him and healed them all."

- Luke 6:17-19

"But when the multitudes knew it, they followed Him; and He received them and spoke to them about the kingdom of God, and healed those who had need of healing."

- Luke 9:11

"Then a great multitude followed Him, because they saw His signs which He performed on those who were diseased."

- John 6:2

We must remember that the biblical notion of a disciple was not someone who followed just the teachings of Jesus or only intellectually assented to His message. A disciple, according to the New Testament, was someone who followed Jesus in every way, doing the same things He did. Therefore a disciple imitated His teacher. In order for us to imitate our Lord, let's examine the ministry of Jesus more closely and discover what some essential ingredients are for healing the sick.

Authority and Power

Compare the words "authority" in Matthew 10:1 with "power" in Luke 5:17.

> *"And when He had called His twelve disciples to Him, He gave them power (Greek: exousia meaning authority) over unclean spirits, to cast them out, and to heal all kinds of sickness and all kinds of disease."*
>
> - John 6:2

> *"Now it happened on a certain day, as He was teaching, that there were Pharisees and teachers of the law sitting by, who had come out of every town of Galilee, Judea, and Jerusalem. And the power (Greek: dynamis meaning power) of the Lord was present to heal them."*
>
> - Luke 5:17

Are they the same thing? How do they each play a role in the way God heals the sick?

While there is some overlap between authority and power, there is an important difference, especially as we consider healing. Authority to heal means the right to heal. Jesus had the right to order sickness to leave a person's body. The sickness had to obey Jesus' authority. Power to heal implies the ability to heal. In Luke 5:17,

Luke wrote, "the power of the Lord was present for him to heal the sick." It seems there were special times and situations when the power to heal the sick was with Jesus (which would imply that there were other times when it was not with Him). Jesus conveyed this when He said that He was not able to do anything apart from the Father (John 5:19).

> *"Then Jesus answered and said to them, Most assuredly, I say to you, the Son can do nothing of Himself, but what He sees the Father do; for whatever He does, the Son also does in like manner."*

The key for Jesus seemed to be the will of the Father, "what the Father was doing."

In the Greek, this difference is even clearer. The Greek word for "power" in Luke 5:17 is "*dynamis*," from where we get our English word "dynamite." It means "power, strength, ability or might." This kind of power is inherent power, power residing in a thing by virtue of its nature, or for example, when a person exerts or puts forth effort. The Greek word for "authority" in Matthew 10:1 is "*exousia*." It means "authority, right or jurisdiction." This kind of authority is the right of influence, the right to rule and govern, or the right to have one's commands submitted to an obeyed by others.

A traffic officer can illustrate the difference between "power" and "authority" in the way we are using them. A policeman or policewoman who is directing traffic does not stop cars by his or her own physical power and might, but by the authority that has been given to him or her by the state. He or she holds up a hand, and the traffic must obey or suffer the consequences. It is absurd to imagine an officer physically stopping each car with just bare hands! In contrast, the general public cannot stop traffic with a raised hand because we do not have the same authority.

This does not mean that authority is all we need in healing. According to the New Testament, Jesus had both the authority and the power to heal the sick.

At the end of Matthew's gospel, Jesus declares that all authority on heaven and in earth have been given to Him (28:18).

> *"And Jesus came and spoke to them, saying, All authority has been given to Me in heaven and on earth."*

Jesus then commands His disciples to reproduce themselves by making disciples of all nations. Along with sharing the gospel and baptizing new converts, His followers were to teach succeeding generations to obey everything He had commanded them (28:19—20).

> *"Go therefore and make disciples of all the nations, baptizing them in the name of the Father and of the Son and of the Holy Spirit, teaching them to observe all things that I have commanded you; and lo, I am with you always, even to the end of the age. Amen."*

That "everything" included Jesus' delegating the authority and power to heal, cast out demons, etc.

He uses us

So, the way that God heals the sick is by using us. He delegates the authority [right] and the ability [power] to heal to His followers. This may be a very different concept from what we have always believed about healing. Many of us picture God doing all the healing directly from heaven as we petition Him. But according to the New Testament, God has given that responsibility to us. He heals the sick through us, His church. It is worth noting that nowhere does Jesus tell His disciples to merely pray for the sick and hope for the best. He tells them to heal the sick!

In Luke 9:1, Jesus gave the disciples both the power and the authority to drive out demons and to cure diseases. When we pray for the sick, there is often a lot of God's power present, and the person receiving prayer and those praying can feel it. But we must keep in mind that we do not possess or own the power to heal. We have been delegated the authority to heal, and when we move in that authority and pray for a sick person, then God sends His power to accomplish the healing.

> *"Then He called His twelve disciples together and gave them power and authority over all demons, and to cure diseases. He sent them to preach the kingdom of God and to heal the sick."*
>
> - Luke 9:1-2

A brief study of the gospels reveals at least ten was that Jesus healed the sick:

- Jesus healed by the Word (Mark 3:1-6, Psalm 107:20)
- Jesus healed by Faith (Luke 7:1-10, Romans 10:8)
- Jesus healed to release those bound by the demonic (Mark 1:23-27)
- Jesus healed to restore life (Mark 1:40-45)
- Jesus healed through the faith of others (Mark 2:1-12)
- Jesus healed through deliverance (Matthew 12:22-37, Matthew 17:14-21, Luke 13:10-17, Mark 5:1-20, Acts 10:38)
- Jesus healed the desperate (Mark 5:25-34, 41)
- Jesus healed the persistent (Matthew 15:22-28)
- Jesus healed to reveal the heart of the Father (John 9:5-34)

- Jesus healed His enemies (Luke 22:49-51

Isaiah saw the nature and power of the atonement in regards to healing when he recorded in Isaiah 53:

> *"Who has believed our report? And to whom has the arm of the Lord been revealed? For He shall grow up before Him as a tender plant, and as a root out of dry ground. He has no form or comeliness; and when we see Him, there is no beauty that we should desire Him. He is despised and rejected by men, a Man of sorrows and acquainted with grief. And we hid, as it were, our faces from Him; He was despised, and we did not esteem Him.*
>
> *Surely He has borne our griefs and carried our sorrows; Yet we esteemed Him stricken, smitten by God, and afflicted. But He was wounded for our transgressions, He was bruised for our iniquities; The chastisement for our peace was upon Him, and by His stripes we are healed."*
>
> - Isaiah 53:1-5

Matthew confirms this attribute of salvation when he writes:

> *"Now when Jesus had come into Peter's house, He saw his wife's mother lying sick with a fever. So He touched her hand, and the fever left her. And she arose and served them. When evening had come, they brought to Him many who were demon-possessed. And He cast out the spirits with a word, and healed all who were sick, that it might be fulfilled which was spoken by Isaiah the prophet, saying: He Himself took our infirmities and bore our sicknesses."*
>
> - Matthew 8:14-18

As does Peter:

> *"...who Himself bore our sins in His own body on the tree, that we, having died to sins, might live for righteousness—by whose stripes you were healed."*

- 1 Peter 2:24

The scriptures also outline at least eleven ways in which the body of Christ operates in the healing ministry.

- The anointing and presence of the gift of healing (Acts 19:11-12; 1 Corinthians 12:9).
- The laying on of hands (Mark 16:8).
- Elders, prayer, and anointing oil (James 5:14).
- Speaking the Word to sickness (Mark 11:23; Psalms 107:20).
- The power of agreement (Matthew 18:19-20; Psalms 133).
- Your own faith (Mark 11:24).
- The name of Jesus (John 14:13-14; Acts 3:1-8).
- Praying for others (Job 42:10).
- The faith of others (Mark 2:5-11).
- Healing through Communion (1 Corinthians 11:22-26; 1 John 1:7; Isaiah 52:5; 1 Peter 2:24; Isaiah 52:14; 1 Corinthians 11:29-30).
- Medicine and the medical profession.

Healing comes in many forms. A simple walk through the book of Acts and we see several dimensions. I love the book of Acts because it reveals the church in action!

- To be strengthened (Acts 3:7)
- To be healed (Acts 3:11)
- To be whole (Acts 3:16)
- To be saved, sozo (Acts 4:9)
- To be cleansed (Acts 4:10)
- To be given therapy (Acts 4:14)

The more we study the New Testament, the more we should be convinced that healing the sick is something God wants us, His church, to do today. As we obey the Lord by praying for the sick, we realize that we cannot operate on our own. We need to recognize the chain of command from the Father, to the Lord Jesus, to us.

We live in a day of incredible urgency. The world looks for a sign that God is with them and for them. You are that sign. Step out and let the healing begin!

We are privileged to have His authority to heal the sick, but we must remain in relationship with Him and focus on His will being done. He has been given the right to govern all the affairs of heaven and earth. We need to obey Him, by the power of His Spirit within us. We need to live as foot soldiers under the command of our King, and like the centurion, say that we are people under authority who have been given authority...to heal. Thankfully, we have His promise to be with us always as we follow in His footsteps.

CHAPTER 14

HEALING & SEEING

"Then your light shall break forth like the morning, your healing shall spring forth speedily, and your righteousness shall go before you; the glory of the Lord shall be your rear guard"

– Isaiah 58:8

Healing and prophetic ministry have been linked together many times throughout the Scriptures. Often times, this happened through prophetic declaration, action, or the command to do something and if you do it you shall be healed.

The story of Elijah and the widow's son is a perfect example of a prophetic action comingled with compassion, relationship, and healing.

> *"Now it happened after these things that the son of the woman who owned the house became sick. And his sickness was so serious that there was no breath left in him.*
>
> *So she said to Elijah, What have I to do with you, O man of God? Have you come to me to bring my sin to remembrance, and to kill my son?*

> *And he said to her, Give me your son. So he took him out of her arms and carried him to the upper room where he was staying, and laid him on his own bed.*
>
> *Then he cried out to the Lord and said, O Lord my God, have You also brought tragedy on the widow with whom I lodge, by killing her son? And he stretched himself out on the child three times, and cried out to the Lord and said, O Lord my God, I pray, let this child's soul come back to him.*
>
> *Then the Lord heard the voice of Elijah; and the soul of the child came back to him, and he revived"*
>
> *- 1 Kings 17:17-24*

In this example we see Elijah responding to the widow's request to heal her son, but literally raise him from the dead. In anguish, he carried the child to the upper room where he was staying. Placed him on his bed and laid on him. While he lay on his breathless body he cried out to the Lord in a deep prayer. At the moment Elijah HEARD the voice of the Lord, the child came back to life. This is a very powerful example of how the "hearing ear" is critical to the ministry of healing, what God is saying regarding the illness.

Another good example of this is found in the book of Numbers. In this book, we find three instances where Moses intercedes for the healing of his people. The first instance is that of Miriam's leprosy:

> *"Then Miriam and Aaron spoke against Moses because of the Ethiopian woman whom he had married; for he had married an Ethiopian woman. So they said, "Has the Lord indeed spoken only through Moses? Has He not spoken through us also?" And the Lord heard it. (Now the man Moses was very humble, more than all men who were on the face of the earth.)*

> *Suddenly, the Lord said to Moses, Aaron, and Miriam, "Come out, you three, to the tabernacle of meeting!" So the three came out. Then the Lord came down in the pillar of cloud and stood in the door of the tabernacle, and called Aaron and Miriam. And they both went forward.*
>
> *Then He said, "Hear now My words: If there is a prophet among you, I, the Lord, make Myself known to him in a vision; I speak to him in a dream. Not so with My servant Moses; He is faithful in all My house. I speak with him face to face, Even plainly, and not in dark sayings; And he sees the form of the Lord. Why then were you not afraid to speak against My servant Moses?*
>
> *So the anger of the Lord was aroused against them, and He departed. And when the cloud departed from above the tabernacle, Suddenly, Miriam became leprous, as white as snow. Then Aaron turned toward Miriam, and there she was, a leper. So Aaron said to Moses, "Oh, my lord! Please do not lay this sin on us, in which we have done foolishly and in which we have sinned. Please do not let her be as one dead, whose flesh is half consumed when he comes out of his mother's womb!*
>
> *So Moses cried out to the Lord, saying, "Please heal her, O God, I pray!"*
>
> *Then the Lord said to Moses, "If her father had but spit in her face, would she not be shamed seven days? Let her be shut out of the camp seven days, and afterward she may be received again." So Miriam was shut out of the camp seven days, and the people did not journey till Miriam was brought in again."*
>
> - Numbers 12:1-15

In this story we see Miriam and Aaron speaking out against Moses regarding his marriage and their justification for doing so rested in the offices that they held. Miriam was a prophetess, and Aaron received revelation by the Urim and Thummim, yet their conclusion was wrong and the result was the judgment of God bringing about Miriam's Leprosy.

Then Moses cried unto the Lord and pleaded with God to heal her. God replied:

> *"Then the Lord said to Moses, "If her father had but spit in her face, would she not be shamed seven days? Let her be shut out of the camp seven days, and afterward she may be received again." (vs. 14)*

This is the command to do something. The implication is, if you put her out for seven days and let my judgment rest I will heal her, and in verse 15 we see obedience to this declaration of the Lord. Another interesting fact about this story is the prophet's ability to only know in part and see in part or see through a glass darkly, and in the case of this book, through visions and dreams. This comes out in the comparison between the ministry of Moses and that of the normal prophet.

Therefore it is critical for the seer to use wisdom's ways and let meekness usher forth as fruit from his spirit, lest he speak presumptuously, resulting in a false word, bringing about hurt to others. For unlike Moses we will only know in part and see in part until we stand face to face with Him who knows all things. Now let's look at Moses receiving a directive that calls for action. It is found in Numbers.

> *"And the people spoke against God and against Moses: "Why have you brought us up out of Egypt to die in the wilderness? For there is no food and no water, and our soul loathes this worthless bread." So the Lord sent fiery serpents among the people, and they bit the people; and many of the people of Israel died.*
>
> *Therefore the people came to Moses, and said, "We have sinned, for we have spoken against the Lord and against*

> *you; pray to the Lord that He take away the serpents from us." So Moses prayed for the people.*
>
> *Then the Lord said to Moses, "Make a fiery serpent, and set it on a pole; and it shall be that everyone who is bitten, when he looks at it, shall live." So Moses made a bronze serpent, and put it on a pole; and so it was, if a serpent had bitten anyone, when he looked at the bronze serpent, he lived."*
>
> - Numbers 21:5-8

Again, we see here sickness because of the judgment of God. So Moses prays and intercedes for the people and the Lord's response to him is twofold, make thee a fiery serpent,, and for the people, who ever looks upon the serpent shall live. Here obedience is twofold. On the one hand, the prophet Moses has a task he must do, and on the other hand, the people have to respond to the Lord by looking upon that serpent of brass.

Therefore, we see conditional healing based upon prophetic obedience and prophetic response. It is also interesting to note that, typologically, the serpent points to Christ on the cross taking the curse upon himself, for by His stripes we are healed. For even here, we see that the testimony of Jesus is the spirit of prophecy.

A study of the gospels reveals that this kind of "action," is also seen in the healing ministry of Jesus. We know that Jesus laid aside his divine nature and took the form of a servant relying completely upon the Holy Spirit for direction. Jesus himself stated, "*I only do what I see the Father doing.*"

In the book of Mark, we read the story of a man born blind who had desired to touch Jesus that he may be healed. Jesus' response to this man is unusual.

> *"So He took the blind man by the hand and led him out of the town. And when He had spit on his eyes and put His hands on him, He asked him if he saw anything. And he looked up and said, "I see men like trees, walking." Then He put His hands on his eyes again and made him look up. And he was restored and saw everyone clearly."*
>
> - Mark 8:23-25

We know that Jesus could have just spoken the word and the man would have been healed but he did not. I believe the reason for this is a response to the Father giving Him an "action" to perform, when completed, then and only then, would the man be made whole. The key here is relationship with God and obedience to all that he commands you to do. It takes a Rhema from heaven for a specific situation to get God's desired results.

We know what God's general will is, that by His stripes we are made whole. Yet, just the proclamation of that truth is not enough. You have to listen, listen, and listen again, keeping your eyes on Jesus for He has said, *"...As the Father has sent me so I send you."* Let's go therefore and follow His example for we are members of His body, but He is the head, the chief cornerstone.

We could also spend time talk of the many wonderful things the Lord has done through his prophets. We could speak of Elisha healing the waters, the healing of Jeroboam and the man of God, Isaiah and Hezekiah's health, but now let me share with you some personal experiences that will elaborate the subject of seeing and healing.

Illustrative Example

Say unto that Mountain, Flee,

In 1981 my wife Jan and I moved to a little town up in the mountains of Southern California. We had been married two years and I had been saved just over a year. As stated earlier, our hope was to find a Calvary Chapel, like Wimber's. We were very excited to find Calvary Chapel Conference Center in Twin Peaks, just outside Lake Arrowhead. Combined with the trees and the serenity of the mountains this was a perfect place to move into a deeper relationship with the Spirit of God.

We arrived at this mountain retreat, shortly after Lonnie Frisbee had been introduced, and a revival had broken out that changed the mountain and the atmosphere of church. It was truly electrifying. Our first summer there I started attending a home fellowship group. During this time, I experienced a presence of the Holy Spirit that I had never encountered before.

One night, while at a home group meeting, in the middle of worship, the Spirit of God came upon me in beautiful waves of grace. I was kneeling down praising God with my hands in the air when Suddenly, the presence of God was all over me. Like electricity over my entire body, I was raptured into His presence. Suddenly, the muscles in my body began to contort and my hands began to fold up in a spastic matter. My eyes started to flutter, my lips began to shake, and my speech was slurred and muffled. The effect was overwhelming, incredible joy mingled with incredible pain. All I could do was praise Him with contorted arms, hands, face, and lips. My speech had left me. I was completely disabled.

This experienced lasted for well over an hour. I didn't really know what was going on but I knew it was God and that the Lord was doing something. This experience happened to me every week during our season in this mountain resort. After about a year, we left Lake Arrowhead and moved to Palm Springs, a desert community south of Lake Arrowhead. We began attending Vineyard Christian Fellowship in Palm Desert. It would be five years later that God would reveal to me what He was doing. At that time it was only on occasion, about every three months or so, that I would feel this intense outpouring of deformity and praise but every time it happened I found myself raptured in intersession.

In the summer of 1986, I attended a conference at the Anaheim Vineyard, Healing 86, with John Wimber and Francis & Judith MacNutt. During the second night of this conference, we were in the middle of worship when suddenly, the Spirit of God was on me more powerful than I had ever experienced before. His presence was just like that season up in the mountains five years earlier only more intense and this time accompanied by visions and words from the throne of God.

I sat in my chair, arms bent, eyes fluttering, fingers, and hands curled in a prenatal position as the power of God moved through my body. The deformity was overwhelming. With slurred speech, all I could do was praise Him. Suddenly, in the midst of this awkward trance-like outpouring, I heard the voice of God,

> *"Say to that mountain, Flee into the sea. Say to that mountain FLEE into the sea, SAY TO THAT MOUNTAIN, FLEE INTO THE SEA!"*

Then I saw the Word of God, larger than life, open against the black of night, then the wind began to blow, moving briskly upon the pages of the Bible and the words came alive as the pages began to flutter, turning, as if the fingers of the Spirit hovered above the Word of God.

I heard the Lord speak again,

> "SAY UNTO THAT MOUNTAIN, FLEE INTO THE SEA., For surely as My word stands and My wind blows, I, the Lord, shall cause it to come about. With every turning of the page so she shall be made whole and as each page quivers before My presence surely I will free this child in bondage. So SAY TO THAT MOUNTAIN FLEE INTO THE SEA!"

Then I saw a mountain, tall and intimidating, beginning to crumble and I looked and the mountain was gone and in its place I saw a mother sitting on the floor with a child's head resting in her lap. The child's body was bent and twisted and the mother was wiping drool from the corner of her mouth. She appeared to be crippled by an extreme case of Muscular Dystrophy or Multiple Sclerosis. It was then that I realized the pain in my body *was her pain* and the bentness I was experiencing *was her bentness*... and tears began to roll down the sides of my face. After that, I saw the same picture of the Word of God as before, with the pages slowly moving one after the other, only this time as each page turned the pain in my body began to disappear and the spasmodic deformity of my muscles slowly began to relax.

Finely the event was over and my speech slowly began to return. When I came to, the worship was over and John Wimber had finished his lecture and was calling for a brief break in the service. I knew with all my heart that this mother with her withered child was at this conference and that God wanted me to find them and share with them my experience. I grabbed my Bible and began walking through the aisles of this crowed auditorium of 5,000 people, looking for this family I saw in the vision.

As I turned down the first aisle, I looked towards the back of the auditorium, in my amazement, I saw on the floor in the back a woman stroking the hair of a young girl and whipping spittle away from her mouth. It was then that I felt the presence of the Lord and I knew that this was the woman in my vision.

With hesitation, I walked up to them and sat beside the mother. All of a sudden, I realized that what I had to say was a prophetic word calling for prophetic action on the part of the mother. She had come to this conference wanting her daughter to be healed and God sent her a message of faith and action pointing to the gradual healing of this lovely young girl. She was to stand firm and the word made Rhema – would move her into a prayer position of saying to that mountain, **FLEE INTO THE SEA.**

We sat together, prayed, talked, and praised the Lord our God. I had reached out for this young daughter's twisted arm and asked the Lord of life to bring the reality of His Word to this young lady. Suddenly, this girl's hand began to move in a way that it never moved before. I looked at the mother and tears began to flow down her checks, she knew what God had spoken will surly come to pass. After an hour, I left this couple and headed back to my seat.

When I got back to my hotel room that night the Lord spoke to me and said,

> *"You will see her tomorrow, ask her, when did this first happen to your daughter?"*

I responded, "Yes Lord."

That night I lay on my bed, blown away by the night's events. In the morning, I rushed to the back of the auditorium eagerly searching for the woman and her child but could not find them. In frustration, I thought to myself, how am I going to find them among all these people. I went to get a cup of coffee. As I headed for my seat, I bumped into someone, when I turned around to apologize; I was staring into that mother's eyes.

She was so excited, jumping up and down saying, "Praise God, Praise God, thank you for that word last night, last night she moved in a way she never moved before, and I know every move of my little girl."

"Praise God," I said not believing my eyes. I looked at her glowing countenance and asked her when her daughter became ill.

She responded, "She's been like this for five years."

Then my eyes began to tear up, the presence of God was all over me. I began to explain to her what happened to me up on the mountain five years earlier. I realized that *the very moment* this girl was struck-down with this devastating illness, the Lord felt her pain, heard her cries, and **took the pain into Himself.** Then, in a way I don't understand, He distributed that pain through His body, the church, and prophetically caused a member of the body of Christ (me) to bear the burden for this wounded child, up on that mountain, **until the day we would meet and God would command that mountain to flee into the sea.**

The flesh can't create this reaction only the Spirit can truly manifest this kind of intense intercession with manifestations of bearing the burdens of others. The Spirit of God intercedes on behalf of the afflicted causing us to partner with Him, like Jesus in the garden of Gethsemane ushering forth tears of blood on the way to the cross. Therefore, in like manner, we come to the garden before we go to the cross so that the blood shed in the garden can be mingled with that precious blood spilt at the cross of the Lord. That action brings about the power of God to the one we bleed for in prayer.

Her response was overwhelming for at that moment, with all the doubts of the past and wondering if God had ever heard her prayers, she was ushered to the omnipotence of ALL MIGHTY GOD. She knew that He who sits on the throne is all-powerful and that He has always been with them working out the answer to her cries.

This experience for me was truly life changing. When I read in the Scriptures about Hosea's entire life being a prophetic word to the nation of Israel I am blown away by the depth of His involvement. When I look at the unusual acts of Jeremiah and Ezekiel, the depth of the actions the Lord uses in dealing with the nation intrigues me. When I read Isaiah 53:4-5 and hear him, speak of the ministry of the Messiah:

> *"Surely He has borne our griefs, and carried our sorrows; Yet we esteemed Him stricken, Smitten by God, and afflicted. But He was wounded for our transgressions, He was bruised for our iniquities; The chastisement for our peace was upon Him,* **and by His stripes we are healed.**"

I know He has made a way for the afflicted. I understand His heart to those in dire need and the depth of His Love blows me away. The seer application is evident, Jesus Christ distributed the pain of this child to His body, the church; He released the spirit of intercession and burden bearing for a space of five years. It was only at that perfect moment in time that He opened the windows of Heaven and revealed His complete plan and purpose for this child. The answer came through a vision during a moment of bliss in His presence. However, the real work, I believe happened during that five-year period where the Holy Spirit cradled this child to the point of breakthrough.

CHAPTER 15

DIRECTIONAL SEEING

"Arise and go to the street called Straight, and inquire at the house of Judas for one called Saul of Tarsus, for behold, he is praying. And in a vision he has seen a man named Ananias coming in and putting his hand on him, so that he might receive his sight."

- Acts 9:11-12

Seeing What to Do

"And he was three days without sight, and neither ate nor drank. Now there was a certain disciple at Damascus named Ananias; and to him the Lord said in a vision, "Ananias."

And he said, "Here I am, Lord."

So the Lord said to him, "Arise and go to the street called Straight, and inquire at the house of Judas for one called Saul of Tarsus, for behold, he is praying. And in a vision he has seen a man named Ananias coming in and putting his hand on him, so that he might receive his sight."

Then Ananias answered, "Lord, I have heard from many about this man, how much harm he has done

> *to Your saints in Jerusalem. And here he has authority from the chief priests to bind all who call on Your name."*
>
> *But the Lord said to him, "Go, for he is a chosen vessel of Mine to bear My name before Gentiles, kings, and the children of Israel. For I will show him how many things he must suffer for My name's sake."*
>
> *And Ananias went his way and entered the house; and laying his hands on him he said, "Brother Saul, the Lord Jesus, who appeared to you on the road as you came, has sent me that you may receive your sight and be filled with the Holy Spirit." Immediately there fell from his eyes something like scales, and he received his sight at once; and he arose and was baptized.", Act 9:10-18*

Often the Lord will use visions or dreams to communicate who he wants to heal and what he wants you to do in reference to this healing. **Remember a condition revealed is a condition to be healed.** This kind of vision applies not only to healing but also to ministerial direction in general. A perfect example of this is found in the book of Acts.

This story like no other in scripture touches my heart the deepest. It brings me back to that Christmas Eve where Jesus confronted me on my own road to Damascus and several weeks later where He entered into my heart, removed the scales from my eyes, and brought me into the kingdom of God. Oh how consistent is the Lord our God, Oh how majestic is His name among those who fear Him.

In this story, we see Saul confronted by the Lord Jesus Christ on his way to persecute the church and due to this Glorious encounter, he is struck blind for a period of three days. After this period of what I suppose was a time of urgent prayer and repentance Saul pours out his heart to the one he meets along the way and is struck with a vision of a man named Ananias laying hands on him that he may receive his sight.

Now, in blindness, he waits for this promise of healing to be fulfilled. He wrestles with the issues of Judgment and Grace. He must have thought this blindness was a fitting punishment for one who lashed out at the Lord with religiously blind eyes. I suppose he never thought of seeing again. Yet for the first time in his life he is about to experience the grace of the cross and for this man of the law it would become the central themes throughout his ministry.

On the other side of this story, we have Ananias. Little is known about this man. We know that he was a disciple living in Damascus. He must have known that this persecutor of the saints was on his way there to destroy the church. Paul tells us later that Ananias was a devout observer of the law and highly respected by all the Jews living.

I find it very fitting to see how the Lord had chosen this potential martyr to be the one who would minister the grace of God to Saul. Ananias was a man who at one time had like passions as Saul but now was a disciple of Christ. In spite of his fear, the Lord chose him to minister to Saul, an enemy of the church. It is also interesting that Ananias is the Greek form of the Hebrew word "Hananyah" meaning "Jehovah has been gracious." You almost see prophetic play on words in this act of ministry to Saul.

Now let's look at the vision itself. It appears that this vision is something very natural. Ananias is not surprised that God is communicating to him in a vision. I am sure Peter's words on the day of Pentecost are fresh within his mind and that the church is the fulfillment of the words of the Prophet Joel. On the contrary he dialogues with the Lord, talking one on one if you will, trying to gain greater understanding on of this commission, and sharing with the Lord his personal fears. In like manner, the Lord responds to his concerns and tells him why he must minister to this man.

So here, we see visions, as a medium of communication to both the one administering healing as well as the recipient of the healing gift.

First, a vision is used by the Lord to communicate to the one being commissioned or sent out to heal, minister, or be the agent in healing.

- He received information as to the nature of the illness.
- He received information as to the identity of the person needing ministry.
- He received direction and the action to be taken when ministering the healing.

Second, vision is used by the Lord to communicate to the person in need of healing, the one on the receiving end of God's grace.

- Which brought about the promise of healing.
- He was shown how the healing will come about.
- He was shown who will be God's instrument in bringing about this healing.

All of which bring about the power of faith in the omnipotent Lord of glory.

Illustrative Examples

Cradle in the wind

Let me share with you another story from my own experience to elaborate on healing and directional seeing. Several years ago while working for Dr. Pat Robertson at the Christian Broadcasting Network in Virginia Beach, Virginia, I had a vision involving my administrative assistant, Janice.

Janice is a sweet spirited young lady who had been suffering with problems in her upper back and legs, which was a kind of scoliosis of the spine. This condition had brought her serious pain. We had prayed for her healing on several occasions but no results. Then, to my surprise, there were conditions of inner healing that the Lord had prioritized over the physical healing of her body.

One night while sleeping, I had a dream. In this dream, I was walking through the employee cafeteria at the Founders Inn and saw Janice sitting at a table eating lunch. The Lord spoke and said, "Go and pray for her that I may heal her." Then I saw myself walking towards Janice. I laid my hand on her shoulder and immediately she stood and began twisting and turning her back. As she was twisting and turning, to my amazement, she was transformed into a young girl. Then I heard the Lord say,

> "I want to heal the child within."

After that, I saw a country road and at the end of the road was a white country church with double doors in the front of it. I walked up, opened the door, and saw Janice siting at an organ playing praises to the Lord. Janice's face was glowing, she had a crown on her head, and on her fingers were rings full of colorful jewels. The Lord spoke to me and said,

> *"Janice's entire life is music to my ears. She has blessed Me with the melody of her heart therefore I have crowned her with the sweetness of My Spirit, that she may play her song to the rest of My Bride. I have placed My rings upon her fingers that she may reach out to others and share what is truly music to my ears."*

Then I woke, and the Lord said,

> *"Fred tell her."*

I was so excited for her, and blown away by the Lord's incredible passionate heart. I rushed to work and found Janise busily working in the office. I shared with her the dream that the Lord had given me and asked her if I could pray for her. With tears running down her face, she bowed her head and we began to pray. In the midst of praying, the Lord gave me a vision.

In this vision, I saw a tree; it was an autumn tree with amber leaves. One of the leaves on this tree started to fall to the ground and I saw the wind rise up, and like a baby's cradle, gently enfolded the leaf and bring it to the ground.

As I shared this picture with Janice, the Lord told me to tell her the following:

> *"Janice, do not be afraid. My love for you passes all understanding, and your life is truly music to my ears. You are in a season of change. I have come to bring life to that child within you... to that little girl that thinks she's not loved... to that child that sits alone... in fear of the hurt she has encountered. You are accepted, you are my child, and as the wind cradles this autumn leaf in change so My Spirit shall cradle and nurture you."*

At that moment, the presence of God was overwhelming and I saw Janice with tears in her eyes slowly overcome with incredible peace. Then as the Spirit of God was cradling her, she slid to the ground resting in the Spirit.

When she came to, she told me about some personal relationships she had and how the Lord was beginning to release her from bondage to this distorted self-image she had of herself. Since that time I have watched Janice truly blossom into a flower of sweet fragrance for the Lord.

In this situation, we see a similar pattern as our previous example. The Lord through this vision showed:

- Who needs prayer
- What the specific ailment was that need focus
- What action needed to be done to flow with the Spirit

He gave faith and hope, dispelling all fear to the one prayed for.

We also see from this example the Lord's heart towards inner healing. The mistake that we can make is assuming that what God desires to heal is that which we see with our natural eye. We need to be careful and listen to the Spirit of God, always seeking to collaborate with Him in what He is doing and not what we think needs to be done before we listen. It wasn't until after the healing of her self-image that her physical healing was manifest.

Proverbs 17:22 says: *"A merry heart does good, like medicine, But a broken spirit dries the bones."* It is clear from this verse that there can be a link between the wounded spirit or soul and physical illness. John, in 3 John 1:2, prays, *"Beloved, I pray that you may prosper in all things and be in health, just as your soul prospers."* He did not say "as your spirit prospers" but as your soul prospers. Again, the point is that a healthy soul can impact the state of your health.

Later we will discuss the Seer and inner healing but for now let me share with you another example that will expound on directional seeing.

An extension of My hands

In 1991, while working at CBN one of my employees had fallen and twisted her ankle. I walked in the office to see what happened and found her sitting in a chair with about eight to ten other employees standing around praying for her foot.

I immediately joined in with silent prayer. While I was praying, I felt this tremendous heat all over my hand. I placed my hand on the shoulder of one of the brothers praying, when he turned and said, "Boy your hand is really hot."

I responded praising God, saying, "The Lord's going to touch her." Then I saw a vision of beautiful meadow. Sitting on the grass of this meadow was this girl. Jesus was standing next to her. He bent over, grabbed her foot, and began praying for her. The serenity of this picture was truly tranquil.

Someone asked her if she had felt that the Lord was doing something. She said that her foot was still in pain. The group finished praying and one brother said, "Sister, we will just claim that healing for you." At that, they all returned to work.

Meanwhile, I was standing by her side, hands on fire and that vision of Jesus stuck in the forefront of my mind. I looked at April (her name) and said, "I think the Lord wants to heal your foot... I don't think we are really done praying yet."

I told April about the vision I had seen, and about the anointing, I had felt in my hands. Then the Lord said, "Fred, be an extension of my hands." That was when I understood that just as Jesus had bent down, held her foot, and began to pray, so in like manner he wanted me to do the same. I did and the warmth of His Spirit was all over April. God had healed her at that moment.

The reason this example is so crucial is here we see a team of brothers and sisters praying with all good intentions for April's healing. The problem was that the prayers went one way. Nobody was really listening to what the Spirit was saying regarding her healing.

We as a people need to learn how to listen to the Spirit of God. We need to learn how to pray in team ministry. When we come together as members of the body of Christ in the process of ministering to an individual's needs we must understand that we are just that, members of His body. That collectively there will be a diversity of gifting. There needs to be a methodology in our ministry time. We need to fine-tune the way we pray for people in order to flow with the Spirit and not walk by Him while he desires to do something else. We need to get trained.

CHAPTER 16

HEALING IN GENERAL

"Along the bank of the river, on this side and that, will grow all kinds of trees used for food; their leaves will not wither, and their fruit will not fail. They will bear fruit every month, because their water flows from the sanctuary. Their fruit will be for food, and their leaves for medicine."

- Ezekiel 47:12

*"Moreover the word of the Lord came to me, saying, Jeremiah, what do you see?
And I said, I see a branch of an almond tree. Then the Lord said to me, You have seen well, for I am ready to perform My word"*

- Jeremiah 1:11-12

The Seer and Healing

Often times, the Lord, when giving information on a specific physical ailment, will give visions in the form of X-Rays. This kind of revelation is a good example of visions as the chosen language of God while receiving a "word of knowledge." It may take place any time during ministry. I have received this kind of revelation, many times, during worship. Let me share with you a few examples.

Illustrative Example

X-Ray

One Sunday a few years ago, I was attending a school of the Holy Spirit class at Vineyard Christian Fellowship in Virginia Beach. While in the midst of worship, the Lord showed me several pictures of what looked like X-Rays.

The first picture I received was the back inside view of a right ankle. As I looked I noticed that all the bones appeared to be intact except for a shadowy area on the inside ankle above the heel. Then the word "tendon" popped in my mind and I knew that the problem with this ankle was a torn or strained tendon and that nothing was broken.

The second picture I received was again a view from the backside, only this time it was the left shoulder blade or scapula bone. As I was staring at this picture, I felt a tremendous pain shooting through the shoulder and neck of this person. Then the thought came to my mind that this was related to muscle strain and possibly a pinched-nerve.

The third picture that came to my mind was the back view of a spinal column. I looked at the center of the spine and noticed a shadowy section closer to the thoracic vertebrae and the word growth popped into my mind. Then I saw a person-walking bent over like someone imitating an elephant. As I pondered this and asked the Lord what it meant, it came to me that this person was

THE PANORAMIC LANGUAGE OF GOD • 221

As to the final vision it was three days later that I meet the woman that this vision was for. That Wednesday I was asked to speak at chapel at CBNs afternoon service. CBN always rotates various speakers each day moving from one chapel to the other giving tremendous variety to the daily services. It was my turn to speak at the corporate support building and this was the largest and most exciting of all the chapels at CBN.

Prior to the service, the Lord impressed me to go throughout the chapel and lay hands on every chair in the room praying for everyone that would sit in the chair. I did this with great enthusiasm. My message that day would was on Jeremiah 17 verses 7-15, where I brought them to the point where they could cry out from their hearts verses 14 & 15:

> *"Heal me, O Lord, and I shall be healed; Save me, and I shall be saved, For You are my praise. Indeed they say to me, "Where is the word of the Lord? Let it come now!"*

As I got up to share this message the Spirit of God came on me very Suddenly, and that picture I had seen the other day flashed in front of my mind. I stood and began praising God for His mighty hand sharing with the crowd how God had impressed me to prayer for each chair in the chapel and that his desire was to touch each member of his body individually with a personal touch from his hand.

Then I shared that vision that I had received a few days earlier. A woman stood who had a lump on the center of her back. She said it was a tumor and she believed the vision was for her. A few people stood around her and we all began to pray for the healing of this tumor. The result of this was her complete healing.

A few days later, it was reported to me by the Chaplin, that several people had been healed at that service, including the woman with the tumor. Here again we see wisdom's ways in the exercise of gifts are the prerequisites to the successful outpouring of God's Spirit. If I had given this word prematurely on Sunday night, I might have discarded it due to the lack of response at Sunday night's service. Again, I say we have to listen, listen, and listen again.

As you can see, visions and dreams can play an important part in the ministry of healing. What is so exciting to me is the creative power of the Lord to speak to His children.

In endless ways, if we listen to the Lord and seek His face and not just His hand, we shall move out in greater dimensions of the Spirit than we have ever known before.

> "But to you who fear My name, The Sun of Righteousness shall arise, With healing in His wings; And you shall go out, And grow fat like stall-fed calves."
>
> - Malachi 4:2

CHAPTER 17

INNER HEALING

"One thing I have desired of the Lord, That will I seek: That I may dwell in the house of the Lord, All the days of my life, To behold the beauty of the Lord, And to inquire in His temple. For in the time of trouble He shall hide me in His pavilion; In the secret place of His tabernacle He shall hide me; He shall set me high upon a rock.

- Psalm 27:4, 5

"Your ears shall hear a word behind you, saying, 'This is the way, walk in it.' Whenever you turn to the right hand or whenever you turn to the left."

- Isaiah 30:21

"For in Him dwells all the fullness of the Godhead bodily; and you are complete in Him, who is the head of all principality and power."

- Colossians 2:9,10

"That He would grant you, according to the riches of His glory, to be strengthened with might through His

> *Spirit in the inner man, that Christ may dwell in your hearts through faith; that you, being rooted and grounded in love."*
>
> - Ephesians 3:16, 17

Often, when one talks about inner healing, a red flag shoots up, on either side of the fence, proclaiming that, this kind of healing is valid, *or* that it is simply fantasy and has no place in the church today. Today, more than any other time in the history of the church, the need for inner healing to the body of Christ is critical. We, as a generation, are wounded, blinded by the weight of sins both past and present.

Many within the church are wounded vessels leaking out sap from the past. They build walls to shield their hurt or hide their pain. Their hearts are scabbed, driving them into stagnancy. This often causes them to run through the same recycled thought processes over and over again. Aspects of their lives are in zombie mode. They are driven by an unseen winds. This is often is due to an onslaught of sin and moral decay that oozes out of the culture we live in.

The effects are widespread, all we have to do is look around at the erosion on society, and we will see God's creation limping and staggering with the heaviness of sin's sludge dripping from every corner of our being. With drug abuse, sexual perversion, violence, abuse, occultism, and new age dabbling into the occult, it's no wonder that the majority of those brought in to the Kingdom of God, come in with excess baggage.

This onslaught of sin, affects every element of our being. It affects the lost and the save alike. Sin can plague bodies with sickness and addiction. Finely, it affects the soul or mind as seen in those who carry the pain of the past, and become psychologically bound by lies that replay in our thoughts like an old record player that constantly skips and replays. Sin affects the whole person, body, soul, and spirit.

Though some contend that man is a Dichotomy, (made up of two parts, body, and soul), this Dichotomous view falls apart in light of scripture and fails to recognize a distinction between the human soul and the human spirit. The scriptures make it very clear we are created as a Trichotomy; there is a distinction in our makeup. Take for example this passage from Hebrews.

> *"For the word of God is living and powerful, and sharper than any two-edged sword, piercing even to the division of soul and spirit, and of joints and marrow, and is a discerner of the thoughts and intents of the heart. And there is no creature hidden from His sight, but all things are naked and open to the eyes of Him to whom we must give account."*
>
> - Hebrews 4:12-13

It is evident from this passage; there is a division between the soul and the spirit. In fact, the Word of God has the power to divide these two natures of our being. The Greek word here for "powerful" is "energes," meaning: "energetic" or "actively at work," in this dividing and discerning process. Here the Holy Spirit shows us a parallel between the dividing of soul and spirit, and the dividing of joints and marrow, and thoughts & intents.

For just as the muscle moves joints and bones, carrying with them the marrow, which dwells helpless within the bone, so the thoughts of the soul drive the actions of the person while the intents of the spirit lay dormant within it. The writer of Hebrews shows us the power of the Spirit's ability to discern what is driven by the soul, compared to what is driven by the human spirit.

This whole dilemma is why Paul in Romans 5, 6, 7 & 8 struggles with the issues of overcoming the sinful nature of the flesh, or the sin infested soul. He went on to say that by putting the soul to death with the cross of Christ one could live in the new nature of the spirit (which was once dead, leaving man as a dichotomy) but is now alive in Christ Jesus (a resurrected spirit bringing about our trichotomous nature). This is further elaborated in another of Paul's writings where we read:

> *"Now may the God of peace Himself sanctify you completely; and may your whole spirit, soul, and body be preserved blameless at the coming of our Lord Jesus Christ."*
>
> - 1 Thessalonians 5:23

It is this process of sanctification that causes us to be transformed into the image of Christ (2 Corinthians. 3:17-18). Paul tells us in Romans:

> *"And do not be conformed to this world, but be transformed by the renewing of your mind, that you may prove what is that good and acceptable and perfect will of God."*
>
> - Romans 12:2

Renewing the mind is the process the Holy Spirit uses to replace the imprint of the world and replace it with the imprint of Christ Jesus. The mind has been programmed with natural "established attitudes." These are the beliefs, thoughts, ideas, opinions, convictions, and prejudices that we have concerning ourselves, others, objects, activities, and God. These can be formed by the influences from of our parents, the educational system, society (through books, television, movies, etc.,) or religious training. These "established attitudes" become permeated with fleshly "personal interest" of selfishness and sinfulness. Because of these imprints, we act out, are driven by them, to achieve personal aspiration, gratification, and reputation, or we react through the fight, fright, or flight modality.

God knows our every thought. The mind needs to be renewed with Godly "established attitudes." When we are born again, we are a new creation. However, as John Wimber said:

> "Everyone who comes to Christ, also come with all kinds of emotional and spiritual baggage. In some cases that baggage will make the job of spiritual formation extremely difficult. They come angry, confused, and bruised. Some of them have been chewed up and spit out by life's difficulties. Many people come from very nominal church background. They may mistrust the church. They may be individualistic, cocky, and arrogant when they walk in the door."

"Established attitudes" develop into a "mind-set" and these mind-sets drive the way we live and relate to the world around us. If our mind-set is healthy, our thoughts and attitudes are in alignment with the Word of God and His truth regarding our identity in Him. When this happens, our soul comes alive and we live through the truth of who we are in Christ. This process is called the renewing of the mind. Remember, "As a man thinks in his soul, so is he (in behavior)" (Proverbs 23:7).

If our mind-set is unhealthy (driven by lies), it will give us a false sense of identity, such as having a persona that is bent with an external orientation, e.g. "How I look," personal guilt through attitudes of worthlessness, or feeling inferior to others. The result is a person who may become self-conscious with an unhealthy desire to please others. We can become inundated with vain imaginations, fears, and phobias. The impact can result in attitudes of anger, impatience, hate, bitterness, resentment, revenge, suspicion, criticism, jealousy, un-forgiveness, blame, depression, co-dependency.

An unhealthy mind thinks differently about God. God may become irrelevant, archaic, and unnecessary or on the other extreme God may become "superstition" or "magical", driving the individual into occult practices or witchcraft, leading to a demonic stronghold.

In Colossians we read:

> *"Therefore put to death your members which are on the earth: fornication, uncleanness, passion, evil desire, and covetousness, which is idolatry. ... Do not lie to one another, since you have put off the old man with his deeds, and have put on the new man who is renewed in knowledge according to the image of Him who created him, ... Therefore, as the elect of God, holy and beloved, put on tender mercies, kindness, humility, meekness, longsuffering;"*
>
> - Colossians 3:5, 9, 10, 12

Elsewhere we are commanded to put on the mind of Christ, in First Corinthians we read:

> *"For "who has known the mind of the Lord that he may instruct Him?" But we have the mind of Christ."*
>
> - 1 Corinthians 2:16

Look at these other verses in relationship to our minds.

> *", be renewed in the spirit of your mind, and that you put on the new man which was created according to God, in true righteousness and holiness."*
>
> - Ephesians 4:23, 24

"Let this mind be in you which was also in Christ Jesus..."

- Philippians 2:5

"Therefore gird up the loins of your mind, be sober, and rest your hope fully upon the grace that is to be brought to you at the revelation of Jesus Christ;"

- 1 Peter 1:13

It is evident here there is a struggle going on within our members. The bible tells us that the flesh is at war with the spirit and the spirit with the flesh. It is this old nature popping out its ugly head, while we are in the midst of trying to walk in the spirit, which causes us to stumble and revert to our old nature. This was Paul's question in Romans:

"For we know that the law is spiritual, but I am carnal, sold under sin. For what I am doing, I do not understand. For what I will to do, that I do not practice; but what I hate, that I do. If, then, I do what I will not to do, I agree with the law that it is good. But now, it is no longer I who do it, but sin that dwells in me. For I know that in me (that is, in my flesh) nothing good dwells; for to will is present with me, but how to perform what is good I do not find. For the good that I will to do, I do not do; but the evil I will not to do, that I practice.

Now if I do what I will not to do, it is no longer I who do it, but sin that dwells in me. I find then a law, that evil is present with me, the one who wills to do good. For I delight in the law of God according to the inward man. But I see another law in my members, warring against the law of my mind, and bringing me into captivity to the law of sin which is in my members. O wretched man that I am! Who will deliver me from this body of death? I thank God—through Jesus Christ our Lord!"

- Romans 7:14-25

Thank God, for Romans chapter eight for in it Paul sets out for us freedom from indwelling sin and the power of being sons of God. Look at the next few verses from Romans 8.

> *"There is therefore now no condemnation to those who are in Christ Jesus, who do not walk according to the flesh, but according to the Spirit. For the law of the Spirit of life in Christ Jesus has made me free from the law of sin and death. For what the law could not do in that it was weak through the flesh, God did by sending His own Son in the likeness of sinful flesh, on account of sin: He condemned sin in the flesh, that the righteous requirement of the law might be fulfilled in us who do not walk according to the flesh but according to the Spirit."*

- Romans 8:1-4

Inner healing is dealing with the residue of our old nature, bringing it to death, that we may live and walk in the Spirit of the living God. The Holy Spirit is in effect rewiring our minds and creating new neurological pathways seeded in the word of God. This is healing of the soul.

When a child is abused and the thought of that pain is too unbearable to deal with, that child will plunge those memories into its sub-conscience mind just to survive, only to find out that throughout all their life they have been driven by unseen thought patterns. Whether they are driven by fear, loneliness, anger, or depression, in order for healing to come, there needs to be a point when they lay the axe to the root of that tree. Proverbs 18:14 says:

> *"The spirit of a man will sustain him in sickness, But who can bear a broken spirit?"*

In Hebrews 12:15 we read:

> *"... looking carefully lest anyone fall short of the grace of God; lest any root of bitterness springing*

up cause trouble, and by this many become defiled;"

The whole process of inner healing is to slay the grip and power that sin has on us. Healing of the physical body is distorting sins grip on a person physically in a given situation. This will ultimately take place at the resurrection and transformation of our bodies on the last day. Healing of the spirit is salvation; by being born again our spirits are quickened to life by His Spirit (1 Corinthians 6:17; 2 Corinthians 5:17). Inner healing is renewing our minds and healing our thought processes taking the axe to the hidden roots of destruction that dwell within us.

Chapter 17

Sozo

"Your ears shall hear a word behind you, saying, 'This is the way, walk in it,' Whenever you turn to the right hand or whenever you turn to the left."

- Isaiah 30:21

"Nor is there salvation in any other, for there is no other name under heaven given among men by which we must be saved (Greek: Sozo)."

- Acts 4:12

The Greek for "*being* saved" is "Sozo." It is used 110 times in the New Testament. It is an action/verb meaning *to be saved* or *rescued* out from under satan's power and to be restored into wholeness, body, soul, and spirit. It has been used to mean:

- Salvation (Acts 4:12; Romans 10:9; Ephesians 2:8).
- Healed from disease (Matthew 9:22; Mark 6:56; Mark 10:52).
- Delivered from demonic oppression (Luke 8:36; 2 Timothy 4:18; Jude 1:5).

- All three of these at the same time (Luke 1:9,10; John 20:21).

To be "sozo" is *to be saved through-and-through*, **saved**, **healed**, and **delivered**, from the clutches of the enemy, and set free in Christ as a new creation. Thank God, the sozo ministry has blossomed as it has today, much thanks to the ministry work of Bethel Church in Redding California. Dawna DeSilva's work in sozo ministry has spanned the globe in not only setting folks free but also equipping the church to carry the sozo torch.

I think it is so important to get a full understanding of this so that we can move out in wholeness and get on with the business of healing this dying world. Inner healing is part of the maturing process. It is not easy, but as Wimber has said:

> *"Christianity doesn't guarantee heaven here on earth. We're going to Heaven- But we may go through hell here on this earth! Maturity does not automatically come with the passage of years; some of the people we work with may be spiritually much younger than their chronological age. A prayer I pray often is: Lord, let me grow up, before I grow old."*

There are many wonderful books out there on the subject of inner healing and sozo. Dawna De Silva has written a dynamic series on the Sozo ministry, and I highly recommend her work (http://store.ibethel.org.)

My purpose here is not to cover the vastness of inner healing. There are much more qualified individuals than myself that have taken up that task. My purpose is simply to show the relationship of visions and dreams in the ministry of inner healing.

Visions, Dreams, and the Ministry of Sozo

Visions and dreams can play an important role in the process of inner healing. God in a moment can cut asunder between soul and spirit showing us the root of the problem. He can also, to the one being healed, visually bring the truth of His love to a situation extinguishing the lies of the enemy with the light of His glory.

As a person moving in the inner-healing ministry, you will encounter a variety of problems. Following is a brief list to name a few.

- The healing of memories
- Shame
- Sexual brokenness
- Masculine/feminine soul identity
- Multiple personality disorders
- Satanic ritual abuse
- The healing of the wounded child
- Broken marital relationships
- The healing of inner vows
- The healing of bitter-root judgments
- Victims of violence
- Addictions
- The healing of cords of iniquity

The list goes on and on, changing with the challenges of every new generation. We are a complex creation in which only Jesus can truly bring healing to our broken places. Jesus has come to set us free from the sin that weighs us down. He comes to take the pain from the past and like unraveling an onion he removes the layers of wounding that have resulted... laying an axe to the core of the problem.

Now let's look at some personal examples involving seeing and inner healing. I share these not to unload my personal history on you but to demonstrate the loving nature of Jesus Christ in the process of healing and to show examples of "how" the Lord uses visionary language to heal the inner man.

Illustrative Examples

Francis and Judith MacNutt

My first experience with inner healing came to me in 1986 at a healing conference sponsored by Vineyard Ministries International. It was held at the Anaheim Vineyard in Southern California. The team of speakers for the week included John Wimber, Francis MacNutt, and Judith MacNutt. Francis and Judith have a very special relationship to the ministry of healing and inner healing. As a team, they minister all over the world bringing the message of Jesus' power to heal, to millions.

On the forth night of the conference, Judith was speaking on rejection and the wounded child. At the end of her message, they called for a time of ministry to all in the auditorium. After a brief time of prayer and inviting the presence of the Holy Spirit to come, Judith began to sing in the Spirit. The power of that song was incredible, it sounded like a lullaby from Father God to my heart. Tears began to roll down my face and I went forward to get prayer.

During the prayer time, I was having a hard time trying to relax. Suddenly, the Lord showed me a vision. I saw my dad standing against a white background. It was as if I was looking at Him through the eyes of God. I saw him as a child. I saw the pain that he had inside and all the hurt and fear that was in his heart.

Then I saw Jesus standing next to him; he was looking at him with overwhelming love flowing out of Him. My dad was looking up at Him with eyes full of love and tears of pain, and joy. Then I saw the Lord take my father's heart and put it in His hand, and with both hands, He began to massage my father's heart. He was healing my father's heart.

I then saw the Lord take hold of my hand and put His hand on my heart. I felt as if I was getting heart surgery. Then He put my father and me together and I rested my head on my father's chest... as the Lord had his arms around the both of us. Tears began to run down my face and a weight was lifted from my heart.

Then I saw a vision of a hospital corridor, I was dressed in white and Jesus was by my side with His arm around me walking me back to my hospital room. The Lord spoke to me and said,

"That's all for now, but you know we're not finished."

When I came out of this trance, I felt like I was walking on air. His presence was so intense I felt a peace that was indescribable. The Lord had given me new eyes to see my father. He showed me how He saw my dad and that was life changing for me. A different kind of love was growing in my heart for my dad. A love that wasn't reactionary... I had always craved his love. I felt that somehow I had to earn it. Now I had a love of compassion. It was a deep love that didn't involve self-hunger... it was holy and pure, like a spring of water flowing from the thrown of God. Like the fulfillment of Malachi 4:6:

> *"And he shall turn the heart of the fathers to the children, and the heart of the children to their fathers, lest I come and strike the earth with a curse."*

I grew up sub-consciously feeling that I had to earn my father's love and that this love was conditional and fragile. This thought process not only affected our relationship but it also affected every area of my life because acceptance in general was based on performance. This was true even about my relationship with Jesus Christ.

At times, the struggle with this was overwhelming. In fact, all through this conference I kept telling the Lord that I wanted to see His face. I didn't want Him to leave me... I wanted to be as close to Him as I could possibly be. That night when I was leaving the conference, I walked to the car and sat in the front seat thinking about the events that had taken place.

Suddenly, the Lord spoke to me very clearly,

"Fred, Behold my Face."

I looked up in the sky and saw an open vision of the face of the Lord. I began to cry as waves of His love flowed through me.

Here we see how the Lord can use visions to reveal a truth about the one being prayed for. The visual symbolism of what He is doing awakens the soul to the light of His glory and cuts to the heart of the situation, laying an axe to the ties that bind. What is also interesting to me is that healing is a process, and the Lord is in no hurry to accomplish this. He chooses the right time and does no more than what needs to be done at that moment. The Lord is gentle when healing the damage of our fragile makeup, more so with inner healing than any other kind of healing.

I had been a Christian for seven years before the Lord began to work on that area of my life. With periodic intervals, God would work on healing my wounded spirit, yet it wasn't until the summer of 2010 that He would finish what he started in 1986. The Lord does not believe in premature healing, this could cause more damage than anticipated. We as ministers to the inner healing grace of the Lord Jesus Christ need to be very sensitive to the Spirit of God when we are ministering.

School Days

Another example from my own personal experience will help to shed some light on how the Lord uses visions to the person being healed in the ministry of inner healing.

In the autumn of 1989, I went through a time of intense inner healing. One night during a healing prayer session, the Lord gave me a vision that opened a wound that was too deep to remember. In this vision, I saw myself walking besides an old stonewall. I came to a corner and turned to my right. In front of me on the right side there was a rod-Iron Gate enveloped by a fog. I stood paralyzed staring at this gate.

Then I saw Jesus walking up to me. He put His hand on my shoulder and asked me if I wanted to go inside. Fear struck my heart. I looked into His warm, gentle, reassuring eyes and said,

"I don't think I want to go in there."

The Lord asked me if I wanted to go for a walk. I took hold of His hand and together we went for a walk. We moved past the gate, still parallel with the wall. The Lord stopped and turned, putting the palms of His hands on the cheeks of my face. When He did this, I noticed that I had changed and turned into a child.

With youthful joy in the sound of His voice, He asked me if I wanted to play. I responded with hesitation, "Well O.K."

With that, I saw the Lord bend down and cup His hands to give me a boost over the wall. The next thing I knew we were running around this old park playing tag, hide & seek, and skipping stones across the stream. The serenity of this park was incredible. With weeping willows, rocks, tall grass, and a stream running through the center of the park we enjoyed the playful surroundings.

We stopped and began to walk along the stream. As we were walking, we came to an area that was enclosed in fog. I stopped at the edge of the fog not wanting to walk any further. Then Jesus looked into my eyes and said,

"It's ok, I will be with you, I will clear the way."

As I walked towards the fog, my heart pounding uncontrollably, I noticed the fog beginning to clear. I continued to walk and Suddenly, found myself on a school playground standing by a tetherball pole. I was five years old and the memory of what had taken place at school started to come back to me.

I saw myself reenacting the event only this time I knew that Jesus was with me. When I was five years old, I went to a private school in Southern California. This uniformed school was very strict on discipline.

One day I got to school late. Not realizing that I was late, I stopped to play tetherball on the playground before class. I wondered where all the kids were, not thinking that school had already started.

When I got to my room, the teacher was very upset. She asked me where I've been. I told her I was playing tetherball. She then grabbed my arm and said, you're going to the hallway. When she said that I started to cry telling her I didn't want to go.

The hallway ran along the back of all the classrooms. It was a place where they stored boxes and chairs and it was the back entrance to the rooms. This hallway was also the place that they put kids to be spanked with a wooden paddle. The hallway had very poor lighting and on the right side of the door in the hallway was a chair that kids who were being punished would sit and wait.

The janitor was assigned to the spanking detail. Jesus brought me back to this classroom. I saw the door that led to the hallway. Fear struck me when Jesus asked me if I was ready to go in there. Then He said that He would go in first and nothing would happen to me because He was with me.

The Lord opened the door and walked in. I clung to His robe and slowly walked in behind Him. He put me in that little chair and stood between the darkness and me. I then heard the sound of a paddle moving across some boxes like the sound one would make if they were running a stick along the side of a fence while they were walking.

I got very scared and started to cry. Jesus turned and wiped the tears from my eyes saying,

"It's ok. I'm with you and nobody is going to hurt you."

I felt a peace come over me. As I looked down that dark hallway, listening to the sound of that paddle against the wall, all of a sudden, the sound stopped and I saw a little man on his hands and knees cowering on the floor moving towards Jesus. It was as if he was trying to hide his face from the light of the Lord.

Jesus turned and looked at me,

"Is this the man that hurt you?"

The tears began to flow again as I responded, "He's the one, he did it!"

Jesus turned and said to me,

"You know what you have to do now don't you?"

"Yes Lord, I do," With my voice all choked up and pain in my heart I looked at him and said, "I forgive you for what you did to me."

I then saw this man move back in shame to the darkness and disappear. I started to cry even harder. Then Jesus picked me up and held me close to Him taking my pain into Himself.

Jesus was beginning to heal the brokenness in my heart. I had replaced the childhood joy of playing with performance for acceptance. The Lord was starting to restore playfulness to that wounded child within me... healing me from the fear of having fun. At that time the Lord never really showed me exactly what this man did in that dark hallway to me. That was a time of healing just one layer of an onion. I would not really experience the fullness of healing until I dealt with the root of what was really happening.

All through this vision it was as if I was a spectator to the events that had taken place. This detachment had its roots in **"Shame"** the act of *"cutting off"* a facet of one's self. In this case, I had cut out that child within me from myself. It wouldn't be until during the preparation of this manuscript and a sozo session I had in 2010 that the Lord began to show me the extent of the damage and heal another layer in that onion, a layer of sexual brokenness in my life. For this man, spanking was a pleasure. What he did in the midst of this punishment I still find hard to discuss. It was during that session that I was fully restored and was also healed in my relationship with Poppa God.

I thank the Lord for His patience in healing. I thank the Lord that this is an ongoing work of wholeness and that the gentleness of His workmanship makes the healing process worth it.

What this man did was inexcusable. However, God had to free me from the hate and the fear of what this man had done to a five-year-old boy. The result of the pain was self-hatred of that child within. I disassociated myself with that part of me. Shattered innocence seems to be a trademark that the enemy loves to use in the sick and perverted days in which we live. How many people are there that are bound up by the brokenness of abuse and victimization? Who hide behind stonewalls they set up in their lives, afraid to enter the fog from the past. Like medieval dungeons in the basements of our minds, we hear the horrifying echo of the past crying out to haunt us. Notwithstanding, to the Lord these are root cellars and he has come to lay the axe at the root of the pain that haunts us. Christ has come to set us free. He has come to bring health and life to the broken places of our past in order that our present can be fruitful and that we may be partakers in the healing of others in the future.

When I was in prayer asking the Lord to heal the shame in me, the Lord spoke to my heart and said,

"Fred are you willing to go into this memory as an adult and face you, as a child?"

I told the Lord that I was willing to do this. When I had said that the Lord gave me a vision of that memory and I was standing in the hallway facing this child that was sitting in the chair scared and trembling. I was yelling at the child. "I hate you for what you did!, Why did you do that? It's all your fault... If you hadn't been playing nothing would had happened. What's wrong with you? You're a stupid, stupid child, I don't like you at all! I hate what you did to me! You are no longer my friend I want no part of you!"

As I was looking at myself yelling at this child, I could feel the hatred that I had for him... for myself. I could feel it in my heart.

Then the Lord spoke to me and said,

> *"Fred... Don't you see... this is sin...? What you are doing is sin."*

"I KNOW, it hurts so much," then I started to cry, "Lord please forgive me for hating this child; Please forgive me for hating me."

When I had finished saying this, the presence of the Lord was all over me and I knew that he had forgiven me. All I could do was cry, thanking Him repeatedly.

Then the Lord spoke to me,

> *"Ask this child to forgive you for hating him. Self hatred is cancerous to your soul."*

I was back in this memory standing before this child. I was worn down, emotionally wiped, as I looked at this little boy sitting scared in the chair.

"Please." The tears began to flow again, as I tried to seek his forgiveness. "Please forgive me for hating you and abandoning you."

This little boy kept holding out his hand to me with tears rolling down his checks. "I forgive you. It wasn't my fault you know. It really wasn't. I just didn't know what to do I was so scared."

Then the Lord spoke to me and asked me,

> *"What does this child need from you?"*

I said, "He wants me to hold him and never leave him again."

> *"Are you willing to do this?"*

"Yes Lord I think I'm ready."

The next thing I saw was Jesus standing between this child and me. He held out His hand towards me and gently pulled me towards this child. With His other hand, He lifted this child from His seat and brought Him to me. With His arms around the both of us He looked up to heaven, his face began to glow, and He cried,

> "Father I thank you for your tender mercy. I thank you that your love endures forever, now Father I pray that these two may be as one even as we are one."

As He said these words, His hands began to glow and the brightness of His being filled the vision that I was seeing. He was merging the two of us together. Then I saw myself kneeling before the Lord and this child was glowing from my heart with his head bowed worshiping in like manner.

Then I saw myself at the Lord's feet. My tears were rolling down my face and onto the feet of the Lord. He reached down, picked me up, and wiped away the tears from my face. As he picked me up, I could see the child within me. The Lord held me and said,

> "I have not rejected you, for I am in you and you are in Me, I love you with an everlasting love."

When this was over, I just sat there and cried.

Sozo, My Love encounter with the Godhead

I would like to close this chapter on the seer and inner healing with a sozo story from my journal, summer, 2010. I wrote this log entry after a Sozo session conducted by Dawna De Silva.

6/11/10

The Lord has been doing a lot of healing in my heart the last three months. And this last week the Lord was working overtime on areas in my life, dealing with my ability to accept his unconditional love. Four days ago, I had a breakthrough with the Lord and He had released such peace in my heart – I could not believe it. The knot in my chest that kept driving me into His healing arms was gone; it had been replaced with peace. Even my breathing changed. He had taken me to a place and was dealing with an issue that had governed my life from the time I was born. He brought me back to some milestones in my life.

He flooded my mind with memories. I remembered when he had started healing this thing, 15 years earlier, at Vineyard in Virginia Beach, when He brought me back to my birth. He told me, he was there the day I was born: When, Suddenly, I was back there in a little 1950s kitchen, my Mom dressed in 50s style cloths with her dark red lipstick and fire red hair. She was so much younger than I had thought and she was pregnant. She was wearing an apron. The scene flashed forward and she was lying on the floor, in pain. Jesus was there in that kitchen, He was kneeling over my mother with his hand on her stomach. She was going into premature delivery. She looked as if she was injured. Hours later, Jan 4, 1957, I was born, 3 lb., 8 oz. and was three months a preemie.

Jesus said,

> *"I have always been with you and I will always be available to you. I was there when they thought you would not live – when you came out, I saw a boxer,"*

He was pointing out all the places of death and destruction in my life, when my Nana passed away. He was there. He was with when my parents were torn apart. He was with me when my little brother tried to kill himself. All these memories kept flooding my mind. He was with me when my older brother Bobbie died, and he walked with me when cancer took my mother and she went to be with Jesus. Then he said:

> *And yes, Fred, I was there with you in your great sadness, the day your son passed away. I will always be there with you. I will always be your comfort and your*

> *rear guard. I will never leave you, nor forsake you; I have got you in the palm of my hands,*

He explained to me how the "**spirit of death**" had governed my life and that He was cutting off the cords of death from me and bringing me into life. I never knew it. I had never seen it. I knew that something had governed my life not to believe. I knew that deep inside I was not accepted but I didn't know why. It was destructive but I could never put my finger on it.

However, now it all began to make sense, I was starting to understand. The spirit of death had tried to rob me from life and from my destiny in Christ. The Lord in that moment had embraced my heart, something broke inside, and I knew I was free, and I began to cry.

Then, the last two days, Jesus kept telling me,

> *"What I show you – I am going to do."*

Over, and over He kept saying it. All day long I would hear him saying,

> *"What I show you, I AM going to do."*

I got so excited when I heard Him say it. I was thrilled at the thought of Him doing what He said He was going to do.

Then the night before last, He said,

> *"Fred, do you believe I am going to do what I show you?"*

It struck me in the heart. I was struggling with this so much. He kept asking me, repeatedly. The knot returned, and I groaned inside. I said, "Lord, I thought we were done? I thought we had taken care of the healing I needed?" In a panic, I went back to my Sozo sessions, trying to find something, anything, to heal my unbelief and bring release to this knot in my chest, but could not. I told the Lord I was going to bed.

In the morning when I woke up, I heard the Holy Spirit singing this song to me:

> *"Come up here, come up here, come up here where I am."*

And I knew what he wanted me to do.

With all my heart, I wanted to move into a place of healing. I was hungry for a touch, to be released. In my heart was the deep desire to have intimacy with the Lord, to go deeper and get as close as possible to Him. I wanted healing, on the inside, of those things that were hindering me from going deeper and having that close – very close relationship with Poppa.

It was about 5:00 AM when I started worshiping the Lord. Shortly thereafter, I decided to continue a Sozo session by Dawna De Silva. I wanted to go deeper with the Godhead. I wanted to allow Jesus to heal me some more. Dawna was walking us through the doorways to the heavenly realm. In that moment, The Lord brought me to a heavenly place. This is what the Lord showed me,

Jesus

As I began to focus on the Lord, I saw Him walking on the beach towards me, smiling. I asked Him a simple question, "Jesus, what do you think of me?"

He smiled tenderly,

> *"I love you so very much. You are the apple of my eye, my soul's delight. You are my friend and I love you dearly. I love being with you."*

I felt his unconditional love for me and it drew me in. It felt so natural. So I thought I would ask him another question, "Jesus, what do you want to show me? Show me that special place."

He took a hold of my hand; we turned, and started to walk. Suddenly, I was standing in heaven, by the river of life. Jesus was standing next to me. He was filled with kindness and Joy. I could sense that He was full of mystery and wonder.

Then He smiled and said,

> "Come, let's go for a walk."

I felt as if I was walking with my best friend. Joy and acceptance filled my heart. Along the bank of the river were pillars. They were ancient pillars, covered with moss and growth.

Jesus said,

> *"These are the pillars of faith. Come let's walk amongst them."*

So we walked between the pillars and talked as we walked. I was staring at them, looking at the care and craftsmanship of their design, their age, and the life that covered them. As we walked, we headed towards the river's edge – to the water line. The river was very peaceful, like a lazy river, like you would see down south, in the delta marshland. Trees surrounded the river with hanging air moss and vines draping down. The place was full of life. Jesus pointed to the plants and the flowers. There was fruit everywhere. It was as if all the foliage, and the bugs, and bees, butterflies and frogs, all worshiped God.

Jesus rolled up His pant legs. He was barefoot. He said,

> "Come on, let's go in."

So I rolled up my pants, took off my shoes, and stepped into the water. It was cool and refreshing.

He said,

> "Oh – doesn't that feel good,, the cold mud between your toes?"

"Yea," I said, "it feels GREAT."

He smiled. He kept pointing life out. A golden fish popped up through the water. Jesus said,

> "Look, look, over there. What a great catch!"

I was watching that gold fish with its massive gills swimming at the surface of the water. I was amazed at the mystery of it all.

We stepped out of the water. Jesus pointed over to a horizon at the bend of the river. In front of the horizon was a mighty archway. He said,

> "See the horizon? It was there, just beyond the edge of heaven that I saw you. Before time and space, I called you forth. I was with you the day you were conceived. I have always been with you and have always loved you. You are my hearts delight. I love you Fred. I desire to be with you and to walk, and talk with you. This is so good, isn't it?"

"Yes Lord, this is very good."

Then He pointed to the horizon, to the archway and said,

> "Look, your destiny, it's just around the bend."

I could feel his love pouring over me. I was captured by His love for me.

Then He took my hand, and said,

"Come, let me take you to the Father."

My heart was in my throat. It was starting to beat fast, as if I was fearful to see Him. I was wrestling with this on the inside. Jesus squeezed my hand. I was so comfortable with Jesus. I knew He loved me deeply and that I was His friend. But the father, that was a little different. We were walking up a road headed to what looked like a castle or something. The landscape had changed. It was like rolling hills with incredible blue and cloud studded white sky.

It almost looked like a scene from the wizard of Oz heading to emerald city.

Poppa

Then all of a sudden, Jesus was gone. I front of me was Poppa, though I could barely make him out. He was so big and swirling around like massive clouds. Then he stopped and I could make out His eyes upon me. Goodness and Joy started to fill the air. I looked up at Him and asked Him a question, "Father, are you pleased with me?"

In a moment, He was in front of me. All I could see was His chest. Hanging around His neck was a beautiful chain with a gold locket around it. He opened the locket and inside there was a picture of me, I was over taken by Him. He showed me His heart. He said,

> *"My heart beats for you. I crafted you and created you. I love every part of you. All your hairs are numbered. Every day has been treasured in my Heart."*

I saw this big animated heart, pumping and beating. It was almost funny, and the father smiled and said,

> *"I love you so deeply. Did you know that before you were born; before the universe was even created, I dreamed of*

> *you? Yes, it's true; I saw you before the earth was formed. I have loved you from the moment I dreamed you into my heart. You are the apple of my eye."*

Then I saw a big book open, and I understood it to be the days of my life. I saw the Father reading the book and turning the pages, as if He was enjoying every moment, as if He was reading a photo album. Then, I saw myself standing before the throne of God and I was dressed in royal attire, bowing before His throne. Then the Father said,

> *"This is what I saw the day I created you. This is what I saw the day you were born." He smiled."*

He took me to the pier in Bahia Beach Florida. The day after my son had died. I was standing at the end of the pier crying out to God. "Why, Why,?" I cried, all night long – My heart was broken.

Suddenly, I saw the Father there at that place, and He wrapped His arms around me and said,

> *"I know how much it hurts. I love you, and JJ is with me. I love you let Me comfort you. You know I am for you, and I am with you, I am with you all the time. I will never leave you nor forsake you; I have you in the palm of My hands."*

I could feel the Father's love. I was starting to warm up to Him. So I asked him a question, "Poppa, what gifts do you want to give me,?"

At that moment, I was overwhelmed by Poppa's eagerness. I saw Him reach out and place a gold and red crown on my head. He took a golden scepter with a large diamond tip, and placed it in my hands. I was overwhelmed. Then He stood me up. It was like we were standing in front of all the kingdom of heaven. Around, everywhere you could look were heavenly palaces and it felt like a mystical wonderful place – full of life!

He stood with a smile on His face. His joy filled the kingdom like the wind of God. He had in His hand a glorious red robe. He cried out in a load voice, as if He was making announcement, like He was presenting me to the nations and to the Kingdom of Heaven,

> *"This is my beloved Son, in whom I AM very well pleased."*

Then He draped the robe over my shoulders, and I stood there and cried. Poppa accepted me. He loved me, He approved of me. Something inside of me broke. I looked in His eyes and saw Poppa – and **I knew He adored me.**

Then, as I looked deeper into His eyes, I could see my eyes – looking into the eyes of others – showing them the Love of Poppa.

Then Poppa Said,

> *"I want to introduce you to someone, to the Holy Spirit."*

I said, "Thank you Poppa for revealing your presence to me, for showing me how much you love and accept me. Poppa, thank you for setting me apart and loving me. Thank you for knowing my name."

The Holy Spirit

Suddenly, I was in a whirlwind. The whirlwind was full of color, like the colors of fire and sunset. We were spinning around faster, and faster. When I stopped, I felt this incredible laughter fill the place. I could hardly recognize the Holy Spirit, but I felt Him, and that I knew Him. He was almost funny and playful.

I stopped and asked the Holy Spirit, "What do you want to impart to me?"

Suddenly, I saw myself standing in front of the Holy Spirit with my hands held out. The word "*Apostle*" was written on my left hand and the word "*Prophet*" were written on my right hand. I stood back and wondered. I looked down at my feet, on the topside of both of feet were written the words "*Healing*." I looked down at my chest and I saw my heart. As I looked, it began to enlarge and expand in my chest. Golden oil began to flow from my heart and it was pouring onto other people.

Then the Holy Spirit said to me,

"Look, learn how to use your robe."

I saw the Holy Spirit with my robe in His hands, He walked up to a body of water and struck the water with the robe, and it parted. Then I saw a storm coming in and the Holy Spirit held up the robe and quieted the storm. Then I saw Him take the robe and drape a family that was shivering in the cold. Then He said,

"Your robe can be a vessel of peace and of comfort."

Then He said,

"Look, this is how you use your scepter."

The diamond on the tip of the scepter began to shoot out beams of white light. The Holy Spirit took the scepter, He swung it like a sword, and it opened up the heavens. He swung it again and it cut into the hearts of men opening them up for the Poppa's touch. He swung it again and rivers of water burst through the earth. Then He said,

"The Diamond glimmers with the nature of God, and it cuts through things like a laser, it becomes His eyes in the hands of one walking in authority."

Then He said,

> *"Go and learn what has been given you. Stir up the deposit and the gifting in your life. Understand your inheritance and your place in the kingdom of God."*

Suddenly, I felt as if I was basting in warm golden oil. When I opened my eyes, I saw all three together in perfect joy, unity, peace, and complete happiness.

As I looked at them I was overwhelmed with how much they truly loved me. The whole experience was about an hour maybe more – but it seemed to be eternal. Thank you Jesus, Thank you Poppa, and Thank you Holy Spirit – I love you!

End of Journal entry.

Healing of relationship with the Godhead is a powerful thing. As you can see, inner healing and God's ability to communicate through visions are very closely related. The Lord also uses visions within the ministry of inner healing in the context of words of knowledge, which we will discuss later. This is information given to a member of the prayer team or counselor about the individual receiving ministry.

Now let me close with the following Scriptures, expressing the heart of the God we serve:

> *"There shall come forth a Rod from the stem of Jesse, And a Branch shall grow out of his roots. The Spirit of the Lord shall rest upon Him, The Spirit of wisdom and understanding, The Spirit of counsel and might, The Spirit of knowledge and of the fear of the Lord.*
>
> *His delight is in the fear of the Lord, And He shall not judge by the sight of His eyes, Nor decide by the hearing of His ears; But with righteousness He shall judge the poor, And decide with equity for the meek of the earth; He shall strike the earth with the rod of His mouth, And with the breath of His lips He shall slay the wicked.*

Righteousness shall be the belt of His loins, and faithfulness the belt of His waist."

- Isaiah 11:1-5

"The Spirit of the Lord GOD is upon Me, Because the Lord has anointed Me To preach good tidings to the poor; He has sent Me to heal the brokenhearted, To proclaim liberty to the captives, And the opening of the prison to those who are bound; To proclaim the acceptable year of the Lord, And the day of vengeance of our God; To comfort all who mourn, To console those who mourn in Zion, To give them beauty for ashes, The oil of joy for mourning, The garment of praise for the spirit of heaviness; That they may be called trees of righteousness, The planting of the Lord, that He may be glorified."

- Isaiah 61:1-3

This is the mighty Lord that we serve, the healer of our body, soul and spirit, Amen!

CHAPTER 18

HEALING OF THE DEMONIZED

"And these signs will follow those who believe: In My name they will cast out demons; they will speak with new tongues; they will take up serpents; and if they drink anything deadly, it will by no means hurt them; they will lay hands on the sick, and they will recover."

- Mark 17:17-18

I cannot dive into the subject of healing without touching upon the Seer and his relationship to healing those bound by the demonic. If you have spent any amount of time praying for those in need, chances are you have, or will, encounter the demonic. When such an encounter takes place, our call is simple: to bind the strongman, proclaim liberty to the captives, and set the prisoners free. Historically we have called this form of ministry "deliverance." It is vitally important for us to have a solid understanding of this ministry. We are living in a time when the hearts and minds of people are under assault like never before. Of course, this is and has always been satan's plan. Yet, today, we are seeing the stage set for a massive increase in his assault on humanity.

In the last fifty years, in western society, we have seen a blending of occult, Eastern mysticism, and materialistic secular humanism that has created, not an organized religion, but a sub-culture or network of individuals, that have penetrated every aspect of society into what is referred to as the "New Age" movement.

This new spiritual or religious humanism commingles the worship of self and the evolutionary id with Eastern or occult powers and pseudoscience. The goal is simple, if secularization wants to crowd God out of the cosmos, the new secularization, represented by the new age, encourages people to equate God with the cosmos – all is god – we are all god. The new age movement is an exceedingly large, loosely structured, network of organizations and individuals bound together by common values, based in mysticism and monism (the worldview that "all is one" and a common vision). This vision is the coming of a "new age" of peace and mass enlightenment, or the "age of Aquarius."

When we pull back the curtain, we see satan and his horde of minions working behind the scenes to bring about this movement. As this cultural shift takes hold and the new age becomes mainstream we can expect a massive rise in individuals being exposed to the demonic realm. This exposure is an open door to demonic possession or oppression. Our job is the same as Jesus, to destroy the works of the devil and set the captives free, for we are His body here on earth.

Our warfare is not against flesh and blood. People are victims, no matter the cause. Paul tells us very clearly in the book of Ephesians that our warfare is against satan and his principalities, powers, rulers of the darkness of this age, and the spiritual hosts of wickedness in heavenly places. This includes ruling fallen angels and demonic evil spirits.

> *"Finally, my brethren, be strong in the Lord and in the power of His might. Put on the whole armor of God, that you may be able to stand against the wiles of the devil.*

For we do not wrestle against flesh and blood, but against principalities, against powers, against the rulers of the darkness of this age, against spiritual hosts of wickedness in the heavenly places."

- Ephesians 6:10-12

The deception of mainstream humanism muddies the waters of clarity as it relates to the occult. Historically, open occultism was easy to spot, but now, thanks to the saturation of the new age movement in society, more and more people have opened the doors to the demonic without realizing it.

My own personal experience with the occult makes this chapter an important part of this book. You see, in my family, the door to the occult world opened up a hundred and thirty years before the current mysticism movement. My family was bound by the cult of Spiritism, and stayed bound for generations, until the Lord drew a line in the sand.

For years, gaining information from the world beyond, communication with the dead (also known as necromancy), and seeking relationship with un-seen entities, plagued my Dad's side of the family. According to my father, my great grandmother was a medium when the Spiritism revival first took place in the 1880s. This was the beginning of my family's involvement in Spiritism.

The only spiritual influence I had as a child came from Spiritism, table moving, and communication with the dead. This was my religion. My Aunt Eva was a powerful medium, she would barely touch a table, and the so-called spirits would be summoned. When I was a kid, my Uncle Bud used to chase us around the backyard of my Aunt's house, by moving wooden picnic benches with only his fingertips touching the tops of the bench. This scared the heck out of me, but at the same time, growing up, I wanted to do that, to be just like my Aunt. There seemed to be so much power in it.

Who were these spirits? I was taught as a child, that they were departed loved ones. In this chapter, I will not only answer that question, but also show you how the Holy Spirit uses the Word of knowledge via the Seer's gift in ministry to the demonized, and show how you can be an effective minister in setting free those that are bound. At the end of this book, I share my personal story and how Jesus set me free from the demonic stronghold that bound my life.

The pursuit of the occult and speaking to the spirit world is rooted in the prideful pursuit for revelation, knowledge, power, and control. As we have seen throughout this book, the secret to revelation is not revelation, its relationship. It does not come through satanically dabbling in the occult. Behind that door lies lying revelation and bondage to demons. True revelation is birthed out of a relationship with the Son of God. It is the "out-flow" of fellowship with Jesus Christ and his Word. To begin this chapter we will start by lying out some foundational truths.

Foundational Truths

We are in a war!

Most Christians never consider the fact that at the heart of the incarnation of Christ was the defeat of satan (1 John 3:8). It is critical to understand this. Everything in this book revolves around that one truth: We are sent to release the captives and set the prisoners free so that their eyes could be opened and they could see the light of our glorious Lord. Our job is to take back the territory that the enemy has seized and usher in the kingdom of God, leaving out this essential truth from gospel message runs in direct conflict with the mission of Jesus Christ. If we are going to be successful in our quest as Christians, this truth must be front and center in all that we do!

Salvation is nothing less than God rescuing humanity from the grip of satan and restoring us into relationship with the living God. Only when we are freed from his grip can we see the truth. You see, once we recognize satan's role in keeping people in darkness, we will awake with a new sense of urgency to bind the works of the enemy, heal the sick, raise the dead, and cast out demons from those that are bound.

demons are satan's foot soldiers. They have one role in the kingdom of darkness: to keep people in darkness. They achieve this goal by invading people's lives and binding them to circumstances or situations through lies and sins until their condition seems to be greater than God's ability and power to forgive and redeem them, leaving victims that feel lost, brutalized, and worn down with no hope of recovery. Due to satan's grip they have become blind to the light of the world, Jesus Christ.

Jesus gave us a clear commission to combat the work of demons when He said:

> *"And these signs will follow those who believe: In My name they will cast out demons;,"*
>
> - Mark 16:17

We can see this reinforced in the commission of the apostle Paul after Christ's ascension:

> *"I will deliver you from the Jewish people, as well as from the Gentiles, to whom I now send you, to open their eyes, in order to turn them from darkness to light, and from the power of satan to God, that they may receive forgiveness of sins and an inheritance among those who are sanctified by faith in Me.'"*

- Acts 26:17-18

I find it so very sad that the world wanders around in the dark; oblivious that satan is the god of their reality and is ruling them with his power. People are not able to "receive forgiveness of sins," without being set free from satan's grasp, demonized or not. To illustrate this truth I will use the action movie, the "Matrix" to illustrate. In this movie, we see the following:

- Computer hacker Neo (pre-Christian in need of salvation)
- Is contacted by underground freedom fighters (Christians engaged in the battle to set the captives free)
- Who explain that reality as Neo understands it (this worlds system) is actually a complex computer simulation called the Matrix (world under satan's rule).
- Created by a malevolent Artificial Intelligence (satan), the Matrix hides the truth from humanity, allowing them to live a convincing (life is good, there is no God, there is no devil), simulated life while machines (demons) grow and harvest people to use as an ongoing energy source.
- The leader of the freedom fighters, Morpheus (the Holy Spirit), believes Neo is "The One" (us, as the body of Christ) who will lead humanity to freedom and overthrow the machines (demonic and works of the devil.)
- Together with Trinity (you get the picture), Neo and Morpheus fight against the machine's enslavement of humanity.

Truthfully, the only reason people remain in their sins is due to the dark forces that keep them blinded to the truth. Their unbelief is not caused by God's unwillingness to awaken them to the truth.

On the contrary, God wants all to come to the saving knowledge of the grace found in Jesus Christ (2 Peter 3:9).

The good news is that Christ has given us the authority and power to bind the devil and stop him in his tracks from blinding the spiritual eyes of nonbelievers. He has sent us out as laborers in a field ripe for harvest (Matthew 9:38) and equipped us with His power and authority to accomplish the task.

Our job: to use the authority and power Christ has given us and stop the enemy for stealing the Word from people's hearts (Luke 8:12). We do this by binding him. When we tell him to stop, he must obey. We turn people from the power of satan's rule by binding his efforts and preaching the gospel to them. This is a battle for the souls of humanity. We are the answer the world is looking for, and God is sending us into the harvest.

It's not just the lost!

> *"But I fear, lest somehow, as the serpent deceived Eve by his craftiness, so your minds may be corrupted from the simplicity that is in Christ."*
>
> — 1 Corinthians 11:3

Why was Paul concerned about the Church at Corinth? Certainly, he was not one easily given to fear. Something was troubling him. Why was he troubled? He feared that satan was leading the church away from the pure and simple devotion to Christ. The enemy's tactics have not changed; they are the same as they were in the garden: to fog, distort, twist, cause confusion, and remove the truth of God's Word from your heart. Deception is a powerful weapon. If satan can cause you to question God's motives, the next logical step is for him to rob you of the Word spoken into your life.

He wants to rob you of your identity in Christ and sabotage your destiny.

Yet, Paul says, "for we are not ignorant of his devices (2 Corinthians 2:11)." The point is, we need to be cognizant of his devices to be effective at waging this war against him. Too many Christians lose the battle with satan because they are ignorant of his plan to destroy their walk with God. The devil will use everything at his disposal to accomplish that end. He is ruthless in his assault. He is cunning and patient, lying in wait for the opportune time, while he weaves a web of entrapment to deceive and cause you to stumble.

Of course, sin is one of satan's most powerful weapons. He uses deception as a means to coerce a person to sin. It's ironic, the devil drives us to sin, and then condemns us for the sin he tempted us to do. It's the same old story. Yet, little did he know, God's plan was to take away our sins and remove all condemnation.

If we get a hold of the fact that:

- We are in an ongoing war for the souls of humanity.
- Jesus has defeated ALL the power and authority of the enemy on the Cross.
- We as believers have the righteousness of Christ as members of His body.
- We have been given the same power and authority in Christ, to overcome the enemy.
- We have been commissioned by Jesus to bind the strongman and take back what is rightfully His.
- Our warfare is not against flesh and blood, but against the powers of darkness.

Then, when these truths settle in our spirits, we will arise with new vigor and might, and take our position as princes in the household of God. Only then can we begin to be effective in our ministry to the lost and demonized.

CHAPTER 19

HEAVEN, ANGELS, AND THE DEMONIC

"For we do not wrestle against flesh and blood, but against principalities, against powers, against the rulers of the darkness of this age, against spiritual hosts of wickedness in the heavenly places"

- Ephesians 6:12

"It is doubtless not profitable for me to boast. I will come to visions and revelations of the Lord: I know a man in Christ who fourteen years ago—whether in the body I do not know, or whether out of the body I do not know, God knows—such a one was caught up to the third heaven. And I know such a man—whether in the body or out of the body I do not know, God knows— how he was caught up into Paradise and heard inexpressible words, which it is not lawful for a man to utter. Of such a one I will boast; yet of myself I will not boast, except in my infirmities. For though I might desire to boast, I will not be a fool; for I will speak the truth. But I refrain, lest anyone should think of me above what he sees me to be or hears from me."

- 2 Corinthians 12:1-5

The Hebrew word for "heavens" is "shamayim," it is plural word meaning "heights," or "elevations." It is found in the first verse of Genesis chapters one and two. The Bible speaks of three heavens. Paul refers to being caught up to the third heaven also called Paradise (2 Corinthians 12:2-4). The fact that Paul describes a third heaven implies that a third heaven cannot exist without a first and second.

The first heaven refers to the atmospheric area of the fowl (Hosea 2:18) and clouds (Daniel 7:13). The second heaven is the area of the stars and planets (Genesis 1:14-18). It is also the abode of all supernatural angelic beings. The Scriptures tell us that there are two locations for evil spirit beings (Ephesians 6:12).

> *"For we do not wrestle against flesh and blood, but against principalities, against powers, against the rulers of the darkness of this age, against spiritual hosts of wickedness in the heavenly places."*
>
> *- Ephesians 6:12*

The first location is mentioned as the darkness of this "age," literally in the Greek, "aion" meaning, "World" or "age." The second location mentioned is wickedness in "heavenly" places, referring to the second heaven. The implication is that some evil spirits dwell on this world, while others reside in the second heaven.

We know from scriptures that satan and a third of the angels were cast out of heaven, when they joined in the rebellion against God, however the heaven they were expelled from was the "third heaven," where God dwells. The third heaven is the abode of the triune God. Its location is not revealed (see Matthew 23:34-37; Luke 10:20; and Revelation 22:2, 20-27).

For our purpose, understanding that there are two locations for evil spirits will help in putting into context the war in which we wage.

Angels

In waging an effective fight against the enemy, it is important to understand that satan is an angel. "Angels" are mentioned almost three hundred times in Scripture, and are only absent from books like Ruth, Nehemiah, Esther, the letters of John, and James. Though other words are used for these spiritual beings, the primary word used in the Bible is "angel."

The Hebrew word for angel is "mal`ach," and the Greek word is "angelos." Both words mean "messenger," and describe one who executes the purpose and will of the one whom they serve. The Holy angels are messengers of God, serving Him and doing His bidding. The fallen angels serve satan (the first fallen angel and the god of this world, 2 Corinthians 4:4).

Angels are created beings and not the spirits of departed human beings. From the following scripture, it is clear that Christ not only created the angels, but also their dominion and sphere of influence.

> *"For by Him all things were created that are in heaven and that are on earth, visible and invisible, whether thrones or dominions or principalities or powers. All things were created through Him and for Him. And He is before all things, and in Him all things consist."*
>
> *- Colossians 1:16-17*

> *"For by Him (Jesus) all things were created that are in heaven and that are on earth, visible and invisible, whether thrones or dominions or principalities or pow-*

> ers. *All things were created through Him and for Him. And He is before all things, and in Him all things consist.*
>
> - Colossians 1:16-17

Angels are personal beings and manifest all the features of personhood. In Job 38:7 they are called "the sons of God." They have:

- Self-awareness (Daniel 10:11)
- Self-expression (Acts 12:7-8; Revelation 22:8-9)
- Moral awareness (Matthew 13:41; Luke 15:10)
- Sempiternity or without end (Matthew 25:41)
- Intelligence (2 Samuel 14:20; Revelation 22:16)
- Desire (1 Peter 1:12)
- Emotion (Job 38:7; Revelation 12:12)
- Accountability (1 Corinthians 6:3)

Angels have an angelic nature. Unlike the trichotomous nature of humans (body, soul, and spirit), angels have a spirit nature (Luke 24:37-39; Hebrews 1:1, 7). Their spirit nature is unique and has some form of a celestial body (Daniel 10:5-6; Matthew 28:2-3; Luke 24:4).

Sometimes they have wings, sometime they are like people, and sometimes they are like fire. From the scriptures, it appears that angels are not confined to any specific form or shape, but assume various forms and appearances according to the nature of the work they are required to perform and the will of God. In many instances, they behave and act just as we do. Look at some of the descriptive information in the Bible.

- They sit down (Judges 6:11)
- They stand (Isaiah 6:2)
- They look like women and have wind in their wings (Zechariah 5:9)

- They look like men; and eat (Genesis 18:2, 8)
- They are masculine in gender (Revelation 10:1-3; Matthew 22:30)
- They are like fire (Psalms 104:4)
- They are spirits (Psalms 104:4; Hebrews 1:7)
- They are capable of learning (1 Peter 1:12; Ephesians 3:10)
- They speak and have their own language (1 Corinthians 13:1)
- They play musical instruments (1 Thessalonians 4:16; Revelation 8:2, 6)

We also learn from the Scriptures that they are many (Daniel 7:10; Matthew 26:53; Hebrews 12:22; Revelation 5:11), they are very powerful (Psalms 103:20; 2 Peter 2:11), and they belong to a more superior order in creation than humans. We also know that angels are indestructible. Being created personal creatures with a definite beginning, they will exist forever as either Holy angels with God (Hebrews 12:22-23) or fallen angels bound in hell for all eternity (Matthew 25:41, 46).

Morally, angels are either Holy or evil. They belong to various ranks (Ephesians 1:21; 6:12; Colossians 1:16), with Michael the archangel as the leader of the warring Holy angels (Revelation 12:7-8) and satan as the leader of evil fallen angels (Matthew 25:41). The words "principality" (rule), "power" (authority), "dominion" (lordship), and "might" (power), indicate various angelic positions or spheres of influence and authority in the administrations of both God and satan.

Holy Angels

As stated earlier, angels, whose name means, "messenger," are active in the service of God.

- They render worship (Revelation 5:11-12).
- They deliver messages (Luke 1:11, 26-27).
- They convey divine revelation (Acts 7:53; Revelation 1:1).
- They inflict divine judgments (2 Samuel 24:16-17; Revelation chapters 8-9).
- They influence governments (Daniel 10:12-11:1).
- They deliver dead humans to their destinies (Luke 16:22).
- They care for God's people (Genesis 19:1-22; 1 Kings 19:5-8; Acts 5:19-20; Hebrews 1:14).
- They observe believers (1 Corinthians 4:9; 11:10).
- They war against the forces of satan (Revelation 12:7-9).
- They are assigned to churches (Revelation 2-3)
- They are assigned as guardians to people (Acts 12:13-15; Matthew 18:2-3, 10).

Understanding what Holy angels are and how they interact with Christians, the church, and the enemy, will help us engage an effective battle. Angels are here to assist us in our life mission. When commissioned, they are actively engaged in war against the enemy on our behalf. Angels also often manifest themselves to those operating with the Seer's gift.

Evil Angels

They Scriptures reveal that satan was created Lucifer – "the shining one" (Isaiah 14:12), "the anointed cherib" (Ezekiel 28:13-14), and that he was perfect in all of his ways until he sinned (vs. 15). Having personhood, he had self-determination and the ability to worship. Yet, struck by his own beauty and pride, he chose to exalt himself rather than the Creator (vs. 17). This self-exaltation was a manifestation of the pride in his heart, the first sin (1 Timothy 3:6). Motivated by burning pride, he set out on an irrational course to seize for himself God's authority over the universe (Isaiah 14:12-14). He became the prince of this world when he led man to sin against God and thus transferred man's rule over the earth to himself (Genesis 1:26; 3:1-6; John 12:31; Colossians 1:13; Acts 26:18).

Following the example and leadership of satan, a third of the angelic host revolted with the devil and became members of his kingdom (Revelation 12:4, 7-9; Matthew 12:26; 25:41), severing their original relationship with God. The Scriptures tell us that there are there are two groups of evil angles, the confined fallen angels, and the free fallen angles.

Confined Fallen Angels

To help us understand the confined fallen angels we need to go back in time to the days of Noah.

> "Now it came to pass, when men began to multiply on the face of the earth, and daughters were born to them, that the sons of God saw the daughters of men, that they were beautiful; and they took wives for themselves of all whom they chose. And the LORD said, "My Spirit shall

> *not strive with man forever, for he is indeed flesh; yet his days shall be one hundred and twenty years." There were giants (Nephilim) on the earth in those days, and also afterward, when the sons of God came in to the daughters of men and they bore children to them. Those were the mighty men who were of old, men of renown.*
>
> - Genesis 6:1

It appears that these "Sons of God" had relations with the "daughters of men" and produced an offspring referred to as giants (Nephilim). It also appears that the women had little to say in the matter. This unnatural union resulted in the procreation of abnormal genetically modified creatures, the Nephilim, translated giants. Due to this alien invasion these "giants" were designated as the principal reason for the judgment of the Flood. Jude and Peter confirm that the angels involved in this unnatural act were judged by God and cast into hell (Tartarus) until the great Day of Judgment (2 Peter 2:4-8; 1 Peter 3:18-20; Jude 6, 7).

Chuck Missler, noted bible scholar, says this regarding Genesis 6:

> *"The strange events recorded in Genesis 6 were understood by the ancient rabbinical sources, as well as the Septuagint translators, as referring to fallen angels procreating weird hybrid offspring with human women- known as the "Nephilim." So it was also understood by the early church fathers. These bizarre events are also echoed in the legends and myths of every ancient culture upon the earth: the ancient Greeks, the Egyptians, the Hindus, the South Sea Islanders, the American Indians, and virtually all the others."*
>
> - Chuck Missler, "Mischievous Angels or Sethites?"

God's judgment in Genesis 6 was an act of the amazing grace of God. By interceding in this matter He kept the human race intact and uncontaminated by satan's attempts defile Christ's bloodline.

If satan had succeeded, Jesus couldn't have been born and the human race would have been lost, forever. By destroying the contaminated race and saving uncontaminated Noah and his immediate uncontaminated family, and by binding the evil fallen angels who participated in this great sin in Hades until the final judgment, God made the way for His plan of Salvation to come about.

From a spiritual warfare standpoint there is no engagement with the confined evil angels, for they are confined, waiting for their final judgment. One thought however, in Revelation 9, John speaks of hearing the sound of a fifth angel, and when it sounded a star fell from heaven to earth, and the key to the bottomless pit was given to him. When he opened the bottomless pit, there arose billows of smoke, and out of the smoke locust like creatures with tails like scorpions, hair like women, teeth like lions, and wings that sounded like mighty horses running into battle, rose and tormented all who were not marked by God. The leader of these creatures was Abaddon, in Hebrew, and Apollyon, in the Greek. Scholars believe this leader is satan. If so, it is very reasonable to believe that these creatures are the confined evil angels from Genesis chapter six.

Free evil angels

We know, according to Jude, that the confined fallen angels that sinned in Genesis 6 were imprisoned in everlasting chains of darkness. However, the Bible also speaks of a time when another group of evil angels will be kicked out of the heaven (Revelation 12:7-9). Whether this event is historical or yet to occur is not clear. Nor is it clear that this verse is speaking of these angels being kicked out of the third heaven. More than likely, these creatures were kicked out of the third heaven when they rebelled against God, and at some point in the future, when the kingdom of heaven advances towards Christ's second coming, these fallen angels will be kicked out of the second heaven, at which time they will invade earth in full force (Revelation 12:7-9, 12). What is clear is that these fallen evil angels are free today and reside in the second heaven.

Yet, just because God expelled these rebellious angels from heaven, does not mean He clipped their wings, changed their celestial angelic nature, or took their individual created gifting from them. The same is true for unsaved humans or backslidden Christians. No, they are still angels, though evil, through and through. These unconfined or free fallen angels are the same angels Paul refers to in Ephesians 6:

> *"For we do not wrestle against flesh and blood, but against principalities, against powers, against the rulers of the darkness of this age, against spiritual hosts of wickedness in the heavenly places. Therefore take up the whole armor of God, that you may be able to withstand in the evil day, and having done all, to stand."*
>
> - Ephesians 6:12-13

In this passage, Paul is telling us that there is a powerful evil network of fallen angels residing in the second heaven under the leadership of satan. These fallen angels are organized, powerful, structured, and bent on the destruction of humanity. Earlier we read how Christ created not only the angels, but also their sphere of influence and authority. How we war against fallen angels is different from how we wage war against the demonic.

Jude and Peter make it clear that there is a certain way one should rebuke them, namely speaking in the name and authority of Jesus, through His rebuke, and not speaking of things, we as humans, do not understand. In God's order, they are still dignitaries, though fallen and evil. Consider Jude's comments regarding Michael the archangel's encounter with satan or Peter's comments regarding how angels, who are more powerful than us, deal with the schemes of the enemy.

> *"Likewise also these dreamers defile the flesh, reject authority, and speak evil of dignitaries. Yet Michael the archangel, in contending with the devil, when he disputed about the body of Moses, dared not bring against him a reviling accusation, but said, "The Lord rebuke you!"*
>
> - Jude 1:8-9

> *",and especially those who walk according to the flesh in the lust of uncleanness and despise authority. They are presumptuous, self-willed. They are not afraid to speak evil of dignitaries, whereas angels, who are greater in power and might, do not bring a reviling accusation against them before the Lord."*
>
> - 2 Peter 2:10-11

Jesus himself gave us an example of resisting satan, a fallen angel, by using scripture in Matthew 4 and Luke 4. The power of the Word brings to life the legal truth that satan and his minions are defeated.

Shifting Atmospheres

The most prominent way fallen angels war against us is how they affect the atmosphere of the World.

> *"And you He made alive, who were dead in trespasses and sins, in which you once walked according to the course of this world, according to the prince of the power of the air, the spirit who now works in the sons of disobedience,"*

- Ephesians 2:1-2

Across the second heaven and into our own atmosphere this highly organized enemy force, works to cause the unsaved to follow the ways of this world. The word "air" in this passage refers to the lowest of spiritual heavens. Fallen angels work to create an atmosphere for demons to do their diabolical work. Fallen angels create the right political, social, religious, and philosophical environment that enables demons to influence, and ultimately control, people in their surroundings. There is one word that best describes this atmosphere and that is "culture." Fallen angels create a cultural environment that makes it difficult for people to be saved or for believers to follow Christ with their whole heart.

Where fallen angels have had success, there is a raise in demonic activity. That is why it is essential that we correctly wage an effective warfare against these spiritual forces of evil. Fallen angels at times may do some of the activities of demons. The devil is also called "the tempter" (Matthew 4:3; 1 Thessalonians 3:5), and he is an angel. Therefore, fallen angels can still tempt us. The primary meaning of the word angel is "messenger." A messenger's job is to convey a message or word from another. Fallen angels are very good at feeding people lies in order to carry out their plans.

Unlike demons, fallen angels are not as easily removed from a person, a church, a region, or a nation. Our work to overcome fallen angels requires great effort. Though we may confront them directly in the name of Jesus, we must often employ additional weapons to overcome their effect. Remember, Daniel prayed and fasted for twenty-one days before he saw the "Prince of Persia" (a fallen angel) pushed back from destroying Israel (see Daniel 10:13).

When evil angels are at work in a person, a church, region, or a nation, it will often take more than a simple rebuke to remove them. They are strong beings and will not be easily dislodged from their assignment. In contrast, demons are relatively easy to drive out with a simple order.

Fallen angels are defeated only through intense spiritual warfare. To understand more clearly our strategy for spiritual warfare against fallen angels, we must first recognize who these beings are, what their tactics are, and how they fight. While demons work directly against us, fallen angels use devices that are more indirect in nature. It is easy to recognize demonic attacks. However, what do we do when the spiritual force in heavenly places attack?

Because we are seated with Christ in heavenly realms, we have authority in this realm (Ephesians 2:6), but how we exercise that authority over fallen angels is different from the way we exercise our authority over demons.

Tom Brown, in his book, Devil, Demons, & Spiritual Warfare, outlines seven very practical steps in dealing with fallen angels.

Cast Out Demons: in order to make any progress against the heavenly forces, you must penetrate their strongholds. Casting out demons breaks down satan's frontline. (Luke 10:17-19)

Intercessory Prayer: God directed prayer is agonizing and intense. It is a wrestling prayer in the spirit and is often associated with fasting. Daniel's example is a good case study (Daniel 10:1-4). Paul describes this type of prayer in Galatians 4:19 as pains of childbirth.

Preach the Gospel: Paul says "For I am not ashamed of the gospel of Christ, for it is the power of God to salvation for everyone who believes," (Romans 1:16). The devils currency is soul. The more souls he has the greater influence he has in the world.

Utilize the Media: Don't wait for the executives in Hollywood to have a change of heart, find ways to use the arts today to shift the cultural messaging in the world. Holy Spirit inspired creativity can influence a community far more than a good sermon from a pulpit (Mark 16:15)

Influence the Schools: Spiritual warfare is more than simply commanding the forces of darkness to leave our nation; it includes engaging the enemy in our schools. We need Spirit filled teachers, administrators, and educators. We need Christians in our libraries, in the PTA, and on the school board.

Get Involved in Politics: Don't believe the lie that Christians aren't supposed to get involved in politics. The terms in Scripture for evil entities are "rulers," "authorities," and "powers." These words come from governmental terms. Even satan is called the "King of Tyre" in Ezekiel 28:12 and the "Prince of Persia in Daniel 10:20. The enemy hates it when true believers get involved in the political process. (See Romans 13:4.)

Obey God: By our obedience we will be ready to punish every act of disobedience (2 Corinthians 10:6). Paul exhorts Timothy that "Moreover he must have a good testimony among those who are outside, lest he fall into reproach and the snare of the devil" (1 Timothy 3:7). Simple acts of obedience will inflict damage on the forces of evil, more than any shouting into the heavens can accomplish.

CHAPTER 20

WHAT ARE DEMONS?

"And these signs will follow those who believe: In My name they will cast out demons; they will speak with new tongues; they will take up serpents; and if they drink anything deadly, it will by no means hurt them; they will lay hands on the sick, and they will recover."

- Mark 17:17-18

"then the Lord knows how to deliver the godly out of temptations and to reserve the unjust under punishment for the day of judgment."

- 1 Peter 2:9

So we have dealt with the topics of angels, both Holy and evil. Now let's turn our attention to demons. To start with, demons are not the spirits of deceased evil humans. The spirits of deceased evil humans are not free to roam but are confined until judgment (Luke 16:19-31; 2 Peter 2:9). Nor are demons merely personifications of evil, or of natural forces, such as the "gods" of nature, as skeptics assume. Nor are demons the superstitious designation for particular natural diseases, such as epilepsy or mental illness, because Scripture clearly distinguishes these disorders from demon possession, although it is possible that both can be present or that demons can induce mental and physical illness.

Unlike angels, demons are never described as winged creatures, and they seem to be limited to the earth. Contrary to popular Christian theory, the fallen angels are not the "demons" of today. The demon inside the madman of Gadara pleaded with Jesus not to send them out of the area (Mark 5:10). Their only choice was limited to roaming the earth. They could not fly away into the second heaven. In fact, Jesus said that when a demon is cast out he wanders through dry places, seeking rest (Matthew 12:43-45).

demons, on the other hand, are often referred to "wicked, unclean, evil spirits" and are usually mentioned in relation to someone who is demonized, and the demon speaks through that person. demons never appear in a bodily form themselves, but always involve a body of a person or animal they are working through.

It is my opinion that demons have their origin in the giants (Nephilim) who existed before the flood. We know from Genesis 6 that the entire Nephilim hybrid race died with the rest of humanity in the Flood except for Noah and his family (Genesis 6:13, 17, 21-22).

We know that the flood destroyed all life that was upon the surface of the earth. The Nephilim were also destroyed. If the fallen angels are being held in chains, they obviously are not the spirits that enslave so many today. The fallen angels already have celestial bodies and don't seek any other bodies to inhabit. However, the Nephilim lost their bodies in the Flood, and are constantly seeking bodies to inhabit.

We know that the spirit nature of a person is passed down through the father (study the following: Genesis 2:7; 1 Corinthians 11:8, 12, 15:21-22, 45; Romans 5:12-32; Hebrews 7:9-10; Ezekiel

18:4, 20; James 5:20.) Jesus is a perfect example of this. Since Jesus did not have a literal, biological father, the sin nature was not passed down to Him. However, since He had a human mother, he was fully human but without original sin. Original sin is passed through the soul from the father. Jesus has two natures: God and man. Colossians 2:9 says, "For in Him dwells all the fullness of deity in bodily form." Jesus received His human nature from Mary, but He received His divine nature through God the Holy Spirit. Therefore, Jesus is both God and man. He was sinless, had no original sin, and was both fully God and fully man.

So, in essence, these hybrids had a genetically altered human body and a sinful angelic spirit like their fathers, the evil fallen angels. Now, they wander the earth as tormented dis-embodied spirits, waiting for their day in judgment where they will join their fallen fathers for all eternity.

There is one last scripture I would like to look at regarding the sinful angelic-spirit-nature of demons. In 1 Corinthians Paul makes an obscure reference to angels when discussing the head covering of women in the church.

> *"For this reason the woman ought to have a symbol of authority on her head, because of the angels."*
>
> - 1 Corinthians 11:10

This reference to angels makes no sense in the context of this passage unless Paul has in the back of his mind the events of Genesis 6. This covering he links to a symbol of authority. The Greek word for authority in this passage is "exousia" meaning "power," "one who possesses authority," or "wears a crown." Many commentators brush over this verse, not knowing how to deal with Paul's statement. However, it is my opinion that Paul, in the context of Genesis 6, is reminding the angelic community that women in the church, these female children of God, are endued with power and authority from the Most High God, are covered by Him, and are princesses in the Kingdom of God. They are not to be looked at in an unholy manor. As well as reminding women in the church of their Holy position and authority in the Kingdom of God.

demons and Necromancy

Necromancy is the sin that entrapped my family for so long. God forbade the Israelites to be involved with various types of magic, familiar spirits, and necromancy (Leviticus 20:27).

According to the Strong's, the word for "familiar spirit" means "ghost, spirit of a dead one, necromancy, one who evokes a dead one, one with a familiar spirit". If one considers that demons are actually the spirits of the dead giants (Nephilim), then it makes sense then that demons are being referenced to as "ghost, spirit of a dead one." Moreover, it is forbidden for God's people to "evoke the spirit of a dead one", or to have anything to do with a demon, let alone to become familiar, gain familiarity, with one. The term for "medium" is "one that has a familiar spirit" and "necromancer," again this is having a relationship with a demon.

> *"When you come into the land which the LORD your God is giving you, you shall not learn to follow the abominations of those nations. There shall not be found among you anyone who makes his son or his daughter pass through the fire, or one who practices witchcraft, or a soothsayer, or one who interprets omens, or a sorcerer, or one who conjures spells, or a medium, or a spiritist, or one who calls up the dead. For all who do these things are an abomination to the LORD, and because of these abominations the LORD your God drives them out from before you."*
>
> *- Deuteronomy 18:9-12*

Some of these same terms are used again in Deuteronomy 18, forbidding the people to practice or to consult with anyone who practiced, having a relationship with a demon. God calls this an abomination, and makes clear that those nations around at the time all did practice these things. Thank God for His amazing grace that He intervened in my family and in my life!

CHAPTER 21

REVELATORY INSIGHT

",to another faith by the same Spirit, to another gifts of healings by the same Spirit, to another the working of miracles, to another prophecy, to another discerning of spirits, to another different kinds of tongues, to another the interpretation of tongues....:

- 1 Corinthians 12:9-10

"But the manifestation of the Spirit is given to each one for the profit of all: for to one is given the word of wisdom through the Spirit, to another the word of knowledge through the same Spirit, to another faith by the same Spirit, to another gifts of healings by the same Spirit, to another the working of miracles, to another prophecy, to another discerning of spirits, to another different kinds of tongues, to another the interpretation of tongues. But one and the same Spirit works all these things, distributing to each one individually as He wills"

- 1 Corinthians 12:7-11

For the Seer, the gifts of the "words of knowledge" and the "discerning of spirits" usually come through the lens of visions and dreams, though visions are the most common. Visions and even dreams can also play a role in your personal preparation and study of effective spiritual warfare. I have classified the following areas as it relates to the Seer's gift and warfare.

Instructional Visions and Dreams: These often occur when the Holy Spirit is guiding you into further study on spiritual warfare. When I first became a Christian, I didn't have a clue as to what was biblical and what was demonic. All I knew was that Jesus loved me. During my first year as a Christian, they Lord would often give me dreams and visions relating to spiritual warfare. All of which, lead me into an in depth study of the scriptures as it related not only to warfare, but Christian apologetics as a whole. Many of the lessons the Lord showed me started in seed form, as He spoke to me in dreams and showed me in visions. Through the prompting of the Holy Spirit and teaching from great mentors, I not only built a strong biblical foundation for my faith, but was awakened to the truth that the Spiritism that I grew up with was in fact, inspired by the demons. This newfound awareness led me in preparation and prayer for freedom of my whole family.

Discerning of Spirits and satanic Generational Assignments: Often the Lord will use visions or dreams to give insight revealing the satanic forces operating in an individual's life and/or family. This can be connected to a curse, the sins of the fathers, or directly related to a door being opened to the occult.

One such event I would like to share involved my family's deliverance from satan's grasp. For the first eighteen months of being a Christian, the Lord would not allow me to confront my family regarding Spiritism and the occult. The night He did release me was indeed an amazing night.

My family had been a burden on my heart for some time. During this season in my life, the Lord had been immersing me in the things of the Spirit. I felt like I was in spiritual boot camp and Jesus was my drill sergeant. The Lord had put me on fast track and was teaching a great deal regarding the scriptures and power of the Holy Spirit in my life. Then one night the Lord showed me the satanic forces that were commissioned to destroy my family and me.

That night I awakened full of the Holy Spirit and praying in tongues. As I sat up, I turned to look at my wife. She was sitting up in bed and her head was shaking violently side-to-side. As I prayed, she slowly stopped and lay back down, continuing her sleep. During this event, she was asleep and to this day, she does not remember the event. As she lay down, I looked beyond her to the door of our bedroom. The presence of the Holy Spirit began to magnify all over me.

Standing in the doorway, I saw, what I understood was a fallen angel dressed in ancient warrior attire. I knew in my spirit that this was the enemy. Next to him was a demon spirit. Instantly, I was aware that this was a high-ranking evil angel and he had authority over the smaller demonic minion. The fallen angel was unable to enter the room. However, he stood his ground for several minutes and appeared to be confident. I also knew that the smaller demon was weaker in power and authority for he could not even look into the room. As I prayed, I felt the presence of the Lord intensify, then suddenly, they both disappeared.

They had come to mess with my family and do harm to my wife. This started my quest towards intersession for my family. As I pondered this event, I felt that they were somehow tied to my background in the occult and were trying to destroy my newly found life in Christ. I was not sure if the Lord had given me an open vision or if He simply opened my eyes to see what was happening in the spirit realm.

A week went by with heavy intersession and study. Then one night the Lord gave me a dream. In this dream, I saw my Aunt's house. I was looking at the back patio door from above. As I watched, I saw my uncle Bill and Aunt Eva arrive home. Suddenly, I saw dozens of spirits flying above them as they entered the house. Then the same creature that was in my house was hovering over them. Then I woke, praying.

Instantly, all the dots began to connect, and I understood that this was the principality assigned to my family for generations. As I prayed, I asked the Lord if I could go down to San Diego and pray for my family. He said, "It's not time." Then, about a week later, while I was worshiping, the Lord spoke to me and said, "It's time."

I instantly called my father and told him I had to meet with the family. When I arrived at my Aunt's house in San Diego, to my surprise, my father had called all his brothers and sisters to come over and listen to what I had to say. I walked into the house, filled with the Holy Spirit. I was greeted with a loving warm welcome and proceeded to the living room where I found all my Aunts and Uncles sitting there waiting for me.

I sat there and began to share my testimony, how Jesus came and set me free. My Aunt knew about the dream the Lord had given me, how He spoke to me two years earlier (see chapter 23 about my story), because I ran to her to find out what the dream meant. At that time, we had a séance and the table went crazy. It actually kicked a bible off the table. That was the last time I had seen my Aunt, up until this moment. Now with newly worn Bible in hand I shared with them the truth of God's Word and the reality of the demonic world.

As I was sharing, I could see the Holy Spirit speaking into their lives. I looked over at my Uncle Paul and he and Aunt Gladis had a big smile on their faces. My Uncle Paul chimed in:

> *"Fred, I know what you're talking about. The spirit activity got so bad in our house that we could not even sleep at night. The furniture would move and the bed would shake. We were scared to death. Then we saw Oral Roberts on TV and he was coming to San Diego. We knew we had to do something so we down to the coliseum and went forward to get prayer. Your aunt and I were saved and healed that night. All of the demonic attacks that happened to us stopped instantly and have never come back. I don't know why we didn't tell anybody. But it's the God's honest truth."*

I was blown away; I knew I wasn't alone in this. After they shared their testimony, I walked my Aunt Eva through the scriptures and shared with them everything relating to the occult. I asked them if they would mind if I pray for them. They all eagerly said yes. As I prayed, I could feel God's presence fill the house. However, I still was not sure of my Aunt Eva's stance on all this.

Later that night, my Aunt Eva was washing dishes in the kitchen. Then I heard her call my name in a sad and weakened voice. When I walked into the kitchen she had her head down on the sink. "Aunt Eva, are you ok?"

The she said, "Fred, please pray for me, and she collapsed to the kitchen floor."

I grabbed her hand and caressed her. Then I began to pray. As I prayed, I spoke to the demons and commanded them to leave her in the name of Jesus. My dear Aunt began to cry even more. I held her and walked her through the steps of salvation. My sweet Aunt went down in tears, came up free, and saved as a child of the King. Together we prayed through renunciation and I shared with her the power of the Holy Spirit and the assurance of salvation. That night started a ripple effect in my Dad's side of the family and all of them came to the Lord. Moreover, my Aunt Eva became my closest confidant in things of the spirit.

You see, my family had opened the door to the occult and for close to a hundred years we were generationally bound to powers in the heavenly realm. All the while God was working behind the scenes to end the power this stronghold had over our family. I am convinced that the hardest part of the battle happened during that year of intersession. I am also convinced that during that time God had commissioned His angelic team to intercede on our behalf and bind the fallen angels and demonic forces assigned to our family.

Discerning of Spirits in General: The Discerning of Spirits is a Supernatural revelation from the Spirit of God, which opens one's eyes to the activities of the spirit realm. The event described earlier is a perfect example of this activity. Through the operation of this Gift one can see Jesus, the Holy Spirit, the similitude of God, Angels, satan, demons and any other spirit beings, objects or spiritual activities. This Gift also enables the possessor to discern the power, good or evil, which prompts certain behaviors in other living beings. (Numbers 22:27-35; Mark 8:33; John 1:47; 6:70)

Anytime an individual experiences a Holy Spirit induced inward vision, open vision, trance, or dream in which the Spirit realm is looked into, the Discerning of Spirits is in operation.

I have experienced the Discerning of Spirits frequently operating with the other Revelatory Gifts on many occasions. I have had visitations of Jesus and Angels through open visions, a trance and dreams. I have been called to intersession by the Lord via dreams and trances where He shared with me the strategies of the enemy in given situation. I have seen the Holy Spirit give insight into the root cause of a man under demon oppression. I have seen open visions of a demonic stronghold over the face of an individual. I have seen in the spirit a demon on the back of an individual.

The Discerning of Spirits is a tremendous Gift indeed and a very powerful gift in dealing with the demonic. Through its operation, come protection, direction, correction, connection, revelation, emancipation and provision.

Words of Knowledge in General: The Word of Knowledge is a Supernatural revelation from the mind of God. It is unrelated to natural, human knowledge. It always has to do with people, places, events, or things. It always, and only, deals with the past or the present. It never has to do with future events. Things revealed in the future fall under the gift of Prophecy. Let's look at an example of the Word of Knowledge from Jesus' Ministry. Jesus met a woman at a well one day. He wanted to prove to her who He was so He challenged her.

> *"Jesus said to her, "Go, call your husband, and come here." The woman answered and said, "I have no husband." Jesus said to her, "You have well said, 'I have no husband,' for you have had five husbands, and the one whom you now have is not your husband; in that you spoke truly." The woman said to Him, "Sir, I perceive that You are a prophet."*
>
> - John 4:16-19

Here Jesus supernaturally revealed part of this woman's past. He told her that she had been married five times. Then Jesus revealed something about her present life. He told her that she was presently shacking up with a man she hadn't even bothered to marry! The woman realized that she was encountering supernatural revelation knowledge.

This is an excellent example of the Word of Knowledge. It has to do with people and events. It also has to do with both the past and the present. Notice something else in this narrative. Jesus only revealed certain parts of this woman's life. He didn't reveal everything about her life. That's why it's called a "Word" of Knowledge. A word is a fragmentary part of a sentence. A Word of Knowledge is only a fragmentary part of all that God knows.

Let me share one example of the Word of Knowledge, as it relates to deliverance.

Several years ago an associate of mine, whom I will call Steve, went off to Bible College in central Florida. I hadn't seen him for several months until one day Steve came by to see me at the restaurant. We got to talk and I could sense that he was troubled and really needed some counsel. I asked Steve if he would like to go for a walk and pray. He said, "yes," so we headed down to the parking garage below the restaurant.

I asked Steve what was going on and he became very erratic. He started crying. I could see shame and fear over his countenance. I asked him what was going on and all he could say was, "I can't think. I can't stop it. I don't know what's wrong with me. I try, and try, and try, nothing seems to help."

I started praying for him and as I was praying I saw a picture of Steve crouched on his knees with his head down chained to a wall. I asked the Lord what this was, and instantly I understood that he was bound to a demonic stronghold. I shared this picture with him, and said that I think he was bound to a lie from the enemy. When I said that, he immediately started weeping. He kept saying in a voice of anguish, "Make it go away." Then he fell to the ground and started shaking violently. All the while I was praying, asking the Lord for more information. At that moment, I felt that his situation was had to do with his sexual identity. I placed my hand on his shoulder and spoke to his spirit to be at peace. He started to relax.

Then I said, "Steve, are you having difficulty in the area of sexuality?"

He started to cry, even more. I told him that I believed that the enemy was binding him to a lie and that Jesus was going to set him free. I told him that Jesus had created him wholly as a man and that the enemy was feeding him lies and driving him to this unnatural lust. He sneered at me. Then I spoke to the evil spirit and commanded it to be silent. Steve just looked up at me with sadness and fear in his eyes. I said, "Steve, do you believe that Jesus is here and that He has come to set you free?"

"Yes," he cried.

Then I spoke to the spirit and said, "You lying spirit of lust, I command you to leave, in the name of Jesus." Steve started to get sick. "You have no authority to punish this man of God." I told the demon, "Jesus said, 'you will know the truth, and the truth will make you free'," and his head perked up. Then I spoke to the demon and said, "I cancel your lies over this brother's mind and command you to leave, now." At that, Steve began to shake and throw-up in the garage. At that moment, the peace of God came over him. I knew that Steve was free. I asked Steve how he felt. He told me it was gone. He explained what was happening to him and how, when he was younger he struggled with his manhood. He had fought this on and off most of his life, but when he started going to Bible School, the struggle intensified.

Steve's situation is like so many others that are held captive to the lies of the enemy. And when we believe the lies we give the enemy permission to punish us because we think the lies are true. Captives are people that have been captured in battle and held as

POWs. Only the truth will release the stronghold of the enemy. It is important to understand how people get bound in order to be effective in setting them free. In Isaiah 61:1 it says:

> "The Spirit of the Lord GOD is upon Me, Because the LORD has anointed Me To preach good tidings to the poor; He has sent Me to heal the brokenhearted, To proclaim liberty to the captives, And the opening of the prison to those who are bound;"

There are two types of people bound in this passage. The first are captives, and the second are prisoners. A captive is taken and imprisoned through lies and deception. A prisoner is a criminal whom a judge sentences to jail. It takes the knowledge of Truth to set a captive free. Prisoners, on the other hand our bound by their own actions.

In Matthew 18:21-35, Jesus talks about forgiveness, and how it relates to being a prisoner.

> "Then Peter came to Him and said, "Lord, how often shall my brother sin against me, and I forgive him? Up to seven times?"
>
> Jesus said to him, "I do not say to you, up to seven times, but up to seventy times seven. Therefore the kingdom of heaven is like a certain king who wanted to settle accounts with his servants. And when he had begun to settle accounts, one was brought to him who owed him ten thousand talents. But as he was not able to pay, his master commanded that he be sold, with his wife and children and all that he had, and that payment be made.
>
> The servant therefore fell down before him, saying, 'Master, have patience with me, and I will pay you all.' Then the master of that servant was moved with compassion, released him, and forgave him the debt.

> *"But that servant went out and found one of his fellow servants who owed him a hundred denarii; and he laid hands on him and took him by the throat, saying, 'Pay me what you owe!' So his fellow servant fell down at his feet and begged him, saying, 'Have patience with me, and I will pay you all.' And he would not, but went and threw him into prison till he should pay the debt.*
>
> *So when his fellow servants saw what had been done, they were very grieved, and came and told their master all that had been done.*
>
> *Then his master, after he had called him, said to him, 'You wicked servant! I forgave you all that debt because you begged me. Should you not also have had compassion on your fellow servant, just as I had pity on you?'*
>
> *And his master was angry, and delivered him to the torturers until he should pay all that was due to him. "So My heavenly Father also will do to you if each of you, from his heart, does not forgive his brother his trespasses."*

It is clear, from the story that un-forgiveness can lead to demonic torment. It opens the door and gives the demonic legal permission to oppress and torture you. Freedom comes from the decree of the King, which in turn give us the authority to command these evil spirits to leave. Without walking a prisoner through the steps of forgiveness, any release from the demonic will only be temporal. It takes the power of the Holy Spirit to get free and stay free of demonic oppression.

The Word of Knowledge in the example I shared help distinguish why Steve was bound. The Word of Knowledge is very powerful. It brings fear and repentance to sinners and blessings to God's people. Most of all, it brings great glory to God.

When you receive a Word of Knowledge, it is important for the Seer to get a clear interpretation from the Lord and understand it application. God gives words of knowledge in several ways:

- Seeing, as in visions and dreams
- Feeling, as in a sharp pain or sensation
- Reading, as in you see words written in your mind
- An Impression, as in thinking or sensing a condition
- Speaking, as in while you are speaking to someone un-premeditated words tumble out of your mouth
- Experience it, as in having a vivid trance or 3D vision, beyond a simple picture

Remember Words of Knowledge can come very fast or be vague. Often the tendency it to brush it off as nothing, learn to focus and tune into what the Holy Spirit is saying. Don't be presumptuous be humble. Be as specific as you can but don't elaborate. Moreover, most of all don't be afraid. Don't let fear rob you and the person who might have been delivered. Faith is a verb, you have to step out. God gives you information because He wants to use you to set people free.

Visions to the One Being Set Free: Sometimes the Lord will use visionary language to nudge a captive in order to move them to a position to be set free. When this happens, it is a beautiful sovereign move by God to display His tenderness and love. To illustrate this let me share one story.

Thanksgiving week, 2004 I got a surprise knock on the door. When I opened it, it was my son Jamisen asking if he could stay with us. I was so excited; I turned our living room into a bedroom and got him a job in the kitchen at our resort. Jamisen broke-up with his girlfriend and was devastated. He said, "Dad, I need to come back to the Lord – would you pray with me." We walked down to the dock, below our house. I told him the story of the prodigal, how the father loved his son so much that he leaped off his porch and came running to his son while he was still far off. He put rings on his fingers, shoes on his feet, and a robe on his back – then he threw him a killer party, fatted calf and all. We sat, cried, and prayed together. I had gotten my son back. What I didn't know was in just a few short months, on January 19, 2005, he would be killed.

The great sadness entered in my life. My boy was gone. He was accidently struck in the back of the head by a bullet. The following months, to help in my grief, I wrote a book called "Reflections from the Kitchen, a look at Christ through the Eyes of a Chef." The folks in my kitchen helped Jan and I walk through our grief. However, the sadness never really goes away.

We didn't have a church in that area. It was very rural. Then a funny thing began to happen. The girls in the kitchen kept coming to my office for prayer. Usually it was for healing or for mending relationship – and you know what? God started answering their prayers. People were being healed. Most of my culinary team was Spanish and my Spanish is what you call "kitchen Spanish." What started with two Marias and Rosa soon became 20 people, praying daily in the employee cafeteria.

This thing was getting big. By now, my cooks were bringing family members to my office. "Con usted permiso jefe, mi moma," I would look over and see a little old Spanish lady standing there who needed prayer because she couldn't walk well, And God healed her.

I said, "God this is crazy, what should I do?" So I started "Cooks for Christ" and began having weekly meetings in our banquet room. I bought cases of Spanish/English bibles and began handing them out. By Christmas of that year, at our first 2006 Cooks for Christmas Party, we had 150 people, families, kids, teenagers, grandparents.

One such teenager was Juana's daughter – Juana used to be called Maria. However, her husband had brutally raped her daughter and they had to go into hiding. She disappeared for a year, returned to Mexico, and came back as Juana. Juana had walked into my office, crying. Rosa interpreted her broken English. She told me what had happened, and that something was wrong with her daughter. She would black out – our just pass out. She asked me to come to their house and pray for them.

When I arrived at Juana's house, her son explained how someone was trying to put a curse on them painting sanetra symbols on their walls in blood. Salendra (not her real name), her daughter had just got home. Juana called her over. "Salendra, this is my chef, he is going to pray for you." We hugged and I asked her to sit down.

When I started to pray for her – she blacked out like a rag doll right in front of me. I thought I was going over for some inner healing or something. I had to pray and get some insight from Poppa. I asked the oldest boy to show me the symbols on the wall. He walked me down the hall to the bedroom and showed me the symbols on the outside wall. What I was really doing was praying in my prayer language and looking for a word from Poppa. I turned to look at Salendra down the hallway and her head suddenly popped up – she was staring at me with her head turned.

"Thank you Poppa." I knew what I was dealing with when I saw the demon's fear in her eyes. I turned and walked back. Immediately, I started to pray, and command this demon to leave her. She started to pass out again. I commanded the demon to release her and loose her mind. She snapped to attention, and after about 15 minutes of back and forth – it was gone. She started to glow. I wanted to make sure it was gone.

She kept saying, "I am free, I am free." Then she said, "It left when I saw you standing before the throne of God singing, and it left." She said when she saw that vision she knew that God loved her and that she knew I was a servant of His.

I knew at that moment that she was indeed free. I led her to Christ in His fullness, and walked her through forgiveness, and she was filled with the Holy Spirit. The demon that had driven her abuser to brutalize her had come upon her, and the Lord, in a way that only He can do, set this child free.

Well at this Christmas party, she had brought ten of her high school friends with her, folks that knew her and witnessed what Jesus had done. Like the woman at the well, she could not contain herself and shared her freedom to all her friends.

CHAPTER 22

DEALING WITH DEMONS

"Then the seventy returned with joy, saying, "Lord, even the demons are subject to us in Your name." And He said to them, "I saw Satan fall like lightning from heaven. Behold, I give you the authority to trample on serpents and scorpions, and over all the power of the enemy, and nothing shall by any means hurt you. Nevertheless do not rejoice in this, that the spirits are subject to you, but rather rejoice because your names are written in heaven."

- Luke 10:17-20

"Then the seventy returned with joy, saying, "Lord, even the demons are subject to us in Your name." And He said to them, "I saw Satan fall like lightning from heaven. Behold, I give you the authority to trample on serpents and scorpions, and over all the power of the enemy, and nothing shall by any means hurt you. Nevertheless do not rejoice in this, that the spirits are subject to you, but rather rejoice because your names are written in heaven."

- Luke 10:17-20

Although satan and his minions are defeated and will ultimately be cast into the lake of fire, the devil is still very active in his warfare against humanity. It is therefore critical that Christians prepare themselves for the battles that is ahead. We do this by:

Be not ignorant of his devices (2 Corinthians 2:11). The enemy takes advantage of our spiritual immaturity and ignorance (Ephesians 4:11-15).

Constantly strengthen ourselves in the Lord (Ephesians 6:10). When we daily feed on the Scriptures and walk in fellowship with the Lord, then we can meet the enemy in the Lord's strength.

Put on the whole armor of God (Ephesians 6:11-18). The armor of God consists of spiritual realities, which we are able to appropriate to our daily lives. These realities are spiritual qualities found in Christ and that manifest Him in our lives. Jesus is the complete armor—He lacks nothing. Let us consider each piece of the armor of God:

Gird your waste with the belt of truth (Ephesians 6:14; John 14:6). The truth here is twofold. First it is the truth of the Word of God and the nature of Jesus Christ. Secondly, the truth is your personal character that you walk in truthfulness and honesty in your daily life. The belt holds up our pants, enabling us to walk in truth and not be hindered or uncovered.

Putting on the breastplate of righteousness (Ephesians 6:14; Philippians 1:11). The breastplate shields the vital organs. Knowing that you have Christ's righteousness (Romans 5:1; 1 Corinthians 1:30) enables you to walk from a kingdom perspective. It is also a call to walk a righteous life.

Wearing the sandals of the preparation of the gospel of peace (Ephesians 6:15; 2 Corinthians 5:20). This refers to our willingness to serve and bear witness to the lost (Acts 16:30-31). This is about motivation of the heart (Romans 1:14-16).

Take up the shield of faith (Ephesians 6:16; Galatians 2:20). Without faith, it is impossible to please God. The Lord wants us to trust Him with all our hearts and believe in all the promises of God. Faith in God, that He is good all the time and He has given us all things in Christ Jesus, will quench the flaming arrows of the evil one.

Put on the helmet of salvation (Ephesians 6:17; Hebrews 13:6). This represents the essential knowledge of salvation and the experience of its deliverance in our daily lives. We need to walk in the assurance of our salvation.

The sword of the Spirit (Ephesians 6:17; John 1:14). This is the Word of God, wielded in the power of the Holy Spirit. To use the Word of God we must learn its content, obey its commands, and depend upon the Holy Spirit to help us to apply it to the various needs of life.

Maintain communication and fellowship with God (Ephesians 6:18a). God is a God of relationship. He desires daily fellowship with Him. We do this through worship, prayer, and reading Scripture.

Be alert for the enemy (Ephesians 6:18b). "Be sober, be vigilant; because your adversary the devil walks about like a roaring lion, seeking whom he may devour"(1 Peter 5:8). He is looking for those who have lost sight of their Lord and have relied upon their own strength in this life. He is looking for chinks in your armor that he can exploit. Our call is to be alert.

Deliverance

"Deliverance" is setting a person free from the oppression of a demonic spirit. demons seek to harass people and, if possible, to move into them. They are restless if they cannot move into a human being. (See Matthew 12:43-45.) When given the opportunity, a demonic spirit will torment or manipulate the host in various ways. Understanding demonic spirits and deliverance is of great importance to the church; because of the adverse effect such spirits can have on believers, on church unity, and on evangelism.

I will use the term "oppression" rather than the term "possession" in the remainder of this chapter, because possession implies ownership and complete control. Since, the Lord Jesus Christ has purchased a believer, he cannot be possessed by the demonic. However, many believers have been host to the demonic prior to conversion, and these evil spirits do not always leave when the host is converted. That is why it is so very important to have in your arsenal the tools for deliverance during times of evangelism. demonic oppression is an enemy of evangelizing, as it prevents the Christian from achieving victory over certain sins, habits, or problems, and thus impairs his testimony as to the power of Jesus to change lives.

Philip is a good model for evangelistic encounters.

> "Therefore those who were scattered went everywhere preaching the word. Then Philip went down to the city of Samaria and preached Christ to them. And the multitudes with one accord heeded the things spoken by Philip, hearing and seeing the miracles which he did. For unclean spirits, crying with a loud voice, came out of many who were possessed; and many who were paralyzed and lame were healed. And there was great joy in that city."

- Acts 8:5-8

Phillip was a gifted evangelist. The signs that accompanied his ministry included miracles, healing, and deliverance. I think the church has often missed this formula for evangelism. The ideal time to set free the demonized lost is during the evangelistic process. By not doing so we end up saving those bound by the demonic, and have not positioned them to be free of their tormentors. First, we should cast out their demons, secondly, we should baptize them in the name of Jesus Christ, and lastly, we should lay hands on them and fill them with the Holy Spirit. Only then will they be able to begin their walk with Christ, unhindered by the baggage they used to carry.

The effect of demonic oppression

A demon may torment the host person with such problems as nightmares, unreasonable fear, general accusations of worthlessness or guilt, shame, pain, depression, irrational behavior, and the like. They can give the host an unwelcome and sometimes apparently uncontrollable desire to sin in a particular way, such as a spirit of adultery, or of pornography, or of anger, or of addiction, as examples.

A demon can push the host person repeatedly into sins and habits he resists and wishes to be free from, and thus be a major cause of disaffection and backsliding. After repeated cycles of committing a particular sin the believer may become discouraged and leave the church, or he may live a life of quiet desperation in the church, not realizing he can be free from such oppression.

demonic spirits sometimes cause disease, and sometimes impede or prevent healing of injuries and disease. Jesus cast out spirits of deafness, dumbness, and epilepsy among others.

demons can carry a weight of spiritual and emotional oppression, which dulls spiritual perception and can cause depression. In Isaiah 61:3, it is referred to as "the spirit of heaviness."

A demon may work steadily in a host person, or it may remain quiet, perhaps for years, and then work strongly in him at a later time, perhaps after the host person has achieved a position of spiritual responsibility and status.

The remedy for demonic oppression is deliverance. Deliverance has always been a sign to unbelievers of the power of God over satan.

Personal Preparation and the Deliverance Process

Below is a list of a few key things to remember when dealing with the demonic.

Love: Behind every deliverance is the heart of God's love for the victim. Seek to be a channel for His love and always minister in God's love.

Order: Demons understand and respect authority. If you are ministering in a team environment, make sure there are clear lines of responsibility. Evil spirits will feed off any dissention or confusion in the ranks.

Understand the Limitations: It is useless to expel a demon against the oppressed person's will. If someone is unwilling to change their lifestyle that caused the mess to begin with and that person is unwilling to renounce their agreement with the enemy, specifically and audibly, if you cast it out, it will return and possibly bring others with it. (See Matthew 12:43-45)

Access: Remember that a demon cannot oppress a person unless some avenue of access has been opened to it, such as unforgiveness, hate, abuse, sin, unclean sex, trauma, or some other circumstance.

Legalistic: Demons are very legalistic, typically refusing to leave a person, unless the host person renounces the avenue of entrance. The objective is to 1: To expel and 2: To close all avenues of access to prevent them from returning.

Flexibility: Remember that the prayee is a hurting person and may have been bound for years. Be ready and open to change gears and focus on the healing of wounds or illness.

Teams: Always work in a team of at least two, and never minister to the opposite sex alone. If there is a need to touch the person, make sure only one person does it.

Priority: Make sure that the victim gets your full attention. Be loving but firm. Be encouraging so the prayee sees hope. Let the victim know that Jesus can set them free. Remember, they may have lost all hope.

Silence: If the spirit is manifesting make it be quiet and submit to you in the name of Jesus.

The Prayee: Establish and maintain communication with the prayee. Don't start to minister until you are in the right frame of mind and you have established communication. Do not speak out or pray loudly. Touching and speaking loudly tends to keep the spirit stirred up. You need the spirit quiet so you can talk to the prayee. Above all, be calm.

Authority: If the prayee gets up and starts to move around, take authority over the spirit out loud, and tell the prayee to come and sit down. If the spirit of the prayee speaks, growls, threatens, argues with you, or gives you orders and ask questions, do not speak to it except to order it to be quiet, in the name of Jesus, and take your legal control.

Freedom: Make sure you ask the prayee if he wants to be free from the situation and try to make sure he actually wants to get free.

Jesus: Make sure the prayee has accepted Jesus as his Savior and Lord.

Interview: Interview the prayee to discover the event or events, or relationship situations that have led to the bondage.

Closing Doors: Lead the prayee in closing all open doors that have given access to the demonic.

Forgiveness: Lead the prayee to forgive the one that hurt them or led them to wrong conduct.

Repentance: Lead the prayee through repentance of each of the prayee's own sins in the situation, and specifically asking for God's forgiveness.

Renounce: Lead the prayee to renounce all the spirits involved, in the name of Jesus.

Bondage: Break the bondage that caused the sin, the conduct, the attitude, the spirit, the vow, or the curse, as indicated, in the name of Jesus.

Cast Out: Cast out the demon or demons in the name of Jesus.

Finish: When you think you have finished, ask the Holy Spirit if there is additional issues that need to be dealt with. If so, cast them out.

Praise: Ask the prayee to praise and thank Jesus for his deliverance.

In Filling: Ask the prayee to pray for the Holy Spirit to fill him, and to fill all the places formerly occupied by evil spirits.

CHAPTER 23

My Story

"Nebuchadnezzar the king, 'To all peoples, nations, and languages that dwell in all the earth: Peace be multiplied to you. I thought it good to declare the signs and wonders that the Most High God has worked for me. How great are His signs, and how mighty His wonders! His kingdom is an everlasting kingdom, and His dominion is from generation to generation.

And at the end of the time I, Nebuchadnezzar, lifted my eyes to heaven, and my understanding returned to me; and I blessed the Most High and praised and honored Him who lives forever: For His dominion is an everlasting dominion, and His kingdom is from generation to generation. All the inhabitants of the earth are reputed as nothing; He does according to His will in the army of heaven and among the inhabitants of the earth. No one can restrain His hand or say to Him, "What have You done?", Now I, Nebuchadnezzar, praise and extol and honor the King of heaven, all of whose works are truth, and His ways justice. And those who walk in pride He is able to put down."

- Daniel 4:1-3, 34-37

The testimony of Jesus is the Spirit of prophecy. This is my testimony, how I came to know Jesus and my walk with Him in the world of the prophetic. Nebuchadnezzar, after encountering God through dreams and the ministry of Daniel, had this to say.

You see, there comes a time in everyone's life, of deep reflection, a time of looking at all the hidden things in your life and assessing where you stand in relationship with the living God. This is a powerful and beautiful experience. Yet, more often than not, it's a two-sided coin.

My own journey into the realm of prophetic dreams and visions didn't come about by a Christian desiring a spiritual gift, though Paul admonishes us to do that. Nor did it come about by being a disciple by the gifted hand of a seasoned prophet in the school of the prophets, yet I would recommend this highly. My journey is more comparable a seed trying to burst through the soil of life. This story is a glimpse through the windows of my heart. How God entered into an impossible situation and replaced the dungeon doors of my life with stained glass windows. Windows that now, with the light of His glory, radiates the splendor of the one who died for my sins.

The story begins, not with me, but with my grandfather, Ernest Asa Raynaud. In a time in history when the world was in a state of confusion and dissolution, World War I had ended. Germany's war efforts were collapsed. Woodrow Wilson had announced his fourteen points for peace, while Charlie Chaplin was bringing laughter to the hearts of many, with his new movie, "Shoulder Arms."

At that time, Grandpa, a stout man with broad shoulders and an iron grip that sent a blow to the handshake of all that greeted him, was working his way through the ring, as a boxer. He had met my grandmother, Alice Mary Lowell, daughter of Adelbert Lowell, who served as a Captain in the US Navy during the Civil War. The Lowell's were an old American family, with ancestors as James Russell Lowell, famous American poet and Statesman, and France Cabot Lowell, who started the first water-powered textile mill in this country, and founded the city of Lowell, Massachusetts.

Grandma's family was aristocratic, but in 1898, when the Spanish-American war erupted, Grandma or Nana as I called her, was sent to a convent in Santa Rosa, California, where she would spend much of her childhood. At the age of seventeen, she moved to San Francisco. It was not long after the great earthquake of 1906 that Grandpa and Nana came together. Both had been survivors of the great quake and, up to the time of her death in 1978, she still received annual letters from the White House honoring her as one of a few survivors.

Gramps had an unshakable love for this woman. She was a petite lady, with gentleness about her. She was a butterfly, timid and meek, and at the same time, afraid and startled at the slightest unexpected move. I think it was this quality that attracted Grandpa, it was different from the rugged way he lived his life.

In 1910, they moved to San Diego, California. They rented a small Spanish style home with a tiny yard. It had a pot-bellied stove and an icebox to store all the perishables. It was an active neighborhood. Often you would see the ice cream man or vegetable man come by in a horse drawn cart. Grandpa's favorite caller was a short black lady, dressed in a white dress and white turban. She would push her cart up the street three times a week, selling hot hominy.

The year the First World War ended my father was born (also known as the Great War). They named him Liberty Earnest Raynaud, third in a family of three boys and one girl. They all grew up during the great depression, yet they did not seem to know it or feel the pain of it. San Diego was different then, and for a kid, life was an adventure. Streetcars would take you to the beach where you could camp or go smelt fishing with a bamboo pole. Now and then, they would take a trip to Young's Cave or hop a freight train and eat dinner at the hobo jungles next to the railroad tracks. The train rides were beautiful; nature came alive with wild flowers, sour-grass, and California poppies everywhere.

It is hard for me to imagine life back then, without all the pollution, noise, and people running around with no place to go. Yet, life was no picnic either, not even close. People were trying to come together, to get back what they had lost during the war where nine million people had lost their lives. All of a sudden, it happened, the great influenza epidemic hit, and people were powerless, standing by while young and old struggled to survive.

In one year, 1918-1919, when the pandemic hit twenty five million people had died around the world and estimated 850,000 men, women, and children died in the U.S. alone. The Bubonic Plague made the War to end all Wars a walk in the park. Eighteen months after the disease appeared, the flu bug vanished and has never shown up again. People wanted to know what happened.

It turns out that while conducting autopsies in 1918, Army doctors had preserved some specimens in formaldehyde. One of these jars contained the lungs of a 21-year-old soldier that died during the pandemic. In 1998, U.S. Army researchers discovered these remains and spent two years extracting seven percent of the genetic code, which provided them with a wealth of information. It appears that the virus passed from birds to pigs, to humans. When the pig's immune system kicks into action, the virus is forced to mutate to survive.

In 1957, the year I was born, we saw it with the Asian flu, ten years later the Hong Kong flu of "68," hit, yet neither of which were as deadly as the 1918 flu. The kicker is, they all came from birds – to pigs – to humans. The scary part is that it could happen again, and we're not prepared for it. Think about the "Bird Flu" talk a few years back.

This country, in its brief history, has seen a lot of war and pain. We have been through two World Wars and perhaps heading to a third World War with this global war on terror, remember 911, and Iran's pursuit of nuclear weapons. That says nothing about the floods, tornados, devastating earthquakes, and the massive hurricanes that have struck our land in recent years. With the onslaught of incurable diseases as Aids, HIV, and the possibility of another "Bird Flu" pandemic, it's a wonder we have any hope for the future. Nevertheless, physical death in the wake of impending danger is the least of our worries. We are in a war that will affect our eternal destination.

Within our borders, a bomb has gone off, more subtle than anything man cooks up. That bomb is the cult and occult explosion. In the previous chapters on Healing of the demonic, I shared how God delivered my family from satan's grip. But there is more to the story. Just to refresh your minds. In my family, the door opened up to the occult world a hundred and thirty years before the current mysticism movement. We were bound by the cult of Spiritism, and stayed bound for generations, until the Lord drew a line in the sand.

My great grandmother was a medium when the Spiritism revival first took place in the 1880s, but it was not until 1930 when great grandmother made a visit to Grandpa's humble home, in San Diego, that communication with the dead became a reality in Gramps life.

According to my father, Gramps was not too sure about spirit communication. He knew his mother was a devout spiritualist, but it was too hard for him to believe that the spirit world could communicate, let alone communicate through a wooden table. As the story goes, that night, his whole outlook changed. They all gathered around the kitchen table. This table was made of solid oak, weighing a good 300 pounds, and Gramps knew that no "hocus-pocus" from his mother could make that table move. Sitting around the table, everyone would place their fingertips lightly on the face of the table. Great Grandmother would close her eyes and concentrate on some loved one from the past. The intensity of her trance caused the blood veins on her forehead to stand out.

The room got quiet, and silence is loud. The only sound heard was the sound of rapid heartbeats, the kind that comes in an hour of fear and uncertainty. Suddenly, a chill filled the air, an unearthly chill that ran down my Grandfather's arms.

"Somebody's trying to get through," Said Great Grandmother, as the table started to shiver.

"I don't believe this!" Grandpa shouted.

Suddenly, the table reared up on two legs, and came slamming down, sliding my grandfather into the corner of the kitchen. Grandpa's heart was in his throat, pumping uncontrollably, as the table pinned him against the wall.

This started the beginning of my family's involvement in Spiritism. For years, this kind of activity, gaining information from the world beyond, and seeking relationship with un-seen entities, plagued my Dad's side of the family. This was my religion, communication with the so-called spirit world. This was my history.

I was fourteen, when we moved to Mission Viejo, one of California's most beautiful communities. Located on the south end of Orange County, this suburban hideaway was surrounded by waves of rolling hills. In the autumn, the hills came alive with the colors of fall. With the tall grasses blowing in the wind, it was as if a magical hand was orchestrating the movement of the golden hills. I loved those rolling hills, but it was not long before all the hills were whipped away and replaced by more houses, Spanish style homes as far as the eyes could see.

The building of that area exploded as the crowded and radical conditions of Los Angeles pushed people southward. It was as if people were running, trying to find their Utopia, and Utopia it appeared to be. Nevertheless, my folks learned fast that things are not always, as they seem to be.

That was the year I discovered a new playmate and drugs became my best friend. My high school years were marked by extreme rebellion caused by my hippy-fied way of thinking. The high school administration officials had labeled me incorrigible and transferred me to Silverado Continuation School during my sophomore year. At the end of that school year, I dropped out. By the time, I was eighteen I was a wreck. It did not take long for the affects of my torn life style to hurt everything and everyone.

I grew up in a family, struggling with alcoholism, drug abuse, Spiritism, and divorce. My parents, though loving, did not know the Lord and their search to fill the void within them lead to many dead ends. The only spiritual influence I had came from Spiritism, table moving, and communication with the dead, except for one thing, the touch of one couple in my life as a child.

I had a Bible believing Aunt and Uncle who lived with us when I was a kid. My Aunt Ida Bell and Uncle Harold were strong Christians and had tremendous faith. They never preached at us but I knew that their life was real. My Aunt was in the choir and had a voice of an angel. On a day, I will never forget, I heard for the first time about Jesus – in a personal way. It happened in front of my house in Huntington Beach, California. I was ten years old. I really liked to talk to my Uncle Harold. He was a peaceful man. He worked the produce section at Vons market and he loved his cigars – they were his quiet time.

Early one evening I saw my Uncle standing on the porch smoking a cigar staring out at the sunset. I walked over to him and started asking him questions about school and stuff. His mind was somewhere else. It was dusk and he was staring off into the distant skies. I asked him what he was doing. He looked down at me and with a big smile on his face said, "One day – Jesus is going to come back and his glory will fill the skies," as he pointed to dusk colored orange skies above us. That was the first time I heard about Jesus in a personal way. I never forgot that day. My Uncle, shortly thereafter, became terminally ill and died that same year. I know that the prayers of my Aunt and Uncle were instrumental in my future salvation.

By 1977 I was a lost, drug infested, longhaired beach bum hippy, living on the beach in Huntington, California. That summer, I bumped into a young catholic girl, by the name of Jan, in a bar on the peer in Huntington Beach. She was a good Midwest girl from Michigan. We spent the whole summer together sleeping on the beach and riding my motorcycle around Southern California. She was on school break from Western Michigan. I was a high school dropout and a cook.

We were polar opposites. Nevertheless, we fell madly in love. At summer's end, she told me she had to go back to school. She said goodbye, thinking she would never see me again. However, to her surprise, a month later, I bought a '66 VW bus, drove to Kalamazoo, and showed up at her dorm room door. She hid me in her dorm room until we could find a place to live off campus. We married on July 1 the following year. I had fallen head over heels for her. For the first time in my life, I let down the walls of my heart to love someone, and in return, let them love me. This experience of being loved and loving someone was the door that God used to soften my heart, and move into my life.

On our honeymoon, many strange things started to happen to me. I found myself struggling with emotions that I never felt before. We were on our way to Travis City in Michigan when I found myself thinking about the existence of God a lot. Everywhere we would go the question of God's existence haunted me. We would drive our old blue and white '66 VW Bus by old country and gothic style churches and I would pull over to the side of the road and take a picture. My wife thought I was nuts. I found myself in debates with people, arguing in favor of Jesus Christ. Though I hadn't, yet known Him, the reality of His existence was becoming clear – something inside was being stirred.

We went back to California for Christmas in 78. One debate took place on Christmas Eve. It was a lively debate with my sister about the existence of God. If you knew my sister, and me, this was a common practice. Everyone finally left the table, due to my stubbornness. With a warm beer in my hand and a dazed look on my face, I sat back at the kitchen table, alone and feeling lonelier. I thought about this day, Christmas, a day that was supposed to be religious, but all we did, as a family, was drink and argue. I pushed my beer aside and left for my room disgusted.

As I lay on my bed, staring up at the ceiling, all I could think about was the reality of God. "Are you real?" I thought. Then sleep caught up with me and I was out like a light. That night was the most incredible night I have ever experienced. I had fallen asleep and dreamed a dream that would change my life forever.

In this dream, I was sitting in my bed and suddenly the room filled with radiant blue and white light. Standing in front of me was Jesus Christ. He had His arms outstretched, as if he wanted to hold me, His whole being radiated with heavenly brilliance. He was beckoning me, calling me. I felt His love drawing me, warmth I never felt before, as if He wanted to hold me, enfold me, and comfort me. I knew that this was the Lord. It was as if He could see right through me, as if he knew all my pain, the deep pain, way inside, that hidden child filled with fear and disbelief.

I woke in amazement and told my family about the dream. My sister said, "Who do you think you are some kind of prophet?" I walked away, wondering about this Jesus. For the next few days, all I could think about was this dream. My life suddenly had no meaning – confusion set in and I began to fall apart. The struggle inside me was mounting. The forces of rage and sin began to flare up within me. I did not know where to go for help.

I went to my Aunt's house to have a séance and find out more about the strange dream that I had. That night the table went wild and towards the close of the night, the table was moving at my touch. This was one of satan's last attempts to pull me all the way into his grip. My Aunt was a powerful medium, she would barely touch a table, and the so-called spirits would be summoned. I always wanted to do that, to be just like her, there seemed to be so much power in it.

My Aunt left the room and went into the kitchen to wash the dishes. I was left at the séance table with my wife Jan and Wendy, a friend of ours. I put my fingertips on the table, closed my eyes, and said, "Come to us now." All of a sudden, the table began to move, sliding in circles to each one of us. I looked up with a blank composure and noticed my wife, startled by what had happened dropping her hands from the table. Then Wendy dropped her hands and I was left solo with the table, moving in circles, slowly... then faster, and faster.

My wife shouted, "Fred you're moving the table." With that, I threw my hands in the air and the table stopped. For the first time in my life, I could move the table by myself. "What did this mean?" I thought to myself. "What does this have to do with the dream I had?" These questions were flying through my mind. I went back home, confused by the nights' events.

Soon I began a downward spiral. By January 15, 1979, I was a complete mess again. We were having a party that night. Towards the end of the party, about 3:00 am, I asked my friends if they wanted to have a séance. Everyone agreed, so I took the table and placed it on top of another table, and within minutes, I was out.

When I came to the room was in a shambles, the table was broken, and my wife was crying. My brother in-law had called the police and my wife cried out, "Get out of here I never want to see you again!"

demonic rage took hold of me. I had tossed furniture around, beaten up my best friend, and threaten everyone in the room. My wife had left me. I found myself running, scared, and alone. I returned to our apartment at Walled Lake and sat on the floor, my mind racing with thoughts of suicidal depression. The pain was bad I wanted to die. The only person I had ever loved was leaving me and the thought of being alone was too unbearable. When suddenly, the dream I had on Christmas Eve was right before my eyes.

In a vision, the Lord was standing before me as before. I looked up to heaven and cried. These words began to form in my mind, "If you're really real, I need you, help me, please help me!" I opened my mouth and got to the "I" in "if" when the presence of the Lord filled the room with warmth like the warmth in my dream. My hair was standing up on end. All I could do was cry. I kept saying repeatedly, "Your real, you're really real!"

The Lord had entered my room and wrapped His arms around me. He took away all my pain, hurt, and sin into Himself and I was, for the first time in my life, forgiven. I was instantly aware that the Lord, He is God! That Jesus loved me, and that He knew me better than I knew myself. I was born again and filled with his Spirit that very minute. Something had happened to me. My eyes were opened for the first time. The demons that bound me were gone. Jesus had set me free. I could see, feel, and hear life for the first time. I knew he had forgiven me of all my sins and I was clean – as white as freshly fallen snow.

My wife had come by the house to pack some clothes and leave. She saw me sitting on the floor and walked right on by. I didn't know how to explain to her what had happened to me. I felt like John Denver in that movie "Oh God." I walked up to her and told her that Jesus came to me... He did something to me. I didn't know how to explain it. I said it would never happen again. Then, by a miracle, she looked at me and forgave me.

That next morning I went to her folk's house. I was sitting in their living room next to a coffee table where they had a big white catholic bible with a picture of Jesus on it. I looked at that picture and tears started to roll down my face. I felt the presence of the Lord all around me, comforting me. I grabbed the bible, opened it, and began to read where my finger hit the page. I read for the first time in my entire life, these words:

> "For God so loved the world, that he gave his only begotten Son, that whosoever believeth in him should not perish, but have everlasting life."
>
> - John 3:16

The tears began to flow again and the Lord spoke to me,

> "Fred, I did it for you!"

I love the Lord so much for that, I love Him more than I can say with words. A few weeks later God was calling us back to my home, to California. On our way back to California, we stopped in a hotel. In the room, they had a Gideon Bible. I began reading it for the first time. I took it with me and held onto it, shoot, I didn't know where to buy one of those things.

Daily I devoured the word. When I read it, the words became alive. The Lord would speak to me, saying, "Fred I have called you to be a prophet to my people, to be a light in a dark place, and a fire before my throne." I did not know what that meant. It was later that I discovered the depth of that call. Of course, we are all called to be witnesses of the resurrected Lord, to be the extension of His hands, to be His voice in a world that is hungry to taste the manna that came down from heaven.

It took me six months to learn what church was all about. I just didn't think in terms like as church and fellowship. All I knew was that Jesus loved me. Daily the Lord would speak to me with that small still inner voice I have come to know and love. At night, I would have the most incredible dreams. We talked, as a friend would speak to a friend. I would see visions and feel his presence daily.

Christian radio was my church for about six months. It did not take the Lord long to bring me into fellowship. It was there that I discovered that many Christians didn't believe that God spoke to His people. I was shocked to find that life in many churches was far removed from what I read in the Scriptures, until I met John Wimber.

My first church was Calvary Chapel in Costa Mesa, under Pastor Chuck Smith. I was immersed in the word. With teachers like Chuck Missler, in depth bible study and worship became my passion. Calvary was the perfect place for being grounded in the word.

That was also the season Bob Dylan was saved. Bob was a hero of mine and when he had been saved I thought, yes God. It blew my mind. It happened at the first Vineyard Church started when Kenn Gulliksen who had brought together two Bible studies groups meeting at the houses of singer/songwriters: Larry Norman and Chuck Girard. This was "Vineyard" before the Wimber years. Bob cut three Christian albums in those years, and they were powerful, "Slow train coming" – "saved", and "shot of love." Well, in my life, I was experiencing so many manifestations of the Holy Spirit in my life, visions, dreams, hearing God, and being filled with the Holy Spirit were just normal. I had no idea that this activity wasn't fully embraced by Calvary or the church in general at that time. I thought – "it's in the book, surely, everyone experiences God like this."

Shortly after that, God was calling us back to Huntington Beach, but I didn't know it, not until Canadian Immigration detained us. You see we did not have work visas, and many folks had split to Canada during the Vietnam War, so Canadian Immigration was cracking down on immigrants. They were tightening up before amnesty kicked in I suppose. You could say I was a snow-back. But we were just a couple of young hippies and thought that this was par for the course. We didn't even think we needed visas, after all it was Canada, and my cousin lived there and was married to a Canadian.

I was doing a banquet for some folks. It turned out that their guest speaker was head of Canadian Immigration. I looked outside in the snow and saw all these undercover cop cars. I thought, wow – a lot of cop cars out there. Moments later, the doors burst open and we were headed down the mountain and placed in immigration holding until we went before the magistrate. Ironically, I was placed in a cell with a man who was from a communist bloc country. He had jumped from a Russian ship and swam to the east coast of Canada, then hitchhiked across the country, ending up in Vancouver. I shared with him the love and power of Jesus and He was saved in that cell.

We soon found ourselves back at home, in Huntington Beach. I was back at Calvary. By this time in my life, though I had only been saved for a merely two plus years, I knew I needed more. It was 1981. That's when I discovered John Wimber at the Canyon High School in Yorba Linda. When I arrived it was shortly after that landmark day in Vineyard history – when on Mother's day, John Wimber asked Lonnie Frisbee to preach and at the end of his message he called all the kids under the age of 25 to come forward and hundreds came up – then he prayed "Come Holy Spirit" and the rest was history. God just fell on the place. That grace filled Mother's Day, was the beginning of the future Vineyard movement.

I found my home. I would spend half my time at Calvary Costa Mesa, learning the word, and half my time at John Wimber's church, just loving Jesus, worshiping, and soaking in the presence. They were meeting at the old Canyon High School in Anaheim Hills, worshiping on bleachers and seeking the face of Jesus. Then, in 1982, Calvary Chapel of Yorba Linda became the Anaheim Vineyard Christian Fellowship.

After a short season back in the OC, God called us up to Twin Peaks, outside Lake Arrowhead, up in the mountains. A month earlier revival had broken out at the Calvary Chapel Conference Center. God had placed Jan and I right up the hill from the center. Chuck Smith had introduced Lonnie Frisbee at a retreat. I believe Calvary Chapel Yorba Linda was there, and the Holy Spirit fell on that place. Young people all over the place were slain with the Holy Spirit. A home group sprung up around that. Some 50 or so people just hung out in an "A-frame" house, praying and seeking God, and God showed up. Folks were hanging on the balcony, lying on the floor, all with one thing in common, a passion for the Lord and His presence.

Well, our hope was to find a church like Wimber's. We were very excited to find Calvary Chapel Conference Center in Twin Peaks. Combined with the trees and the serenity of the mountains this was a perfect place to move into a deeper relationship with the Spirit of God. The revival that had broken out was still alive, active, and new. It changed the mountain and the atmosphere of church. It was truly electrifying. Many amazing things happened on that mountain, some of which I shared in this series.

After about a year, we left Lake Arrowhead and moved to Palm Springs, a desert community south of Lake Arrowhead. We began attending Calvary of Palm Springs.

By this time, Yorba Linda was now Vineyard Anaheim. I would split my time at Calvary and then drive from Palm Springs to Anaheim Vineyard. Vineyard was alive with the presence of God. You would simply walk in and the presence of the Holy Spirit was upon you.

- Folks were getting healed left and right
- The demonized were being set free everywhere
- Miracles, signs and wonders were part of this new vibrant body of believers
- The worship was alive with the breath of God
- Kinship groups were training camps of fellowship were folks learned to practice the gifts of the Kingdom

The non-pretentious, un-religious message and nature of John Wimber was refreshing for so many of us. We just wanted God to be God. I would try to take folks from Palm Springs with me, so they could experience what I was experiencing. One couple I took was from the Church of Christ. They didn't even believe in instruments being used in the church. Here they were, in a Holy Spirit infused atmosphere of presence and worship, when a young lady in front of us manifested a demon and a ministry team began dealing with that critter. The wife, of my friend, saw that, jumped to her feet and ran out of the church.

Then a new Vineyard plant happened, and Vineyard of Palm Desert was born. I had a new home. Now my Anaheim visits were shorter, maybe once a quarter, and for every conference, "Power Healing," "Power Evangelism," and "Signs & Wonders and Church Growth."

John had a passion and a mission to train, equip, and deploy, and he had a vision to take the message of "doing the stuff" and "everyone gets to play" to world. This naturally supernatural message was affecting denominations around the world.

Like Lonnie Frisbee before him, John was on fire for a personal relationship with the power and presence of Jesus Christ. John put into words everything I believed and was experiencing in my life. His passion for Jesus and his emphases on Christians being authentic, filled, and "doing the stuff, was exactly what my spiritual DNA was crying out for. John Wimber developed a model of ministry that he had dubbed "naturally supernatural" and it reinforced in my heart the Lord's desire to live from a kingdom mindset. His model took ministry off the platform and allowed all of us to participate in lending a hand to "what the Father was doing."

John Wimber was a professional musician who played the Las Vegas circuit for 5 years. John later signed with the Righteous Brothers. When God gripped John in 1963, he was a "beer-guzzling, drug abusing pop musician, who was converted at the age of 29 while chain-smoking his way through a Quaker-led Bible Study.

One of my favorite stories of John's was when he recalled his first years as a believer. He became a voracious Bible reader and after weeks of reading about life changing miracles in the Bible and attending, what he called "boring" church services. John asked a lay leader at that "boring" church:

> *"When do we get to do the stuff? You know, the stuff here in the Bible; the stuff Jesus did, like healing the sick, raising the dead, healing the blind – stuff like that?"*

He was told that they didn't do that anymore – only what they did in their weekly services. John replied, "You mean I gave up drugs for that?"

John used to always emphases, "Everyone gets to play," which meant that all of us could participate in "doin' the stuff." It wasn't just for the pastors and preachers; it was for folks in the pews, folks like you and me. We soon learned that the "real meat was in the street" and Jesus was about to send all out and spawn a church growth movement that was simply remarkable. Everyone being allowed to do the stuff, the emphases on worship, and fellowship through "kinship" groups became part of the guiding foundation, hallmark, and marching orders of the Vineyard Movement in the early years. When I look back at some of the highlight of those years, I yearn for the fundamentals of the early Vineyard, to flood through the Vineyard of today.

- Sold out relentless worship, passion for Christ, and doin' the stuff – 80s – 90s
- Equipping the Saints and kinship empowerment – 80s onward

- Church planting & VMI – 83 onward
- Power healing – 84 onward
- Power evangelism – 85 onward
- Signs, Wonders and Church Growth – 85 onward
- The prophetic – 86 through the 92

John taught me that the most important thing in my life was intimacy with Jesus. That single core value has been my guiding pursuit for much of my Christian walk. I can say with full conviction that John was my true father in the faith, thank you John!

For the next 30 years, the Lord moved my family all around the country and every transition were filled with ecstasy, or pain, or both. It seemed that everywhere we went, we always ended up at a recently planted Vineyard. We would be there for a season – then the wind would blow and off we were again to another location. For me going to church was a treat, a special gift. The life of a chef allows very little time to meet the schedule of church attendance. Weekends, and holidays are our busiest times, so we fit it in where we can.

We would find ourselves living in Milwaukee, Florida, Virginia at the Virginia Beach Vineyard with Todd Hunter during my CBN years with Pat Robertson, Texas, Minnesota, Las Vegas, San Diego and Orlando. In 2003 I ended up on the Gulf Coast of Florida at a resort in the farming community of Ruskin. This pristine coast would be our new home until we came to DC.

Thanksgiving week, 2004 I got a surprise knock on the door. When I opened it, it was my son Jamisen asking if he could stay with us. I was so excited; I turned our living room into a bedroom and got him a job in the kitchen at our resort. Jamisen broke-up with his girlfriend and was devastated. He said, "Dad, I need to come back to the Lord – would you pray with me." We walked down to the dock, below our house. I told him the story of the prodigal, how the father loved his son so much that he leaped off his porch and came running to his son while he was still far off. He put rings on his fingers, shoes on his feet, and a robe on his back – then he threw him a killer party, fatted calf and all. We sat, cried, and prayed together. I had gotten my son back. What I didn't know was in just a few short months, on January 19, 2005, he would be killed.

The great sadness entered in my life. My boy was gone. He was struck in the back of the head by a bullet when a gun accidently went off. The following months, to help in my grief, I wrote a book called "Reflections from the Kitchen, a look at Christ through the Eyes of a Chef." The folks in my kitchen helped Jan and I walk through our grief. However, the sadness never really goes away.

We didn't have a church in that area. It was very rural. Then a funny thing began to happen. The girls in the kitchen kept coming to my office for prayer. Usually it was for healing or for mending relationship – and you know what? God started answering their prayers. People were being healed. Most of my culinary team was Spanish and my Spanish is what you call "kitchen Spanish." What started with two Marias and Rosa soon became 20 people, praying daily in the employee cafeteria.

I was blown away when I started to pray for our Poppa, our King to stand in our midst, using broken Spanish and sign language, and I would look around at our group and people were just weeping. Rodney, a new cook, with a biker headband and tats, walked by the cafeteria and stood frozen at the door, tears streaming down his face. He turned and ran away. I walked back to the fry station to talk to him. "Are you ok?"

He looked at me and said, "That was the most beautiful thing I have ever seen." He asked me to pray for him. We left the kitchen and walked down to the pier and God just came upon him.

This thing was getting big. By now, my cooks were bringing family members to my office. "Con usted permiso jefe, mi moma," I would look over and see a little old Spanish lady standing there who needed prayer because she couldn't walk well, And God healed her.

I said, "God this is crazy, what should I do?" So I started "Cooks for Christ" and began having weekly meetings in our banquet room. I bought cases of Spanish/English bibles and began handing them out. By Christmas of that year, at our first 2006 Cooks for Christmas Party, we had 150 people, families, kids, teenagers, and grandparents. Previously I shared the story of Salendra, which occurred during this season in my life.

You see, what I learned about the moving of God's presence, visions, dreams, and the prophetic, was born out of relationship with Jesus. It came from a God who said, "I no longer call you my servants but friends." It was birthed in the living room of a dying young man, whom the Lord decided to visit one day. Upon that visitation, there arose a friendship, not that I loved Him, but that He first loved me; and a friend like that is truly worthy of all that we can offer him, namely, our lives.

For decades, satan had bound my family with lying revelation. Yet, I have seen the Son of God turn the table on this deceiver and over the years usher many within my family to the knowledge of His saving grace. The Lord saved my Dad at age 65 and healed our relationship at Vineyard's Healing 86 Conference. My mother received salvation on her deathbed while dying in my arms from cancer as I read to her Psalms 23. My older brother Bob was saved as a teenager. His salvation sustained him while his body was being ravaged by terminal illness. My sister Jean and her husband Greg were saved by observing Christ move in the lives of their children, Chase and Andrea. They were saved as teenagers while staying with us one summer.

My Aunt Eva, former spiritist, was saved after the Lord gave me the opportunity to witness to my Dad's entire side of the family. I had confronted my Aunt about the dangers of table moving, some two years after I was saved. Jesus set her free, and she never picked up or participated in a séance since. Her compassion, faith, and belief in Christ's ability to sustain me were an inspiration. I saw God save my cousin Jim at Vineyard's Power Evangelism conference in 1985, and walk with him while he struggled with cancer. I watched as Jesus wrapped His arms around all of us when my son went to be with the Lord after a terminal head wound. I have seen the renunciation of seeking false revelation, and the love of Christ filled that void in my own life.

I have heard the whisper of the Spirit within my ear wooing me to Him who sits upon the throne. No channeler, no séance, no crystal, or any other lying wonder can stand next to the revelation of Jesus Christ, our true hope! You can be as close to God as you want to be, just let Him in and believe He rewards those who diligently seek Him.

I pray that this book blesses you in your relationship with Jesus Christ and will help equipped you to be more effective in your service to the world. Embrace your call and bring it to the streets.

Part 3: The Seer & Prophecy

CHAPTER 24

THE SEER & PROPHECY

"Saying, "Do not touch My anointed ones, and do My prophets no harm."

- Psalms 105:15

"'And it shall come to pass in the last days, says God, That I will pour out of My Spirit on all flesh; Your sons and your daughters shall prophesy, your young men shall see visions, your old men shall dream dreams. And on My menservants and on My maidservants I will pour out My Spirit in those days; and they shall prophesy."

- Acts 2:17-18

In light of the hour in which we live, this book excites me the most. We are living in a prophetic time, a season of the ushering forth of the Kingdom of God... a time of the Elijahs of God to take their stand, with golden trumpets of proclamation upon their lips and holy fire in their eyes.

This excitement does not stem from an immature view of fringe supernaturalism. Nor does it stem from the frail hearts of those who run to teachers desiring to have their ears tickled. It lies in the root word of "excitement," which has its essence in the idea of an "exodus." It is this exodus of the church, which so parallels the exodus of the Jews to the Promised Land that stirs my heart.

To know that we, as members of the body of Christ, are advancing the Kingdom of our God and are forerunners to the dawning of a new order – a Kingdom not made with hands is a wonderful thing. We are partakers and forerunners to the return of our Lord and savior Jesus Christ. Like John the Baptist, we are the voices of many crying out in the wilderness, Prepare the way of the Lord.

We are prophetic people. We are the oracles of the living God and now more than ever, the time has come to proclaim from the mountaintops, behold the Lord is coming with the clouds and every eye shall see Him. For surely our God desires to speak to His church and woo His bride to the wedding feast of the Lamb; to call her garments white, wash her in His blood, and to remove every spot and wrinkle. However, the voice of the bridegroom will not stop at the church. For nations shall hear, Our God Reigns. Truly, the time has come for the Elijahs of God to step forth and introduce the nations to our God.

Prophecy Defined

Vine's Expository Dictionary of New Testament Words defines prophecy as a noun that:

> *"Signifies the speaking forth of the mind and counsel of God. It is the declaration of that which cannot be known by natural means. It is the forth-telling of the will of God, whether concerning the past, the present, or the future."*

Dr. Bill Hamon states that:

> "A truly, divinely inspired prophecy is the Holy Spirit expressing the thoughts and desires of Christ through a human voice."

Derek Prince says that:

> "The gift of prophecy is the supernatural imparted ability to hear the voice of the Holy Spirit, and speak God's mind or counsel. Prophecy ministers primarily to the assembled group of believers but also to individuals. Its three main purposes are:
>
> 1. To edify, meaning to build up and strengthen, to make more effective.
>
> 2. To exhort, meaning to stimulate, or to encourage, or to admonish.
>
> 3. To comfort or to cheer up.

John Wimber wrote,

> "Prophecy is declaring the message of God to His church for the purpose of edification. It is not a skill, aptitude, or talent. It is the actual speaking forth of words given by the Spirit in a particular situation and season, this may be given in a poetic form or even in a song."

We can see here various definitions to prophecy, telling us various aspects of the prophetic. Vine's say's that prophecy contains the mind, counsel, and or will of God. Derek Prince points out the purposes of prophecy in the ministry to the church while Wimber brings in the variety of prophetic that includes poetic, oracle, and song. Prophecy is a wonderful gift to the body of Christ. Healthy prophecy in a healthy prophetic has the ability to stir the hearts of God's children and plant destiny into their souls. Prophecy is so important to the church that Paul in 1 Corinthians 14:1-5 says that we are to desire the prophetic gift due to the power of its ability to edify, exhort, and comfort the Church:

> *"Pursue love, and desire spiritual gifts, but especially that you may prophesy. For he who speaks in a tongue does not speak to men but to God, for no one understands him; however, in the spirit he speaks mysteries. But he who prophesies speaks edification and exhortation and comfort to men. He who speaks in a tongue edifies himself, but he who prophesies edifies the church. I wish you all spoke with tongues, but even more that you prophesied; for he who prophesies is greater than he who speaks with tongues, unless indeed he interprets, that the church may receive edification."*

We see this in action when Paul exhorts Timothy to take heed to his ministry and calling when he says:

> *"Let no one despise your youth, but be an example to the believers in word, in conduct, in love, in spirit, in faith, in purity. Till I come, give attention to reading, to exhortation, to doctrine. <u>Do not neglect the gift that is in you, which was given to you by prophecy with the laying on of the hands of the eldership.</u> Meditate on these things; give yourself entirely to them, that your progress may be evident to all. Take heed to yourself and to the doctrine. Continue in them, for in doing this you will save both yourself and those who hear you"*
>
> - 1 Timothy 12-16

Yet for some in the church, prophecy is something to be feared. They don't understand it and therefore turn their backs on it, which is contrary the Lord's desire. This is sad really because a healthy body of believers is one in which all its members function in unison and health. When all the gifts and offices are functioning in the church, the church is healthy and vibrant. Thank God we live in a day where there is good sound teaching on the subject and the prophetic is being revived in the church. For Peter's-sake, don't you know the church was birthed with the promise that its hallmark would be a prophetic people speaking as oracles of God and proclaiming what they see through visions and dreams, as declared by Peter:

> "And it shall come to pass in the last days, says God, that I will pour out of My Spirit on all flesh; Your sons and your daughters shall prophesy, Your young men shall see visions, Your old men shall dream dreams. And on My menservants and on My maidservants I will pour out My Spirit in those days; And they shall prophesy"
>
> - Acts 2:17-18

In fact, the Lord declares that He does nothing unless He reveals it to His servants the prophets:

> "Surely the Lord GOD does nothing, unless He reveals His secret to His servants the prophets. A lion has roared! Who will not fear? The Lord GOD has spoken! Who can but prophesy?"
>
> - Amos 3:7, 8

A church that embraces the prophetic is not only healthy it is endowed with reward, as Jesus declared:

> "He who receives a prophet in the name of a prophet shall receive a prophet's reward."
>
> - Matthew 10:41

However, to facilitate this desire for a healthy vibrant church I think it would be helpful to glean insight on the nature and personality of your typical prophetic person.

The Prophetic Person

Let's be honest, prophets are weird, and seers, weirder still. As Loren Sanford said:

> *"Who among those in the charismatic wing of the Church has not found at least some prophetic people to be 'a few French fries short of a Happy Meal'. They can be wonderful, but they can also come across as confusing, extreme, crusty, unbalanced, defensive and moody."*

I think church leaders struggle the most with prophetic people. They have a hard time learning how to pastor this kind of gift or personality. The regular folks in the church usually fall in two camps.

In the first camp you will find people that are overly attracted to them because of their supposed spirituality and its potential benefit to them, and in the second camp you will find people who are repelled by them for reasons they barely understand. Real acceptance is rare and when it happens, it is precious.

Loren Sanford, in his book "Understanding Prophetic People," Chosen Books (available on Amazon.com), points out some common characteristics found in prophetic people:

Rarely Content: at least until they have served long and made peace with their gift. Seasoned prophetic people who have persevered over time in seeking the presence and heart of God and have allowed suffering to effect their character changing it in ways it was intended to, come at last into a deep abiding peace and joy that are not easily shaken.

Burden Bearing: All prophetic people are burden bearers. They deeply feel everything in the hearts of people around them. Some feel it for nations, some for regions or the church, but they all feel. Without growth and understanding of what it means to bear burdens of the Lord, a prophet can become depressed or even isolated. They may think the emotions they are experiencing are their own and spin out in guilt or confusion. Only growth and maturity on how this gift functions will balance the roller coaster ride of feelings. They need to remember that Jesus is the burden bearer and not the prophet. Prophets are just servants co-laboring with Christ.

The Gift of Weakness: Often the path of a prophet is filled with bliss comingled with pain. It is in the painful places that Christ develops character. Paul said it best in 2 Corinthians 12:7-10:

> *"And lest I should be exalted above measure by the abundance of the revelations, a thorn in the flesh was given to me, a messenger of satan to buffet me, lest I be exalted above measure. Concerning this thing, I pleaded with the Lord three times that it might depart from me. And He said to me, 'My grace is sufficient for you, for My strength is made perfect in weakness.' Therefore most gladly I will rather boast in my infirmities, that the power of Christ may rest upon me. Therefore I take pleasure in infirmities, in reproaches, in needs, in persecutions, in distresses, for Christ's sake. For when I am weak, then I am strong."*

Eccentric Personalities: Prophetic folks are a bit strange. They don't think, feel, or act like the rest of the church. They are often misunderstood, and even rejected. At times, they don't even understand themselves. A church that has built a prophetic culture, allows room to grow and love prophets nurturing a space that values all the giftedness within the body of Christ.

Self-Protections: This can be a very harmful place to be in. Rejection, can lead to the sin of protectionism, which can result in seeing through the eyes of mistrust, thus filtering all that God is saying. When this happens it can lead a prophetic person to reject the very fellowship that would be so healing to his soul. This desire to protect by running away may feel like a safety net but in fact will bring about isolation and despair.

Loneliness and Isolation: Prophetic folks will often ask questions about life and faith that do not seem to matter to others, and they begin to wonder off into dreamland, as the rest of the world passes them by. They are impatient with things they deem shallow. Their quest consumes them and they may seem aloof. Because of the lack of common perspective, they have trouble relating to people and peers. They live as forerunners. They are usually one-step ahead of the rest of the body of Christ, and when the rest of the body of Christ catches up, and are filled with joy of being in this new season, the prophet has moved on to that next place. Because of this, a prophet may feel alone. If the prophetic person is unbalanced in their maturity of this gift, it will lead to isolation and deeper loneliness. This is a dangerous place to be, and prophets need to guard their hearts in this regard.

Unusual Experiences: When I first was saved, I thought all Christians experienced what I was experiencing. I didn't grow up in church, so my idea of Christianity came for the Scriptures and my own experiences. It would take me years to come to grips with the fact that not everybody sees or experiences what I do. Let's face it; trances, visions, dreams, burden bearing, contortions, strange healing modalities, and such are not typical for most people. Although, I sense this is changing in the body of Christ. People, in general seldom relate to these experiences. As a young prophet I walked alone, still do most of my time, but today it is in the right context, and within a healthy relationship in my church and family. A prophet needs balance, love, and correction from those who walk in other gifts.

Awareness Deficits: Prophetic people rarely think about how their actions, weird behavior, and the way they communicate are viewed in the eyes of other people. In general, people have a hard time understanding why prophetic folks do what they do. Just examine the lives of John the Baptist and Ezekiel and you will understand that God's view of normal is much different from that of society. Normal folks would never do what the prophets of old would do.

The Fruit of Rejection: Prophetic people will face rejection. They always have. Jeremiah was thrown down a well. Elijah fled for his life to escape death at the hands of Jezebel. His brothers sold Joseph as a slave. Prophetic people who have not made peace with their calling and have not honed their life balance through the healing hand of God can appear to be angry and defensive, geared up to take on the next assault. They will misread and misinterpret what people are saying. Prophetic people, like all of us, are a work in progress. It is extremely important for the prophet to be as forgiving as Jesus, and let love be their guiding motivation. Compassion and understanding always wins the day. Listen to the words of Jeremiah.

> "O Lord, You induced me, and I was persuaded; You are stronger than I, and have prevailed. I am in derision daily; Everyone mocks me. For when I spoke, I cried out; I shouted, "Violence and plunder!" Because the word of the Lord was made to me a reproach and a derision daily.
>
> Then I said, "I will not make mention of Him, nor speak anymore in His name." But His word was in my heart like a burning fire shut up in my bones; I was weary of holding it back, and I could not. For I heard many mocking: "Fear on every side!" "Report," they say, "and we will report it!" All my acquaintances watched for my stumbling,

saying, "Perhaps he can be induced; Then we will prevail against him, And we will take our revenge on him."

- Jeremiah 20:7-10

Life-Threatening Events: It is not uncommon for those that have a high calling of God on their lives to be born in some type of trauma, especially as children. The enemy of our souls has a stake in cutting off our destiny before it can happen, especially if that destiny will affect the lives of many. It has always been that way. Just read "Fox's Book of Martyrs" or DC Talk's "Jesus Freaks" and you will get a glimpse at the warfare struggle.

Too serious about Life: Prophetic people are always serious. Everything has a sense of urgency to it. They are driven by destiny and urgency all of their lives. Consequently, life balance is difficult for them. They never seem to find time to play or room to laugh. It is only after years of being seasoned in what I do that I have learned to enjoy life in all its fullness.

How to deal with and nurture prophetic people

In light of this it is imperative that prophetic people be mentored and blossom in a church that has a prophetic culture of honor and love. Pastors and leaders must nurture prophetic people with gracious understanding, without taking offense at their quirks or brokenness. Prophetic people need loving friends, folks that will drive them to balance, laugh with them and teach them to play. The church also needs prayer warriors – watchmen on the wall, who hold up the prophets and other leaders in the church, and cover them with intersession.

Finely, the church needs to foster a prophetic culture. A prophetic culture is one where the prophecy is as normal as the rest of the gifts and offices are. It does not elevate it nor dismiss it. Weighing and testing happens naturally at a grass-roots level. There is a culture of peace and not fear or confusion. It encourages growth and mentorship. Equipping the saints for ministry is a high core value. The body is alive with worship and their only goal is to seek the face of Jesus and love Him.

Types of Prophetic People

Often, there is confusion regarding how much authority prophetic gifted people carry. People often ask, "Doesn't the prophetic add to the scripture and if so isn't that wrong?" The simple answer is no. Let's look at the Scriptures and examine the activity of the prophets and their ministry to get a clearer understanding of this answer.

In the Old Testament

In the Old and New Testaments, we find two levels of the prophetic given. We see the ministry of certain prophets in the Old Testament and Apostles in the New Testament whose ministry was used to give us the Scriptures. These men spoke the very Words of God. On the other hand, we see the ministry of certain prophets in the Old Testament and prophets in the New Testament who ministered to fellow members of the community. These men spoke a message from God to one another but their words were the words of men inspired by God.

In the Old Testament, the prophets who spoke the very words of God were messengers sent by God. This is seen in the following verses:

> "Then Haggai, the Lord's messenger, spoke the Lord's message to the people, saying, "I am with you, says the Lord."
>
> - Haggai 1:13

> "The vision of Obadiah. Thus says the Lord GOD concerning Edom (We have heard a report from the Lord, and a messenger has been sent among the nations, saying, 'Arise, and let us rise up against her for battle.')"
>
> - Obadiah 1:1

> "And He sent word by the hand of Nathan the prophet: So he called his name Jedidiah, because of the Lord."
>
> - 2 Samuel 12:25

You can see from these verses that God divinely sent these men to the people. They were called messengers and ambassadors of the Lord God. We also know that their very words were God's words. In Deuteronomy 18:18 the Lord says:

> "I will raise up for them a Prophet like you from among their brethren, and will put My words in His mouth, and He shall speak to them all that I command Him."

And in Jeremiah 1:9:

> "Then the Lord put forth His hand and touched my mouth, and the Lord said to me: "Behold, I have put My words in your mouth."

In Ezekiel 2:7 we read:

> "You shall speak My words to them, whether they hear or whether they refuse, for they are rebellious."

These men spoke the very words of God. Their mission was to be the very mouthpiece of the Lord.

In addition to being sent by God as messengers of the Lord and speaking the very words of God, their words carried absolute divine authority. In Deuteronomy 18:19 we are told that the Lord required obedience to the words spoken by this kind of prophet, for they were God's words, and in rejecting the words of the prophet, you are rejecting God (1 Samuel 8:7). The disobedience of the people to the Lord's prophet often brought judgment and the wrath of God (2 Chronicles 25:16; 18:1-34).

In addition to the prophets that spoke the very words of God and give us the Scriptures, there were other prophets in the Old Testament who spoke with the words of men (that is to say their words did not generate scripture.)

A good example of this is found in the ministry of Elijah and Elisha in the books of Kings. The record of their ministry shown in the Kings is there to illustrate the use of the prophetic in the Kingdom of God. It is a historical narrative of the Kings from Solomon to Zedekiah, from a Kingdom in tranquility to the fall of Judah and exile to Babylonia. We see the ministry of these men as they interact with the Kings of this nation and the nations of others.

We also see in this historical narrative, there were companies of prophets at various locations (1 Samuel 10; 2 Kings 2:3, 5, 7; 4:38; 6:1).

> *"Now the sons of the prophets who were at Bethel came out to Elisha, and said to him, "Do you know that the Lord will take away your master from over you today?"*
>
> *And he said, "Yes, I know; keep silent!"*
>
> *Then Elijah said to him, "Elisha, stay here, please, for the Lord has sent me on to Jericho."*

> But he said, "As the Lord lives, and as your soul lives, I will not leave you!" So they came to Jericho.
>
> Now the sons of the prophets who were at Jericho came to Elisha and said to him, "Do you know that the Lord will take away your master from over you today?"
>
> So he answered, "Yes, I know; keep silent!"
>
> - 2 Kings 2:3-5

These prophets, found in the book of Kings, were there when Elijah was taken to heaven. They watched as the mantle of anointing was passed to Elisha. In this, we also see a hierarchy in prophetic authority. It appears that the prophetic ministry of Elijah and Elisha were greater than that of the other prophets. They appear to be the elders or teachers to the sons of the prophets as illustrated in the following verses.

> "Now when the sons of the prophets who were from Jericho saw him, they said, "The spirit of Elijah rests on Elisha." And they came to meet him, and bowed to the ground before him."
>
> - 2 Kings 2:15

> "And Elisha returned to Gilgal, and there was a famine in the land. Now the sons of the prophets were sitting before him; and he said to his servant, "Put on the large pot, and boil stew for the sons of the prophets."
>
> - 2 Kings 4:38

> "And Elisha the prophet called one of the sons of the prophets, and said to him, "Get yourself ready, take this flask of oil in your hand, and go to Ramoth Gilead."
>
> - 2 Kings 9:1

Here we see the prophets not only giving reverence to the ministry of Elisha but taking orders and being directed by the prophet

Elisha. The younger prophets ran errands for Elisha (2 Kings 9:1-13). Yet the Lord tells us that he used the ministry of all the prophets to speak to the nation of Israel, and Judah, as seen in the following verse.

> *"Yet the Lord testified against Israel and against Judah, by all of His prophets, every seer, saying, 'Turn from your evil ways, and keep My commandments and My statutes, according to all the law which I commanded your fathers, and which I sent to you by My servants the prophets.'"*
>
> - 2 Kings 17:13

We also see that Nathan delivered messages from God (2 Samuel 12:1-14) and that David had court prophets, which were in his service, to help him make decisions (2 Samuel 7:1-17). Baalim was also a prophet who got messages from God for the people (Numbers 22-25). Prophets of less stature are throughout the Scriptures. We have Ahijah who prophesied against Jeroboam (1 Kings 14:1-18), and the man from Judah who prophesied against the altars at Bethel (1 Kings 13:1-32). In the Old Testament we see traveling Prophets, who were Seers of the Lord, i.e., Samuel, Elijah, and Elisha. We also see Temple Prophets such as Ezekiel and Jeremiah; and Court Prophets, Nathan, Gad, Asaph, Heman, Jedthun who were David's Seers. Finely we see the Free Prophets who held no priestly or court office, such as Amos, Hosea, Micah, and Isaiah.

In the New Testament

In the New Testament, we see Apostles whose function was similar to the same as the Old Testament prophets who gave us the Scriptures. These men were messengers of Christ (John 20:21; Acts 22:21; 2 Corinthians 5:20). They spoke the very words of God (Galatians 1:11-12; John 14:26; 16:13-14; 2 Peter 3:2; 1 Thessalonians 2:13; 2 Peter 3:15-16). The level of gifting from God in their lives was to complete the cannon of Scriptures and lay the foundation that the church would be built on.

In addition to the Apostles we also see another kind of prophetic activity found in the New Testament. These prophets ministered to the church speaking the heart of God through the words of men. Their purpose was not to give us the Scriptures but to operate in the body of Christ.

In Acts 11:27-29 we have Agabus predicting a famine in Antioch.

> *"And in these days prophets came from Jerusalem to Antioch. Then one of them, named Agabus, stood up and showed by the Spirit that there was going to be a great famine throughout all the world, which also happened in the days of Claudius Caesar. Then the disciples, each according to his ability, determined to send relief to the brethren dwelling in Judea."*

We also see in Acts 21:9-11 where Agabus warns Paul about impending persecution from the Jews in Jerusalem.

> *"Now this man had four virgin daughters who prophesied. And as we stayed many days, a certain prophet named Agabus came down from Judea. When he had come to us, he took Paul's belt, bound his own hands and feet, and said, "Thus says the Holy Spirit, 'So shall the Jews at Jerusalem bind the man who owns this belt, and deliver him into the hands of the Gentiles."*

Prophetic gifting is also found in relationship to the commission of Paul and Barnabus for a special mission (Acts 13:1) and with Judas and Silas at Antioch (Acts 15:32). The Prophets predicted Paul's trials (Acts 20:32), and warned Paul of trouble at Jerusalem (Acts 21:4). Phillip's daughters are said to be prophetess (Acts

21:9), and Timothy learns of his gifts through prophecy (1 Timothy 1:18).

> "This charge I commit to you, son Timothy, according to the prophecies previously made concerning you, that by them you may wage the good warfare,"

And in 1 Timothy 4:14-16 we read:

> "Do not neglect the gift that is in you, which was given to you by prophecy with the laying on of the hands of the eldership. Meditate on these things; give yourself entirely to them, that your progress may be evident to all. Take heed to yourself and to the doctrine. Continue in them, for in doing this you will save both yourself and those who hear you."

It is evident in scripture there are varying degrees of authority attributed to different levels of prophetic utterance. The New Testament Apostles were functioning in a similar role as that of the Old Testament prophets that gave us the Scriptures. Yet, in the Scriptures, we also see another level of Prophetic activity that occurs in both the Old and New Testaments, these were the prophets that spoke the words of men. Their prophetic activity was initiated by the Spirit of God, was spoken through human words or actions, and was a mixture of the Spirit and humanity. These prophets who spoke the words of men did not leave us the Scriptures. Their purpose was on the day-to-day activity of the church in the lives of individuals. Agabus, Silas, Judas, Phillip's daughters, and the prophets in the church at Corinth demonstrate this.

For the Church today, prophecy operates at the second level. The prophets and Apostles handed down to us the Scriptures that were the very words of God and have supreme authority in the church. Prophecy spoken today does not carry the same degree of authority as the Scriptures.

CHAPTER 25

Prophetic Layers

"Surely the Lord GOD does nothing, unless He reveals His secret to His servants the prophets. A lion has roared! Who will not fear? The Lord GOD has spoken! Who can but prophesy?"

- Amos 3:7, 8

"For there is nothing hidden which will not be revealed, nor has anything been kept secret but that it should come to light. If anyone has ears to hear, let him hear. Then He said to them, 'Take heed what you hear. With the same measure you use, it will be measured to you; and to you who hear, more will be given. For whoever has, to him more will be given; but whoever does not have, even what he has will be taken away from him.'"

- Mark 4:22-25

The gifts and callings of God come from Him. He is the one that calls and distributes as He wills. Jesus illustrated this when He told His disciples:

> "You did not choose Me, but I chose you and appointed you that you should go and bear fruit, and that your fruit should remain, that whatever you ask the Father in My name He may give you."
>
> - John 15:16

It is Christ that gives the ascension gifts:

> "Therefore He says: "When He ascended on high, He led captivity captive, and gave gifts to men."
>
> ... And He Himself gave some to be apostles, some prophets, some evangelists, and some pastors and teachers, for the equipping of the saints for the work of ministry, for the edifying of the body of Christ,"
>
> - Ephesians 4:8, 11-12

This is further elaborated on in Paul's letter to Corinth:

> "And God has appointed these in the church: first apostles, second prophets, third teachers, after that miracles, then gifts of healings, helps, administrations, varieties of tongues."
>
> - 1 Corinthians 12:28

We are told to desire Spiritual gifts and to desire the gift of prophecy yet it is God who places the offices in the church.

Mike Bickle, in speaking about contemporary prophetic ministry gifts, identifies four levels of prophetic ministry. His outline of the prophetic is very helpful in identifying the ingredients of development in prophetic ministry. This four level framework is simply a starting place to look at the function of the prophetic within the church today. Mike Bickle clearly states that this is just a starting place and after further research, it may become apparent that more levels are needed.

Simple Prophecy

The first level is that of Simple Prophecy, that is someone who speaks something that God brings to mind. This kind of prophecy is illustrated in Acts:

> "And it shall come to pass in the last days, says God, that I will pour out of My Spirit on all flesh; Your sons and your daughters shall prophesy, your young men shall see visions,
>
> Your old men shall dream dreams. And on My menservants and on My maidservants I will pour out My Spirit in those days; And they shall prophesy."
>
> - Acts 2:17, 18

Paul adds to this where he says that:

> "For you can all prophesy one by one, that all may learn and all may be encouraged."
>
> - 1 Corinthians 14:31

This level of gifting is from the Holy Spirit to equip the church for edification, exhortation, and comfort, to one another (1 Corinthians 14:3.) This gift is available to all believers.

Prophetic Gifting

The second level is that of Prophetic Gifting. This gift falls into the same category as level 1 of simple prophecy but it differs in that the person operating in this gift is beginning to bud forth more of a prophetic anointing. This level is the starting point of the separation of simple prophecy, available to all, and the Gift of Prophecy is exercised on a regular bases. An individual moving in this realm should be honed for leadership and be discipled and nurtured on a regular base. His main purpose is still to edify, exhort, and to comfort.

Prophetic Ministry

The third level is that of Prophetic Ministry. These are individuals who have been released by the church for ministry. Their gifting is much broader than that of the 1 Corinthians 14 model for in this level there is a measure of authority within the local assembly, but they may travel outside the local church to minister to other members of the body. Often those moving in this level also will operate with many of the other sign gifts, i.e., healing, miracles, and deliverance. In addition, there is strong insight into directional and correctional ministry.

Office of Prophet

The fourth and final level is that of the Office of Prophet. These individuals have a far-reaching ministry to the body of Christ. Their influence is more international, and natural signs (as in the Old Testament) often confirm their words. Their words carry much authority and they often move in the signs and wonders gifts. They have a current flow of revelation to include angelic visitation, and open visions. At times, they will speak of things that are not spiritual, i.e., natural events and things that speak to the nations. There is also revelation regarding future events and moves of the Holy Spirit worldwide.

Growing as a prophet

Learning to grow in your prophetic gift involves more than simply hearing and seeing, it involves lifestyle change and a Godly character built upon the word of God. Here are a few keys to your success.

Immersed in the Word: To grow as a prophet of the Lord it is imperative that you be filled with the word of God. Study the Scriptures. Meditate on the texts concerning prophecy. This takes a disciplined life style.

Prayer: There needs to be strong emphases on prayer and intersession.

Character: Your Christian character is very important. The words of a prophet are judged first by the fruits of a prophet. Learn to weigh prophecy, both yours and others. Ask God to grant you wisdom (James 1:5). You must desire to walk blameless before all men letting your light shine forth as outlined in 1 Timothy and Titus.

Correctable and teachable: You must be correctable, teachable, and fall under the leadership of your church or governing body. It is very important to be in a learning environment such as a home group at your church. Search out elders within your church who will help you grow up in your gift. Recognize the value of prophecy in the church (1 Corinthians 14:3).

Seek and Release: Ask God for the gift of prophecy. We are encouraged to seek after and desire to prophecy (1 Corinthians 14:1,39). Ask your pastor to lay hands on you to receive the gift of prophecy (Romans 1:11; 1 Timothy 4:14; 2 Timothy 1:6). Finely you must be in love with Jesus Christ. Be obedient if God releases prophecy to you. Respond to the Holy Spirit.

Forms of Prophecy

> *"So Samuel grew, and the Lord was with him and let none of his words fall to the ground. And all Israel from Dan to Beersheba knew that Samuel had been established as a prophet of the Lord. Then the Lord appeared again in Shiloh. For the Lord revealed Himself to Samuel in Shiloh by the word of the Lord."*
>
> - 1 Samuel 3:19-21

In the bible, we see various forms of the prophetic. Like a painter's palate the rainbow of colors in which God expresses Himself to His people is a reflection of His divine creative nature. The colors are as vast with variety as the personalities traits found in His people.

The Prophetic Oracle

In Isaiah 49:5-7, we see "The Prophetic Oracle."

> *"And now the Lord says, who formed Me from the womb to be His Servant, to bring Jacob back to Him, so that Israel is gathered to Him (For I shall be glorious in the eyes of the Lord, and My God shall be My strength), Indeed He says, 'It is too small a thing that You should be My Servant to raise up the tribes of Jacob, and to restore the preserved ones of Israel; I will also give You as a light to the Gentiles, that You should be My salvation to the ends of the earth. Thus says the Lord, the Redeemer of Israel, their Holy One, To Him whom man despises, To Him whom the nation abhors, To the Servant of rulers: "Kings shall see and arise, Princes also shall worship, Because of the Lord who is faithful, The Holy One of Israel; and He has chosen You."*

This can also be seen in the New Testament in Acts 13:1-3.

> *"Now in the church that was at Antioch there were certain prophets and teachers: Barnabas, Simeon who was called Niger, Lucius of Cyrene, Manaen who had been brought up with Herod the tetrarch, and Saul. As they ministered to the Lord and fasted, the Holy Spirit said, "Now separate to Me Barnabas and Saul for the work to which I have called them." Then, having fasted and prayed, and laid hands on them, they sent them away."*

The word "oracle" in the Greek is the word "Logion." It is a diminutive of the word "logos" meaning a word, narrative, or statement and it is divine in that it is a message from God to His people. In the New Testament the use of the word "oracle" can be seen in 1 Peter 4:10-11.

> *"As each one has received a gift, minister it to one another, as good stewards of the manifold grace of God. If anyone speaks, let him speak as the oracles of God. If anyone ministers, let him do it as with the ability which God supplies, that in all things God may be glorified through Jesus Christ, to whom belong the glory and the dominion forever and ever. Amen."*

Here we see oracle and its relationship to the full council of God, or totality in teaching. This I would say is the call for walking and living a life founded upon the Logos thereby causing the Rhema of God to come forth. This is not an addition to scripture as we discussed earlier. Let's look at a Prophetic Oracle found in the book of Acts.

> *"Now in the church that was at Antioch there were certain prophets and teachers: Barnabas, Simeon who was called Niger, Lucius of Cyrene, Manaen who had been brought up with Herod the tetrarch, and Saul. As they ministered to the Lord and fasted, the Holy Spirit said,*

> "Now separate to Me Barnabas and Saul for the work to which I have called them."
>
> - Acts 13:1, 2

Prophetic Exhortation

In Isaiah 12:1-6 and Acts 15:30-35, we have an example of "The Prophetic Exhortation." The meaning of exhortation denotes the idea of calling one to one's side, to entreat, an appeal, encouragement, and consolation. Let's look at these two examples of the "Prophetic Exhortation."

> "And in that day you will say: "O Lord, I will praise You; Though You were angry with me, Your anger is turned away, and You comfort me. Behold, God is my salvation, I will trust and not be afraid; 'For YAH, the Lord, is my strength and song; He also has become my salvation.'" Therefore with joy you will draw water from the wells of salvation. And in that day you will say: "Praise the Lord, call upon His name; Declare His deeds among the peoples, make mention that His name is exalted. Sing to the Lord, for He has done excellent things; This is known in all the earth. Cry out and shout, O inhabitant of Zion, for great is the Holy One of Israel in your midst!"
>
> - Isaiah 12:1-6

Here the prophet is giving a prophetic word of encouragement, hope, and future blessing. We can also see this type of prophetic word in the book of Acts.

> "So when they were sent off, they came to Antioch; and when they had gathered the multitude together, they delivered the letter. When they had read it, they rejoiced over its encouragement. Now Judas and Silas, themselves being prophets also, exhorted and strengthened the brethren with many words. And after they had stayed

there for a time, they were sent back with greetings from the brethren to the apostles. However, it seemed good to Silas to remain there. Paul and Barnabas also remained in Antioch, teaching and preaching the word of the Lord, with many others also."

- Acts 15:30-35

In this example, we also get an explanation of the impact of Judas and Silas's words "exhorted and strengthened the brethren."

The Prophetic Prayer

In Nehemiah 9:6-37 we have an outstanding picture of "Prophetic Prayer." This kind of prayer is an anointed prayer where the Spirit of God steps in as intercessor and bubbles forth the heart of God. Linked to Prophetic Prayer is the prayer of intersession. When intersession is combined with Prophetic insight, it becomes much more powerful, cutting through the heart of the matter and cries out God's solutions to a given situation. Let's look at Luke 1:67-69 for an example of Prophetic Prayer.

> *"Now his father Zacharias was filled with the Holy Spirit, and prophesied, saying: "Blessed is the Lord God of Israel, for He has visited and redeemed His people, and has raised up a horn of salvation for us in the house of His servant David,"*

The Prophetic Song

Now let's look at prophecy in the form of a song. The song of Moses, found in Deuteronomy 32:1-43, is a beautiful example of "The Prophetic Song." Paul tells us in 1 Corinthians 14:15, "What is it then? I will pray with the spirit, and I will pray with the understanding also: I will sing with the spirit, and I will sing with the understanding also." Moreover, in Ephesians 5:19 "Speaking to yourselves in psalms and hymns and spiritual songs, singing and making melody in your heart to the Lord"; In Deuteronomy 31:30 we see that Moses sang to the people of God. "And Moses spake in the ears of all the congregation of Israel the words of this song, until they were ended." In Isaiah 42, we see the prophet Isaiah break into song in the midst of prophecy.

> "Sing to the Lord a new song, and His praise from the ends of the earth, you who go down to the sea, and all that is in it, you coastlands and you inhabitants of them! Let the wilderness and its cities lift up their voice, the villages that Kedar inhabits. Let the inhabitants of Sela sing, let them shout from the top of the mountains. Let them give glory to the Lord, and declare His praise in the coastlands. The Lord shall go forth like a mighty man;
>
> He shall stir up His zeal like a man of war. He shall cry out, yes, shout aloud; He shall prevail against His enemies."
>
> - Isaiah 42:10-13

Personal Prophecy

There is also an aspect of prophecy that takes the form of "Personal Prophecy." The "Personal Prophecy" is not only very popular today but controversial as well. I believe this kind of ministry is very important to the body of Christ. Yet, like anything else there needs to be balance. "Personal Prophecy" is a prophetic Rehma word from God to an individual. "Personal Prophecy" may cover topics concerning gifts, callings, ministries, God's will in a situation, romance or marriage, births, geographical moves, or simply your walk with God.

A good prophetic culture creates guidelines for how to administer personal prophecy and frowns upon what we call "parking lot" prophecies. Like all prophecy, the word needs to be judged and confirmed in the body of Christ with the understanding that "Personal Prophecy" is always "in part" and not the whole picture. And it always will stir a witness of the Holy Spirit in the heart of the receiver. Let's look at 2 Samuel 12:1-7 where we have an example of "Personal Prophecy."

> "Then the Lord sent Nathan to David. And he came to him, and said to him: "There were two men in one city, one rich and the other poor. The rich man had exceedingly many flocks and herds. But the poor man had nothing, except one little ewe lamb which he had bought and nourished; and it grew up together with him and with his children. It ate of his own food and drank from his own cup and lay in his bosom; and it was like a daughter to him. And a traveler came to the rich man, who refused to take from his own flock and from his own herd to prepare one for the wayfaring man who had come to him; but he took the poor man's lamb and prepared it for the man who had come to him."
>
> So David's anger was greatly aroused against the man, and he said to Nathan, "As the Lord lives, the man who has done this shall surely die! And he shall restore fourfold for the lamb, because he did this thing and because he had no pity."
>
> Then Nathan said to David, "You are the man! Thus says the Lord God of Israel: 'I anointed you king over Israel, and I delivered you from the hand of Saul."
>
> \- 2 Samuel 12:1-7

Here we see Nathan giving a personal prophecy of correction to David. He does so through the vehicle of a story. In it God draws shows David the depth of his sin. In the book of Acts 21:9-11 we have, another "Personal Prophecy" combined with "Prophetic Action." Let's read.

> *"Now this man had four virgin daughters who prophesied. And as we stayed many days, a certain prophet named Agabus came down from Judea. When he had come to us, he took Paul's belt, bound his own hands and feet, and said, "Thus says the Holy Spirit, 'So shall the Jews at Jerusalem bind the man who owns this belt, and deliver him into the hands of the Gentiles.'"*

> - Acts 21:9-11

Prophetic Action

The "Prophetic Action" is found all throughout the Old Testament. This kind of Prophetic communication is a physical acting out what the Lord is saying. It is dramatic and is always done at the Lord's command and not at the whim of an individual. In Jeremiah 13:1-11 we have a good example of the "Prophetic Action."

> *"Thus the Lord said to me: "Go and get yourself a linen sash, and put it around your waist, but do not put it in water." So I got a sash according to the word of the Lord, and put it around my waist. And the word of the Lord came to me the second time, saying, "Take the sash that you acquired, which is around your waist, and arise, go to the Euphrates, and hide it there in a hole in the rock." So I went and hid it by the Euphrates, as the Lord commanded me.*

> *Now it came to pass after many days that the Lord said to me, "Arise, go to the Euphrates, and take from there the sash which I commanded you to hide there." Then I went to the Euphrates and dug, and I took the sash from the place where I had hidden it; and there was the sash, ruined. It was profitable for nothing.*

> *Then the word of the Lord came to me, saying, "Thus says the Lord: 'In this manner I will ruin the pride of Judah and the great pride of Jerusalem. This evil people, who refuse to hear My words, who follow the dictates of*

their hearts, and walk after other gods to serve them and worship them, shall be just like this sash which is profitable for nothing. For as the sash clings to the waist of a man, so I have caused the whole house of Israel and the whole house of Judah to cling to Me,' says the Lord, 'that they may become My people, for renown, for praise, and for glory; but they would not hear.'"

- Jeremiah 13:1-11

Prophetic Action is drama. It is parabolic in nature and demonstrates the word of God metaphorically. Jeremiah is a perfect example of this in action. His action with the sash was parabolic to the nation's condition and God's word to them, "For as the sash clings to the waist of a man, so I have caused the whole house of Israel and the whole house of Judah to cling to Me,' says the Lord, 'that they may become My people, for renown, for praise, and for glory; but they would not hear."

Chapter 26

PROPHETIC DREAMS & VISIONS

"Then the Lord came down in the pillar of cloud and stood in the door of the tabernacle, and called Aaron and Miriam. And they both went forward. Then He said, "Hear now My words: If there is a prophet among you, I, the Lord, make Myself known to him in a vision; I speak to him in a dream."

- Numbers 12:5, 6

"He sought God in the days of Zechariah, who had understanding in the visions of God; and as long as he sought the Lord, God made him prosper."

- 2 Chronicles 26:5

As you can see, the prophetic word of God can come in many forms, shapes, and sizes. I would like to zoom in on the use of visions and dreams in the prophetic. Prophetic visions and dreams are all throughout the Scriptures. In Deuteronomy 13:1 a Prophet is referred to as a "Dreamer of Dreams." In Numbers 12 we read:

> "Then the Lord came down in the pillar of cloud and stood in the door of the tabernacle, and called Aaron and Miriam. And they both went forward. Then He said, "Hear now My words: If there is a prophet among you,
>
> I, the Lord, make Myself known to him in a vision; I speak to him in a dream."
>
> - Numbers 12:5, 6

Prophetic Seeing

A good example of "Prophetic Seeing" is found in Isaiah 6:1-8. Let's read:

> "In the year that King Uzziah died, I saw the Lord sitting on a throne, high and lifted up, and the train of His robe filled the temple. Above it stood seraphim; each one had six wings: with two he covered his face, with two he covered his feet, and with two he flew. And one cried to another and said: "Holy, holy, holy is the Lord of hosts; The whole earth is full of His glory!" And the posts of the door were shaken by the voice of him who cried out, and the house was filled with smoke. So I said: "Woe is me, for I am undone! Because I am a man of unclean lips, and I dwell in the midst of a people of unclean lips; For my eyes have seen the King, the Lord of hosts." Then one of the seraphim flew to me, having in his hand a live coal which he had taken with the tongs from the altar.
>
> - Isaiah 6:1-8

Another example of "Prophetic Seeing" is found in the book of the Prophet Daniel. Let's look at Daniel's dream (-Daniel 7:1-15).

> "In the first year of Belshazzar king of Babylon, Daniel had a dream and visions of his head while on his bed. Then he wrote down the dream, telling the main facts. Daniel spoke, saying, "I saw in my

vision by night, and behold, the four winds of heaven were stirring up the Great Sea. And four great beasts came up from the sea, each different from the other. The first was like a lion, and had eagle's wings. I watched till its wings were plucked off; and it was lifted up from the earth and made to stand on two feet like a man, and a man's heart was given to it.

"And suddenly another beast, a second, like a bear. It was raised up on one side, and had three ribs in its mouth between its teeth. And they said thus to it: 'Arise, devour much flesh!' "After this I looked, and there was another, like a leopard, which had on its back four wings of a bird. The beast also had four heads, and dominion was given to it. "After this I saw in the night visions, and behold, a fourth beast, dreadful and terrible, exceedingly strong. It had huge iron teeth; it was devouring, breaking in pieces, and trampling the residue with its feet.

It was different from all the beasts that were before it, and it had ten horns. I was considering the horns, and there was another horn, a little one, coming up among them, before whom three of the first horns were plucked out by the roots. And there, in this horn, were eyes like the eyes of a man, and a mouth speaking pompous words.

"I watched till thrones were put in place, and the Ancient of Days was seated; His garment was white as snow, and the hair of His head was like pure wool. His throne was a fiery flame, its wheels a burning fire; A fiery stream issued and came forth from before Him. A thousand thousands ministered to Him; Ten thousand times ten thousand stood before Him. The court was seated, and the books were opened. "I watched then because of the sound of the pompous words which the horn was speaking; I watched till the beast was slain, and its body destroyed and given to the burning flame. As *for the rest of the beasts, they had their dominion taken away, yet their lives were prolonged for a season and a time.*

"I was watching in the night visions, and behold, One like the Son of Man, coming with the clouds of heaven! He came to the Ancient of Days, and they brought Him near before Him. Then to Him was given dominion and glory and a kingdom, that all peoples, nations, and languages should serve Him. His dominion is an everlasting dominion, which shall not pass away, and His kingdom the one which shall not be destroyed. "I, Daniel, was grieved in my spirit within my body, and the visions of my head troubled me."

Illustrative Examples

Now let's look at a few personal examples of visions and dreams, relating to various aspects of Prophetic Ministry.

Illustration One: Personal Prophecy

Not too long ago while praying with Debbie, a friend of mine, the Lord gave me a vision. In this vision, I saw a wooded area with a stream running through it. Debbie was running along the side of the stream, shooting and darting through the woods. The look on her face was intense and urgent.

Next to her in the river was a salmon swimming upstream. As I looked at Debbie running she suddenly stopped, as if she was in pain. She reached down and took hold of her foot. She was wearing a pair of moccasins. I noticed there was a hole in the bottom of one of her moccasins. Debbie had a rock or something in her moccasins that was causing her to stumble.

As I began to share this vision with Debbie, the presence of God was all over me. I began to speak as the Lord gave me utterance.

> *"Child you have sought Me with all your heart and you have ran the race that I have set before you with diligence and perseverance. Yet every time you stumble, you beat yourself up with condemnation feeling that I have rejected you. Yet it is this rejection and pain that I have come to heal.*
>
> *For I have not rejected you, says the Lord. I have purchased you for a price more precious than Gold, I have paid for all the pain and the hurt, and I have come to give you life and that more abundantly. I have come to take away the pain of that which causes you to fall and give you a new pair of shoes, fitted for you and the race that I have called you to.*
>
> *For as the salmon swims up stream to give birth to that which I have put in him, so you shall run and give birth to that which I have put in you. For your feet shall be as hinds feet, set upon a Rock. That Rock is the Rock of your salvation. No longer shall the stubble of this thing, cause you to stumble, for I have broken the curse that has clung to your path and given you new shoes to run with, says the Lord."*

The outcome of this personal prophecy to Debbie was truly a point of breakthrough for her. Over the following months, this word from Lord had revitalized her walk with Him. The Lord had healed the spirit of rejection that weighed her down and given her a new vigor. Today she works full time in ministry with Mercy Chefs.

Illustration Two: Personal Prophecy

Let me share with you another example of a personal prophecy that will help to illuminate visions and the prophetic. A few years back while ministering personal prophecy at a church in Richmond Virginia, during one of their School of the Holy Spirit nights, I received a vision for a gentleman in the church.

In this vision, I saw a boat floating on a lake. The boat had several life preservers along its side. This man was trying to sit in a lounge chair and relax but every time he began to sit down the waves of the lake began to rise up and he could never sit.

I shared the vision with this brother and the Lord gave me this word to give to Him:

> *"All your life you have been a protector to your children. You have taught them the ways of the Lord and have given them My light that they may serve Me. Just as you have been a life preserver to them in a time of trouble so I AM to you. Trust Me to be your Father. Trust Me to be that life preserver that takes care of all of you. For surely I shall watch over your children. I shall protect them and help them in the time of need. Yet know I have come to help you, says God. I have come to refresh your soul and give you a season of rest from the worry that rises up against you. Trust Me O child of mine and I shall be your skipper, your anchor, and your quiet place. Now be refreshed. Be released from so much responsibility; and know this, that I, the Lord, today, have given you rest. Receive my Spirit and know that my peace shall refresh your soul, says God."*

As I shared this word to this dear brother, I could see waves of the Spirit refresh him, as tears rolled down the sides of his face. God desires to speak to His children. He desires to touch them right where they are, and give them abundant life in this hard world that we live in.

Illustration Three: Personal Prophecy

One final example of personal prophecy will suffice for our purposes here. One day several years ago while ministering to a group of employees at CBN the Lord gave me a vision for a dear lady named Lola. In this vision, I saw the hand of the Lord upon Lola. On His hand, he was wearing a ring with various stones in it. In His other hand, He held a scepter with sparkling jewels that shined forth-tremendous light. Lola was standing with her head down sadness filled her countenance.

The Lord spoke to my heart and said,

> "This ring on My finger is Lola's family and every stone within it are the birth stones of her children."

I shared this vision with Lola and then the Lord gave me this word to give her.

> "Daughter of Mine, I am the lifter of your head, the God of your salvation, the Lord of Comfort in your time of need. You have worried about the destiny of your children, whether they will serve me or serve the fallen one, and sadness has filled your heart. Know this, that I am for you, says the Lord, and I have heard the tears of your sorrow. For with every tear that falls to the ground I have caused it to water the seed that is within your children. Do not fear for their souls for My hand is upon them even as My hand has been upon you. I have placed them upon the ring of My finger and with My scepter I have upheld the desires of your heart.
>
> For the jewels on My finger have become the jewels on your crown, for you are my faithful one and your children are set into sockets of pure gold tried in the fire and they shall illuminate the light of My glory. Remember My ways are not your ways; but know this that the way that I have chosen is truly the best way for I am the way the

truth and the life, and today I have given you a crown of promise to cover your household. So lift up your head and behold the God of your salvation."

With teary eyes, Lola lifted her head in praise unto God. The power of His presence pierced through hopelessness and despair, bringing about faith in the author and giver of life. Oh how wonderful are His ways, how majestic is His name among those who love Him.

Prophecy and Directional Seeing

Directional seeing is the process in which the Lord shows you something that is specifically related to gaining understanding regarding direction. This may be for you or for someone else.

Illustration One – Directional Seeing

Let me use this example to illustrate directional seeing. In 1980, I was attending fellowship at Calvary Chapel of Costa Mesa in California. Every Friday night Pastor Chuck Smith would host a Christian concert through Maranatha Music to minister to the youth. One night, after the concert was over the lead singer for the band made a call to all who would like to participate in "One Day at a Time Prison Ministries." The Lord touched my heart so powerfully that I shot out of my chair and went up to volunteer for that ministry. Over the next several weeks we went to local jails and prisons, ministering to those incarcerated. During that time I met a gentleman, I'll call Bob (not his real name). Bob was a professional businessman and was very involved in the political arena and revitalization projects in Orange County. Bob and I became good friends.

My time in prison ministry was cut short when the Lord called my wife and me to Canada to open a Hotel. The next six months we spent our time in the icy cold of Canada. When we returned from Canada, the Lord placed it upon my heart to get a hold of Bob. For the next few weeks I looked for Bob, and finally I left a message at his office. A few days later, the Lord gave me a dream. In this dream, I saw the architect drawings or blue prints of Orange County Airport. They were very detailed and written across the drawing were the words "John Wayne International Airport." I woke blown away by this dream.

I was standing in the kitchen of my mother's house telling her about the dream when the phone rang. Mom answered it. She looked at me and said, "It's for you. Do you know someone by the name of Bob?"

"Yes," I said. I took the phone and said, "Bob, How are you doing? I have been trying to reach you."

"Good Fred, good, what can I do for you?"

"Well," I said, "I'm not really sure. I had this dream last night." I proceeded to tell Bob about the dream, when we got in town, and how the Lord had placed him on my heart.

"Praise God," Bob said, "You know I sit on the board of the County Commissioners her in Orange County? Well I have been seeking the Lord's guidance regarding something. You see – we are looking at rebuilding Orange County Airport and it has been recommended that we rename the airport to 'John Wayne International Airport.' I have been praying if this is the right thing to do. Praise God brother, I believe God just gave me the green light."

I was so blown away at what transpired I just stood in my mom's kitchen praising the Lord, and today, if you fly into Orange County, an eight-foot bronze statue of John Wayne will greet you as you pass through the gates of "John Wayne International Airport."

So what's the lesson here? One brother is praying for guidance. Another brother is 1,000 miles away driving down the coast heading back to California. God stirs my heart to get a hold of that brother, but not knowing why. After multiple attempts – it was the night before he reached me that the Lord spoke via a dream regarding this brother's situation. It was all, so very naturally supernatural. This is the simplicity of the language of visions and dreams. The Father desires to move in our day-to-day lives. He wants the freedom to pour out the spirit of revelation and understanding in very practical and common ways. He is looking for hearts that are not bound up by a religious spirit but hearts set free to walk with him in simplicity. The God of the everyday is speaking every day.

Prophecy and the Gathered Assembly

Often times the Lord desires to speak to His people as a group. This is different from what He proclaims in a personal prophecy. When prophesying to the gathered assembly it is very important that all things are done decently and in order (1 Corinthians 14:40). Order deals with timing and the leadership of your church can let you know what is acceptable to your specific church. Remember that the spirit of the prophet is subject to the prophet (1 Corinthians 14:32). That means that you control the "when" and "how" of prophesy. Be teachable and open to correction. Assembly prophecy should fallow the 1 Corinthians 14:3 purpose. Remember that revelation given to you by God while you're at church does not mean that the revelation is necessarily for the whole group. With every revelation there needs to be an interpretation and an application. It is God's application that let's you know the "who," the "where," and the "when," of a revelation.

Illustration One – Prophecy and the Gathered Assembly

Let me now share with you some examples of prophetic vision from my own experience. In August of 1990, during CBNs "Seven Days Ablaze," I was in worship in front of the studio headquarters building when the Lord gave me this vision.

The Lord spoke to me very loud and clear saying,

> *"What I am doing in the church today is world-wide and I am calling My people to be trees of righteousness, a planting of the Lord, and all My trees shall clap their hands."*

Then I saw this Vision.

I was looking up to heaven praising Him. The presence of the Lord was truly overwhelming. All of a sudden, I saw the throne of God, high and exalted. Around about the throne were the trees of the Lord. They were blowing in the wind, moving and swaying in worship to the Lord. Then I saw a White Mountain of solid rock, like marble, or jasper. It filled the whole earth, as it shot up into heaven in brilliant splendor. There were large crevasses in the sides of the mountain. As I looked, I was overcome with the splendor of the shape of this mountain. As I looked up, I realized that the crevices in the sides of this mountain were the creases in the majestic robe of the Lord Jesus Christ. Then the Lord said,

> *"My trees shall be petrified trees of solid rock. Trees planted not of this world but trees planted on Me."*

Then I saw these trees planted on the mountain of the Lord and the mountain was Christ. Trees of stone, hallelujah! Then I was standing next to a tree, a tree that shot up so high in the mountain. As I was looking up into the tree, I saw the Holy Spirit, as a dove, flying up over the top of the tree. Then the Lord said,

> *"Look at the place I've called you to. Look at the place I've called you to."*

Then I opened my eyes and I saw the mountain of God surrounding the place where we were standing, it was surrounding everything, everywhere, and the Lord said,

> *"BEHOLD THE MOUNTAIN OF THE LORD AND THESE TREES SHALL BE PLANTED UPON THIS MOUNTAIN!"*

The Spirit of the Lord was all over Me.

Pat Robertson sensed that some people had received a word from the Lord and asked if we would like to share. Then I shared parts of this vision to the crowd gathered at this assembly, as the Lord had lead. The following day Pat spoke on the book of Daniel and "the Mountain, cut without hands."

This vision had a threefold purpose. Part of it was for the gathered assembly, part was to Pat, possibly confirming his message for the following day, and part of it was a personal word to me. In this setting, the Lord would only have me share that which was for the group and for Pat.

Illustration Two – Prophecy and the Gathered Assembly

Let me now share with you one more vision that deals with public prophesies to gathered assemblies. On night, a few years ago, I attended a small group meeting at a friend's house. During worship at this meeting, the Lord gave me the following vision.

In this vision, I saw the oceans of the world at dusk. There were naval ships moving across the face of the waters coming from all directions. Then I saw a ballerina beginning to dance across the floor. Her beauty and purity was uncanny. Her stature was as an Olympian with perfectly toned muscles and her face had a look of intense seriousness about it. With every move she made there was a sense of perfect form and balance. Then the Lord spoke,

> "BEHOLD THE DANCE OF THE BRIDE!"

As He was speaking, I saw the Earth suspended in clear blue space. This ballerina was standing at the top of the Earth in a starting stance with her hand held up to the heavens. Then I saw the Hand of the Lord reach down and take hold of the ballerina's hand. With perfect orchestration, He began to spin the bride in a dance. Faster and faster He spun, moving the bride across the globe. Then He said,

> "BEHOLD THE DANCE OF THE BRIDE!
>
> *For surely she shall dance and surely I shall come. For the dance, that I have called her to is a dance of holiness and power, to shake the foundations on which this world stands. Like a mighty army my bride shall come. From the north even to the south, and from the east to the west, so she shall dance. For greater things than these shall ye see. For my table is set and my wedding shall be, but the dance of my bride this world shall see, for I am coming for the Holy ones. I am coming, GOD THE SON!"*

At the end of this word, we experienced an outpouring of the Spirit that was truly over whelming. We read in Revelation 19:7, 8:

> *"Let us be glad and rejoice and give Him glory, for the marriage of the Lamb has come, and His wife*

> has made herself ready." And to her it was granted to be arrayed in fine linen, clean and bright, for the fine linen is the righteous acts of the saints."

And in Hosea 2:19, 20:

> "I will betroth you to Me forever; Yes, I will betroth you to Me in righteousness and justice, in loving kindness and mercy; I will betroth you to Me in faithfulness, and you shall know the Lord."

And finally in Isaiah 62:5:

> "For as a young man marries a virgin, so shall your sons marry you; And as the bridegroom rejoices over the bride, so shall your God rejoice over you."

So Paul adds to this in Ephesians 5:32 where he has been expounding on marriage says:

> "This is a great mystery: but I speak concerning Christ and the church."

The bride of Christ shall prepare the way for the return of her Husband. She shall get her house in order and sweep through this planet with Holy fire as the extended arm of the Lord. The power of God shown the church during apostolic era has not ended. As a matter of fact the dance of the bride shall be like nothing before it, For as one man ushered forth the proclamation of His first coming, a company of believers shall bring in his second coming. For this is the time of the bridal shower, where the later rains shall mingle with the former rains, bringing down a shower that will flood the earth. Like a title wave of His presence the earth shall again be flooded but this time with the rain of His glory.

Gifts and Callings

Often times the Lord will prophetically confirm the gifts and callings to an individual through prophecy. This is illustrated by Paul, in Romans 1:11:

> *"For I long to see you, that I may impart to you some spiritual gift, so that you may be established."*

Paul adds to this idea when he addresses Timothy in 1 Timothy 4:14:

> *"Do not neglect the gift that is in you, which was given to you by prophecy with the laying on of the hands of the eldership."*

Later Paul tells Timothy in to stir up that gift was given him:

> *"Therefore I remind you to stir up the gift of God which is in you through the laying on of my hands."*
>
> - 2 Timothy 1:6

In 2 Samuel 7:8-17 we have a good example of this kind of prophecy.

> *"Now therefore, thus shall you say to My servant David, 'Thus says the Lord of hosts: "I took you from the sheepfold, from following the sheep, to be ruler over My people, over Israel. And I have been with you wherever you have gone, and have cut off all your enemies from before you, and have made you a great name, like the name of the great men who are on the earth.*
>
> *Moreover I will appoint a place for My people Israel, and will plant them, that they may dwell in a place of their own and move no more; nor shall the*

> *sons of wickedness oppress them anymore, as previously, since the time that I commanded judges to be over My people Israel, and have caused you to rest from all your enemies. Also the Lord tells you that He will make you a house.*
>
> *"When your days are fulfilled and you rest with your fathers, I will set up your seed after you, who will come from your body, and I will establish his kingdom. He shall build a house for My name, and I will establish the throne of his kingdom forever. I will be his Father, and he shall be My son. If he commits iniquity, I will chasten him with the rod of men and with the blows of the sons of men. But My mercy shall not depart from him, as I took it from Saul, whom I removed from before you. And your house and your kingdom shall be established forever before you. Your throne shall be established forever.*
>
> *According to all these words and according to all this vision, so Nathan spoke to David."*

Illustration One

Let me now share with you a personal experience that will illustrate how visions relate to this kind of prophecy. One night while ministering prophecy at a church in Virginia the Lord gave me a vision for a young lady sitting in the congregation.

In this vision, I saw this young lady standing on a dusty dirt road. The road looked like it was in Jerusalem. In her hand was a bowl of milk. She knelt down in the center of the street and placed the bowl of milk on the ground. All of a sudden, I saw little kittens from all over the city running up to this bowl to get milk. They were all huddled around that bowl, lapping and drinking all they could get. Then I saw this young lady standing on this road surrounded by children.

I shared this vision with that young lady and the Lord gave me these words to give to her.

> *"Daughter of mine I have placed a sweet anointing of My Spirit within you and I have called you and chosen you to be a missionary and teacher to My children. For the milk, that I have placed within you is true milk indeed, sweet and pure. For this milk shall draw all that I put in your path to come to you. You shall be a refuge to the children and nourishment to their souls. For I know, Daughter, that you shall go wherever I send you. It shall be even as kittens are drawn to milk so these children shall be drawn to you, says the Lord God."*

We all then prayed for this young Lady and called down God's blessing and anointing upon her. As we prayed, the presence of God was all over her and she was slain in the Spirit (meaning falling down due to the presence of God), falling to the ground with His sweet presence. I later found out her father was a pastor and that she had been seeking God about being a missionary and going to Israel. God had confirmed the desires of her heart, and in fact had placed that desire within her, Himself.

Summary

Prophecy can touch many accepts of our lives. The Lord desires to speak to our day-to-day needs even as He desires to plant hope for our future and bring us into the gifts and callings of our lives. I have seen God speak to people regarding geographical moves, major decisions, business endeavors, romance, pregnancies, financial endeavors, and future events. God at times has even spoken words of correction and though this is rare, it is always spoken in love; nonetheless it happens for whom the Lord loves He also chases and chastises. The Lord desires to woo His bride unto himself. Jesus is jealous for His own and He will not share His bride with the spirit of this world.

The bible speaks very clearly about prophecy in the scripture. We are told not to despise prophecy or give it a lesser role than is appropriate. At the same time we are commanded to prove all prophecies, and hold fast to that which is good (1 Thessalonians 5:20, 21).

Even beyond all this, we are commanded to desire and earnestly covet the prophetic ministry:

> *"But earnestly desire the best gifts. And yet I show you a more excellent way. Pursue love, and desire spiritual gifts, but especially that you may prophesy. Therefore, brethren, desire earnestly to prophesy, and do not forbid to speak with tongues"*
>
> - 1 Corinthians 12:31; 14:1, 39

To respond properly to the prophetic it is important that we learn to judge properly what has been said. But more importantly is to judge a prophet as a person by the quality of his life. This entails the fruit of his ministry, his message, the maturity in his life, the methods he employees, his moral character, and motives of his heart. Motives are high on God's discernment list. Samuel declared that when anyone manipulates prophecy for his or her own gain, that person is guilty of the sin of witchcraft (1 Samuel 15:22, 23).

It takes faith

Responding to something that God has given you takes an element of faith. In Hebrews 4:2 we read:

> *"For indeed the gospel was preached to us as well as to them; but the word which they heard did not*

> *profit them, not being mixed with faith in those who heard it."*

If a prophetic word is received with an attitude of faith and acceptance, then the rhema that is heard will create faith for the fulfillment of that word. In Romans 10:17 it states that:

> *"So then faith comes by hearing, and hearing by the word of God."*

In the Greek, the "word" here is "rhema." A word from God quickened to you for that moment. Faith is foundational. Without faith, it is impossible to please God. However, with faith all things are possible.

True faith produces the ability to obey and obedience is better than sacrifice. James tells us to be doers of the word, and not hears only. And in Deuteronomy 29:29 we read:

> *"The secret things belong to the Lord our God, but those things which are revealed belong to us and to our children forever, that we may do all the words of this law."*

And in Romans 2:13 it is the doers of the law that shall be justified and not just the hearer. So James tells us in 4:17:

> *"Therefore, to him who knows to do good and does not do it, to him it is sin."*

Finally let patience, humility, meekness, and submission be the foundation on which you respond to a true word of prophecy. Humble obedience is the ignition key that starts the fulfillment of what God has spoken to you. Let the prophets of God arise and proclaim this world for the Kingdom of our God!

CHAPTER 27

GUIDELINES FOR PROPHETIC MINISTRY

"Having then gifts differing according to the grace that is given to us, let us use them: if prophecy, let us prophesy in proportion to our faith; or ministry, let us use it in our ministering; he who teaches, in teaching; he who exhorts, in exhortation; he who gives, with liberality; he who leads, with diligence; he who shows mercy, with cheerfulness."

- Romans 12:6-8

Guidelines are not laws etched in stone. They are guardrails that keep us on a path of etiquette and peace, where the fruit of the word can flourish. Kris Vallotton, an incredible prophet with Bethel Church in Redding, California, said it well:

> *"Guidelines are intended to give some banks to the river. Without banks, the river becomes a flood. In a flood, the water typically does more damage than good."*

A prophetic culture creates riverbanks so the water can flow freely. The Scriptures say clearly in 1 Corinthians 14:39-40 that:

> *"Therefore, brethren, desire earnestly to prophesy, and do not forbid to speak with tongues. Let all things be done decently and in order."*

As I shared earlier what the Word stated, "the spirits of the prophets are subject to the prophets" (1 Corinthians 14:32). What that means that you are in control of discerning the **"who, when, where, and what."** Your motivational guidepost is edification. In 1 Corinthians 14:26 we read:

> *"How is it then, brethren? Whenever you come together, each of you has a psalm, has a teaching, has a tongue, has a revelation, has an interpretation. Let all things be done for edification."*

Kris Vallotton, in his book "Basic Training for the Prophetic Ministry" outlines the following examples to illustrate when it is inappropriate to give a prophetic word.

Out of anger: When we are angry or have strong, negative emotional feelings toward the person or people for whom we have a prophetic word.

Personal platform: When we use prophecy as a "platform" to validate our personal doctrines or belief system. Example: "I, the Lord, say to you tonight thou shall not go to the movies!"

No relationship or accountability: When we have no relationship or accountability to the person or group of people receiving our prophecy. It is important for prophetic people to have relationship with the people to whom they are ministering. Too often people have an "us" and "them" attitude toward the people they are ministering to. This is unhealthy and dishonoring. Healthy relationships build bridges for effective ministry.

When delivering a prophetic word it is important to speak in your normal voice, through your personality. Some folks invoke the

"King James" language to validate the word. This is silly. Talk normal and in humility. Dial down; let the peace of God carry your mood. Like my wife always says, "**breathe**." The essence of your language and demeanor should be equal to the Holy Spirit's.

It is seldom necessary to yell or raise the level of our voice, as if that will increase its authority. Authority comes from God and what God initiates, God validates. The tone we communicate with says just as much as the words we use. Using phrases like "Thus says the Lord" or "I the Lord say to you," really aren't necessary. Follow your churches guidelines in delivering a prophetic word. Remember love should be at the center of all we do.

Love and ethics in prophetic ministry are so incredibly important I thought this would be a good place to insert a document produced by a dynamic team of prophetic leaders to guide the church in the area of the prophetic.

Convergence Council's Principles, Ethics, and Protocols

Originally compiled by John Paul Jackson and Marc Dupont with editorial guidance from: John Paul Jackson, Marc Dupont, Loren Sandford, John Sandford, Jim Goll and Bobby Connor, this document outlines prophetic protocol for those involved in the prophetic ministry.

Use these guidelines as a foundation tool for the prophetic ministry in your church. The work is well thought out and gives Godly guidance to those who desire to serve from a heart of love, compassion, and accountability.

Biblical Principles Concerning Ethics and Protocols Relating to New Testament Prophetic Ministry

The Preamble

Within the contemporary church the term, "prophetic ministry," can mean a great many things. Therefore we have attempted to outline a brief description of biblically based values and practices for New Testament prophetic ministers and prophets. The following are intended primarily for those called to trans-local ministries to the church at large. However, we also acknowledge many of these principles can be applied to individuals whose prophetic work does not extend beyond their local church.

Some persons labeled as "prophets" may be more accurately categorized as "prophetic ministries." While they may minister to the church at large, they primarily operate within the occasional "charisma" gift of prophecy. Others are called to bear the ministry of a prophet consistently as a primary calling.

An established prophet will not only operate in the gift of prophecy, but will carry seasonal prophetic burdens and messages from God the Father to the wider church, and sometimes even to nations. His or her emphasis may be much more "the word of the Lord," as opposed to "words from the Lord." They may, at times, even give a prophetic rebuke or warning to the church, which should always be a message of grace, postured within the Father heart of God.

Our heart in preparing and submitting these values is neither to police, nor to correct any known individuals or situations. Rather, we are simply endeavoring to articulate biblical standards that can help ensure long-term fruitfulness both for prophetic ministries and the recipients of those ministries. Revelation 19:10 states: "The testimony of Jesus is the spirit of prophecy." Therefore, we wholeheartedly believe that the overriding theme, goal and vision of any biblically based New Testament prophetic ministry should be to make known the Person and ways of Christ Jesus. And while a prophetic ministry may often be accompanied by revelatory words, signs and wonders, healings and miracles, a true prophet will always seek to champion the Person of Christ, the gift-giver, more than the gifts.

Because God's will is for each disciple of Christ to be conformed to the image of Christ, we believe, as well, that God calls those who represent His will, voice, and ways to be living testimonies of Christ-like integrity, lived out within the context of healthy relationships that provide accountability.

The goal of our presentation is Christ-like love and service from a pure heart. We do not present these principles and protocols from an assumed posture of authority or elitism. The spirit in which we present them is two-fold; Firstly, we desire to offer this as an appeal for Christ-centered unity of purpose among current prophetic ministries. Secondly, we wholeheartedly desire to see our colaborers bear witness to who Jesus is in every facet of ministry as they seek to prophetically serve the Body of Christ.

Biblical Principles Concerning Ethics and Protocols Relating to New Testament Prophetic Ministry

I. Concerning Beliefs and Practices

1. The Bible, as the perfect revelation of Jesus and the infallible word of God, is the absolute standard for weighing and assessing all revelation (2 Timothy 3:16, Colossians 2:18-19, John 1:14).

> A. While I treasure spiritual experiences from the Holy Spirit, I will not place subjective experiences and discern-

ment above the Bible (Revelation 19:10; Colossians 2:18-19).

B. I will not allow my emotions or pride to rob me of utilizing the Bible as my standard for weighing a revelation and any interpretation I may attach to a revelation.

C. I will always speak a Bible-centric message.

D. I will seek to draw all who hear me toward a greater relationship with the Father through Jesus, and to make the name of Jesus known in a biblical way.

2. God values His Word as the expression of His name and nature (Psalms 138:2). Therefore, we hold truth as a necessity in prophecy.

A. I will always try not only to speak truth, but to speak prophetic words in a way that reflects the loving heart of God.

B. I will determine to always lovingly speak prophetic correction in such a way as to avoid condemnation toward those who receive the prophetic word.

C. I will intend to always communicate hope for change through the transforming power of Jesus.

D. I commit to reflect the nature of my God by loving people more than my gift.

E. Prophecy is a word from God. I will try to speak it with both humility and confidence.

F. While fearing God, I will not fear man. Whenever God directs me to release revelation I will not hold back through fear of man, fear of offending those with whom I am in relationship, or fear of losing popularity and/or opportunities to minister (Galatians 1:10, Proverbs 29:5).

G. I commit to God's call on my life to proclaim the ways and will of God ahead of the "success" of my ministry in the eyes of man or the church.

3. I believe that prophetic accuracy is essential. I believe that the method and manner of delivery (the heart) of a prophecy is also important.

A. I understand that voicing words from God is a responsibility not to be taken lightly. I aspire to have 100% accuracy in all I say.

B. I will admit when I am wrong and take steps to acknowledge, repent and make restitution for my error in a prophecy or its delivery, in a manner appropriate to correct the error and the reason for the error.

C. Repentance and restitution must also be appropriate to my sphere of influence and the scope of the prophetic word (Psalms 138:2).

4. If I do give an errant prophecy, I commit to full repentance. This will include:

A. An apology. If I gave the prophecy to a private party, my apology must be to that party. If the prophecy was given to a group such as a church or the public, the apology must be given to that group.

B. Biblical repentance does not mean saying, "I'm sorry" only to God, but also to those I have hurt. Most importantly, I must communicate that I am deeply concerned about the harm I have done or the hurt I have inflicted, and I will do whatever else is needed to help heal the wounds I have caused.

C. With the help of wise counsel, I will seek to find if there is anything in my heart that caused this error, and deal with it through confession, repentance and action.

D. I commit to continuing in accountability to a safe and loving authority whom I believe will support me and help me walk in integrity. I will not remove myself from this process even if painful to me and/or it seems that those to whom I am accountable are not treating me fairly.

E. I believe there are consequences to all actions. If my error is particularly serious or repeated, I will be willing to take time off from prophetic ministry until I and those in authority over me have discerned that I am ready to resume ministry.

5. Concerning supernatural manifestations, I will not substitute the seeking of angels, angelic activity, or other supernatural manifestations, over the seeking of God, His presence, and the truths contained in Scripture. The source of all truth is the Holy Spirit (2 Corinthians 11:14; Colossians 2:18-19).

A. I believe that the character of Christ in me is more important to the Kingdom than my gift. It is the application and manifestation of God's Word in my life.

B. I will not fall prey to idolatry by seeking to generate, initiate or exaggerate supernatural manifestations, no matter what may be expected by the church culture in which I speak.

C. Likewise, I endeavor to allow the Holy Spirit to initiate how and when He releases supernatural manifestations and/or ministry through me.

D. If God does speak to me through angels, or causes certain manifestations, or gives particular types of revelation, I will communicate what I hear and see only as God directs. I will do so without elevating myself, my experience or revelation in any way that might detract from the Person of God Himself.

6. Understanding a prophetic word is vital to its implementation. Therefore, I commit to being open to discuss, with appropriate leaders within the Body of Christ, the prophetic words I receive and interpretations of those words. I will endeavor to do so because prophetic gifts are given to serve the people, not to promote the one who prophesies.

7. Words from God should encourage, train and equip the Body of Christ to conform to the image of Christ (Ephesians 4:11-16). I will endeavor to always help the Body of Christ perceive the Person of Christ more clearly and to hunger for Him and His ways (Colossians 1: 8-10, Ephesians 1:17-18).

8. Ephesians 4 ministries are to equip the Body of Christ to receive, develop and mature, rather than to cultivate an audience of spectators for our gifting. Thus, we hold in high regard the priesthood of each believer in Christ (1 Peter 2:5; Romans 8:14; Isaiah 61:6).

A. I commit to preaching sound doctrine rather than dividing the Body of Christ through non-scriptural doctrines designed to amaze my audience and develop a following (2 Timothy 4:3-4).

B. I will not use the gift God has given me in a reckless manner that might cause others to stumble or misunderstand God and His ways (Jer. 23:32).

C. I commit to help Christian leaders and trainers discern between the operation of God-given spiritual gifts and human psychic abilities (Daniel 2:27-28; 4:8-9).

D. I commit to help train the Body of Christ to discern between true, Holy Spirit-inspired revelation and mere human intuition, New Age pseudo-spirituality or psychic abilities (1 John 4:1).

E. I will intentionally try to communicate revelation and the interpretation of revelation in ways that encourage strengthen, and comfort the recipient(s) of the word (1 Corinthians 14:3).

F. I will seek to avoid prophesying anything that controls or manipulates the lives of others.

G. When giving a prophetic word, I will seek to always encourage hearers to biblically and prayerfully weigh it rather than to take it without consideration (1 Corinthians 14:29).

9. I commit to help train the Body of Christ to discern between genuine encounters with God and other pseudo-spiritual experiences, as well as to help the Body of Christ understand the various degrees of revelation and their relative levels of importance.

10. I commit to refusing to prostitute the revelatory gifting God has given me by attaching a fee to a prophetic word* (Micah 3:11).

A. I will not use a prophetic word or prophetic ministry to manipulate people to give financially to me, and or the ministry I lead (2 Peter 2:15).

B. I will not lead people to believe that the prophetic word will be triggered or influenced by a gift.

*Accepting honorariums, gifts or travel remuneration is acceptable. This is different than prophesying for an agreed amount of money, and is equivalent to a pastor receiving a salary.

II. Concerning My Life in Representing Christ Jesus Prophetically

1. I commit to living, modeling and championing the character of Christ. I believe Christ-like character to be more important than operating out of gifting (2 Corinthians 7:1).

    A. I choose to consistently promote and model the ways of Christ more than simply communicate revelation.

    B. When it comes to representing Christ Jesus, I believe that I not only have a message, but that I am the message.

2. I believe that wisdom from above is "reasonable and peaceable." I will place high value on Christ-like humility, and shun prophetic arrogance (James 3:17).

3. I commit to having an accountability group in place to whom I will hold my lifestyle, marriage and ministry accountable.

    A. I commit to living a life free of substance abuse, love of money, extra-marital sex, pornography, pride and unforgiveness/bitterness.

> B. I commit to living out God's high value of love and covenant emotionally, spiritually and physically with the "spouse of my youth," to the best of my ability.
>
> C. I will guard my heart and make a covenant with my eyes not to look upon another in a lustful manner.

4. I commit to being free from both the love of money and the love of appearing successful in the eyes of man. I commit to choosing venues to host my ministry, based on the leading of the Holy Spirit as opposed to the size of the crowd or financial remuneration.

5. I commit to being not only a person of prayer and worship but a continual student of the Bible and the ways of God.

6. I commit to honor the Lord by honoring and strengthening His delegated authority in the Body of Christ.

> A. I will honor and strengthen local pastors and church leaders as God's-appointed shepherds and gatekeepers for their local congregations.
>
> B. I will not usurp the authority of the local leadership in the Body where I am called to speak.

7. I commit to perceiving myself as a servant to both the church at large and the local church as God gives me opportunity.

> A. I will not view congregations and other ministries as mere platforms, or tools to facilitate my vision and calling.
>
> B. I will not steal another leader's people or leadership in order to build my ministry.

8. I commit to financial, ethical and moral purity, and will not use the Body of Christ to advance my ministry nor build my own em-

pire. My endeavor is to imitate Jesus' example of servant hood, and only do as I see the Father doing.

III. The Nature of Authentic Prophetic Ministry

Bible-centric — Bear/bare witness, expose, declare and establish the truth of Scripture.

Salvation-centric – Declare, teach and demonstrate the gospel of the Kingdom of God with signs and wonders following (Mark 16:20).

Jesus-centric – Edify, comfort, encourage and exhort believers and the church in the way to Jesus as well as the way of Jesus.

God-centric, Demonstrate in word, deed and manner the character of the Father: love, righteousness, justice, compassion, mercy, majesty and holiness.

Sovereignty-centric, Bring glory to God alone. His name, His acts, and His Glory are inseparable. He exercises His will through His Omniscience, Omnipotence, Omnipresence, Immutability, and Eternality, as He chooses.

I agree

> *I, Fred Raynaud, (insert YOUR name) agree with the Convergence Council's Principles, Ethics, and Protocols as written by John Paul Jackson and Marc Dupont and the editorial team of Loren Sandford, John Sandford, Jim Goll and Bobby Connor.*
>
> *I join my agreement with my other brothers and sisters in prophetic ministry:*
> - Don Wayt
> - Robert Fetveit

- Andrea Bareither
- Scott Evelyn
- Aaron Evans
- Jeannine Rodriguez
- Giulio Gabeli
- Dan Mosely
- Marc Lawson
- Brendan McCauley
- Stacey Campbell
- TOV Rose
- James Goll
- Howard Espie
- Shannon Tolbert
- Shelton Davidson
- Duncan Graham
- John and Ruth Filler
- Patricia King
- Rod and Marie Holt
- Tom and Jean Blasi
- Rick and Cynthia Hayes

Part 4: Words to the Church

CHAPTER 28

SECTION INTRODUCTION

"Your ears shall hear a word behind you, saying, 'This is the way, walk in it,' Whenever you turn to the right hand Or whenever you turn to the left."

- Isaiah 30:21

"Having then gifts differing according to the grace that is given to us, let us use them: if prophecy, let us prophesy in proportion to our faith; or ministry, let us use it in our ministering; he who teaches, in teaching; he who exhorts, in exhortation; he who gives, with liberality; he who leads, with diligence; he who shows mercy, with cheerfulness."

- Romans 12:6-8

Introduction

The purpose of this book is to cause change. The purpose of this writing is to help equip the saints for the work of ministry. The purpose of the book is to illuminate an aspect of God's communicative workings that seldom receive attention. Paul said, **",that which we know we declare unto you,"** that which I know I share with you, that you will run, and having run, obtain. For truly our work has only begun.

As I come to the last section of this book, my heart burns within me, not because of the words contained in this section but because of the work God has laid out before us. The following chapters are devoted to **demonstrating** the language of visions and dreams and how the Seer's gift operates. I will do this by sharing words, visions, and dreams the Lord has given me. I have also selected words that speak to the heartbeat of our Lord Jesus and His passion for this generation and the call of the hour.

As you read the following chapters, let your hearts be stirred. Look for the nuggets of revelation that spark your hearts with fire. Revelation 19:10, reminds us *"the testimony of Jesus is the Spirit of prophecy."* What that means for you, is you can hear the word of testimony and claim that word for yourself. By taking hold of a word that ignites your heart, you can say, **"that word is for me!"** If it blesses you and lights a fire in your soul, and your life and heart is marked by change and a revived passion, then I have accomplished what I have set out to do. Be blessed, in His precious name.

CHAPTER 29

SEASON OF THE CORN

"Proclaim ye this among the Gentiles; Prepare war, wake up the mighty men, let all the men of war draw near; let them come up: Beat your plowshares into swords and your pruning hooks into spears: let the weak say, I am strong...
Put ye in the sickle, for the harvest is ripe: come, get you down; for the press is full, the fats overflow; for their wickedness is great. Multitudes, multitudes in the valley of decision: for the day of the LORD is near in the valley of decision."

— Joel 3:9, 10, 13, 14

"Ask ye of the LORD rain in the time of the latter rain so the LORD shall make bright clouds, and give them showers of rain, to grass in the field."

— Zechariah 10:1

"Also I heard the voice of the Lord, saying, Whom shall I send, and who will go for us? Then said I, Here am I; send me."

- Isaiah 6:8

We are living in a prophetic day, an hour when the Spirit of God is moving within His Church with incredible urgency. We have seen the fires of revival burn on the landscape of Africa. We watched in amazement as the Spirit of God rose against the walls of communism and opened the doors to people that were shut out by a political stronghold. We have seen the blind receive their sight, the deaf hear, and the lame leaping for joy. All of these miracles, signs, and wonders are just the beginning of the outpouring that God desires to rain down upon us.

Nonetheless, we as a people, in the midst of tremendous grace and wanting more, have fallen into a type of spiritual complacency. We have grown accustom to the little rain we have received and settled in thinking that where we are at is good enough, it will sustain us.

Yet, God would say,

"This is not rain but a mist, a sprinkling of My presence."

You see, God wants so much more than anything we can imagine. His desire for the church of this age is so far beyond or ability to think and imagine. That is why the Lord refers to this current season as a mist. There's more church. There is so much more.

A while back, when I started to prepare for this chapter the Lord gave me a vision. In this vision I saw a landscape, parched with dryness, similar to the soil of a riverbed that was once flowing and alive, but now dry, hard, and cracked, because of the lack of water and the intensity of heat. In the horizon sat the sun, flaming red, as if at sunset. As I looked, all of a sudden, the land began to quake, and the ground opened up with flames of molten lava clinging to its sides. From the midst of the crack, people began to come forth.

Their eyes upward, and faces aglow with the glory of God, they began to march out of a hell that bound them to eternal darkness.

I asked the Lord what this meant. He replied,

> *"The time has come for a quaking in the Land, not as in the day of Korah's rebellion. For surely I will cause a quaking to come, not a quaking unto judgment, but a quaking of release..., I will set free them that are bound and call forth the dead of this age... bringing life to those held captive by the evil one."*

All of a sudden, the horror of those headed for the gates of hell paralyzed me. I thought of the sadness that fills the heart of God when he looks upon those enslaved by the devil. That is when I heard the Lord say,

> *"I, the Lord, have come to set the prisoners free."*

The purposes of God are always Kingdom purposes. His gifting has not come to tickle our ears at a weekly prayer meeting. He did not send His Spirit that we should sit in pews, week after week, waiting for the next thrill, or the next guest speaker, or the next healing, or the next prophecy. He sent His Spirit into the world that the Kingdom of our God would invade the kingdom of this world. That He would usher in the fullness of the kingdom to come. For in truth, there is an ending in the Bible. There is a time of the consummation of all things, when our God will fill the whole earth even as the train of His robe, now, fills the temple. Let it fill our temple God!

God is calling us to a new maturity. God is seeking people weaned from foundational milk – He's looking for meat seekers. He is looking for the framers to build on a foundation already laid (Hebrews 6:1). For the time is coming when the plowman shall overtake the reaper, and the treader of grapes, him who sows seeds... for the eyes of the Lord are upon us. Even now, the former and latter rains are merging to become one and the reception of that rain will only come to a lamp-trimmed-bride without spot or wrinkle. God is calling forth an army for these last days. The Lord is fulfilling what He spoke to the Prophet Joel 2:1-3, 11:

> *"Blow the trumpet in Zion, and sound an alarm in My holy mountain! Let all the inhabitants of the land tremble; For the day of the Lord is coming, for it is at hand: A day of darkness and gloominess, a day of clouds and thick darkness, like the morning clouds spread over the mountains. A people come, great and strong, the like of whom has never been; Nor will there ever be any such after them, even for many successive generations. A fire devours before them, and behind them a flame burns; The land is like the Garden of Eden before them, and behind them a desolate wilderness; Surely nothing shall escape them., The Lord gives voice before His army, for His camp is very great; For strong is the One who executes His word. For the day of the Lord is great and very terrible; Who can endure it?"*

There is a quaking in the land, our God is shaking us to wake-up to the call of the Bride, to hear the voice of the Bridegroom as he beckons her to the dance,

> *the Dance of the Bride that will fill the whole earth. For the trumpet shall sound, and the flute shall play, and the Bride shall dance in these final days.*
>
> *As we stand by listening, we hear the prophet sing, crying out, and urging the Lord's Bride to be. What is this voice that I hear, Words of prophecy, loud and clear,! It is the voice of our God heard throughout the land, It is the voice of the Lord, when He begins to stand, to take back creation from the fallen one. It's a time of possession. His time has begun!*

As I sat writing this heaviness rested on my heart. I didn't understand it so I cried out to God. As I cried, I looked out at the clouds above my patio and saw written in the heavens, "Prophecy to My people." At that moment the Lord said to me,

> "What I whisper in your ear, shout it from the roof tops. What I reveal in your heart proclaim upon the mountaintops. I have called you to be a prophet to my people, a watchman on the wall."

After He spoke those words, I saw the Wailing Wall around Jerusalem and I was standing at the entrance of a gate. I looked and saw people, lame and crippled, going in and coming out through the gate. Around them were God's people, watching, but doing nothing. Then I remembered Peter at the Gate Beautiful and I cried, **"God change me!"**

God is breathing life into a new generation of Christians whose eyes have been turned upward, whose ears have been honed by the Holy Spirit to listen to what the Spirit is saying to the churches, and whose voices have been oiled with the sweet anointing of proclamation.

Lately, the Lord has been showing me pictures of corn, ears of corn, as far as the eyes can see. Everywhere I look, when my mind is searching and reflecting on the majesty of the Lord of all Glory, I would see stalks, tall and full of rich sweet corn. My mind would wonder as I explored the concept of corn, *the maize, meaning life*, as the Indians called it.

Suddenly I saw Jesus standing tall in a field or mighty valley. He was taller than the mountains that spanned the background of this image. Jesus had been walking the length of the valley. He had a nap-sack over His shoulder and in His hands were seeds. As He walked through the valley, he was sowing seeds. Everywhere he walked, He scattered seeds. Then He stood at the base of the mountain, looked up towards heaven, and **called for the rain, and it rained**. Then He **called for the sun, and it shined brighter than the noonday**. Then He **called for the wind... and there arose a breeze from heaven that blew across the landscape of the valley**. It wasn't a mighty wind but a soft wind. Its force was more like a mother hen nurturing her chicks as the soft breeze brushed away the surface dirt across the landscape.

Then Jesus stood, taller than the mountains. He started to bend over. In slow motion, I saw Him bending down. He was bending over looking at a single blade of a leaf in the dirt. It was so small compared to His size, how big he was. He was looking at it with such intensity, as if He was searching for life from the scattered seeds of His labor. He was looking to see what was sprouting. When He saw that single blade breaking forth from the ground He reached down to examine it more closely. Then I saw that leaf turn into a large ear of corn, thick, rich, and plentiful. Then He spoke to the earth and more leafs sprang up and instantly they were transformed into corn. Rows and rows of corn filled the valley where He stood.

As I sat there pondering the ears of corn I heard a mighty popping sound. The ears of corn began to pop like popcorn. Then the Lord said,

> *"These ears of corn that you see are ears to hear, and the sound that your hear are nuggets of revelation exploding into fulfillment upon the landscape of humanity."*

I understood that these kernels were indeed the rehma of God ignited in the hearts of His children.

Then the Lord spoke this into my spirit,

> *"I am calling for the harvest of the corn, the ears of my body, to stand up, and proclaim all that I have birthed*

within them. The day of the corn has come – and all my corn is ripe for the popping – exploding upon the scene of humanity, white nuggets of proclamation from My throne, eagerly waiting for the day of their destiny.

I have planted them. I have watered them. I have caused My glory to shine upon them and I am the one who calls for the wind and the rain. They have been prepared for the day of proclamation. They have been drenched in the butter, from the altar of my presence.

These kernels of mine have been prepared for a moment such as this. My desire is to fill the earth with the sound of My Spirit and the popping that you hear in the land is the beginning of my proclamation for I am turning up the heat – and releasing the "Kernels," – those who are ready – waiting to explode, explode upon the sea of humanity. I have come so that you will hear the sound of my call, and usher into the frying pan of My altar, an altar whose coals have been burning from the foundation of all creation.

This altar, My altar, is a place where the tongue is touched by the fire of My desire and lips are sealed into the covenant of praise and proclamation. It is a place where dross is removed and what is left is refined into pure silver, a ring for My finger that will touch all that I touch, pure gold, a garment for My raiment – a coat of many colors, colors of promise and purpose.

Yes My corn is **not** "yellow" – it does not retreat at the sound of My popping – it plunges in, passing through the fire, reaching out for all that I desire, it is like the maize – Indian corn of many colors accomplishing all that I desire and require.

Yes, I am the keeper of the corn. I am He, who whispers in your ears and causes you to hear all that I speak into it. More than that, I am He who brings life to My proclamation, for the I AM – I AM the LOGOS, I AM the Son of God – I AM the whisper in your ear and as a hand full of *kernels fills a bag of popcorn to overflowing so My word shall not return to Me void but will fill abundantly more.*

He who has ears to hear – let him hear what the Spirit is saying to the churches. Today is the Day of the Corn."

Chapter 30

Let it Rain

"And I heard, as it were, the voice of a great multitude, as the sound of many waters and as the sound of mighty thunderings, saying, "Alleluia! For the Lord God Omnipotent reigns! Let us be glad and rejoice and give Him glory, for the marriage of the Lamb has come, and His wife has made herself ready."

- Revelation 19:6, 7

"Therefore, since all these things will be dissolved, what manner of persons ought you to be in holy conduct and godliness, looking for and hastening the coming of the day of God, because of which the heavens will be dissolved, being on fire, and the elements will melt with fervent heat? Nevertheless we, according to His promise, look for new heavens and a new earth in which righteousness dwells. Therefore, beloved, looking forward to these things, be diligent to be found by Him in peace, without spot and blameless.", 2 Peter 3:11-14

As I write this my eyes keep glancing out the windows of my office to the horizon, I see flashes of lightning and thunder. Now, in the natural, it is a lovely day, 80 degrees and sunny, but in my spirit I see storm clouds coming, great and mighty storm clouds, unlike any day the world has ever seen before, nor shall ever see again. I sense a day upon us unlike any time in history. It is a season of transfiguration, a time of the kingdoms of this world to collide with the Kingdom of our God! A rapid moving of the consummation of all things is at hand. I can hear the beckoning of the Lord Jesus crying out,

> *"Come My children, for truly the harvest is plentiful but the laborers are few. Come to Me My children, for this is the hour that My prophets spoke of, A time of the end of all things, as you know them. A new season has begun and the balances are in My hands, to weigh the hearts of my children.*
>
> *No longer will you say it is the beginning of spring and we have plenty of time until winter falls upon us, for I tell you that today is the day of the winter storms of Heaven. Today is the day of the early rains of spring. Now is the time for the latter rain of My presence! Walk with Me in this rain, or you will be washed away by the foolishness of your willful hearts. For no longer shall I wait to heal the dryness of this earth, prepare for the rain of God!"*

After Jesus had walked with His disciples for nearly three years and was reaching the end of His redemptive mission here on earth, He spoke these words to His disciples,

> *"For the Son of Man will come in the glory of His Father with His angels, and then He will reward each according to his works. Assuredly, I say to you, there are some standing here who shall not taste death till they see the Son of Man coming in His kingdom."*
>
> - Matthew 16:27, 28

He then took three of His disciples, Peter, James, and John and brought them to a high mountain where He was transfigured before them. His face begun to shine like the brilliance of the sun and His raiment was as white as light. Then He said to His disciples, **"Arise, and do not be afraid."**

> *"Lord, have mercy on my son, for he is an epileptic and suffers severely; for he often falls into the fire and often into the water. So I brought him to Your disciples, but they could not cure him." Then Jesus answered and said, "O faithless and perverse generation, how long shall I be with you? How long shall I bear with you? Bring him here to Me." And Jesus rebuked the demon, and it came out of him; and the child was cured from that very hour."*
>
> *- Matthew 17:15-18*

When I read this scripture I asked myself; what was Jesus saying? This sounds like a strong rebuke coming from the Lord. What does He mean when He says, "How long shall I be with you?"

This is what I believe Jesus was saying here. After nearly three years of intensive training, demonstrating for them the works of the kingdom and teaching them how to move in the Spirit, to heal the sick, raise the dead, and cast out demons, he arrives at the final chapter of His life here on earth. He is transfigured in front of their eyes while having a conference with the Father, Moses, and Elijah, regarding I suppose, the weeks that lie ahead, and the cross. He proclaims to them His impending death and resurrection. He tells them about the glory of His second coming and the end of the age.

Then, He is confronted with the progress of His disciples. Its report card time and Jesus being dissatisfied over the outcome, cries out, "...How long shall I be with you?" In other words, don't you realize the hour in which we live? My time is short. You have been with Me for over two years and still you do not know how to operate in the Kingdom. Class is over kids and the time for kingdom advancement is now. Where is your faith? This is their wake-up call. This is a hearts cry to stand at attention and pay attention. This is exactly where we are today.

We are at a time such as this, and God is wooing the bride to awake from her sleep. How long does it take us to be trained? How long does it take us to move out in Kingdom power and resurrect this dead world? God is calling us to stand, to listen, and to learn. In the global economy of God's timing, School is almost over. Individually, if it has not begun, it needs to start now. If it has, then we need to move beyond head knowledge and start doing the works of the kingdom. You might be asking yourself, how do I know if I'm ready? That's easy. The prerequisite to doing the works of the kingdom are outlined by Jesus comments after His rebuke in Matthew 17:

> *"So Jesus said to them, "Because of your unbelief; for assuredly, I say to you, if you have faith as a mustard seed, you will say to this mountain, 'Move from here to there,' and it will move; and nothing will be impossible for you."*
>
> - Matthew 17:20

He is looking for recipients of mustard seed faith. He is looking for servants that have tilled the soil of the hearts and prayed "**God plant that seed in me.**" He is looking for folks that will take what they have and be "**doers**" of the kingdom. The heart cry of Jesus is that whatever measure we have been given – we would spend it all and be spent by Him. It is in the doing that the increase comes. By spending the measure of faith we have, He will fill us with more. It takes a little action to get a reaction. He is looking for saints that see the big picture and in seeing... they will discover the power of His resurrection and the Kingdom of heaven. This is a small investment... to do such mighty works... a little seed can move mountains.

It doesn't get much easier than that. We have become too professional in our outlook of the church. If Peter waited to graduate from seminary to do the works of the kingdom, we would have never read about Peter in the Scriptures. We have to get back to the simplicity that is in Christ Jesus and leave big business and professionalism to the rulers of this world. Remember the greatest in this Kingdom are those that have become as little children.

For the last several decades, the church has been anticipating a tremendous harvest for the Kingdom of God. We have looked upon the landscape of this world spinning out of control, and prayed, "Father, send us revival." We watch as the separation of light and darkness draw lines in the sand and the culture war wages on, lashing out at values that were once the norm. We bow our knees in prayer as we see the horror of global terrorism, war, and the crisis of the Middle East. We pray all the more, as this world quakes its way towards destruction. We grab hold of each other, searching for the hem of His garment as earthquakes, tsunamis, hurricanes, and natural disasters, shake this planet, all the while the world seems to be heading down a path of no-turning-back.

Yet, through it all we press in and press on, knowing that Our God Reigns. So we call out for the rain of His presence... we cry out for the Latter Rain of His Glory, and we, in Holy Spirit desperation, pray "Father, THY KINGDOM COME... on Earth, now, as it IS in Heaven!" We are looking for that End Times breakthrough, that only the Lord of all Glory can bring.

You know, in the fall and winter months, the Mediterranean world reverberates with excitement and anticipation of the olive harvest. As they should, olives take time to grow. The average tree can take up to seven years to produce enough fruit to yield a harvest... and even then, each tree only produces three to four quarts of oil. That's the buzz, You can hear it in the streets, "the olives are ripe, and abundant, the Harvest is at hand." You want to shout it from the rooftops.

Listen dear saints, dear keepers of the oil, prepare your hearts for the harvest, for today the olives are ripe for the pressing. Yet, remember dear ones, dear keepers of the oil, each tree will only yield enough oil for itself. Be mindful, be fruitful, and keep your jars full, wicks trimmed, and hearts set ablaze, for the groom is about to leave His chamber to embrace His bride, and the bride He desires to embrace is an "extra" virgin bride whose decanter is full and whose light is set ablaze.

Yes, we are very much like the olive grower waiting for that final harvest. We watch as the orchard moves and sways to the changes in the weather. We cry out to God when drought is upon the land for fear that the harvest won't come. We cringe, and then pray, asking the Lord of the harvest to send forth the spring rains. We wait and we fertilize, crying out for the winter rains.

Yet, through the years of waiting, we are suddenly struck with that promise from Heaven...

> *",Let us now fear the LORD our God, who gives rain, both the former and the latter, in its season. He reserves for us the appointed weeks of the harvest"*
>
> *- Jeremiah 5:24*

Therefore, we press on and pray the more.... We can sense, in the Spirit, the times they are a changing, so we stand with the words of Joel:

> *"Fear not, O land; Be glad and rejoice, for the Lord has done marvelous things! Do not be afraid, you beasts of*

the field; For the open pastures are springing up, and the tree bears its fruit; The fig tree and the vine yield their strength. Be glad then, you children of Zion, and rejoice in the Lord your God; For He has given you the former rain faithfully, and He will cause the rain to come down for you—The former rain, and the latter rain in the first month. The threshing floors shall be full of wheat, and the vats shall overflow with new wine and oil."

- Joel 2:21-24

That is what we are waiting for... we are waiting in anticipation for a Holy Spirit outpouring like no other... a Latter Rain visitation of Jesus upon this earth. I hear constantly, "the rain, we so long to see, is coming." You can feel it in the air, like the stillness before a storm, the moisture level has risen, the barometer is off the charts, and the climate is changing before our very eyes. We all want revival, we all want the Word of God to go forth in power and transform the lost and the destitute in a final wave of His presence.

Yet the Lord would say *there is a precursor to the out-pouring of this rain.* Jesus is so full of rain it coming out His pores... like the great drops of blood bursting through His flesh in the Garden. Nonetheless, to the breaking of His heart, He holds back the rain. Though the waters are ready to burst through the heavens – He says – *Not yet, Hold back a little longer, the time is now but My bride, she's not ready.*

You see, for several days, every time I went to pray the Lord kept showing me this picture. In this vision, I saw a massive stone wheel; slowly turning... the picture was so vivid I could almost hear the sound of crushing as I watched the intensity of this stone wheel turn. I asked the Lord what it was. He spoke these words into my heart:

"The hour has come for My anointed ones.... My olives, which stand before me, are now, this day, ripe for the

> crushing. The season of new oil is upon you and you shall go forth and pour yourselves out upon this land; for I have seen the agony of My people – I have heard the cries of My saints. Within their bosom lies the fruit of My labor, To birth in them a tsunami of My presence, and in their labor they shall birth the deluge of My deliverance and My love.
>
> Their labor has reached its final hour and the birth of this out-pouring is that of New Oil... Golden Oil from the olives of My Latter Rain, for know this day, that I have called you to a new place. I have called you to lie beneath the stone of my pressing. I have watered My olive trees with visions of My Latter Rain and now they have grown ripe with the hope of My outpouring. This day I have begun the shaking.
>
> This day I have begun to gather My olives. For at My feet lie olives, ripe for the pressing. Now, this day, My Spirit will begin to gather.... So listen to Me now... your services are needed. Come with Me, lie down upon the floor of My alter, come with Me, lie down beneath the Stone of my pressing. For the oil from this press will usher in My Latter Rain."

As I pondered upon His words, I saw again that massive stone... and then the picture zoomed out and I saw a spigot or gutter extending out from the base of the stone. Out of the stone, dripped Golden Oil. As the stone wheel turned, the oil went from dripping to pouring.

Below the spigot was a bucket. It had become so full it was overflowing. The flow soon turned into mighty splatters. Looking from above the bucket, I saw the heavens and the earth below – then the bucket burst open, releasing its contents upon the face of the earth. Then I saw the legs of people standing upon the earth. They were looking down at their feet in amazement. They all were standing in this Golden Oil, and the oil began to rise, amazed they looked up to Heaven, eyes beaming with the Glory of God.

Then the voice of the Lord spoke,

> *"A new glory is rising and shall cause your feet to be transformed from bronze to iron."*

That was when I saw a new strength enter the people of the Lord, and then I saw Jesus rise above all and begin to walk through the Land. His stature was mighty and His body filled the whole earth.

The Call of Jesus in this Hour

God is calling us into a new day. He has planted within our heart the desire to see His glory. He has placed within us the cry and the prayer to call forth the Latter Rain – to usher in the deluge of His presence. However, there is something vital that needs to happen in this ushering.

He is not only calling us to press in... **but to be pressed, crushed, under the presence of His Holiness**. You see, without the complete yielding of our hearts to Him, the Oil cannot come, and it is the Oil that brings forth the rain and the rain becomes as golden oil. So what does it mean to be pressed, to yield us to Him completely?

Just yesterday, the Lord spoke to my heart and said,

> *"The fire you desire is My desire, but that torch is only lit on Heaven's alter of worship."*

You see pressing happens in His presence. When we press in and worship the lover of our souls we are crushed by the incredible nature of His love for us. Worship is a lifestyle. Worship is adoration. Worship is a lover pressing into to Him with such urgency, because she can't do anything else, she has to be with her Lover. Jesus adores you. Jesus is so in love with you that He wants you to be with him and the door to His kingdom is worship. Worshipers are lovers; they are so sold out to be in His presence that they constantly have their eyes upward looking for Him and His presence. Worshipers are like the Shulamite bride of the Song of Solomon.

> "Let him kiss me with the kisses of his mouth—For your love is better than wine. Because of the fragrance of your good ointments, Your name is ointment poured forth; Therefore the virgins love you. Draw me away!"
>
> - Song of Solomon 1:2-4

The kisses of the King draw us. The heartbeat of His presence changes us. Through intimacy with our Lord, we can proclaim, like the Shulamite, **"The king has brought me into his chambers. He brought me to the banqueting house, and his banner over me was love."** You see Jesus is looking for a people so hungry for Him, so thirsty for Him, so desiring Him, that they are as lovesick as He is, and when they hear the sound of His voice their hearts leap inside of themselves. Listen to the words of the Shulamite.

> "The voice of my beloved! Behold, he comes leaping upon the mountains, skipping upon the hills. My beloved is like a gazelle or a young stag. Behold, he stands behind our wall; He is looking through the windows, gazing through the lattice. My beloved spoke, and said to me: "Rise up, my love, my fair one, and come away. For lo, the winter is past, the rain is over and gone. The flowers appear on the earth; The time of singing has come, and the voice of the turtledove is heard in our land. The fig tree puts forth her green figs, and the vines with the tender grapes give a good smell. Rise up, my love, my fair one, and come away!"
>
> - Song of Solomon 2:8-13

Since our destiny is set to be the bride adorned in white and married to the King of all creation, we might as well start now, adorn ourselves with His presence, and pursue Him. It is only in worship and adoration for Him that will bring us into the hour of great anointing. He invested everything, His very life is to create a people that are lovers, that will be an extension of His hands, doers, that will see what He sees and march out, full of the Holy Spirit, and heal this land.

I had a dream, in the dream I was standing on the beach with some folks, and it was dark, like a red sky. All around us were zombies, the walking dead, trying to devour us and kill us. The tide came in. It was a red tide. We were splashing water with an oar on the zombies. As soon as the water touched the zombies they began to dissolve. I saw the red tide cover the beachhead and thousands of zombies started dissolving into the sea. Then I heard the voice of two zombies dissolving in the waters. One said, "I can feel the Holy Spirit's presence."

Then the other said, "Well that makes sense, He created us."

Then I watched as the tide receded, like a tsunami inhaling, drawing back to the belly of the ocean. When it did, I looked at the beach and more zombies popped up out of the ground, attacking and aggressively pursuing us. In a panic, we started running for our lives. I looked to the left and saw soldiers running as well, some were riding Segways, and others were simply running. Everyone was running towards a wall trying to jump over. Then I saw a man with no legs riding a motorcycle. He was trying to help a child over the wall, but couldn't because he had no legs. Then I woke.

As soon as I woke I heard the Holy Spirit say,

> *"Not by might, nor by power, but by My Spirit says the Lord."*

You see a powerless church has no legs to stand on. When the tide of His presence recedes for a season, if we aren't filled with His presence, with living water, with the golden oil of anointing, we cannot stand. Our fight is weak and tiring. We spend more time running for our lives than we do changing the lives of the walking dead.

It's important to get this. The very DNA of humanity was designed to respond to the presence of the Holy Spirit. They will melt in the heart of His presence when they feel the red tide upon them. We are in warfare, and this fight is not against flesh and blood, but against principalities, powers, and forces in dark places.

The Lord has positioned each of us in strategic places around the planet. Whether individually, or as an organization, we are encamped like clusters of grapes, being prepared to engage in this Holy battle. However, it is only in Him and through Him that hearts, souls, and minds of this world will be changed. This is not a political fight. It is a spiritual fight. We are called to bring life to the walking dead. However, know this, a tide that recedes, recedes only for a season, and the tide that is coming back, is a tsunami of Christ's blood that will flood and saturate the land.

God's strategy: You

Awhile back, the Lord spoke to my heart about the strategic planting of His people in strategic places upon a battlefield. I was in a trance, and the scene that I saw was, as one would see if they were watching an old civil war movie, watching a camp of Union soldiers strategizing their advancement into battle. These outposts of His kingdom were placed strategically about at various locations, waiting for their next move to engage the enemy. Even now I can see the white tents clustered together with soldiers moving about, lighting fires to warm their coffee, and preparing their weapons for battle as the morning sun begins to rise and the dew lifts from the landscape.

Suddenly, the Lord showed me the valley of the battlefield. I was looking up at the skies above the valley and saw massive storm clouds covering the sky like a powerful blanket, shaking and moving with incredible intensity. Then the Lord spoke to me very powerfully and said,

> *"Call to the winds."*

Then the sky began to move, and He said,

> *"Call to the North, Call to the South, Call to the East, Call to the West."*

Then the skies began to move, and blow, and thunder.

So, I cried out to the winds. I cried out to the North winds, and the South winds, and the Winds of the East and the West. I cried – "Lord, send your power," and the sky began to turn like the development of a mighty hurricane.

Then the Lord showed me a lake that was overshadowed by the storm. Then he showed me a massive drop of rain hitting the lake. When it hit, mighty ripples flowed out from it, and the Lord said,

> *"Call to the rain!"*

And I cried out, "Send your rain oh God." I kept crying out, "I call to the wind, I call to the rain, I call to the North, the South, the East and the West. Send your rain oh God." Then the Lord showed me the hurricane that was building above the valley and out of the hurricane came forth-small cyclones, waterspouts. Suddenly these tornados landed upon His people, individually, like little cyclones spinning in the hearts of men.

Then the Lord said,

> *"Speak to the rivers and the streams, call to the ground to release the waters of My presence."*

And I saw people standing on the ground and suddenly, water came forth from the earth like what would happen if someone squeezed a wet sponge, and the people were getting soaked, and the water turned into a stream, into a river unstoppable.

Then the Lord showed me a Bell Tower. It was a like an old Spanish mission bell tower, (like Taco Bell) and the Lord was standing next to the bell tower with a staff in His hand. He took His staff and began to hit the bell. With incredible force and rhythm he hit the bell, and the sound of the bell went out throughout the Land.

Then I heard a voice say,

> *"Blow a trumpet in Zion, sound an alarm upon My Holy mountain. Call for the elders, let the saints come out of her chamber. Blow a trumpet across the land."*

Then I heard the Lord say as He swung and hit the bell.

> *"This is My mission bell and I am on a mission, I have a mission to complete."*

Poppa loves you dearly. He wants to rain down His presence upon you and move in the lives of your families, communities, and the region you live in. The Lord has called and placed churches and people around various regions around the world like outpost of the Kingdom of Heaven, strategic outposts positioned with purpose to advance His plan in this day and hour. There is a great outpouring on the horizon. The Lord is on a mission to bring about a great work.

The Lord would say to us,

> *"Listen Sweet Vine, Sweet Vineyard of mine, you are the winds,, you are the mighty winds of change,"* and the Lord would say to you, if you rally to His heart's cry and respond to the sound of the mission bell, *"I the Lord, the King of Heaven, will blow upon you with such a sweet,*

> sweet, fragrant wind that you will become (collectively) the force that I will use to usher in the hurricane of Heaven upon this land."

Please know that today is a day of refreshing. Today is a day for setting the captives free. The Lord is looking for the bride to come together in a unified force and call for the rain of God. His promise to you is to:

> "Ask for rain in the time of the latter rain. The Lord will make flashing clouds; He will give them showers of rain, grass in the field for everyone."
>
> - Zechariah 10:1

When you call, He will answer. "**Yes!**" He will respond with massive drops, one for each of you. Then He will cause a rippling to take place. The cyclone will be His passion, His power, the ripples will be the outflow of His love, and this outflow will become a highway in the midst of dry land and the people will begin to hear a sound – a fresh sound in their ears, a tune and a melody from heaven designed especially for them. For He is about to paint the landscape in living color, He is about to paint the land with His glory and play a melody of mercy to this generation.

The Lord is saying,

> "Arise you elders, you tribes, arise, and come to My sanctuary. Say to the mountains, 'Bow before the Lord of Glory.' Call to the rivers, Call to the streams – Release the waters of salvation, release the waters stored up for this hour. For I have a plan and a purpose, my flower, I have a plan for power in this hour."

Press in this day to the pressing of the Lord. Only then will we walk with Him in this final hour. The promise is that of a new filling, a new glory. When we yield, He will not only release this anointing, He will trade our feet of brass (representing the need to be cleansed and healed all the time) for feet of iron (representing His strength, where we transition from the healed to the healers). We will become a people ready to walk in this final hour.

Zechariah, in chapter four, when desiring to see the restoration of Judah and the temple, was caught-up in a vision. An angel approached him, awakened him from his sleep, and said, "What do you see?" Zechariah responded, telling the angel what he saw, and then he asked the angel what it meant:

> *"Now the angel who talked with me came back and wakened me, as a man who is wakened out of his sleep. And he said to me, What do you see?*
>
> *So I said, I am looking, and there is a lampstand of solid gold with a bowl on top of it, and on the stand seven lamps with seven pipes to the seven lamps. Two olive trees are by it, one at the right of the bowl and the other at its left. So I answered and spoke to the angel who talked with me, saying, What are these, my lord?*
>
> *Then the angel who talked with me answered and said to me, Do you not know what these are?*
>
> *And I said, No, my lord.*
>
> *So he answered and said to me: This is the word of the Lord to Zerubbabel: Not by might nor by power, but by My Spirit, Says the Lord of hosts"*
>
> - Zechariah 4:1-6

Now the angel was taken back, he should have known what olive trees and the golden olive oil were, but he didn't. The angel said, "Do you not know what these are?"

Admittedly, Zechariah said, "No, my lord."

Then the Angel said, **"Not by might nor by power, but by My Spirit, Says the Lord of Hosts."**

You see we have something that Zechariah did not have. We have the Holy Spirit, the resurrected Lord of all glory, and the Father of all creation living inside us. You see, the lesson form Zechariah is, unlike an oil lamp, an olive tree has an endless living supply of oil, forever producing, forever replenishing. Our desire is the same – only bigger.

Let's not stand before the Lord and ask, what are those olive trees? If we are going to press in we must be pressed in His presence. Only then we shall watch as the Lord anoints His tabernacle (Exodus 40:9-11) and fulfills the words of Jesus, as we proclaim His kingdom to the ends of the earth (Acts 1:4-8). For the call to His church, in this last hour, is to have lamps filled with oil, lamps that burn without ceasing (Exodus 27:20; Mathew 25). This is what all of creation is groaning for (Romans 8:22-27). Consider the words of Jesus, and ponder and pray regarding these things. Seek His face.

> "Then the kingdom of heaven shall be likened to ten virgins who took their lamps and went out to meet the bridegroom. Now five of them were wise, and five were foolish. Those who were foolish took their lamps and took no oil with them, but the wise took oil in their vessels with their lamps. But while the bridegroom was delayed, they all slumbered and slept.
>
> And at midnight a cry was heard: 'Behold, the bridegroom is coming; go out to meet him!' Then all those virgins arose and trimmed their lamps. And the foolish said to the wise, 'Give us some of your oil, for our lamps are going out. But the wise answered, saying, 'No, lest there should not be enough for us and you; but go rather to those who sell, and buy for yourselves.' And while they went to buy, the bridegroom came, and those who were ready went in with him to the wedding; and the door was shut.

> *Afterward the other virgins came also, saying, 'Lord, Lord, open to us!' But he answered and said, 'Assuredly, I say to you, I do not know you.'*
>
> *Watch therefore, for you know neither the day nor the hour in which the Son of Man is coming."*

- Matthew 25:1-13

Now is the time to look up!" A new season has begun. God is on the move and He is searching for His bride to take her place and arise, to be the voice of one crying out in the wilderness, Prepare ye the way of the Lord, for the Kingdom of God is at hand! It is time to move-on folks.

Chapter 31

Mercy Drops are Falling

Then He said, "I will make all My goodness pass before you, and I will proclaim the name of the Lord before you. I will be gracious to whom I will be gracious, and I will have compassion on whom I will have compassion."

- Exodus 33:19

A while back, the Lord kept showing me a picture. it wasn't a dream or a trance. It was simply one of those panoramic visions. In the vision I saw a massive drop of golden liquid hanging in the air. It was translucent and glistening, and it was rich thick like honey. As I walked into worship and began to sing and pray, the Lord gave me the following vision. I was looking up to the heavens and suddenly the sky above me was covered with a sheet of honeycomb. The honeycomb stretched from one end of heaven to the other and the pockets of honey were vibrating to the sound of worship. Then, as I was looking in anticipation, the Lord changed my perspective and I was watching the honeycomb from heaven's side.

As I was looking at the throne room, I saw Jesus standing there in Kingly attire. The entire room was filled with His glory and draped in golden light, as if everything was made of translucent gold. Jesus was standing on the backside of the honeycomb. It was as if a sea of honeycomb stretched across the heavens. He had a golden staff in His hand and He took His staff and pounded the honeycomb floor three times.

Suddenly, I was back, watching the honeycomb from the ground. The sky started to shake and then, with a massive thrust, the combs burst open and sky began to rain down massive drops of golden honey. I watched as people began to be covered with honey. Joy fell upon all as they lifted up their eyes and began to rejoice over the richness of the outpouring. They were reaching out and touching others. The honey was sticky and clung to everyone it touched. Like a golden impartation, the honey was distributed to all. Much like "pay it forward" – the commission was to reach out and touch somebody, sweeten their lives, and let the anointing stick to them and draw them to Him.

I asked the Lord what the honey was and He said,

> *"The honey is my sweet tender Mercy. Just as Moses sought to seek my face and to see my glory, I made all my GOODNESS pass before him, and I proclaimed My name before him. For I am gracious upon whom I am gracious and I will have compassion on whom I have compassion. For I am clothed in tender mercy, and my kingdom stands upon that mercy, for I am good all the time and My goodness is starting to pour out.*
>
> *Mercy drops are falling, are falling – yes,*
>
> *Mercy drops are falling, are falling.*
>
> *I will drape you with tender mercy. You will go out and come in with sweet mercy upon your lips – and you will take My mercy to the streets, to the highways, and byways, and My mercy will flow. My mercy is endless. My grace is more than sufficient for you. My desire is that you would be vehicles of My peace and power – that you*

will touch the downcast and the broken hearted and release My tender mercy.

The people are rigid; they don't see Me as the lifter of their heads. My Mercy is endless; it sets free them that are bound. They need to see Me in all My goodness, for I Am GOOD all the time and My mercy is from everlasting to everlasting. I laid down My life so that My honey would fall and fill the earth with My glory.

Mercy drops are falling, are falling.

And this drop is for you."

The cry of the Lord in Isaiah 49:8-13, amplifies His heart and mercy:

> *"Thus says the Lord: "In an acceptable time I have heard You, and in the day of salvation I have helped You; I will preserve You and give You as a covenant to the people, to restore the earth, to cause them to inherit the desolate heritages; That You may say to the prisoners, 'Go forth,' To those who are in darkness, 'Show yourselves.'*
>
> *"They shall feed along the roads, and their pastures shall be on all desolate heights. They shall neither hunger nor thirst, neither heat nor sun shall strike them; for He who has mercy on them will lead them, even by the springs of water He will guide them. I will make each of My mountains a road, and My highways shall be elevated.*
>
> *Surely these shall come from afar; Look! Those from the north and the west, and these from the land of Sinim." Sing, O heavens! Be joyful, O earth! And break out in singing, O mountains! For the Lord has comforted His people, and will have mercy on His afflicted."*

Let Your mercy fall upon us. Let our hearts be merciful. To know the love nature of God is to know the heartbeat of mercy. God is love. **God is good. He is good ALL the time.** If grace is getting what we don't deserve, mercy is not getting what we do deserve.

Mercy is a two-sided coin. On one side, we have our own testimony of God's mercy and grace towards us, how we were once blind, but now we see. On the other side, we have the responsibility to give away what we have received, the love of God and His mercy. When we, as a people, learn to embrace the love nature of Christ and move out in a non-judgmental way, radiating the love of Christ, the world will take notice. They will see that we aren't looking to manipulate them into the Kingdom. **Love will draw them.**

Jesus is calling us to be the "**Love Feast**" for the world to dine. When they see honest love in action, they will taste and see that He is good. We will be sticky like honey bringing sweetness to the lives of those around us. In these last days, our Lord wants a bride that is fragrant with His nature. Love releases the Kingdom.

God is calling us to a new place, a higher place, and nothing we have known from the past will be sufficient for this new season. We are moving into a place much like Moses was in Exodus 33. Moses lived his first forty years in royalty in the house of Pharaoh and forty years tending sheep on the backside of the desert. At 80 years of age, he was confronted by God and commissioned into his life mission. This reluctant, stammering, excuse-making fugitive was called back to Egypt to lead the Hebrews out of captivity. Now this broken-down sheepherder became the man of the hour and for the next forty years, he would see the mighty hand of God deliver a ragtag motley assembly of complaining, unbelieving, and rebellious tribesmen into a nation.

From the beginning, the very nature of Moses' relationship with God was one of "**presence.**" From the days of the burning bush to the heights of the unveiling of the law on Mt Sinai, Moses would have a face-to-face relationship with God. His relationship with God was unlike any before him in scripture. He witnessed the miraculous deliverance of Israel from the grip of the Pharaoh. He saw the grand exodus take place and the power of the Passover blood on the doorposts of God's children turn the page of Pharaoh's 430-year grip on Israel. Now it was ending. He witnessed the miraculous journey to Sinai, with deliverance at the Red Sea, provisions of manna and quail provided in their desert wanderings, and protection from the hostile Amalekites. He had encounters with God, so powerful, that his face literally glowed with the Glory of God.

Then in Exodus 33 we see the heart of Moses revealed when the Lord commands him to depart from Sinai and go to the Promised Land.

> *"Then the Lord said to Moses, "Depart and go up from here, you and the people whom you have brought out of the land of Egypt, to the land of which I swore to Abraham, Isaac, and Jacob, saying, 'To your descendants I will give it.'"*
>
> *- Exodus 33:1*

Moses is promised that God would send His angel before him. Here's the catch, God said He would not go himself lest He wipe out this stiff-necked people from His presence.

> *"And I will send My Angel before you, and I will drive out the Canaanite and the Amorite and the Hittite and the Perizzite and the Hivite and the Jebusite. Go up to a land flowing with milk and honey; for I will not go up in your midst, lest I consume you on the way, for you are a stiff-necked people."*
>
> *And when the people heard this bad news, they mourned, and no one put on his ornaments. For the Lord had said to Moses, "Say to the children of Israel, 'You are*

> *a stiff-necked people. I could come up into your midst in one moment and consume you. Now therefore, take off your ornaments, that I may know what to do to you.'" So the children of Israel stripped themselves of their ornaments by Mount Horeb.*
>
> *Moses took his tent and pitched it outside the camp, far from the camp, and called it the tabernacle of meeting. And it came to pass that everyone who sought the Lord went out to the tabernacle of meeting which was outside the camp. So it was, whenever Moses went out to the tabernacle, that all the people rose, and each man stood at his tent door and watched Moses until he had gone into the tabernacle.*
>
> *And it came to pass, when Moses entered the tabernacle, that the pillar of cloud descended and stood at the door of the tabernacle, and the Lord talked with Moses. All the people saw the pillar of cloud standing at the tabernacle door, and all the people rose and worshiped, each man in his tent door. So the Lord spoke to Moses face to face, as a man speaks to his friend. And he would return to the camp, but his servant Joshua the son of Nun, a young man, did not depart from the tabernacle."*
>
> - Exodus 33:2-11

Moses was grieved in His heart. All he knew of God was birthed in His presence. The very thought of God taking them into the next season of their destiny without the presence of the Almighty, was too much to bear. He moves in closer to God. He starts to pull on His heartstrings. From the depth of his being Moses says in Exodus 33:12-14:

> *"...See, You say to me, 'Bring up this people.' But You have not let me know whom You will send with me. Yet You have said, 'I know you by name, and you have also found grace in My sight.' Now therefore, I pray, if I have found grace in Your sight, show me now Your way, that I may know*

> *You and that I may find grace in Your sight. And consider that this nation is Your people."*
>
> *And He said, "My Presence will go with you, and I will give you rest."*

Moses, in essence is drawing a line in the sand. His heart is aching for more of God. He had been to the mountaintop and his face had radiated with the glory of God. He walked with God like no other, yet in this moment he is relentless, saying, "If Your Presence does not go with us, do not bring us up from here." His desire to live in the presence moved the Lord to relent and give Moses the desire of his heart (Exodus 33:15-17).

> *"Then he said to Him, "If Your Presence does not go with us, do not bring us up from here. For how then will it be known that Your people and I have found grace in Your sight, except You go with us? So we shall be separate, Your people and I, from all the people who are upon the face of the earth."*
>
> *So the Lord said to Moses, "I will also do this thing that you have spoken; for you have found grace in My sight, and I know you by name."*

Even at this, Moses is not satisfied. His hunger for God is unstoppable. His mind is not on the mission ahead or the future promised land. He is not thinking about his call or his duty. All he wants is more of God. He wants to see Him in all His glory. It is at that moment that God is moved to answer the heart cry of Moses and show him His glory. Only the surprising thing is, when God responds to Moses about His glory He points him to His nature, He says (vs. 19):

> *"Then He said, "I will make all My goodness pass before you, and I will proclaim the name of the Lord before you. I will be gracious to whom I will be gracious, and I will have compassion on whom I will have compassion."*

In essence, God is saying,

> "My identity, My nature, who I am, reveals My glory, and that is My goodness, that is My name, it is the revelation of the understanding who I am, and the love nature of My being that displays My glory. When you see and understand that, you are ready."

The Exodus story continues (33:18-23):

> *"And he said, "Please, show me Your glory."*
>
> *Then He said, "I will make all My goodness pass before you, and I will proclaim the name of the Lord before you. I will be gracious to whom I will be gracious, and I will have compassion on whom I will have compassion." But He said, "You cannot see My face; for no man shall see Me, and live." And the Lord said, "Here is a place by Me, and you shall stand on the rock. So it shall be, while My glory passes by, that I will put you in the cleft of the rock, and will cover you with My hand while I pass by. Then I will take away My hand, and you shall see My back; but My face shall not be seen."*

At that moment, Moses is given a gift, and the gift is the revelation of the nature of God, His name, His goodness, and His overflowing compassion. God takes him and places him in the cleft of the rock-of-our-salvation. He is hidden, as it were, in Christ, and then, when God removes His hand, he sees the back of God.

I would suggest to you that the back he saw was the back of Jesus himself, scourged on Calvary at the whipping post. It is that place of complete surrender and desire to see God face to face, knowing that nothing else matters in life but that one desire is the platform for God to draw him in.

God is bringing us to that place. He is changing our desires and drawing us to a place of transformation. Each one of us, personally, is at a crossroad. Do I go to the left, and settle for His angelic covering as I move forward in life? Or, do I stop and say, *"God, I can't go anywhere, unless you go with me. I need to know You completely, in all Your fullness. I need to see Your glory. Father, reveal to me Your nature and Your name. Let me be saturated with the knowledge of Your incredible love and compassion."* You see, when His love nature and goodness burns inside us, we can change the world.

The Lord hinted at His nature when He gave Moses the schematics of the tabernacle in Exodus 25. What's interesting in this set of instructions is that God does not start with exterior of the tabernacle and work inward. He instead starts at the most Holy place of all, the "Holy of Holies."

The first furnishing of that place is the Ark and the Mercy Seat. The Mercy Seat was the cover that rested on top of the Ark. It was made of pure gold and had two golden Cherubim that bowed on each end.

The Mercy Seat was more than a covering for the Ark, it was the place of His presence, for between the Cherubim, the cloud and fire of His presence would hover just above the Mercy Seat. It was the space between the Cherubim, which represented God's presence among the people.

This seat of pure gold, could not be controlled by man. It was a Holy place. The Mercy Seat conveyed to the Israelites the idea that God was in their midst. The Ark then becomes a foundation of the Mercy Seat and the place where His presence rests.

However, we don't get a full revelation of this until the resurrection of Christ. John's record of this is very interesting. We read in chapter 20 a very unusual encounter Mary has at the tomb.

> *"But Mary stood outside by the tomb weeping, and as she wept she stooped down and looked into the tomb. And she saw two angels in white sitting, one at the head and the other at the feet, where the body of Jesus had lain. Then they said to her, "Woman, why are you weeping?"*
>
> *- John 20:11-13*

It is here, and nowhere else in the gospels, we see the actual Mercy Seat, mentioned in Exodus 25. Mary peers into the tomb and she stops down and sees the spot where Jesus had been laid. At each end of that space were Angels, one at His feet and one at His head. At this moment, the essence of the Holy of Holies and the Mercy Seat becomes clear.

From the time that Moses built the tabernacle and the Priests carried the Ark of the Covenant before the people, what they were actually carrying was a living prophecy of the Lord Jesus Christ, their Messiah, resurrected on Easter morning. The space between the Angels was indeed the place where Christ raised from the dead, and in His resurrection He conquered sin and death and brought us into His presence and into the Holy of Holies. This is a powerful revelation. When God gives Moses the schematics of the tabernacle, He starts with a picture of the resurrected Lord.

The first act of Mercy on that Easter morning, 2,000 + years ago was a presence encounter with Mary. Like Moses, Mary was hungry for her Lord. She was disheartened. Her Jesus was gone. The man who freed her from seven demons, the one who healed her heart, and forgave her of all her sins, was gone. She woke that morning, crying inside. She had to be with Him, even in His death. She took off running, probably before dawn and ran to the tomb. It was probably still dark outside. Didn't matter, she had to be with Him. And when she arrived she found herself at an empty tomb, face to face with the Mercy Seat.

"Where have you laid Him," she cried.

Nevertheless, the tomb was still empty. That empty tomb is the place we find ourselves today. When all of our preconceived ideas and thoughts about God's nature are placed in the tomb, crucified if you will, then we are in a position to, like Mary, hear Him call out our name, and like Mary, we shall see Him for who He really is. He will show us His love nature. His love nature will bring about the change we are seeking. He will bring us into that Holy place. His love nature will transform us into a Bride ready for a wedding.

> *"Now when she had said this, she turned around and saw Jesus standing there, and did not know that it was Jesus. Jesus said to her, "Woman, why are you weeping? Whom are you seeking?"*
>
> *She, supposing Him to be the gardener, said to Him, "Sir, if You have carried Him away, tell me where You have laid Him, and I will take Him away."*
>
> *Jesus said to her, "Mary!"*
>
> - John 20:14-16

You see, everything we are, and everything we do is wrapped up in the resurrection of our Lord. At the heart of the sacrificial act lies the tender heart of the Father and His Mercy towards us. His incredible love and mercy draw us. It is His undying commitment to forgive us, woo us, and draw us into His presence that sustains us. We go from glory to glory in His love. With every step we take, the revelation of His loving kindness takes us deeper into Him. This deepness is always birthed out of resurrected mercy and love.

It is also interesting that the Hebrew name for the Mercy Seat is "kapporeth," which is best rendered in English, "propitiatory," meaning, having power to atone for or offered by way of expiation or propitiation. In other words, the very name points again to the atonement and the redeeming power of Christ's forgiveness extended to us.

The first time my eyes were opened to the truth of how much the Father perpetually loves me happened thirty years ago. I was a young Christian, still carrying luggage from my past on my back. I had sinned, I had gotten in an argument with my wife, and the weight of my guilt was crushing me. Up to this point in my life, I had felt that salvation was something I had to work at, as if it was fragile, and I needed to toe the line or it was over.

I was feeling so dreadful. I felt ashamed. The shame in my heart was smothering me. I couldn't even talk to the Lord about it. I was driving home from work along a road that parallels the mountains, along the desert, from Palm Desert to Palm Springs, California. The sun was starting to set, and the sky was starting to turn orange. I was crying inside. Then, without thinking about it, I mumbled to the Lord, "**I feel like dirt.**"

Suddenly, in a moment, I was in a trance. You have to understand I was driving. The Lord must have had some Angel take over at the wheel, because I was caught up in the most incredible vision. Here's what I saw:

I was standing in the middle of a field on a farm. Jesus was standing in front of me. His long hair was blowing in the wind. He was dressed in overalls. He looked at me intently. Then, very gently, He reached down and scoped up some dirt in the palm of His hand. He brought His palm up close to His mouth, staring at the dirt. Then He stretched His arm out, palm facing up, and spun around. As he was spinning, He began to blow upon the dirt in His hand. Instantly, the dirt flew out of His hand and scattered across the land like seeds being scattered. Instantly, as the dirt hit the ground, crops began to shoot up, as far as the eyes could see. Then looked at me with soft tender eyes, very close, and said,

"Boy, what I can do with dirt."

I was blown away, crying my heart out. He, in a moment, when I expected rejection and the firm hand and discipline of a father, He showered me with love and favor. Like Mary, I wanted to run to Him and cling to Him. I had found my Lord in the midst of my pain. I came to, still driving, and cried and praised Him all the way home. His love nature drew me in. His tender mercy and compassion caused me to want to go deeper. I knew one thing, His love for me was unshakable, and it caused me to love Him even more.

When we get this, we will truly be able to show the world the love of Jesus Christ. The resurrection is wrapped up in love and mercy. Like the sons of Aaron, we are called to carry the Ark of resurrection and presence before us in battle. That Ark is, in essence the Ark of tender mercy and love wrapped up with His presence and His power. Paul reminds us of this very thing when he says in 1 Corinthians 13:1-10:

> *"Though I speak with the tongues of men and of angels, but have not love, I have become sounding brass or a clanging cymbal. And though I have the gift of prophecy, and understand all mysteries and all knowledge, and though I have all faith, so that I could remove mountains, but have not love, I am nothing. And though I bestow all my goods to feed the poor, and though I give my body to be burned, but have not love, it profits me nothing. Love suffers long and is kind; love does not envy; love does not parade itself, is not puffed up; does not behave rudely, does not seek its own, is not provoked, thinks no evil; does not rejoice in iniquity, but rejoices in the truth; bears all things, believes all things, hopes all things, endures all things. Love never fails. But whether there are prophecies, they will fail; whether there are tongues, they will cease; whether there is knowledge, it will vanish away. For we know in part and we prophesy in*

> *part. But when that which is perfect has come, then that which is in part will be done away."*

The last day's bride is a lovely bride. She will move out with incredible grace, mercy, peace, and love. She is so lovely that she will literally draw the Lord of Glory to return for her. Be lovers dear children. Seek what Moses sought. Be as eager as Mary, and lay your preconceived ideas at the doorstep of the tomb. Embrace Him like John the beloved at the last supper. Be clothed by Him like Gideon of old. Run to Him and don't stop until you have a life changing love encounter with Him. Only then can you be His eyes, hands, feet, and heart to this dying, hungry planet. He needs your loveliness.

CHAPTER 32

THE HOUSE OF BREAD

"The average church has so much machinery and so little oil of the Holy Spirit that it squeaks like a threshing machine when you start it up in the fall after it has been out in the field all year."

- Billy Sunday (1862–1935)

The problem with many churches today is the same problem we see in many of our restaurants. The French were the first to coin the word "Restaurant." In the Dictionnaire de Trevoux, in 1771, defined the word restaurateur:

> *"Someone who has the art of preparing true broths, known as 'restaurants', and the right to sell all kinds of custards, dishes of rice, vermicelli and macaroni, egg dishes, boiled capons, preserved and stewed fruit and other delicious and healthy-giving foods."*

It wasn't until 1786 that the word restaurant was used to describe an eating-house. The simplicity of the early eating-houses was nothing like the restaurants of today. They were the local hangouts – places that served comfort food – honest and home-made, at a value that was friendly to the common folk. What started out as a simple house-of-bread suddenly became more complex.

Today, restaurants are big business and we are inundated with them. Like merchant-booths in an ancient marketplace, waiting for the crowds to sample their wares, we have them on every street corner and every inch of space between. These cookie-cutter concepts unfold, pop-up, and spread out across the landscape like settler's tents across the prairie planes. No longer is the sole-proprietor standing at the door to greet you. No longer do you walk into a neighborhood café and have intimacy with the owner and your neighbors as well. The corporate Big Buck and the bottom line drive it all.

The days of the independent owner who had only one goal in mind, to fill the place with well nourished, extremely stuffed, and happy consumers is over. It doesn't matter what you call it... a Café, Bistro, Brasserie, Tavern, Diner, Coffee Shop, or Restaurant, if there's one on every street corner you can be guaranteed that the menu as well as the experience is carved out of the boardroom and not from the heart of a chef proprietor.

The days of the community restaurant beating with the heart-felt passion of an independent neighborhood owner is gone in most communities. In times past, the independent owner saw their restaurant as a place with purpose. People would come in; they'd eat and be satisfied beyond their expectations. Their experience is so fulfilling, so wonderful, that they leave feeling full and content. They want to come back again. Not only do they come back – they become a marketing-campaign unto themselves. They tell their friends, their neighbors, anyone who will listen... what a grand experience they had in your restaurant.

The sad reality is that many independent restaurants today struggle to survive. They strive while going up neck to neck with the big boys. They can't compete with the glitz and glitter of the well-staged cookie-cutter concept of their corporate counterpart. The corporate giants on the other hand have it down pat. They have the educated experience, corporate marketing, project planning, a solid infrastructure of controls and training, with a so-called pulse on the consumer, and the corporate cash to back up their enterprise. They have done their homework, and they know the demographics of the area where to put their hot branded concept. The problem with these corporate institutional giants is not their expertise and business acumen, the problem is passion.

Without passion, even though you have all the ingredients of success, you will soon become a whitewashed tomb of a restaurant. You will be a colorful balloon – bright and shiny on the outside – but inside – full of hot air serving up dribble to a consumer that has lost their ability to taste real food. They have bought into the picture on the billboard with its thick and juicy representation of a dish that in reality is not even close to the picture. Thank heaven for glitz and glitter... if you spin it right, strong theme, lots of energy and glitzy decorative elements to distract them from the product – maybe the folks won't notice, and the sad thing is – most don't.

A while back, Jan (my wife) and I were sitting around trying to decide what to eat for dinner, when, like a moment of marital oneness; we looked at each other and said, "Breakfast." That was it, nothing like breakfast for dinner. We hopped on my motorcycle and shot over to a nearby chain coffee shop that had recently opened. The building and design package of the facility was nice. They had all the extra consumer hooks one would anticipate these days, retail merchandising at the entrance, walk-up to-go counter for easy pick-up, counter seating with contemporary table-lamps, positioned appropriately, and a warm comfortable interior broken up with a modest ratio of booths to tables. Decorative pony walls and partitions infused with a few plants breaking up the space to create the right environment without causing you to feel you were eating in a banquet hall.

"So far so good," I thought to myself, as I reached for the menu to scan the offerings. The menu was, from a corporate standpoint, perfectly engineered. All the items were well placed, descriptors were well written, layout was crisp, and for a café, the offerings sounded appealing. My choice was easy... steak and eggs to feed my craving, and flapjacks – there's nothing like a pancake supper with a good steak and a side of eggs to fill that void. Well, so much for fantasy.

My food arrived and it was awful, I mean BAD, and I haven't said that in a long time. Sitting on my plate was the most puny, over-cooked, soggy (figure that one out), piece of what they referred to as a steak. Next to that boil-in-the-bag piece of meat, was a small pile of little pale, un-seasoned, cubed potatoes, called home fries, and two pale looking eggs, at least they were over easy.

Now, as I get older, I have grown to focus more on the company than the meal, but this time I couldn't. I felt like Howard Beale, the acclaimed news anchorman for UBS TV in that 1976 movie "Network." I wanted to stand up and look at rest of the patrons in the restaurant and say, "look at your food – look at it will you and ... get up now. I want all of you to get up out of your chairs. I want you to get up right now and go to the window, open it, and stick your head out and yell, I'm as mad as hell, and I'm not going to take this anymore!" Ah but alas, I contained myself. With a loss of appetite, I returned my food, and sat there with a cup of old warm coffee. I continued a nice dialog with my wife while waiting to depart.

You see this place with all the components to make a modern day restaurant a success, lacked one serious ingredient. They could not deliver what they had promised – good food. It takes passion to make good food. Someone in the kitchen has to be on his or her knees before a hot stove and find out how and what to cook. Passion is the key that separates real food from a cheap imitation. Passion is the door, the driving force, which brings all the right elements together. Passion will pull you to the consumer's table to check the pulse of their experience. Passion will drive you into the kitchen causing you to work endlessly on a dish until it is just right, its taste, texture, aroma, layers of flavor, presentation, all of it, are perfect. You will tear it apart and build it back up again – as many times as needed until it's right.

Passion is contagious. It's contagious with the staff and the patron. People are drawn to your passion. People want to be around people that believe… people that are truly excited about what they do. They want to brush up against you and get close to you. They want to catch a glimpse of something, they want to glean a new understanding, a new depth of what you're doing. They want an imparting of something. They want your mantel, so to speak. They want a double dose of the fire that is burning inside of you. They want to draw from the wellspring of your experience. They desire to taste of something grand. They want their cups to overflow.

Now listen. This is very important. I am NOT talking about restaurants and the consumer. I am talking about the answer to the greatest mystery of the 21st century. **I am talking about the Church.** I am talking about the great commission. I am talking about Jesus Christ and His desire to set a table in the community where you live and serve up a meal that is fit for Priests and Kings. **I am talking about Passion and the Pulpit.** I am talking about the ingredients needed to reach a dying world. I am talking about the difference between a lukewarm or a dead church and one that is alive on the inside with the presence and heartbeat of Jesus Christ.

The restaurant, in a real way, is parallel to our church buildings today. We build them on every street corner. We offer up verbal menus from the word of God for all to come and feast. We desire to restore man back into fellowship with their loving Father and introduce them to the "bread of life." Even the word "Restaurant" has its root meaning "to restore; a food that restores." Haven't we been given the great commission to restore mankind and bring them back into fellowship with their creator, to feed them real bread, living bread, the bread of life?

How often have we, the church, bought in to this corporate model. Instead of spending time on our knees before the hot stove of God's presence, we are in search for the right hook, a good program, and a new way to increase the tithe and raise the membership. Our real model is closer to Jesus in the garden of Gethsemane, than the hanging gardens of Babylon. We don't need spin. We need to be spent. Like change in the pocket of an Almighty God, we need to be sold out to Him. We need to seek Him until we sweat, as it were, great drops of blood. Only then will we have a message that is birthed in travail. Only then will we communicate the "Passion of Christ."

We get caught up in our various programs and events, how well we say the same old message, while forgetting what the fundamental mission was that brought us here to begin with. At times such as this, we have to go back to our first love and receive from Him the passion and simplicity that we knew when we first believed – where the mission was fresh and simplistic – the goals were souls and not much more.

That is not always a simple task. People have a tendency, no matter where they are or in what state they are in, to get comfortable. They settle into complacency and loose the desire for a deep love relationship. It becomes a forked-road marriage where each partner is headed in opposite directions. Neither a marriage nor the church will be able to survive in such a state. We, the bride of Christ, must be in submissive obedience to His master plan. Our churches need more of Him and less of us.

It's just like that; cookie-cutter, restaurant Jan and I ate at. It looked good, had all the spin but in the end – there was nothing solid to eat. It had become a "house-of-stale-bread" or a "house-of-bread" serving no bread at all, just old dried crumbs ground into the carpets from patrons long forgotten. When a restaurant runs out of its ability to serve food – people stop coming. The sad thing is that these people are hungry – they are thirsty – they are looking for someone somewhere to open their doors and invite them to come in and feast at the table of abundance.

Tragically, many churches have ended up in the same condition. A house-of-bread where the only mandate is to reminisce about the bread of the past – speculating how good it must have tasted. Yet, there are no ovens to bake what people want or need. It becomes a history lesson about bread. People come in hungry for the bread of life. They want to sink their teeth into savory hot loaves of freshly baked bread. They hunger and desire manna from heaven but all they get is a menu they can never order off.

Oh, there's talk about how wonderful the bread once was – they even sing about bread – but serve it fresh and hot – no way. All of this brings about a spiritual famine in the land. People go about their day hungry and thirsty for a living vibrant relationship with the bread of life – but are left unfilled and hopeless. The sad thing is that Jesus is now, more than ever before, ready to send fresh hot loves of His presence into their midst – if they would only seek His face and give Him back His church.

So what happens to the communities where we live, our neighborhoods, and our cities? What happens to our children? What happens to all the starving people around us desiring to sink their teeth into spiritual food that has substance and life giving power? They go hungry and the famine becomes more rigorous. Our churches become fast food outlets – scattered about on every street corner – but nothing of substance is really served there. What do people do when their spiritual hunger becomes spiritual malnutrition? They flock to anything or anyone that offers something resembling a loaf of bread. They window-shop on the streets of our cities and taste the offerings of the new age movement, Eastern mysticism, or the occult, in search for hot bread. They seek out astrologers and tarot card readers hoping to find living water to quench their dying souls.

People are a lot smarter than we think. If one of our churches lit the ovens of the Holy Spirit and started cooking hot loaves from heaven... word would travel, it would get around, people would do anything to get real bread... hot freshly baked bread... especially in times of great famine.

Consider the story of Ruth, found in the book of Ruth in the Old Testament.

> *"Now it came to pass, in the days when the judges ruled, that there was a famine in the land. And a certain man of Bethlehem, Judah, went to dwell in the country of Moab, he and his wife and his two sons.,*
>
> *, Then she arose with her daughters-in-law that she might return from the country of Moab, for she had heard in the country of Moab that the Lord had visited His people by giving them bread."*

- Ruth 1:1,6

Naomi and her family left home and moved to Moab because there was a famine in Bethlehem. Bethlehem was the city of David; Bethlehem was the birthplace of the Messiah; Bethlehem was the birthplace of the bread of life. Bethlehem was the last place on earth you would think of as a place of famine. Even the literal translation of the word "Bethlehem" in the Hebrew means "the House of Bread." It should not have been a place of famine, but famine came, and Naomi left because they were hungry. They left because the House of Bread had no bread at all.

Why do people leave or never come into our churches – because there is no bread. Bread is the substance for life. The Jews knew the power of bread – they used its symbol during the Passover (feast of unleavened bread), the showbread was an integral part of the tabernacle and proof of the presence of God in the temple. In the book of Numbers, chapter four, it was called the bread of the Presence. The showbread literally means – show-up bread – the evidence that God has shown up in this place.

Naomi and her family are symbolic of the people that never enter, or leave, many of our churches today. They left Bethlehem and went to Moab trying to find bread. Oh, what lengths people will go through in search of some hot bread in times of famine. We see it all around us – people flock to nightclubs, casinos, and bars, in search for bread that will fill the void in their souls. They become slaves to sin, drugs, mental or physical abuse, and they accept it – believing it is their cup in life. Why do they believe this? The answer is simple – we have let them down, we have failed them and not offered them the reality of the living truth and the power of a gospel that will change their lives forever. We have become a franchise of the fast food gospel.

The good news is we do not have to except this state of spiritual melancholy. Jesus is more than ready to rain manna from heaven upon us. He wants His church back and is more than ready to hang a sign outside the "House of Bread" stating – "**Welcome... Under New Management!**" The turnaround is simple:

> *"If My people who are called by My name will humble themselves, and pray and seek My face, and turn from their wicked ways, then I will hear from heaven, and will forgive their sin and heal their land."*
>
> - 2 Chronicles 7:14

There is no other way. God wants to bake loaves of hot bread and serve them up to a people hungry for His presence. This really hit home for me one Sunday morning at church while taking communion. I walked up to the communion table to take communion. I stood there, held the bread in my hand, and began to thank the Lord for what He did for me. My heart was set on really digging into the moment. Suddenly, the Lord gave me an incredible vision.

The Vision of the Bread of Life

I fell into a trance and saw myself standing in a café. The café was full of life, action, and buzzing with excitement. To my right was a large hearth stone oven. Right next to me was a chef with a wooden peel in his hand. He was pulling out of the oven large loaves of hot bread and tossing them into baskets. Waiters were moving about the café handing out loaves of this hot fragrant bread. Everyone was filled with incredible joy. The place was alive with enthusiasm and energy – and they were all smiling.

The counter in front of the oven was an "L" shape that wrapped around to the front of the café. In the corner next to floor-to-ceiling windows were two very large wine barrels – Napa Valley style. The wait staff was pouring wine from the spigots into large beer pitchers. They were running around pouring glasses of wine – smiling all the way. The front to the café was all windows, and the door was open.

The street in front of the café was alive with people rushing over to enter the café. A paperboy was riding his bike had stopped in front of the café with a paper in his hand. He had an incredible smile on his face, almost animated. The paper was the "*Good News Journal*" and the headline across the front-page read, "**This Is That**," echoing Peter's famous words from Acts chapter two, in explanation of the out-pouring of the Holy Spirit on the day of Pentecost.

I asked the Lord what was going on, and He said,

> *"Religion has taken My communion and placed it in a box of lethargy. It lies dormant at the foot of the cross, never moving to the place of resurrection and life. Yet, My kingdom is full of Life, where Mercy flows continuously from the vats of heaven and is waiting to be poured out and served up in Kingdom Café.*
>
> *Heaven is so full of My grace that it comes out of the oven of My presence like loaves of warm bread, eagerly desiring to be served up, and full of life and abundance. When My people embrace the abundance of grace and mercy that I desire to pour out – people will flock in groves to get into My Kingdom and Joy will be the hallmark of My waitstaff.*
>
> *The fire has been lit, the ovens are hot, the dough has been prepared for this hour, and the vats are already overflowing with My mercy. The bread and the wine point to the glory of what I have done, what I am doing, and what I will be doing in the days and months ahead. The gift of My atonement did not stop at the cross – it is perpetual – it moves to create a Kingdom here on earth, as it is in Heaven, full of royalty – a royal priesthood – sons and daughters of God reflecting the Glory of who I AM and what I AM doing, ageless, ceaseless, full of life and abundance.*
>
> *The Kingdom Café is open – tell them to come – come to My banqueting table, the table has been set, destiny is*

today, see what I see – behold the beauty and the glory of the Kingdom Café. Oh how I love the life in this place."

The next time you drive down the restaurant district of your neighborhood pay attention to all the types of restaurants you find there. Look at the ones that have a two-hour wait, in contrast to the restaurants whose parking lots are empty. Count the number of fast food outlets and cookie-cutter chains and see how many cars are lined up in the drive-thru.

Look at the churches in your neighborhood and use the same kind of guidelines you would to find true, hot, passionate food, try to find the one with a two-hour wait – to get in. I tell you, if a great restaurant opened its doors and served hot-out-of-the-oven bread, you would have to fight them off with a stick to stop them from coming in.

I challenge you – if people are willing to stand in line for two-hours to have a burger – how long will they stand in front of a church that is overflowing with the presence and power of the Holy Spirit. **The bread-of-life will draw them.** The new wine will keep them. No coupon, groupon, BOGO, or two-for-ones will bring them in. No early bird specials will cause them to beat down your doors. However, bread, life-giving bread, just out of the oven bread, served hot and fresh for this generation – will.

Humanity has a bread-shaped hole in its heart and the only thing that will fill it is Jesus. Let's get back to the culinary basics and bring forth hot bread to the nations. I look forward to the day when the lines outside our churches go on for blocks. I can't wait for the sweet aroma of the freshly baked bread of His presence to float through our streets filling the air like incense, drawing all those who are tired and needy. I look forward to the time when restaurant owners have to close down their restaurants because the ovens are turned up at the church down the street – fresh bread is being served and the entire town is eating it up. Let's get on with the task at hand. **Light the fire – kindle the stove – turn up the heat – let Jesus show up and bring to the world the bread of His presence.**

> *"When the hour had come, He sat down, and the twelve apostles with Him. Then He said to them, "With fervent desire I have desired to eat this Passover with you before I suffer; for I say to you, I will no longer eat of it until it is fulfilled in the kingdom of God."*
>
> *Then He took the cup, and gave thanks, and said, "Take this and divide it among yourselves; for I say to you, I will not drink of the fruit of the vine until the kingdom of God comes."*
>
> *And He took bread, gave thanks and broke it, and gave it to them, saying, "This is My body which is given for you; do this in remembrance of Me."*
>
> *Likewise He also took the cup after supper, saying, "This cup is the new covenant in My blood, which is shed for you."*
>
> - Luke 22: 14-20

CHAPTER 33

COFFEEHOUSE OF HOPE

"Give ear, O my people, to my law; Incline your ears to the words of my mouth. I will open my mouth in a parable; I will utter dark sayings of old, which we have heard and known, and our fathers have told us. We will not hide them from their children, telling to the generation to come the praises of the Lord, and His strength and His wonderful works that He has done."

- Psalm 78:1-4

"And He said to them, "To you it has been given to know the mystery of the kingdom of God; but to those who are outside, all things come in parables, so that 'Seeing they may see and not perceive, And hearing they may hear and not understand; Lest they should turn, And their sins be forgiven them.'"
And He said to them, "Do you not understand this parable? How then will you understand all the parables?"

- Mark 4:11-13

The Parable... Given in a Dream

The following parable was given to me in a dream.

Once there was a Barista that loved his profession and took great care and pride in the coffee he brewed, so much so, that he said to himself, *"I am going to build me a café that serves up the finest coffee in all the world. In fact, my café is going to be so warm and welcoming that all who come in will taste of my cup and their lives will be filled with comfort and joy. It will be a place where people will gather and find rest for their souls."*

Well, as any good businessman would do, he surveyed the competition and assessed the needs of the marketplace. He was struck by the indifference of the people, how they would run into any coffeehouse and drink no matter the quality or how watered down it was. Some were running after instant coffee. Others wanted the sweeter varieties, like a caramel macchiato or vanilla latte that was so diluted all flavor was lost. And the beans, well no one knew the quality of a good beans, or the care it takes to produce the perfect cup, so he said to himself, *"I am going to change things. My coffee house will not be like this, for in my house – I will serve only the finest of beans, and I will pour only the finest cup,"* this desire to serve burned deep with-in his soul.

So he bought some land and built himself a coffeehouse. And when it was done the Barista stood back and marveled at the beauty, warmth, and simplicity of his new café, it was wonderful. He was now ready to open the doors to his new café. There was one problem he had no coffee. Now this troubled the café owner, *"How can I sell the finest cup and not have the finest bean?"* So he looked to the bean traders to see what they offered, but did not care for the quality, their beans were either picked too early, or the wrong variety. For this Barista only the high mountain Arabica beans would do. Other beans were either low-mountain beans and often over roasted or burnt and lost all the essential oils, flavor, and aroma. So, he said to himself, *"I will head out myself and gather the beans I need."* So he closed the doors to his café and went on a journey in search for the finest of beans.

The Barista traveled to a far away land. Its landscape was mountainous and terrain dangerous. In fact, this land was made up with some of the highest mountain ranges in the world and many were volcanic and active. The Barista knew that the best beans grew in regions such as this, so he picked the tallest volcanic mountain he could find and set out on his journey in search for the finest beans. After several days of hiking through the thickest of forests, he finely reached the summit. He searched and searched but found no beans, only ash and hardened lava, remnant for its last eruption. Then, as he circled the peak of the mountain, he came across a path that led him to a small luscious valley. On the edge of the valley was a single Arabica bush, but the bush had no life for it had been scorched in the heat of the eruption. He stood disheartened. Then, as if by fate, he glanced down at the base of the tree and saw nestled in the ashes, five little beans. *"I know what I will do,"* he said, *"I will plant the beans and wait for them to grow."* So he gathered the beans in the palm of his hand, and took some soil mingled with ash and journeyed to the center of the valley where he found a cluster of tall shade trees. There he planted his beans under the shade and safety of the trees.

For seven years, he waited for his trees to grow. Through rain, and wind, and cold, and heat he camped at the side of his bushes looking for the fruit he so longed to see. Then one day, as the sun was breaking through the mist that had covered the mountain top he saw it, his trees began to blossom. They were covered with the most incredible white flowers he had ever seen. And the aroma, like jasmine, filled the mountainside. But after four days the flowers were gone, leaving behind them perfect dark green berries.

"*Alas*," the barista said, "*the berries I so long to see*," and he knelt down and thanked the God of Heaven for yielding a harvest. But he knew that if he wanted to create the perfect cup he must not pick them to soon or they will produce a bitter cup, not fit for drinking. So he waited until they began to ripen, at first to yellow, then light red and finally darkening to a glossy deep red. Now it was time. He laid gunnysack at the base of the bush and vigorously he shook the tree until all the ripe berries had fallen onto his gunnysack. Likewise, he did to all five trees. After gathering his berries, he knelt down and sorted the good from the bad. Then placing the good berries into massive bags he tied them off and threw them over his shoulder and carried them down the mountain heading home with a wonderful harvest.

When our Barista arrived at his café his eagerness to open his doors and serve his first cup was overwhelming, but he had to slow down, the time was not ready. He had to prepare the berries for roasting. First, he had to remove the flesh of the berry revealing the seeds or beans as we call them. Then he fermented them to remove the slimy film still present on the bean. When the fermentation was finished, he washed them with fresh water and laid them out to dry. But the work of the Barista was not done for the cup he desired to pour had to have a rich dark and aromatic flavor. To get to this level of excellence the beans needed to be roasted.

The roasting process was crucial as it developed caramelization, color, nuttiness, and most of all; it brings out the essential aromatic oils, which give the coffee its true flavor and aroma. Our Barista knew for the perfect cup, he did not want to over-roast it but still wanted a deep smooth cup with a subtle sugary flavor.

Alas, the coffee was ready for cooling. Once cooled, he packed his beans in an airtight container until it was time for brewing.

Now, it was time. Now he could open the doors to his café and begin serving that perfect cup. So he went over to his espresso machine and placed his beans in the grinder. After grinding the beans he placed ground beans into the hopper and with a tamping device, he pressed the ground very tightly forming a puck, locked it into place on the espresso machine, and hit the brew button causing very hot water, under extreme pressure, to press its way through the grounds. The result produced a rich, almost syrupy beverage by extracting and emulsifying the oils in the ground coffee. He looked down at his little demitasse cup and said, "Perfect! This is just what I was looking for: a well-balanced cup with a reddish-brown crema. Now I can open my doors."

The story and its interpretation.

"My dear children listen to this story and understand. Do you not know that I would climb the highest mountain for you? Do you not know that I would search for you and bring you unto Myself?

Yes, I have called you unto Myself. I found you and pulled you out of the ashes and placed you in the palm of My hands. I held on to you as My own, and planted you under the shadow of My wings, and have protected you. I nourished you and watched as you grew.

I was there on the day you blossomed. Your faith in Me has been a sweet aroma in My temple. Your love for one another has been as jasmine, an aroma of adornment. I know the shaking you have endured, but I have gathered you up as a fine treasure and carried you upon My back, and brought you to this place inside of Me.

Do not fear or be dismayed. I have come that you might have life – and that more abundantly. But I want you to know that My presence and work in your life did not stop on the day you bloomed. Nor, did it stop when I saw the fruit of your love. No, it is because of your love and desire to draw closer to Me that I have pressed into your lives.

The work that I do calls for deep preparation. The value of the cup that I desire to pour is far richer than instant espresso. My gift for you is built upon perseverance. My desire for you is beyond anything you can imagine. Do you not know that everyone is seasoned with fire, and the fire you have experienced is the fire of purity?

I, Myself, have brought you to the roaster. I am the one that called you to that place. For though you walk through the flames of trial, the stench of the smoke shall not harm you. For what I am doing is for your benefit. For it is through this fire that the flesh is dried out, so that the oil of My presence within you would be drawn to the surface.

Yes, it is that oil that brings the flavor and fragrance of My Kingdom to others. I am preparing you. My desire is to pour you out upon the nations, so press in, and press on, know that in the end you shall be called blessed of My Father.

I know that many of do not understand this grinding process. Yet it is by this process that you, become We, for it is the rock of My presence that has brought you to this place. I have called you to cast all your cares upon Me – yes even your very lives. And when you fall upon this rock you will be broken, but out of your brokenness will arise a heart set apart for Me, so press in, and press on, to that place that I have called you.

The pressure is on. You have been pressed on many sides, this I know, and this I understand. But please understand Me when I tell you, it is by this pressure and by this tamping, that My cup is created.

Do not fear and do not worry, cast your cares upon Me and let patience do its perfect work. Trust Me My child, you shall come through this time and you shall be a cup of blessing, for I have brought you unto Myself, and the cup I desire to pour – is a cup of blessing. This, My beloved, is the heart of the matter, press-in my love, press-on my beloved, for soon you will see the doors of My café open. My cup is full, and your cup shall surly overflow. Its' espresso time My children. Press-in, and press-on."

Chapter 34

The Shaking

"The poor and needy seek water, but there is none, their tongues fail for thirst. I, the Lord, will hear them; I, the God of Israel, will not forsake them. I will open rivers in desolate heights, and fountains in the midst of the valleys; I will make the wilderness a pool of water, and the dry land springs of water. I will plant in the wilderness the cedar and the acacia tree, the myrtle and the oil tree; I will set in the desert the cypress tree and the pine and the box tree together, That they may see and know, and consider and understand together, that the hand of the Lord has done this, and the Holy One of Israel has created it."

- Isaiah 41:17-20

"Along the bank of the river, on this side and that, will grow all kinds of trees used for food; their leaves will not wither, and their fruit will not fail. They will bear fruit every month, because their water flows from the sanctuary. Their fruit will be for food, and their leaves for medicine."

- Ezekiel 47:12

In the seasons ahead there is going to be a gracious shaking in the kingdom of God. The shaking is a shaking of release into greater levels of love, mercy, and tenderness. This season is a season of harvest. This harvest is the harvest of the fruit trees of heaven. From across spectrum of the kingdom, trees that have been fertilized, growing, and soaking in the sun of His presence are moving into realms of release and fruit-fullness. Let me explain.

During prayer a short while back, the Lord brought me to a quiet place. All around me, I saw ripples of water, as if I was submerged in an ocean and my eyes were just above the waterline. I was looking at the water and the water was vibrating all around me with the presence of Jesus.

As I watched the ripples, suddenly, I saw the face of Jesus. It looked as if he was sleeping with his face against a golden silken pillow. However, as I watched, I realized he wasn't sleeping at all. He was tenderly embracing the surface of the water. I understood the water as being the water of your life as a child of His.

Your life was infused with the water of His life. His life was fluid and it covered you. He was so enveloped in tender love and passion, for His desire over you, that, as He laid down, in tenderness, and He began to breathe upon the surface of the water. As He breathed His breath moved upon the water it causing ripples, and the ripples became waves – and the waves rolled out until they became a tsunami that flooded the whole earth.

Then I heard a song, a tender lullaby,

The breath of the Lord is upon the waters

The breath of the Lord is upon the waters

His tender love is upon me

His tender love is embracing me

He is caressing me with the depth of His embrace

His love for me is stirring, stirring, stirring the deep places of my heart.

As I listed to that melody I was over come by the heart of the song...

> *His love is fluid. His fluidity will overcome you in this season. His flowing love will bring rapture to your souls and a release of revelation and knowledge of Him, His heartbeat, passion, and love. His peace and presence will move upon you like waters upon the surface of the deep. His breath will be upon you like the dance of the wind, shaking, shaking, and shaking the very pillars of your soul.*
>
> *He is wooing you to a deeper place, a place of saturation, yes, marination, Marination that will bring transformation.*
>
> *The ripples He is sending from you will be a proclamation to the nations.*
>
> *What is produced in this season of tenderness and love will yield incredible fruit. During this season of marination and transformation, lives are going to change and fruit that has been ripening upon the vine in the last season is about to be released upon the face of the earth.*

Let me explain,

As I was watching the water, it all became quiet and dark like the night sky. Then I heard the Lord say,

> "I am shaking and shifting the structures of the earth and calling for fruit in this season. I am bringing in the harvest and causing My voice to sound out in the highways and byways. Like a mighty whisper I am penetrating the hearts of many, and many, many, many shall hear and come unto to me. Byways shall become highways, crooked places shall be made straight. Plow horses are being sent out and the breaches are being repaired."

Then he gave me a glimpse of the garden of His delight.

Almond Trees: Then I looked and saw Almond trees shaking in the wind and as the almonds fell to the ground branches sprung up and the almond branches began to bloom. The Lord said, "I am calling forth My almond branches, my royal priesthood, and they shall begin to bloom in the land and cause a fragrance to fill the air and begin to change the atmosphere."

Apple Trees: Then I looked and saw Apple trees shaken by the wind of His presence. Apples started to fall to the ground. As they fell, I saw workers of the harvest, the gathers collecting baskets of apples. The apples were collected and brought into the kitchen of the Most High God. There they were prepared, and the aroma of simmering apples began to fill the atmosphere of heaven, apples laced with cinnamon and raisins. Apples laced with sugar and spice. He took these fragrant apples, wrapped in the bread of His presence and baked them as pies, and then cut into wedges, and He said,

> "With these wedges, I will pry open the dark places and transform doors that were once closed, windows of heaven; this is the process of My presence."

And the Lord said,

> "You are the apple of my eye and the desire of My heart and I am preparing you and enfolding you with My presence and for My purpose. I am about to serve you up to

this planet and invade those that are, so-called, hard to reach, and to those hard to reach places. And they shall open their doors to you because you bear my fragrance. You are sweet because I have simmered you in My love."

Date Palms: And then I looked and saw the mighty Date palms of the desert, and they began to shake. I saw dates falling from the mighty palms. Then I heard the Lord Say,

"I have planted some of you at the gate of the desert and you have flourished in the dry places and have grown in the desert places and now I am beginning to release your fruit." And the Lord said, *"In this desert place, I have courted you, yes, I have dated you and showered you with My adoration and My love. Because you have grown in the desert place, I will cause you to become a river of life, and this desert will be transformed into fertile fields. And gardens will grow and harvest will come, and your branches will be as shade to the broken."*

God is shaking the desert places, bringing sweetness to the barren lands, making you as date-nut bread to a hungry people.

Fig Trees: Then I looked and saw figs falling in the orchard and the figs were transformed into Fig-Newton, flakey and rich in flavor and aroma. And I heard the Lord say,

"I am releasing my figs upon the land and opening realms of creativity and invention. My people will be a catalyst of creation, speaking creative life into this season."

Pine Trees: Then I saw tall pine trees lining the Mountain of the Lord and the Pine trees started to shake, and pine-cones started to fall and when they fell they revealed pine nuts, and the pine-cones became cones of protection, and the pine nuts began producing trees, that became ladders for others to climb the high mountain places of God.

Then I saw pesto blended with the basil of praise. I saw shrimp marinating in the pesto and God was calling those who were small in their own eyes to change their identity. And He said,

> "The small are about to become great in might. No longer consider yourself as shrimp in my Kingdom, for you are monster prawns, yes giants in the land, and you are flavorful prawns, prawns in the hands of a master chef who is about to serve you up as a new course for this generation. You are mighty pine trees planted upon the mountain of the Lord."

Tomatoes: Then I saw the Lord walking in the tomato fields. As He walked, ripe tomatoes began to fall to the ground, and the Lord said,

> "This is a new fruit in the land, a new crop that will penetrate the public places. They are a savory fruit, and the meat of their calling will stretch across boundaries and touch the high places, yes even the pinnacles of power. And they shall release the flavors of Heaven to those that many say, cannot be reached, But I say, these have been created, to reach into that place and to transform that dominion into the dominion of Heaven."

Ancient Seeds: The tide is turning and the geographical plates of the planet are shifting and realigning, glory, glory, glory. I looked and saw the mighty plates of the earth beginning to move and shift. As they shifted I saw mighty seeds being exposed, sprout, and grow. They were "Ancient seeds" planted from the hand of the Ancient of Days, and these seeds are about to be released into the earth, and the Lord said,

> "My people are about to bring forth a mighty root system in the earth that will shake the very foundation of the land. Trees, trees, trees are being shaken, and fruit is coming forth. Heritage and inheritance is being released. Fruit from the past is being grafted into the fruit of the

present. I am creating super fruit that will produce super food loaded with the nutrients and DNA of Heaven."

This is a new season. This is a season of change and transformation. Press into his tenderness towards you. Press into the waters of life. Drink from the ocean of his love until your branches are so plump with his heartbeat – that your fruit falls into arms of the nations – ripe and ready for a hungry people.

This is your season. This is the year of fruitfulness, Press on Church and let His love overcome you.

CHAPTER 35

The Anointing

"You shall put the turban on his head, and put the holy crown on the turban. And you shall take the anointing oil, pour it on his head, and anoint him"

- Exodus 29:6-7

"Then you shall take the garments, put the tunic on Aaron, and the robe of the ephod, the ephod, and the breastplate, and gird him with the intricately woven band of the ephod. 6 You shall put the turban on his head, and put the holy crown on the turban. 7 And you shall take the anointing oil, pour it on his head, and anoint him."

- Exodus 29:5-7

A butterfly landed on my armchair. I was in Florida, and it was gorgeous outside, so I wasn't surprised, except that butterflies speak so deeply to my heart. They speak of destiny and transformation. I had been sitting there wondering about life and destiny, and there it was, this little winged angel gazing up at me. I was immediately reminded about a word the Lord shared with me one summer.

For weeks that summer, the Lord had been sending me butterflies. When I asked Him what it meant He said,

> *"Transformation – pollination – impregnation, impartation. I am transforming My children to be a people called out by My name, to be a changed people – people that pulsate with the glory and beauty of My Kingdom. No longer will My children crawl around like caterpillars with their identity rooted in this world. They – have been transformed – renewed in their minds – a people that reflect My very nature – a people that have been transformed from this realm to the Heavenly. They have become butterflies of My reflective glory – they have taken flight, and in their flight they will pollinate the world around them with My kingdom, with My glory, with My love."*

A short while later, while I was at work, preoccupied with something, the Holy Spirit began to sing into my spirit. The volume of the singing was loud and getting louder. As I was walking towards the elevator His presence was increasing and the sound kept coming – then I stepped into the elevator and it became heavier – so much so, it took my breath away. Then the Lord said,

> *"I am taking you higher – Step into My presence – I am accelerating the timetable – I am taking you up higher – enter in – choose the penthouse – the pinnacle of My palace – step in and rest in my Glory."*

When I got home that night, I was sitting on my patio looking at the sun set between some tall pine trees by my house. Suddenly, I saw the Lion of the tribe of Judah – golden and powerful – filling the sky between the trees. He was moving towards me – big, fast, and powerful. As He moved closer, I could feel His presence increase – so much that I was startled and jumped back. I thought I was going to be overwhelmed and fall to the ground. This happened several times, and then it stopped – and my heart cried out – more Lord – I need more of You.

All that the Lord said was,

> *"Suddenly, Suddenly, Suddenly,"*

But my heart wanted suddenly right now – and for days and days this hunger lingered – crying out, More of you.

Then that Friday night, a few days later, as I sought the Lord – praying for more, suddenly I saw the throne of God. Brilliant white light was shining from the throne. In front of the throne I saw Angels standing before a massive vat filled with golden oil. They were stirring this vat with very large paddles. Then Jesus stepped off His throne and stood before the vat. He peered into the vat until His reflection permeated the oil and His face covered the surface of the oil like a mirror. Then He bent over and dipped His face into the oil. When He stood back up His entire body was enveloped with golden oil. Then it was as if He was the oil – as if He was golden liquid. He began to shake His hands and massive drops of oil began to fall from the heavens.

I was lying down and saw this massive drop falling towards me – almost in slow motion. Then I heard the Lord say,

> *"I AM the anointing – I AM the Christos – I Am all that you need – I have poured out Myself to release My anointing upon you – I AM all you need." Then the drops kept falling and as I look at these incredible golden drops – first the drops looked as if they were falling from an inverted golden crown – from the tips – then they appeared in the shape of keys – golden keys of oil."*

And the Lord said,

> *"My anointing is the key to unlock My presence with-in you – to unlock your destiny,"*

And suddenly, it was as if I was looking into outer space and the heavens were filled with golden keys of oil – everywhere – like stars and planets move through the heavens.

Then the Lord said,

> "Behold the endless possibilities of My presence. Behold the endless possibilities of My presence in you. Today is the day of destiny. Today is the day that I unlock your tomorrows – your tomorrows are today – enter into My glory and know that I am He who holds the keys of David – who holds the keys of life and of death. Unlock the treasure chest within your spirit and release upon this land My Love, My power, My glory – for I AM glorified in you."

Isaiah 61 we read:

> "The Spirit of the Lord GOD is upon Me, because the Lord has anointed Me to preach good tidings to the poor; He has sent Me to heal the brokenhearted, To proclaim liberty to the captives, and the opening of the prison to those who are bound; To proclaim the acceptable year of the Lord, And the day of vengeance of our God; To comfort all who mourn, to console those who mourn in Zion, to give them beauty for ashes, the oil of joy for mourning, the garment of praise for the spirit of heaviness; That they may be called trees of righteousness, The planting of the Lord, that He may be glorified."
>
> And they shall rebuild the old ruins, they shall raise up the former desolations, and they shall repair the ruined cities, the desolations of many generations. Strangers shall stand and feed your flocks, and the sons of the foreigner shall be your plowmen and your vinedressers. But you shall be named the priests of the Lord, they shall call you the servants of our God. You shall eat the riches of

the Gentiles, and in their glory you shall boast. Instead of your shame you shall have double honor, and instead of confusion they shall rejoice in their portion.

Therefore in their land they shall possess double; Everlasting joy shall be theirs. "For I, the Lord, love justice; I hate robbery for burnt offering; I will direct their work in truth, and will make with them an everlasting covenant. Their descendants shall be known among the Gentiles, and their offspring among the people. All who see them shall acknowledge them, that they are the posterity whom the Lord has blessed." I will greatly rejoice in the Lord, My soul shall be joyful in my God; For He has clothed me with the garments of salvation,

He has covered me with the robe of righteousness, as a bridegroom decks himself with ornaments, and as a bride adorns herself with her jewels. For as the earth brings forth its bud, as the garden causes the things that are sown in it to spring forth, so the Lord GOD will cause righteousness and praise to spring forth before all the nations."

Rise up dear friends and be transformed, mount up on the wings of a butterfly, and slide into your destiny!

CHAPTER 36

THICK OIL FOR A CHOSEN GENERATION

"'The glory of this present house will be greater than the glory of the former house,' says the Lord Almighty. 'And in this place I will grant peace,' declares the Lord Almighty."

- Haggai 2:9

Something inside me is burning. I can't let it go. I yearn for that touch of the Master's hand that will shake the very foundation of my life and the lives of those around me. My heart is pounding in anticipation for Jesus to encounter His church like never before. I long for revival, true revival that is sustained for the long haul, a revival that grows from glory to glory, and does not dissipate through the years. I long for a touch of God on the land that will be greater than anything before it. I burn inside to see this generation leak with the presence of God. I long to see the reflection of Jesus on the face of His bride. I long to hear his heart beat and feel his embrace.

I grew up in the church in the midst of revival. The year was 1979. The Jesus movement was in transition from a beach salvation movement to a power encounter movement. John Wimber of Vineyard Christian Fellowship had sparked something inside my heart that would forever change me. John had taught me that I could get as close to God as I wanted to, that I could serve Him with a level of intimacy that would overflow with prophecy, healings, signs, and wonders, to a starving broken planet. He taught me that "doing the stuff" was my birthright as a child of God, and that pursuit of His presence was the Kingdom.

Vineyard was birthed from a handful of burnt out pastors to become a major force in equipping the church worldwide to passionately seek the face of Jesus and reach out to the world through power encounters. We truly believed that when we pray, **"thy kingdom come, thy will be done, on Earth as it is in Heaven,"** we meant it, and so did Heaven! We were a church in the midst of revival.

Since the days of Pentecost, great revivals and awakenings have occurred throughout the centuries. But they have always faded away between the generations. Sure they have left their residue and incredible benefit to the body of Christ, but the burning heart nature of what we call revival – that heart pounding desire to seek his face – fades, and so often, in the wake we are left with another denominational spin off, but the heart of what birthed the revival disappears.

People have always asked, **"Why in the space of a couple generations do revivals dissipate?"** They go from a blazing fire of Glory to barely a flicker, then nothing – a puff of smoke – and it's gone. We haven't changed much since the times of Joshua. In Judges 2:7-11 when Joshua became leader, the bible says:

> *"So the people served the Lord all the days of Joshua, and all the days of the elders who outlived Joshua, who had seen all the great works of the*

> *Lord which He had done for Israel. Now Joshua the son of Nun, the servant of the Lord, died when he was one hundred and ten years old.*
>
> *And they buried him within the border of his inheritance at Timnath Heres, in the mountains of Ephraim, on the north side of Mount Gaash. When all that generation had been gathered to their fathers, another generation arose after them who did not know the Lord nor the work which He had done for Israel. Then the children of Israel did evil in the sight of the Lord, and served the Baals;"*

To be honest, that is my fear for this generation. The truth is, faith, anointing, ministries, mantles, gifts, and mighty moves of God cannot be transferred from generation to generation without personal power encounters and the desire of a people to burn for and seek after, with all their hearts, the face and presence of Jesus.

The good news, for this generation, is that God is on the move. There is a sense in the air that something big is about to happen. The gap between revivals is getting shorter and shorter. God is agitating our hearts. He is stirring the pot of our souls. He is shaking our very foundations. He so longs for a sustained move of his presence that he is not letting go; He is relentless in His pursuit. Really, He has taken hold of the hem of our garment, and will not let go, until the healing has begun. He is causing a desperation inside many that is truly making us miserable and it will not yield until we see and receive the fullness of what He longs for in this new era.

In my lifetime alone, since that incredible day in January 1979, when Jesus yanked me from the fires of hell and brought me into his presence as a child of the King, we have seen revival hit in pockets around the world. We saw the birth of revival in the Vineyard movement; we saw the flames of fire hit Toronto, Pensacola, Redding, Kansas City, Charlotte, and Mobile. This isn't just a western move. Today, God is beginning to take nations. He is establishing his Army around the world for a global harvest. However, what we are seeing today is just a trickle.

What Jesus desires to do for this generation is far beyond all of the moves of God in history. Jesus is waking the bride of Christ. We are so overdue. The coming move of God will be the sustained move of God. It will be unlike any before it. He is going to do a new thing. He is about to put his imprint on cities, states, regions, and countries, and, he is going to do it through everyday people. There is a personal outpouring that is going to take place that will reach the ends of the earth, and it will come through and be upon "average Joes", as we say in the states, people like you and me.

Repeatedly the Lord keeps showing me this very thing. He has not conceded, and I cannot shake it. Just yesterday, while driving to work, the Lord gave me a vision of the Shekinah Glory of God coming as a cloud. As I looked at the cloud it became a funnel cloud, and I heard the Lord say,

> *"I am about to pour out my Shekinah glory on the individual. Like a funnel in the spout of a bottle, I shall pour My presence upon them and in them and they shall see and know My glory like no other generation."*

This personal outpouring will be rich with power and authority, but it will be wrapped up in a people, who, like Moses, have been to the mountain top, and have seen the lover of their souls, face-to-face. The anointing that is about to fall on the bride is thick with His presence, and will come upon all who seek after him and the beauty of His being.

The power and personal nature of this next move of God was reinforced in a dream the Lord had given me recently. In this dream, I saw a faucet in a bathroom like one would see in a typical home. The faucet was turned on, full force, and out poured thick black oil, like petroleum. When I saw it, I knew in my spirit that it was the oil of anointing. When I woke, instantly I saw visions of the earth, and inside the earth, I saw caverns of the deep filled with hot molten oil. They were just under the surface and scattered throughout the earth. As I looked, I saw oil wells sprouting up across the land. I saw layers of black shale just under the surface of the earth and the children of God holding clumps of shale in their hands. As they held the shale, it liquefied and flowed from the palms of their hands.

When I asked the Lord why the oil was black, he said,

> *"Just as the blood of Able cried out from the ground for justice, so the residual anointing, life missions, ministries, destinies, and dreams from all of history are, even now, crying out to me. I have reserved, for this generation, an anointing that is so thick it reeks with the history and legacy of My saints. Every lost dream, every shortened life call, every unfulfilled destiny, every mantle from every martyr, every mandate from every missionary, from every child in My house who has gone before you is stored up in me and is ready to be released upon the land.*
>
> *That is why it is thick and black like oil, like petroleum. It is full of energy and power and this generation, more than any before it, knows what it means to be without it and the high cost it takes to obtain it. This anointing is redemption oil, redeeming all the lost anointings of history."*

Then he said,

> *"Do you understand?"*

"Yes Lord," I responded. And in that moment I understood the thick blessing and rich heritage of the saints. I understood that this anointing was an answer to the heart cry of the saints in Revelation chapter 6:9-11.

> "When He opened the fifth seal, I saw under the altar the souls of those who had been slain for the Word of God and for the testimony which they held. And they cried with a loud voice, saying, "How long, O Lord, holy and true, until You judge and avenge our blood on those who dwell on the earth?" Then a white robe was given to each of them; and it was said to them that they should rest a little while longer, until both the number of their fellow servants and their brethren, who would be killed as they were, was completed."

I understood that the judgment of God in these last days would begin with the love feast of the bride. It would begin with the fresh release of all the anointings throughout history, reduced and condensed into a mega-blast of his presence. I understood that Jesus would take the surplus from all who came before us and smear us with it, like smearing butter on hot toast.

He is about to give payback to the enemy. He is throwing down the trump card and the power and presence of the past will be more than our floor; they have become seeds, commingled and germinated for a new generation. You are God's secret weapon.

I also understood that we have to press in and remember and honor all that God has done before us. That we have to declare and decree with hearts of fire, that greater is He that is in us, than he that is in the world. God is about to flood the marketplace with saints smeared with his anointing. However, we have to remember how great and awesome our God is and believe His testimony. The bible says that the testimony of Jesus is the spirit of prophecy. All his wonders are available for release in our lives, today!

The word says:

> "Remember the days of old, consider the years of many generations. Ask your father, and he will show you; Your elders, and they will tell you:"
>
> - Deuteronomy 32:7

And again in Joel 2:25...

> "So I will restore to you the years that the swarming locust has eaten, the crawling locust, the consuming locust, and the chewing locust, My great army which I sent among you."

Paul understood the heritage of the saints when he counseled Timothy in 2 Timothy, chapter 1:5-7:

> "When I call to remembrance the genuine faith that is in you, which dwelt first in your grandmother Lois and your mother Eunice, and I am persuaded is in you also. Therefore I remind you to stir up the gift of God which is in you through the laying on of my hands. For God has not given us a spirit of fear, but of power and of love and of a sound mind."

And in Colossians he says:

> "For this reason, since the day we heard about you, we have not stopped praying for you. We continually ask God to fill you with the knowledge of His will through all the wisdom and understanding that the Spirit gives, so that you may live a life worthy of the Lord and please Him in every way: bearing fruit in every good work, growing in the knowledge of God, being strengthened with all power according to his glorious might so that you may have great endurance and patience, and giving joyful thanks to the Father, who has qualified you to share in the inheritance of His holy people in the kingdom of light. For He has rescued us from the dominion of darkness and brought us into the kingdom of the Son He loves, in whom we have redemption, the forgiveness of sins."

> - Colossians 1:9-14

Even the writer of Hebrews in chapter 11, understood the power of this rich thick anointing when he points us to the great cloud of witnesses.

> *"All these people were still living by faith when they died. They did not receive the things promised; they only saw them and welcomed them from a distance, admitting that they were foreigners and strangers on earth."*
>
> - Hebrews 11:13

He continues in verse 32:

> *"And what more shall I say? I do not have time to tell about Gideon, Barak, Samson and Jephthah, about David and Samuel and the prophets, who through faith conquered kingdoms, administered justice, and gained what was promised; who shut the mouths of lions, quenched the fury of the flames, and escaped the edge of the sword; whose weakness was turned to strength; and who became powerful in battle and routed foreign armies. Women received back their dead, raised to life again. There were others who were tortured, refusing to be released so that they might gain an even better resurrection. Some faced jeers and flogging, and even chains and imprisonment. They were put to death by stoning; they were sawed in two; they were killed by the sword. They went about in sheepskins and goatskins, destitute, persecuted and mistreated— the world was not worthy of them. They wandered in deserts and mountains, living in caves and in holes in the ground. These were all commended for their faith, yet none of them received what had been promised,"*

And get this...

> *"...Since God had planned something better for us so that only together with us would they be made perfect."*
>
> *- Hebrews 11:32-40*

So His heart cry to us is this... in Chapter 12:1...

> *"Therefore, since we are surrounded by such a great cloud of witnesses, let us throw off everything that hinders and the sin that so easily entangles. And let us run with perseverance the race marked out for us,"*

You see...

> *"By faith Abel brought God a better offering than Cain did. By faith he was commended as righteous, when God spoke well of his offerings. And by faith Abel still speaks, even though he is dead."*
>
> *- Hebrews 11:4*

But in Hebrews 12:22-24 he says...

> *"But you have come to Mount Zion, to the city of the living God, the heavenly Jerusalem. You have come to thousands upon thousands of angels in joyful assembly, to the church of the firstborn, whose names are written in heaven. You have come to God, the Judge of all, to the spirits of the righteous made perfect, to Jesus the mediator of a new covenant, and to the sprinkled blood that speaks a better word than the blood of Abel."*
>
> *- Hebrews 12:22-24*

The blood of Jesus is speaking today. The blood of all the saints is speaking today. It is Christ's joy to anoint each of you, and your household with his payback plan.

When I was worshiping at church after the Lord had given me the dream of the faucet being turned on, I saw Jesus, in a bedroom with a pillow in his hand. He was having a pillow fight. The room was filled with joy as he swung the pillows around. The pillows were so stuffed full that as he swung they burst open and feathers were flying around everywhere. The room was so full of feathers that all you could see was a cloud of soft white feathers.

When I was praying about this I understood that trapped inside the pillow were dreams, dreams that that the Lord had placed in the hearts of his children, dreams of destiny and purpose, and the Lord's desire to bring breakthrough and release to long forgotten dreams.

As I was praying for a release of destiny in the lives of people in the church I saw the Holy Spirit fly in like a dove. His wings were dipped in the dark oil. As he flew over, a single oil dipped feather began to float down. As it approached, it became a quill pen. I then saw the pen begin to write. It was writing a signature – like a John Hancock, if you will.

I understood that the Holy Spirit was writing the dreams of promise, identity, and purpose on the hearts of his people. That He was engraving His purpose in their lives and signing His very name to it, like a decree. Like the signature on a check, you can take this check and deposit it, for it is decreed in heaven and engraved upon your hearts.

> *"Whoever has ears, let them hear what the Spirit says to the churches. To the one who is victorious, I will give some of the hidden manna. I will also give that person a white stone with a new name written on it, known only to the one who receives it."*
>
> - Revelations 2:17

The Lord wants to tar-and-feather us, and send us out of the church building and into the streets. He is so concerned with our destiny, and the impact that this generation will have on the world, that He has not, and will not relent until his bride looks like Him. He is redeeming the time. You are a chosen generation. Do not underestimate the impact that you, as an individual, will have on this planet.

The last picture the Lord showed me regarding this anointing I saw an ocean size pool of this oil cover the whole earth. Then one drop fell from Heaven into the ocean of anointing causing ripples to flood the planet. Don't underestimate the impact of one drop upon your life can make. In the physics of God, drops become oceans.

Let us cry out and be smeared, tarred, and feathered!

> "The Redeemer will come to Zion, to those in Jacob who repent of their sins," declares the Lord.' As for me, this is My covenant with them," says the Lord. 'My Spirit, who is on you, will not depart from you, and My words that I have put in your mouth will always be on your lips, on the lips of your children and on the lips of their descendants—from this time on and forever,' says the Lord."
>
> - Isaiah 59:20-21

Reread Joel Chapter 2 for a snapshot of your destiny!

CHAPTER 37

DRINK, MY BRIDE

"You, God, are my God, earnestly I seek you; I thirst for You, my whole being longs for You, in a dry and parched land where there is no water. I have seen You in the sanctuary and beheld Your power and your glory. Because Your love is better than life, my lips will glorify You. I will praise You as long as I live, and in Your name I will lift up my hands."

- Psalms 63:1-4

"I'm simply done with life. 57, not terminal or depressed. I was going to use the plastic bag, but too many failed attempt stories. I live in an apartment bldg, in California USA & if someone hears me moaning inside the bag & calls the police, it's BAD news for me. I've tried dehydration 4 times & have always failed & had water., I'm on another attempt at dehydration. Something always came up to deter my plan. It's going much better this time.

After 3 days of no food, I have no more hunger. Having no liquids is a lot tougher, but I've built up my courage & determination. I'm more willing to suffer dry-mouth, & I won't "cheat" by eating frozen grapes (they contain enough liquid to delay death). I've lost 50 pounds so there's not much for

> *my body to live on itself. Some people might find this an agonizing way to die. It suits me., I'm very much at peace. I've made amends to all my friends & family. I've been an Atheist, but talked w/ several religious people about death. I believe I'll go to a nice place, & I'll recognize those I knew in some way. The dry-mouth is the hardest part of this method. At times it's really hard to swallow. So I go to sleep for a while.,"*
>
> – From the Suicide Project, http://suicideproject.org

When I first read those words, it broke my heart. I found myself praying for her, asking God to give her living water, to show up and pour out his Spirit and open her eyes to the beauty of life in Christ. I'm sorry; I don't know the outcome of the writer. I pray she is still alive. She posted her journey on the Suicide Project website. That is all she wrote, two paragraphs of death, despair, and defeat. I pray someone at Suicide Project found a way to reach her, so very sad.

I found this story by accident. I was searching for stories about dehydration. When I was first diagnosed with diabetes I was in a state of dehydration. The sugar level in my body was killing me. I was constantly thirsty due to frequent urination. My mouth was dry. I experienced nausea, cramping, fatigue, confusion, sleepiness, and blurred vision. However, unlike the person above, I wasn't trying to kill myself. When my wife finely took me to the doctor's office, my blood sugar was 530. Thank God we caught it before I went into a coma. It's been five years, and I have had to make many life style changes – but all is good.

What really troubles me about the story above is that it does not have to be that way. We, the body of Christ, have the answer that this lady is searching for. We carry in us Kingdom life. Why did she want to die? Why wasn't someone there to give her hope? Where were the anointed ones? Sometimes I feel that we, the church, are a bit dehydrated and its hard to offer someone else water when you, yourself, are running on empty. I think we have gotten so used to running on empty that we don't realize we're drying out. Are we truly equipped to make a difference? Have we reached our full potential in Christ?

Unlike dehydration in the natural, spiritual dehydration may be harder to detect. In the natural, our bodies tell us we need water and instantly we move to fulfill that need. In the spirit realm, it's not as easy.

Signs like sexual immorality, impurity, and witchcraft, are obvious. It's the subtle signs of spiritual dehydration like complacency, jealously, fear, anger, selfish ambition, dissension, and discord that we often miss. Worse, we blame it on "quirks" in our personality or cultural upbringing. I think the number one sign so often missed is the lack of true thirst, that heart aching hunger for intimacy with Jesus. This one is so easily brushed off. If we aren't in "blatant sin" and are living a pretty good and decent life, then all is good, right? Not quite.

Many unsaved folks live good and decent lives. I believe the real test is our love meter with Jesus. A love meter measures your intimacy, hunger, and relationship with Christ. How hungry are we for him? Without an intimate relationship with Jesus, one that is constantly thirsting for more, we become like the old story of the frog in the water. If you throw a frog into boiling water, he will instinctively jump out to save its life. If, on the other hand, you drop him in ambient water (consider the lukewarm nature of the church of Laodicea in Revelation 3:14-22), then slowly turn up the heat; the frog will swim around until it boils to death.

You see a life that isn't constantly being filled with the love of God through relationship and intimacy will loose their ability to discern the true state of their condition, and find themselves floating in a sea of loneliness and spiritual isolation. And like that frog, in the end, if not caught in time, they will boil to death. For the Christian, a love relationship with Jesus is the life-line. In the book of Revelation, to the church at Ephesus, one of the greatest churches of the New Testament era, Jesus said this:

> *"I know your works, your labor, your patience, and that you cannot bear those who are evil. And you have tested those who say they are apostles and are not, and have found them liars; and you have persevered and have patience, and have labored for My name's sake and have not become weary. Nevertheless I have this against you, that you have left your first love. Remember therefore from where you have fallen; repent and do the first works, or else I will come to you quickly and remove your lampstand from its place—unless you repent."*
>
> - Revelation 2:2-5

We know the truth of this in the natural. Ask anyone who is married, what their relationship would be like if their spouse was not madly in love with them, if they were complacent and took their mate for granted, if they never showed affection, or never showered them with love and attention. They would tell you the marriage is doomed, it's on the rocks. Sadly, it will end either in divorce or in the prison of unloving routine, two people trapped and separated by the invisible wall of hurt, hate, pride, and self will.

Let me ask you a question: *Are you personally, at this time in your life, at a deep and agonizing level, hungry for more of the Lord? Are you so thirsty for him that, like the heartbeat of the of the bride in the Song of Solomon, if you can't find him, you're incom-*

plete? Does your thirst cause you to and groan for Him? Do you dig and search for him, like a thirsty soul digging for water in a desert, not stopping until he finds water?

You see Jesus is looking for a bride that truly craves him, one that is so in love with him she will do anything, just to be in his presence. The good news is we don't have to stay in that dry place. We don't have to live that way. But we do have to repent. We do have to change the way we think about Jesus. We have to change the way we approach Him. Jesus is so eager to embrace us and fill us with his presence. He is in fact, chomping at the bit to do so. He is standing at the door, ready to fill us again, and again, and again. And that filling is pure bliss. So much so, that Peter, in the book of Acts responded to the crowed like this....

> *"When the day of Pentecost came, they were all together in one place. Suddenly a sound like the blowing of a violent wind came from heaven and filled the whole house where they were sitting. They saw what seemed to be tongues of fire that separated and came to rest on each of them. All of them were filled with the Holy Spirit and began to speak in other tongues as the Spirit enabled them. Amazed and perplexed, they asked one another, what does this mean? Some, however, made fun of them and said, they have had too much wine. Then Peter stood up with the Eleven, raised his voice and addressed the crowd: Fellow Jews and all of you who live in Jerusalem, let me explain this to you; listen carefully to what I say. These people are not drunk, as you suppose. It's only nine in the morning!"*
>
> - Acts 2:1-4, 12-14

These folks were so filled with new heavenly wine they appeared to be drunk! Living water changes us. Being filled with the presence of Jesus rocks our world. We become undone. The good news is, when we drink and are full, we thirst even more. The Kingdom works that way. No, wonder the first miracle recorded in the book of John was the wedding feast at Cana, where he turned water into wine to reveal his glory.

In the summer of 2010, I saw a vision of Jesus. He was leaning against an ancient well, like Jacob's well, with a cup in his hand. He looked at me, with a smile on his face, and said:

> *"Drink! – Come!*
>
> *All who are thirsty come to the living waters and drink, drink until your cup is overflowing.*
>
> *Drink until you are so full it flows into the streets. Drink until the land is saturated with my presence. Drink, My bride.*
>
> *Drink that I might shower you with My love.*
>
> *Drink that I might fill you with My presence, and endow you with My power and My passion.*
>
> *Drink My bride to overflowing and My glory shall rest upon you."*

I looked around and saw some folks really craving for more of Jesus, but others were not. It could have been fear or just uneasiness, but at the end of the day, the presence of Jesus was there to fill His children. I think that is the key, "being children, being childlike." Jesus wants us to come to him like a child. When we abandon all, and just want to seek his face like a child – the windows of heaven open up and the rain begins to fall – the floodwaters start to raise and the wonder and beauty of the lover of our souls, rushes in. You see children know how to dream. They aren't shackled by duty. They aren't preoccupied to fill a series of repetitive tasks and projects. They just want to play with their Poppa. They just want to soak in the waters of life. They just want to be held by Daddy.

Sometimes folks feel the Lord's presence or listen to a word from the Lord and it really resonates in their hearts, but that resonation soon dissipates, and is replaced with another activity. That encounter moment is taken away, they have robbed themselves of the true purpose of resonation: to draw them in and closer to Jesus; to be filled with the healing work of His hand; to be immersed into the living water – and be changed. Instead of allowing time to baste in the moment through worship, or quietness, or meditation, or simply waiting, they rush off to the next task and that Holy Spirit moment of filling, passes them by. They miss the rich blessing that only comes through marination and patiently waiting on the gentile grace-fullness of Holy Spirit. The modern demands of our cultural and the rigidness of tight schedules can kill off the move of God as much as anything else.

Yet, Jesus still needs to go to Samaria. He still stands at Jacob's well looking for someone to take the drink from His hand. Jesus told the woman at the well in the forth chapter of John:

> *"If you knew the gift of God and who it is that asks you for a drink, you would have asked him and he would have given you living water.", "Everyone who drinks this water will be thirsty again, but whoever drinks the water I give them will never thirst. Indeed, the water I give them will become in them a spring of water welling up to eternal life."*
>
> - John 4:10, 13-14

And in John chapter 7 in desperation, he cried out,

> *"On the last and greatest day of the festival, Jesus stood and said in a loud voice, "Let anyone who is thirsty come to me and drink."*
>
> - John 7:37

This burning desire to drink and be filled with the presence Jesus is unstoppable. Everywhere I turn the Lord keeps saying the same thing. I can't shake it. Then (summer of 2012), I saw the following:

In the vision, I saw myself standing backstage, as it were. I was peering at the side of the stage looking at a soft cream-white curtain. I approached the curtain and reached out to touch it. As I touched it, I was struck by its softness. I looked up to see how high the curtain went and saw the curtain shoot straight up into the heavens. As I was peering into the heavens, I realized it wasn't a curtain at all, it was the robe of Jesus. I was holding the hem of his garment. I was overcome with the Holy Spirit, and I heard the voice of Isaiah:

> "In the year that King Uzziah died, I saw the Lord, high and exalted, seated on a throne; and the train of his robe filled the temple,"

> - Isaiah 6:1

And like Isaiah, I was undone. Then I heard the Lord say,

> "The stage has been set. The time has arrived. My Spirit yearns to fill My temple, and I shall fill My temple, until the whole earth is filled with My Glory. Don't you know that you are the temple of the Holy Spirit? Open up your hearts and let me in,, open up your hearts and let me in. Open the doors of your hearts and let ME IN."

And I cried out in my spirit – **have your way God, have your way!!!!** Fill us God fill us to overflowing. And I looked around again and knew the Spirit of the living God was there to fill his bride to overflowing. I wanted to shout it out – wake up oh bride – be filled with His glory, be filled with His fullness, be filled and see the glory of the Lord! But the time wasn't right, so I sat there, filled, yet sad inside. The heart cry of Jesus hovered over that place like the Shekinah glory, but the bride was still sleeping.

Moments later the Lord showed me the oceans of the world and farmers were plowing on the surface of the ocean. They were in rows, all plowing in unison. As I watched the farmers were transformed into people riding wave-runners riding the wake of His presence.

Instantly I understood the riders were His Last Days messengers, preparing the way for His coming, preparing for the next great wave of His presence. They were the sent-out-ones. They were the voices of those shouting in the wilderness, "prepare ye the way of the Lord." They were the forerunners on wave-runners, riding the wave of his Glory, a wave so big, like a tsunami, it will flood the land.

You see the Lord's cry is no different than what He spoke to the prophet Malachi...

> *"I will send my messenger, who will prepare the way before me. Then suddenly the Lord you are seeking will come to his temple; the messenger of the covenant, whom you desire, will come," says the Lord Almighty. But who can endure the day of his coming? Who can stand when He appears? For He will be like a refiner's fire or a launderer's soap."*
>
> - Malachi 3:1-2

The Lord is getting us ready, but this season requires a bride whose lamps are full and lit and whose cups are overflowing. While I was praying about this I saw the Lord standing in Heaven. His head was bent down towards the earth. His mouth opened and water came gushing out like a waterfall. I looked at the waterfall and saw salmon swimming upstream, towards Jesus. I heard the Holy Spirit say, "Swim to me my children, swim and spawn a new generation, spawn life." And I knew that Jesus was birthing something that has generational impact, and this move will reach generations to come (Psalms 36:9).

> *"For with you is the fountain of life; in your light we see light."*

Jesus is calling us into a new level of oneness that will have everlasting impact....

> *"My prayer is not for them alone. I pray also for those who will believe in me through their message, that all of them may be one, Father, just as you are in me and I am in you. May they also be in us so that the world may believe that you have sent me. I have given them the glory that you gave me, that they may be one as we are one — I in them and you in me—so that they may be brought to complete unity."*
>
> - John 17:20-23

> *"For I will pour water on the thirsty land, and streams on the dry ground; I will pour out my Spirit on your offspring, and my blessing on your descendants. They will spring up like grass in a meadow, like poplar trees by flowing streams."*
>
> - Isaiah 44:3-4

After this the Lord showed me trees weeping golden sap, and I knew that all,

> *",Creation waits in eager expectation for the children of God to be revealed. ... We know that the whole creation has been groaning as in the pains of childbirth right up to the present time."*
>
> - Romans 8:19, 22

Then I saw the wooden floors of an old shack. I looked at the floor with all its grain exposed, and saw that even the floors were weeping. Then I saw the walls of the shack, and I saw the grain in the wood, and I knew that the grain was revealing years of brokenness. It was revealing a people bound by a structure of pain and fear.

Then I saw Jesus peering through a knothole in the wall. Outside was the wondrous beauty of his presence. It lit up the sky. I knew that the Lord had come to bring healing and restoration. I knew that the Lord was releasing healing and restoration to His church. I knew that he was breaking the walls that bound and shaking the wooden foundation that is stopping His children from obtaining their potential. I understood that He was peering inside our hearts and asking us to open up to Him and trade the shack of shackles for a mansion on a hill.

Then I saw Jesus walking quietly on a green hill, dressed in a simple cream-white robe, like a monk would wear, only cream-white, no gold, it was common, and simple. He removed His hood revealing His crown; it too was soft and simple, almost understated like a whisper. It had the words faithful and true inscribed on it. Large red rubies were studded between the words and around the crown.

As I was looking, I felt that the Lord was coming in quietness, almost like He was coming in secret. And the Lord brought this scripture to my mind:

> *"You go to the festival. I am not going up to this festival, because my time has not yet fully come." After he had said this, he stayed in Galilee. However, after his brothers had left for the festival, he went also, not publicly, but in secret."*
>
> - John 7:8-10

I knew that this season was also a season of the quietness of Christ. Jesus is coming to us quietly and in secret. He will whisper in our ears, and He will share with us His secret things. This is the place of being still before Him. He will show up when we least expect it. He will enter situations that we think He has no interest in. He, himself will spy out the land. He, himself, will ride the wind like a whisper and invade our hearts in a new intimate way. He will show us a side of His nature that we have never seen before. We will look upon Him, and see a completely new revelation of His presence. Know this:

> "The secret things belong to the Lord our God, but the things revealed belong to us and to our children forever, that we may follow all the words of this law."
>
> - Deuteronomy 29:29

And

> "I will give you hidden treasures, riches stored in secret places, so that you may know that I am the Lord, the God of Israel, who summons you by name."
>
> - Isaiah 45:3

This experience will be like that of John in the book of Revelation. John was the beloved. John was the youngest of the disciples; he had walked with Jesus for three years. He was there when Jesus was transfigured. He had his head on the breast of Jesus at the last supper. He stayed by him at the foot of the cross, and raced Peter to the tomb on that Easter morning. He was there at Pentecost, and served Him for nearly 70 years, as a church father, until his exile on the isle of Patmos.

Yet, as a man who knew Jesus so well, who walked with him so long, he was about to encounter Jesus like he never did before. Check it out...

"I, John, your brother and companion in the suffering and kingdom and patient endurance that are ours in Jesus, was on the island of Patmos because of the word of God and the testimony of Jesus. On the Lord's Day I was in the Spirit, and I heard behind me a loud voice like a trumpet, which said: "Write on a scroll what you see and send it to the seven churches: to Ephesus, Smyrna, Pergamum, Thyatira, Sardis, Philadelphia and Laodicea."

I turned around to see the voice that was speaking to me. And when I turned I saw seven golden lampstands, and among the lampstands was someone like a son of man, dressed in a robe reaching down to his feet and with a golden sash around his chest. The hair on his head was white like wool, as white as snow, and his eyes were like blazing fire. His feet were like bronze glowing in a furnace, and his voice was like the sound of rushing waters. In his right hand he held seven stars, and coming out of his mouth was a sharp, double-edged sword. His face was like the sun shining in all its brilliance.

When I saw him, I fell at his feet as though dead. Then He placed his right hand on me and said: "Do not be afraid. I am the First and the Last. I am the Living One; I was dead, and now look, I am alive forever and ever! And I hold the keys of death and Hades. "Write, therefore, what you have seen, what is now and what will take place later."

- Revelation 1:9-19

We are moving towards a new encounter with Christ. We shall see Him like we've never seen him before, Get ready church.

After this I saw cream-white sheets hanging on a clothesline and the wind was blowing them dry. Spring aroma filled the air, and then I saw the face of a bride behind a cream-white veil, She was getting ready to step out from behind the veil.

I understood the Lord was drying out our garments, getting them ready to wear – His bride is at the door and in His heart, He is crying out...

> "Gather the people, consecrate the assembly; bring together the elders, gather the children, those nursing at the breast. Let the bridegroom leave His room and the bride her chamber."
>
> - Joel 2:16

> "Let us rejoice and be glad and give him glory! For the wedding of the Lamb has come, and his bride has made herself ready."
>
> - Revelation 19:7

And we shall join Him in His cry...

> "The Spirit and the bride say, "Come!" And let the one who hears say, "Come!" Let the one who is thirsty come; and let the one who wishes take the free gift of the water of life."
>
> - Revelation 22:17

And He will rejoice over us...

> "For Zion's sake I will not keep silent, for Jerusalem's sake I will not remain quiet, till her vindication shines out like the dawn, her salvation like a blazing torch. The nations will see your vindication, and all kings your glory; you will be called by a new name that the mouth of the Lord will bestow.
>
> You will be a crown of splendor in the Lord's hand, a royal diadem in the hand of your God. No longer will they call you Deserted, or name your land Desolate. But you will be called Hephzibah, and your land Beulah; for the Lord will take delight in you, and your land will be married. As a young man marries a young woman, so will

your Builder marry you; as a bridegroom rejoices over his bride, so will your God rejoice over you."

- Isaiah 62:1-5

Be filled dear children. Drink until you're full and overflowing. Let him whisper in your ear. Let him heal the brokenness in your heart. Let him rebuild the foundations of your life. Let him drape you with clean cream-white garments and give you the season of the bride. So you can fulfill "who" you are in Christ. It's your destiny.

Chapter 38

Verily, Verily

"And he saith unto him, Verily, verily, I say unto you, Hereafter ye shall see heaven open, and the angels of God ascending and descending upon the Son of man."

- John 1:51, KJV

I find it fascinating, every time I read these two little words from Jesus, "verily, verily." This duet appears 25 times in the New Testament and only in the book of John, and only spoken by Jesus. You lose the impact of this combination in the newer translations such as the NIV, where they use the words "Very truly," or "Most assuredly" in the NKJV. The Greek here is actually the word "amēn." Its origin is Hebrew. It is often translated trustworthy, surely, so be it, amen, truly, and verily. According to Strong's, it has been called the best-known word in human speech. The word is directly related, in fact, almost identical, to the Hebrew word for "believe" (amam), or faithful, and it carries the notion of being "firm." Thus, it came to mean "sure" or "truly," an expression of absolute trust and confidence.

What strikes me is when the word is spoken twice, as a lead-in to a statement or proclamation. In scripture, Jesus is the only one to use that pairing. Listen to some of the statements Jesus proclaimed with this pairing:

"Jesus answered and said unto him, Verily, verily, I say unto thee, Except a man be born again, he cannot see the kingdom of God."

- John 3:3, KJV

"Then answered Jesus and said unto them, Verily, verily, I say unto you, The Son can do nothing of himself, but what he seeth the Father do: for what things so ever he doeth, these also doeth the Son likewise."

- John 5:19, KJV

"Verily, verily, I say unto you, He that heareth my word, and believeth on him that sent me, hath everlasting life, and shall not come into condemnation; but is passed from death unto life."

- John 5:24, KJV

"Verily, verily, I say unto you, The hour is coming, and now is, when the dead shall hear the voice of the Son of God: and they that hear shall live."

- John 5:25, KJV

"Jesus answered them and said, Verily, verily, I say unto you, Ye seek me, not because ye saw the miracles, but because ye did eat of the loaves, and were filled."

- John 6:26, KJV

"Jesus said unto them, Verily, verily, I say unto you, Before Abraham was, I am."

- John 8:58, KJV

"Verily, verily, I say unto you, He that believeth on me, the works that I do shall he do also; and greater works than these shall he do; because I go unto my Father."

- John 14:12, KJV

Each of those statements, are powerful, foundational, statements of our faith. They breathe of the eternal manifest presence of Jesus and His kingdom! In ancient Hebrew, if I was going to describe to you, say, a "hole" in the road, if its size was average, I would say, "hole," however, if it was a large hole, I would say, "hole, hole". If it was a massive crater, I would say, "hole, hole, hole." The importance of this is the weight Jesus puts in what he is about say, "Verily, verily, I say unto you." In other words, He is saying,

> *"listen up, what I am about to tell you is extremely important and it is critical that you believe it."*

This truth is magnified even more when we read in the book of Revelation the following:

> *"And the four beasts had each of them six wings about him; and they were full of eyes within: and they rest not day and night, saying, Holy, holy, holy, Lord God Almighty, which was, and is, and is to come."*
>
> - Revelation 4:8

You cannot help but notice the repetition of the word "Holy." Here the bigness of God's Holiness is magnified by the unending proclamation of the living creatures surrounding His throne. The very thought of that makes you want to lie prostrate and simply worship and soak in His presence.

This thought hit home with me recently when I was reflecting on all that God had been speaking into my spirit recently. There has almost been a speed, a sense of urgency to what He has been saying. Generally, God has always driven me to the same three core messages when He speaks – pointing believers to their destiny, pointing believers to Heaven and driving them into His presence – and pointing out the hour in which we live and the call to the Bride of Christ.

These three themes have been a general message of my life. I think they are hard-wired into my system, who I am as a Christian and a prophet. However, in this current season there is a real sense of urgency. In the fall of 2011 the Lord gave me a word to the church, the Lord emphasized the powerful anointing that has been set aside for this generation in this place and time. He has also emphasized the place of the Bride in this hour, and the need for her to press in, and be filled with His presence. It has been a call to get equipped, if you will, for the task that is in front of her. Both messages are consistent with my life theme. What was different is the speed and repetition that the messages were coming; I mean daily, several times during the day.

Let me illustrate this with just a few of the words the Lord has spoken to my heart.

A short time after the above incident, while driving to church I saw a vision of intense rain. The rain was so forceful it was horizontal. I was soaking wet, running into the rain. I had an incredible sense of joy as I forced myself forward into the rain. I knew in my spirit that this was the latter rain of God that He was coming like a storm upon us. I also knew that this rain was a driving rain pushing us forward into our destiny, but more so, into His presence. The words of Hosea and Joel filled my mind.

> *"Then shall we know, if we follow on to know the Lord: his going forth is prepared as the morning; and he shall come unto us as the rain, as the latter and former rain unto the earth."*
>
> - Hosea 6:3

> *"Be glad then, ye children of Zion, and rejoice in the Lord your God: for he hath given you the former rain moderately, and he will cause to come down for you the rain, the former rain, and the latter rain in the first month.*

> *And the floors shall be full of wheat, and the vats shall overflow with wine and oil. And I will restore to you the years that the locust hath eaten, the cankerworm, and the caterpiller, and the palmerworm, my great army which I sent among you."*
>
> - Joel 2:23-25

Joel actually summed up what the Lord had been speaking to my heart. Not only was His presence coming in intensity but the outflow of that move would be a global harvest (the wheat) bringing about the filling of His children (vats of wine) and the anointing (vats of oil) from His presence. I saw the tables turned on the enemy and a restoration of all things to King Jesus, brought about by His great and mighty army. When I was reflecting on this, I heard the Lord say,

> *"Proclaim this to My children. Blow a trumpet in Zion, sound an alarm on My Holy Mountain. I am coming like the rain, and every eye shall see Me, and the wetness of My presence shall saturate everything in My path."*

A short time later, I looked up and saw, what looked like the sky dissolving. It was like those old movie film clips, where, at the end of the movie, the heat from the projector bulb burns the filmstrip and you watch as the film dissolves in front of your eyes. I instantly understood that what I was seeing was the kingdoms of this world dissolving and making way for the Kingdom of Heaven to fill all. Then I remembered the words of Peter:

> *"But the day of the Lord will come as a thief in the night; in the which the heavens shall pass away with a great noise, and the elements shall melt with fervent heat, the earth also and the works that are therein shall be burned up. Seeing then that all these things shall be dissolved, what manner of persons ought ye to be in all holy conversation and godliness, Looking for and hasting unto the coming of the day of God, wherein the heavens being*

> *on fire shall be dissolved, and the elements shall melt with fervent heat? Nevertheless we, according to his promise, look for new heavens and a new earth, wherein dwelleth righteousness.*
>
> *Wherefore, beloved, seeing that ye look for such things, be diligent that ye may be found of him in peace, without spot, and blameless."*

- 2 Peter 3:10-14

This was a message of seriousness. A wake-up call, if you will, to be mindful and diligent during the hour in which we live. It was reminiscent of the words of Isaiah and John:

> *"All the stars in the sky will be dissolved and the heavens rolled up like a scroll; all the starry host will fall like withered leaves from the vine, like shriveled figs from the fig tree."*

- Isaiah 34:4

> *"I watched as he opened the sixth seal. There was a great earthquake. The sun turned black like sackcloth made of goat hair, the whole moon turned blood red, and the stars in the sky fell to earth, as figs drop from a fig tree when shaken by a strong wind. The heavens receded like a scroll being rolled up, and every mountain and island was removed from its place."*

- Revelation 6:12-14

Then a short time later, I saw Jesus. I could only see His feet up to His calves. He was wearing old worn-out work jeans like overalls. He had on construction-style work boots that were worn and dusty. He was walking between the rows of crops on a farm, examining the harvest. Then the words of Jesus filled my mind:

> *"The harvest truly is plentiful, but the laborers are few. Therefore pray the Lord of the harvest to send out labor-*

ers into His harvest.' Let both grow together until the harvest, and at the time of harvest I will say to the reapers, 'First gather together the tares and bind them in bundles to burn them, but gather the wheat into my barn'"

- Matthew 9:37-38, 13:30

Then I heard the Lord say,

> "See how fat the kernels of wheat are? See, even now they are bursting at the seams. I have walked the fields of harvest. I have seen the seeds of My labor. Look, the time is ready, even at hand, for the Son of Man to reap the wages of His sacrifice. The Harvest is ready; the kernels are ripe for the threshing floor. Come my children; let us gather together the harvest of My labor."

Can you sense the urgency of the message? It is a call to press in and co-labor with our Lord and Savior, for the harvest is ripe and ready to reap.

Then, a short time later, I saw a revolutionary patriot digging in the dirt. I thought he was digging for water, so I asked the Lord what he was doing. He said,

> "He is not digging for water, he is barring treasure for a future generation. You are that generation. It is the inheritance of this generation sowed into the soil of this land. Release the treasure, that this country may seek me again, and I will pour out a blessing on them that will flood the whole earth."

And I knew that the revival that birthed the founding of this nation would come again, like the rain, and renew the land for a great and mighty harvest.

Then, as I was reflecting on all that the Lord had spoken He showed me the following:

I saw the horizon just after dusk. On the horizon were twelve massive candles burning. I asked the Lord what they were. He said,

> "These are the guardians of transition. The governments of this world shall be relinquished and the Government of My Kingdom shall fill the earth even as the oceans of this world cover the surface of the deep. For the heavens shall roll up like a scroll and every mountain shall flee, and everything that exalts itself against Me shall be humbled. Nothing shall stand against the tsunami of my presence. I am coming, and My watchmen and guardians are standing by, ready, and brightly lit."

The power of this vision was breathtaking. The bigness of the word echoed deep in my soul. I could hear the thunder of His footsteps. I could feel the atmosphere of the planet changing. I knew that we were entering into a new season, a season unlike any other. I understood that the candles were the church. I was reminded of the words of John in Revelation 1:12-15,

> "Then I turned to see the voice that spoke with me. And having turned I saw seven golden lampstands, and in the midst of the seven lampstands One like the Son of Man, clothed with a garment down to the feet and girded about the chest with a golden band. His head and hair were white like wool, as white as snow, and His eyes like a flame of fire; His feet were like fine brass, as if refined in a furnace, and His voice as the sound of many waters"

But, then it hit me, yes it was the church, but in the context of this vision it was the church dressed in Bridal attire and she was fully engaged in what the Groom was about to do. Listen to the words of John in Revelation 21:9-27.

> "Then one of the seven angels who had the seven bowls filled with the seven last plagues came to me and talked with me, saying, "Come, I will show you

the bride, the Lamb's wife." And he carried me away in the Spirit to a great and high mountain, and showed me the great city, the holy Jerusalem, descending out of heaven from God, having the glory of God. Her light was like a most precious stone, like a jasper stone, clear as crystal. Also she had a great and high wall with twelve gates, and twelve angels at the gates, and names written on them, which are the names of the twelve tribes of the children of Israel: three gates on the east, three gates on the north, three gates on the south, and three gates on the west.

Now the wall of the city had twelve foundations, and on them were the names of the twelve apostles of the Lamb. And he who talked with me had a gold reed to measure the city, its gates, and its wall. The city is laid out as a square; its length is as great as its breadth. And he measured the city with the reed: twelve thousand furlongs. Its length, breadth, and height are equal. Then he measured its wall: one hundred and forty-four cubits, according to the measure of a man, that is, of an angel.

The construction of its wall was of jasper; and the city was pure gold, like clear glass. The foundations of the wall of the city were adorned with all kinds of precious stones: the first foundation was jasper, the second sapphire, the third chalcedony, the fourth emerald, the fifth sardonyx, the sixth sardius, the seventh chrysolite, the eighth beryl, the ninth topaz, the tenth chrysoprase, the eleventh jacinth, and the twelfth amethyst. The twelve gates were twelve pearls: each individual gate was of one pearl. And the street of the city was pure gold, like transparent glass.

But I saw no temple in it, for the Lord God Almighty and the Lamb are its temple. The city had no need of the sun or of the moon to shine in it, for the glory of God illuminated it. The Lamb is its

> *light. And the nations of those who are saved shall walk in its light, and the kings of the earth bring their glory and honor into it. Its gates shall not be shut at all by day (there shall be no night there). And they shall bring the glory and the honor of the nations into it. But there shall by no means enter it anything that defiles, or causes an abomination or a lie, but only those who are written in the Lamb's Book of Life."*

Isaiah captures the same type of urgency:

> *"Awake, awake, O Zion, clothe yourself with strength. Put on your garments of splendor, O Jerusalem, the holy city. The uncircumcised and de-filed will not enter you again. Shake off your dust; rise up, sit enthroned, O Jerusalem. Free yourself from the chains on your neck, O captive Daughter of Zion. For this is what the Lord says: You were sold for nothing, and without money you will be redeemed...Listen! Your watchmen lift up their voices; together they shout for joy. When the Lord returns to Zion, they will see it with their own eyes. Burst into songs of joy together, you ruins of Jerusalem, for the Lord has comforted his people, he has redeemed Jerusalem...Depart, depart, go out from there! Touch no unclean thing! Come out from it and be pure, you who carry the vessels of the Lord. But you will not leave in haste or go in flight; for the Lord will go before you, the God if Israel will be your rear guard.*
>
> - Isaiah 52:1-3, 8-9, 11-12

So the beauty of the Bride, as Heaven sees her, is breath taking, is unshakable, untouchable, full of God's glory, covered with fine jewels, and pearls, and her gates are open to all. Angels stand guard at her gates. She is simply glorious, without spot or blemish.

So I ask you, how serious does the Lord get? I mean, seriously folks, how serious is He when He keeps saying the same thing over, and over? Do you sense that we are in new a season of transition? Do you hear the sound of Heaven calling you to a higher place? Do you feel the sound of drum beat? Do you hear footsteps of the King? I do and I want to call you to a place of listening, and pressing in to the throne room.

Sometimes, when we hear words that seem so big and so broad, we don't really know what to do. We say to ourselves things like, "that was cool," or "awesome God," and we continue to go about our day. Alternatively, we find ourselves feeling inadequate, unable to respond. I have good news for you.

The Lord never speaks to us about great promises, only to dangle them in front of like carrots on a stick, with no real desire to bring about what He has promised. Sure, He responds to our hunger and thirst for him, and He does call us to seek him, to knock, and to dig. He responds to our worship, yes, in a very powerful way, but it is His joy to bring us the Kingdom.

It is His joy to set our hearts ablaze. It is His heart's desire that we would be transformed into that beautiful Bride and He longs to make that happen. However, this pursuit is not something we have to struggle with or muster up in the flesh. More than anything, He wants us to come to Him like little children, free from the fear of performance, free to leap in to Poppa's lap and enjoy His companionship.

The last vision I had this week before writing this sums up the "**How**" of moving into the place of intimacy. I saw Jesus sitting on the throne. He was full of joy, to the point of laughter. He was sitting like a grandpa calling his grand kids to jump into his lap. There was such eagerness in His expression. He was so proud of the growth of His kids. He was so pleased with them how they were learning and how they responded to the simple things. He just wanted to hug on them and cuddle with them. He wanted to play with them and give them all the joy that was in His heart.

> "But Jesus called them unto him, and said, Suffer little children to come unto me, and forbid them not: for of such is the kingdom of God. Verily I say unto you, Whosoever shall not receive the kingdom of God as a little child shall in no wise enter therein."
>
> - Luke 18:16-17

The key to moving in this next move of God will be the intimate manifestation of the Church being like Children, in their love towards Jesus, for such is the Kingdom of God!

One last thing, on the way to Church this morning, the Lord gave me a vision of storm clouds. I saw the sky and it was dark with a massive thick black cloud. As I was watching the cloud suddenly, from the center of the cloud, it burst open, exploding the cloud into hundreds of smaller clouds. The smaller clouds looked like men's hands with lightning bolts in each fist. The clouds were heading in all directions, north, south, east, and west. I knew that clouds represented the church. I understood that the rain of His presence that was about to come was going to transform us, we were going to move from rain seekers to rain delivers. We were not only going to bring the rain of His presence to the world, but like the lightning bolts, we were bringing the power of God with signs and wonders, thunder, and lightning.

A couple of hours later, I was standing in the doorway that leads outside to my porch. I was watching the rain literally hammer the backyard. The wind was blowing, leaves were flying, and now, the Holy Spirit came upon me and said,

> "As you see in the natural, so shall you see in My Spirit. Prepare for rain." I started to praise God, crying out, "Send your rain God, and rain down on us!"

Then I recalled the words of Elijah:

> *"Then Elijah said to Ahab, 'Go up, eat and drink; for there is the sound of abundance of rain.' So Ahab went up to eat and drink. And Elijah went up to the top of Carmel; then he bowed down on the ground, and put his face between his knees, and said to his servant, 'Go up now, look toward the sea.'*
>
> *So he went up and looked, and said, 'There is nothing.' And seven times he said, 'Go again.'*
>
> *Then it came to pass the seventh time, that he said, 'There is a cloud, as small as a man's hand, rising out of the sea!' So he said, "Go up, say to Ahab, 'Prepare your chariot, and go down before the rain stops you.'"*
>
> *Now it happened in the meantime that the sky became black with clouds and wind, and there was a heavy rain. So Ahab rode away and went to Jezreel."*
>
> - 1 Kings 18:41-45

I propose to you that Elijah was not only seeing the natural rain for Ahab, and the nation, but was seeing the rain of God in these last days, and the church transformed. Get ready church, prepare for rain, and we, like Elijah's servant, will look faithfully, until we see the first cloud.

CHAPTER 39

Last Thought

"My heart is overflowing with a good theme; I recite my composition concerning the King; my tongue is the pen of a ready writer.

You are fairer than the sons of men; Grace is poured upon your lips; Therefore God has blessed You forever. Gird Your sword upon Your thigh, O Mighty One, with Your glory and Your majesty. And in Your majesty ride prosperously because of truth, humility, and righteousness; And Your right hand shall teach You awesome things. Your arrows are sharp in the heart of the King's enemies; the peoples fall under You.

Your throne, O God, is forever and ever; A scepter of righteousness is the scepter of Your kingdom. You love righteousness and hate wickedness; Therefore God, Your God, has anointed You with the oil of gladness more than your companions. All Your garments are scented with myrrh and aloes and cassia, out of the ivory palaces, by which they have made you glad. Kings' daughters are among Your honorable women; at Your right hand stands the queen in gold from Ophir.

Listen, O daughter, Consider and incline your ear; Forget your own people also, and your father's house; so the King will greatly desire your beauty; because He is your Lord, worship Him. And the daughter of Tyre will come with a gift; the rich among the people will seek your fa-

> *vor. The royal daughter is all glorious within the palace; her clothing is woven with gold. She shall be brought to the King in robes of many colors; the virgins, her companions who follow her, shall be brought to you. With gladness and rejoicing they shall be brought; they shall enter the King's palace.*
>
> *Instead of Your fathers shall be Your sons, whom You shall make princes in all the earth. I will make Your name to be remembered in all generations; therefore the people shall praise You forever and ever."*

- Psalms 45

They call this Psalm "The Glories of the Messiah and His Bride." A poetic prophet of the sons of Korah wrote it. It was set to the tune of the "Lilies," pointing us to love writings of the Song of Solomon, and speaks of the passion of the King for His bride. In fact, the writer calls this psalm, "A song of love." It was a royal wedding song and was more than likely sung at the wedding of King David or Solomon and one of his princesses. Charles Wesley was so moved by this psalm he paraphrased it in his hymn, "My heart is full of Christ, and longs its glorious matter to declare." Prophetically, it speaks of Christ and His love for the church.

The first nine verses speak to the glorious nature and splendor of the King and His might against all falsehood, pride, and injustice. The next five verses speak directly to the bride. The writer is calling her to the high place; he is exhorting her to forsake her old life and accept her new position as queen, with all its sacrifices, duties, rewards, and pleasures, but above all to yield herself fully to the King.

It is fitting to end this book on the Bride of Christ. In fact, I thought I was done with this book after completing the previous chapter. However the Lord had another idea. You see He woke me up out of an incredible dream the other day, and for the last two days I haven't been able to shake it.

In the dream I was taken to the throne room of God. I saw myself walking up to the throne to embrace my King. Above the throne was a banner with the word "commission" written across it. I saw myself walk between two pillars that lead to the throne. Then I saw myself exit the throne through two other pillars on the right. I was dressed in a white bridal gown with boots on. The time between entering the first two pillars and exiting the second set of pillars my mind was filled with incredible revelations regarding the Bride of Christ and her commission and destiny. I understood that the foundation of her commission was found in the loving embrace of her King, and in that embrace, in her love fellowship with her husband, she would be endued with power and glory to fulfill her call.

Then, as I walked away, in my new bridal attire, instantly I was standing in the workplace, holding the elbow of a young lad. I looked down at his elbow and saw the residue of scar tissue from surgery, where they pieced together his elbow with metal pins. I began to pray and commanded the metal to leave his body.

As I was praying this young man jumped back with a startled look and said, "What are you doing to my arm?"

I watched as the Lord began to miraculously recreate his elbow and remove all the metal from his body. They boy was smiling ear-to-ear, blown away at what was happening. Then I looked out to the crowd and said,

> *"Join with me loved ones, say the name of Jesus, and watch the Glory of the Lord."*

Instantly, everybody began to say "Jesus" in perfect harmony. Their voices filled the atmosphere like a Holy choir from heaven.

As they spoke I saw the metal plate in the boy's head dissolve and eject from his body. Then I woke.

Taken-back by the dream, I began to pray, and my prayers continued throughout the day. At the time I didn't know what the dream meant... whether it was literal, in the sense that I would see this boy and bring the King's healing gift to him, or whether it was something more.

By noon, as I was standing outside reflecting on the dream's meaning, the Lord spoke to me very load and clear. *"Tell them..."* He said,

> *"Tell them how much I love them, how much My heart burns for My bride. Tell them that My love for them is unshakeable, it is so deep that My heart beats with passion at the very thought of her. Tell My bride that I am head-over-heals for her, and in this hour, I shall take her into the wedding chamber and there she will know the tenderness of My touch. I shall wrap My arms around her and caress her with Holy love and with fire. In my embrace I will shower her with My desires. I shall cover her with My presence and trade her earthly garments with the wardrobe of heaven. I will put rings on her fingers and bells on her toes. I shall engrave her heart with My image and she shall see what I see. She shall feel as I feel. She shall touch others even as I have touched her. She shall be a queen in My kingdom, and her garments will radiate her beauty because she has looked upon the face of her lover.*
>
> *In this hour, this hour of the Bridal Shower, I shall wrap myself around her in My embrace, she shall see My heart for her and for humanity and in so doing, she will rise with a burning conviction, yes with a Holy commission, and return to the land that I send her, and there she shall reach out and bring the love touch to all she encounters.*

Yes, My love touch is amazing, for in that touch is wrapped up all the mysteries of creation. She shall speak and limbs will be created. She shall whisper and the ears of the deaf shall be restored. Where ears do not exist, they shall be created at the breath of My bride. For this is the hour of the Bridal Shower, and the rain she has so longed to see will come even as the wind blows upon the garment of my bride, as she walks amongst the hosts of heaven. Her aroma is like sweet raspberries. The very taste of her brings healing to the land, for she has been to the wedding chamber and felt My embrace. She has kissed the lips of her lover and has left changed into the beauty I saw the day I created her. This is how I feel about My bride, she is the lover of My soul. Prepare for the bridal shower My bride and come to me. Let me embrace you and give you My heart."

As He spoke those words to me I could feel His love flow over me like warm oil. Liquid love covered my heart and I, like the psalmist, took up the pen of a ready writer. As I began writing I was suddenly caught up in the Spirit to the worship song "Dying to Return," by Vineyard. As the sounds of this song flooded my heart, I saw Jesus in this incredible montage. As I heard these words His love filled my heart.

"He walked with a smile"

I saw Him as the Son of Man, strong and eloquent, walking along dusty roads, smiling and touching all along the side of the road. His features radiated with mission and purpose. With every touch His face beamed with the most incredible smile. Then He turned, looked into my eyes... and smiled. The song continued.

"He walked with peace"

And I was overcome by His peaceful nature. Peace flowed out from Him like waves of light flooding the atmosphere. Then, it was as if he was looking around, but no one really understood the true meaning of His life mission. He was listening to the hearts of those around Him. The road was lined with people, some wanted food, others healing, others just desiring to see miracles, and there were others there, mocking Him in unbelief. Yet, in all, it seemed that no one understood. Then, like before, He turned and looked at... and smiled. It was a smile that said,

> "I know, and they will soon know... when its finished."

And the song continued.

"But His heart cried out"

And when I heard those words I could see His heart pour out to the Father, the only one that knew the road He was one, the only one that truly understood. Then He bowed His head as if He heard the words from His Poppa respond back to Him,

> "All is well My Son ... it is almost finished, your almost there."

Then He lifted His head in perfect peace and strength, and with Holy confidence He looked over at me again, and smiled, and His smile carried so much weight in it. It was like a smile of assurance in the outcome of His destiny. And the song continued.

"He was alone"

And instantly I saw Him in His loneliness on this planet. His heart was in perfect unity with His Father and the Holy Spirit, but He walked as a man alone. I could feel the ach in His heart, desiring the lover of His soul, to be united with her so that she would see and understand fully His love for her. The song continued.

"He broke the world, Made all things new"

And I saw Him on the road to the cross, as venomous words spewed out of the mouths of all around Him. His heart was torn at the blindness of the crowed. Yet, again, at that moment He turned and looked in My eyes, and smiled. My heart tore with His love and I was overtaken and undone. The lover of my soul was hurting, and in His hurt was the soul desire to embrace me. As the onlookers mocked Him, and tried to crush His spirit, He stood silent, and then turned again to me... and smiled.

"And He tore my heart as He stood silent,"

And I was overwhelmed by His beauty and His tenderness, His love and desire for me was killing me and I saw Him, in His sacrificial journey, to redeem me and bring me to Himself, and I was undone.

"So beautiful, So beautiful"

And I saw Him as His heart cried out in the garden, and I saw Him as they spit on Him, and the cat-of-nine-tails came ripping down, tearing open His flesh. And with every scourge, I could see His eyes, His incredibly tender and loving eyes. I saw the strength of His perseverance, as the whip ripped across His back... Then as before, He turned and looked again, and the whip came lashing down, and as His eyes met mine... He smiled. I was undone.

Then I saw them as they mocked Him and put that scarlet robe upon His back and pressed that crown of thorns into His skull. I saw blood began to run down the sides of His face, and onto the ground, onto the earth that He created.

And I saw Him as they nailed nine-inch spikes into His hands and feet and hung Him on the cross. And I saw Him, as He cried out:

"Where are You?"

"Where are You?"

"My God why have You forsaken me?"

And I was so moved, my body began to shake, and tears filled my heart at the sight of this perfect man hung between heaven and earth... alone.

"Up there alone this perfect man"

And my heart was overcome at the sight of His sacrifice and I watched, as He turned, and once again, looked at me in my eyes... and smiled. Then He turned and said, "It is finished... I'll be back," and He smiled again. And I saw Him as He gave up His Spirit to the Father.

"Dying to return the Son was killed"

And I understood like never before, the words of the writer of Hebrews when he wrote:

> *"Therefore we also, since we are surrounded by so great a cloud of witnesses, let us lay aside every weight, and the sin which so easily ensnares us, and let us run with endurance the race that is set before us, looking unto Jesus, the author and finisher of our faith, who for the joy that was set before Him endured the cross, despising the shame, and has sat down at the right hand of the throne of God."*
>
> — Hebrews 12:1-2

The same passion and love for you that drove Him to the cross is the same passion and love that drives His desire for you today. It is that same unshakeable passion that desire to embrace His bride, the lover of His soul. He will not stop until He can embrace you and wrap you in the wedding garments of His good pleasure. Consider the words of John.

> "And I heard, as it were, the voice of a great multitude, as the sound of many waters and as the sound of mighty thunderings, saying, "Alleluia! For the Lord God Omnipotent reigns! Let us be glad and rejoice and give Him glory, for the marriage of the Lamb has come, and His wife has made herself ready." And to her it was granted to be arrayed in fine linen, clean and bright, for the fine linen is the righteous acts of the saints.
>
> Then he said to me, "Write: 'Blessed are those who are called to the marriage supper of the Lamb!'"
>
> - Revelation 19:6-9

Readiness happens in His presence. Readiness takes place in intimacy. Transformation takes place when we snuggle up to Him and open our hearts to receive the fullness of His love for us.

The commission of this next season will be the commission of the bride, it will usher in the power of God like never seen before, and it will be birthed from a Lover, to the beloved, and will change humanity forever.

> "Then I, John, saw the holy city, New Jerusalem, coming down out of heaven from God, prepared as a bride adorned for her husband. And I heard a loud voice from heaven saying, "Behold, the tabernacle of God is with men, and He will dwell with them, and they shall be His people. God Himself will be with them and be their God. And God will wipe away every tear from their eyes; there shall be no more death, nor sorrow, nor crying. There shall be no more pain, for the former things have passed away."
>
> - Revelation 21:2-4

Your destiny is calling you...

> *"And the Spirit and the bride say, "Come!" And let him who hears say, "Come!" And let him who thirsts come. Whoever desires, let him take the water of life freely."*
>
> - Revelation 22:18

I looking for the day the rain comes down in sheets of liquid love. I am looking for the season of the saints where the bridal shower of the Bride shakes the very foundations of the earth. Where limbs are created where there were no limbs. Where eye sockets are filled with the creative love touch of Jesus. Where the deaf hear, for the first time, the voice of Jesus as He whispers in their newly created ears how much He loves them. I am looking for the day when average Joes step out in thunderous power and change the face of nations. I am looking for the day that the lover of our souls embraces us with His passion and pushes us into our destiny. I'm waiting for the rain of God! Let's move the heart of God and worship Him on His throne. It's time church. Get ready, get ready, get ready!

My prayer is that this book series has helped to light a fire in your soul and push you to that higher calling of our Lord – so shake the dust off your feet and don't look back. This is the season of the bride.... Rise up dear ones and embrace your King, for He is madly in love with you.

PART 5: THE SEER'S GUIDE TO SYMBOLISM

CHAPTER 40

SIMILITUDES, METAPHORS, & SYMBOLISM

"As I walked through a great wilderness I came to a certain place where there was a Den, and I laid myself down in that place to sleep: and as I slept I dreamed a dream.
I dreamed; and I thought that I saw in my dream a man standing with his face turned away from his own house. He was clothed in rags, a book was in his hand, and a great burden was on his back.
Then I saw him open the book and read; and as he read, he wept and cried out, 'What shall I do?'."

- John Bunyan, The Pilgrim's Progress

This part of the book is devoted to the symbolism that the Holy Spirit uses to speak to us in dreams and visions. I wrote this section as a reference tool. I encourage you to return to this section of the book as many times as needed and ponder the various ways the Lord speaks to our hearts.

When I first started thinking about this chapter I was drawn to that incredible pilgrim and warrior in the faith, John Bunyan. He is best remembered for his book "*The Pilgrims Progress*" which he says, was "*Delivered under the similitude of a DREAM.*" He wrote it from a prison cell almost three hundred fifty years ago (1678). John Bunyan's dream story has become the most famous allegory in English literature. It has been read by more people than any other religious book in history, second only to the Bible, and it has been translated into more languages than any other book in the English tongue.

In the book of Hosea we read:

> "*I have also spoken by the prophets, and I have multiplied visions, and used similitudes, by the ministry of the prophets*"
>
> - Hosea 12:10, KJV

The Hebrew word for "similitude" in this verse is "dama" meaning to liken, to compare, to imagine, think, a symbol, or similitude. To that definition I would include the words, metaphor, allegory, simile, and parable. As you can see from this book series the Lord loves to speak through stories. His language is so broad and wide it defies our linier mindset. In this chapter let's explore the language of similitudes and give examples on the various ways the Lord uses symbolism and metaphor to speak into our lives.

The following examples are meant as a general guideline for possible interpretation of visions and dreams and are in no way definitive. **Your number one source for interpretation is the Holy Spirit and the Word of God.** These insights simply come from the commonality found by many in the body of Christ as well as my own personal experience. *They are here to stimulate your thinking and cause you to ponder as you explore the depth of the language of God. Remember, everything is about context. The context of your* *of your dream or vision will help define its meaning and application.*

This is **not** a complete glossary of pectoral symbolism. I have simply chosen a few for the purpose of illustration. For those who want a more in depth look, James Goll's "Dream Language" is a great place to start. Another great resource is the ministry of John Paul Jackson and his class on "The Art of Hearing God." It is designed to train students to hear the voice of the Lord and to develop greater intimacy with Jesus Christ.

(http://www.streamsministries.com).

Moving in dreams and visions is available to every believer in some degree or another. While everyone is not called to the ministry of the seer-prophet, **all** can move to some extent in this realm.

In this book I have tried to show the value of metaphor and teach you how God uses the language of visions and dreams to speak to you. I want to encourage you to learn to think metaphorically. Consider the way God speaks. Much of the Old Testament is given to us veiled in allegory, shadows, types, and metaphor. From Genesis to Revelation we see the fundamental truths of the Gospel and the face of Jesus woven throughout the Scriptures like nuggets of revelation tucked away in the melody of the Word.

The main reason people miss interpretations is by thinking in literal rather than metaphorical terms. God uses symbolism that is familiar to your life. He knows every aspect of your being and will speak through your makeup and the things that have marked your life experience. He knows your life, your makeup, which you are, and what you do. He knows your passions, and interests, He is interested in you. If you are a mechanic, God may speak to you along those lines. If you are a Chef, God may show you an area that you can relate to. Jesus spoke to the people of His day in parables that they could relate to. As an agrarian society that worked the land and fished in the Sea of Galilee they understood when Jesus spoke of tilling the soil and casting out nets for a catch.

God may show you the same type of symbols and their meaning and be very consistent in their use, interpretation, and application. For instance, in the Word of God a lamb is a common symbol that has a consistent thread of meaning throughout Scripture. Whenever certain symbols manifest pictorially to you, it will become fairly obvious what they mean.

On the other hand God does not want us to turn His creative voice into a formula. His desire is to stretch us and cause us to dig for truth through fellowship with Him. He wants us to be constantly dependent upon Him and His Word. As soon as we think we have it down pat, He will show us a symbol that we thought we knew, and suddenly it make no sense at all. The Lord does this to keep our dependency on Him. Always seek Him and His Word to search out the meaning of His speech. John Paul Jackson put it this way regarding visionary interpretation:

> *"The closer we can maintain our intimacy with the Holy Spirit, the better we can begin to hear His voice in understanding what He is speaking to us. We can learn all the mechanics and they are immensely helpful, but after that we must depend upon His voice to lead us."*

Follow Daniel's lead. Daniel knew that "*Interpretations belong to God*" and He sought the Lord through prayer and the Lord revealed the meaning of the dream (Daniel 2). In the end, it is hearing His voice that brings the revelation.

Symbolism found in visions and dreams are often similar, however, the interpretation may be quite different. Often visions operate through the gifts of "*the word of knowledge,*" "*discerning of spir-*

its," or "*prophecy*" and the interpretation and application may come quickly, as God speaks to your heart regarding the matter. Dreams on the other hand may need more digging and often revolve around your life destiny, mission, life, and God's desire for you personally. I will try to bring this to light as we discuss similitudes.

As you learn the metaphorical language of the Holy Spirit your ability to see will reach new heights. Proverbs 25:2 says that,

> *"It is the glory of God to conceal a matter but the glory of kings (or man) is to search out a matter."*

God places great value on our seeking out the things that He conceals. Us this section of the book as a reference tool to spark your mind to think metaphorically. Press in and press on dear saints. The Lord desires to speak to you!

Chapter 41

A

Angels

Remember, angels are here to help and minister to us. They are messengers of God sent to declare God's purpose for your life and destiny. Angels are warriors of God and fight on behalf of the Saints of the Most High. They are actively engaged in the purposes of the Kingdom of God. In book two of this series, "The Seer and Healing," I address the topic of angels at great length.

Angels can come to us in many ways. You may see or discern their presence during worship. You may physically encounter an angel. The writer of Hebrews states,

> *"Do not forget to entertain strangers, for by so doing some have unwittingly entertained angels."*
>
> - Hebrews 13:2

Angels can come to you in a dream or see them in a vision. The following are just a few of the possible reasons for angelic visitation.

Declaration or Proclamation: Angels are messengers sent by God to speak and declare truth regarding some aspect of your life. They come to confirm and proclaim your destiny and call of God. They take God's word over your life and speak it into your spirit. This is a solidifying moment. God wants you to receive and understand his word for you. This is seen throughout the scriptures.

Direction and Guidance: Angels can come with specifics regarding guidance or direction. They may tell you what to do or where to go. They may give you wisdom or insight about something you're going through. In Acts 8:26 an angel spoke to Philip and gave him direction on where to go.

Faith, Healing, and Deliverance: Angels can come to impart to you a level of anointing or to release faith into your life. Faith is the fuel that activates your spirit into action. The Word says, that without faith it is impossible to please God. We see Sarai's faith ignited in Genesis 16:7-11.

Angels can come and minister healing (See John 5). Angels can come and bring deliverance. In Psalm 34:7 it says,

> "The angel of the Lord encamps all around those who fear Him, and delivers them."

In Isaiah 63:9 we read,

> "In all their affliction He was afflicted, and the Angel of His Presence saved them; In His love and in His pity He redeemed them; And He bore them and carried them all the days of old."

Protection or Warning: Angels can be sent to warn you (Matthew 1:20; 2:13; 19-20) or bring protection in a time of need. They are sent to show you how to react or what to do regarding an impending harmful situation. You may see angels engaged in battle on your behalf. When you see this type of activity, pray in prayers of intersession. In Psalm 91:11-12 reads,

> "For He shall give His angels charge over you, to keep you in all your ways. In their hands they shall bear you up, lest you dash your foot against a stone."

Revelation and Understanding: Angels can come bringing revelation and prophetic insight. An angel communicated the entire book of Revelation to John. Daniel experienced such incredible Revelation that only an angel could interpret it for him (see Daniel 8:15-26; 9:20-27).

Strength and Comfort: Angels can come to you to impart strength or give you comfort. Angels came to strengthen Jesus after Hid 40 day fast (See Matthew 4:11; Mark 1:13). Daniel experienced the strength of God through angels (Daniel 10:18). Elijah, after he defeated the prophets of baal (1 Kings 19:5-8).

Worship or ushering in the presence of God: Angels can change the atmosphere of a place and usher in the presence of God. They were created to worship God and they carry with them the atmosphere of Heaven. God's holiness is so vast it latterly electrifies the atmosphere of a place with holiness. Angels can't help but bring the weightiness of His holiness when they show up.

Animals

Animal symbols are interesting. The animal kingdom is wide and diverse. They may be seen in a vision or a dream. What they are doing or your interaction with them is just as important as their species. Remember, everything is about context. Here are a few examples of animals and their possible meaning.

Bats: Often symbolize demonic activity.

Cats: Cats are self-willed, stealthy or sneaky, and un-trainable. Seeing a cat may speak of attitudinal adjustments that need to be made in your life. They are predators and prowl around in search for pray. A black cat may speak of demonic activity.

Deer: Deer are tranquil and can often speak of comfort, peace, or longing (see Psalm 42:1).

Dogs: Dogs can be positive representing fellowship, companionship like that of a brother, or faithfulness. On the other hand they can represent unbelievers or evil men (Psalm 22:16). Dogs that are growling or barking can represent demonic attack or oppression.

Donkey: A donkey can represent the spirit of deception (Numbers 22:22). They may speak of being stubborn or mulish (Job 11:12) or, on the other hand, they may speak of humility (Luke 19:28-

44). A donkey can also mean harvest such as plowing or working a farm. A donkey with a pack on its back may mean burdens and worry, the weight of the world on your shoulders.

Fox: Seeing a fox can represent one who is crafty or cunning (Luke 13:332). It can also represent the demonic, robbing the hen house of those newly born again.

Frogs: Frogs often represent the demonic (Revelation 16:13-14). However, they can also represent agility such as a frog leaping across a pond on Lilly pads or compliancy and a sleepish soul such as a frog swimming in a pot of boiling water.

Goats: Goats often represent the demonic, occult, false prophet, or the lost (Matthew 25:33).

Horse: A horse often represents strength, power, or conquest; a horse ready for battle is a good example. Horses can also represent your ministry or God calling you to join His army.

Lamb or Sheep: Sheep and lambs represent Christ or His people (Psalm 78:71; John 10:15). You may see Jesus caring for a sheep, or leaving the 99 to pursue the one. He loves and cares for the sheep of His fold. For example, if you see Jesus shaving a sheep, it may mean He is cleaning you up and striping away the debris in your life.

Lion: A Lion can represent Jesus and His royalty (Psalm 17:12). Or, it may represent the enemy seeking to devour you (1 Peter 5:8).

Ox or Bull: An ox can symbolize service, harvest as in farming, slaughter (Proverbs 7:22), or strength (Proverbs 14:4). Bulls on the other hand can symbolize persecution, spiritual warfare, opposition, or threat (Psalm 22:12).

Aroma

Often, in a vision, dream, or even in the natural you may smell an aroma or a fragrance. Pay attention to the smell. Aromas are vast and their meaning is just as vast. They can usher in the presence of the Lord or tap your history or heritage and bring comfort. They can symbolize warning or atmospheric conditions. The following is just a sample of some of the aromas you may experience:

Cooking odors: Often cooking aromas come from your personal experience and draw upon memories that are meaningful to you. The smell of cinnamon and apples may bring you the comfort of your mother. Smelling the aromas of an outdoor BBQ may signal times of fellowship and family unity. Sweet aromas may be a call to go deeper into your intimacy with the Lord.

Floral aromas: Can symbolize the presence of Christ (Song of Solomon 3:6) or the love of God in your life (Ephesians 5:2). For example, the smell of roses can symbolize God pouring out His love and blessing on a person or an increase of His presence in the atmosphere of a gathering.

Foul odors: Can symbolize demonic activity or sin. For example, smelling rotten eggs (sulfuric) may be a call to intercede and change the atmosphere, binding the demonic from a situation or place.

Seductive aromas: Perfume can symbolize a warning regarding temptation, seduction, or deception (Proverbs 7:7, 10, 13; Ecclesiastes 10:1).

Art

Artistic symbols are fascinating. The range from paintings to sculptures, clay to wood, and completed works to works in progress. Art is always about beauty. They can be personal or prophetic. They can symbolize transformation, sanctification, or mission.

The artist is just as important as the art. You may see something that you are painting or you may see Jesus sculpting clay. The first speaks of your dreams and your destiny the latter speaks of Christ's work in your life.

What is being created or painted is also significant. Is it a landscape, a city, or a person? Pay attention to the details. Paintings can also mean "covering." For example, you may see your house being painted speaking to you being covered by His presence or renovating so to speak you as the temple of the Holy Spirit.

A potter's wheel is symbolic of being molded or shaped. Pottery is symbolic of a Godly vessel. Painting can also be negative such as a whitewashed tomb (Matthew 23:27). Context is everything.

Authority Figures

Authority symbols may include your boss, a parent, teacher, guardian, law enforcement, official, judge, politician, or doctor, each of which carries its own meaning and is often easily understood. Consider the following:

Attorney: Seeing yourself as an attorney can be a call to stand in the gap for a people group and intercede on their behalf. Jesus is not only our Judge (Psalm 51:4) he is our Advocate (1 John 21:1) and in Christ all judgment has passed through Him and. He has freed us from the power of sin and death.

Boss: Seeing your boss may symbolize your relationship with authority. All authority is given and ordained by God (Romans 13:1-3). We are called to be servants to all. Your ability to honor those in authority is critical to being mature and having a heart this is in right relationship with those around us.

Counselor: Seeing a counselor may represent not only the need for getting counsel about something but to receive the counselor. In Isaiah 9:6 Jesus is called our Counselor. Jesus referred to the Holy Spirit as the Counselor (John 14:16 AMP).

Doctor: Jesus is our Great Physician (Luke 5:31). Seeing a doctor can range from the need to be healed and God's desire to touch you, to being called into the ministry of healing. See medical for more symbols regarding healing.

Judge: The context of seeing a judge can range form standing before the judgment seat of Christ (Romans 14:10) to seeing balances (Psalm 62: 9), a courtroom, or standing before a judge. Often forgiveness is at the heart of the situation. A judge can also symbolize God making a judgment regarding a situation you are going through.

Jury: Seeing a Jury can speak to the weighing of evidence or passing judgment (James 5:9).

Law Enforcement: Seeing officials in this arena represent earthly or spiritual authority (1 Peter 2:13). Depending on the context, it can point to a violation in your life and God is graciously warning you to turn and change your ways. A jailer on the other hand may point to being oppressed by the demonic. Being in Jail can symbolize being in bondage spiritually or mentally.

Teacher: Seeing a teacher often points to being teachable and seeking knowledge and wisdom. Jesus is referred to as our Teacher (Matthew 23:10). Jesus refers to the Holy Spirit as our Teacher (Luke 12:12; John 14:26,

> *"But the Helper, the Holy Spirit, whom the Father will send in My name, He will teach you all things, and brings to remembrance all things that that I said to you."*.

Parent or Guardian: Seeing a parent may represent the need for reconciliation, generational blessing, or inner healing. However, a parent can also represent God. Sometimes seeing your mother may represent the Holy Spirit and His desire to nurture and comfort you. Likewise, seeing your father may represent Father God and His desire to heal the Father, Child relationship.

Pastor: Seeing your pastor or a pastor can have several meanings. You may be called as a pastor. You may need to deepen you relationship with your pastor. God may be calling you to care for and build your relationship with the flock of God.

Chapter 42

B

Birth, Pregnancy, Babies, and Children

Symbolism involving pregnancy, birth, babies, and children are vast and range from having a child in the natural to God birthing something new in your life. Here are a few symbols with their possible meaning.

Adoption: Romans 8:15-17 says,

> *"For you did not receive the spirit of bondage again to fear, but you received the Spirit of adoption by whom we cry out, "Abba, Father." The Spirit Himself bears witness with our spirit that we are children of God, and if children, then heirs—heirs of God and joint heirs with Christ, if indeed we suffer with Him, that we may also be glorified together."*

God has adopted us. We are part of the Royal family of heaven. Adoption speaks to your identity in Christ. He is a father to the fatherless. Our destiny is in Christ as dear sons (Romans 8:15).

Baby or Infant: We know that babies are a gift from God (Psalm 127:3) and that often they symbolize something new God is doing in your life. However, babies are also dependent, helpless, innocent, and sometimes messy. Babies take a lot of work. They need to be fed and nurtured (1 Corinthians 3:1).

Every new work, in its beginning is the same way. It takes time, patience, and perseverance. God may be calling you to use be a wise parent and train care for this new thing like an infant. God may also be calling you to be dependent upon Him like a baby and nourish yourself on the milk of His word.

Child or Children: Children can often symbolize childlike faith and a call to simplicity and faith. God wants us to be as little children, to be filled with innocence, faith, and joy in Him. He wants or trust and dependence to be on Him. He wants to comfort us like a father to a child and release joy and playfulness in your spirit.

Giving Birth and Labor Pain: Giving birth often symbolizes the dream or ministry is about to take place. Often travail, struggle and pain accompany the birthing of a new thing. It calls for perseverance and endurance. What God has spoken to you in private is now ready to be manifested to the world.

If you see, for example, an umbilical cord can signify the need to detach yourself from something or to cutoff an aspect or occupation in your life. Labor can also symbolize great pain and travail (Jeremiah 6:24).

Miscarriage or Abortion: Symbols regarding a miscarriage or abortion may be speaking to a personal healing that needs to take place in your life. On the other hand, it could represent a graceful warning regarding a work in your life that needs change. Head in one direction and dreams are aborted; head in another direction and the child come to full term.

Pregnancy: Seeing yourself or someone else pregnant may refer to a desire to have a child and God's desire to fulfill that dream. However, more often than not, it refers to God planting the seed of a dream or ministry in your life (Isaiah 42:9; 66:9). Pregnancy is a time of intimacy with the Lord. It is a season to nurture your dream and envision its scope and attributes, what it will look like, who it will touch, how it will function.

Beverages, Drinking

The symbolism of beverages or drinking is vast and can range from drinking living water from the cup of His hand to being bound by addiction. Here are a few common examples.

Alcohol: Drinking alcohol can symbolize a struggle with addiction or residue from a former addiction (Proverbs 20:1). It can also speak of being controlled or under the influence of the demonic, playing the fool, being rebellious, or even witchcraft (Ephesians 5:18; Proverbs 14:16). Being in a bar speaks to a bad or worldly environment.

Simple Beverages: Drinking simple cool beverages can speak of refreshing and good news (proverbs 25:25). For example drinking champagne can symbolize victory, celebration, or christening (to send out).

Vinegar: Drinking vinegar can speak of being mocked or slandered (Psalms 69:21; Matthew 27:48).

Water and Wine: Water and wine, are powerful symbols. The first miracle by Jesus in the book of John was changing water to wine at the wedding in Cana (John 2). Water and wine are powerful images of the church, His bride, being filled with the Spirit of God. Water also speaks of new life in Christ and being filled to overflowing with living water (John 4:7-15; 7:38). Of course wine speaks of the redemptive work of Christ on the cross and the power of the blood (Matthew 26:28).

When we see the cup of blessing often God is calling us to live in the fullness of the salvation we have received and to be filled with new wine, to be as it were drunk in His Spirit with power and anointing.

Water of Service: We also see water as a symbol of service and the call to serve (John 13:5; Matthew 10:42). This can be a powerful call to missions and to the poor.

Birds

Birds are powerful symbols. Their meaning is wide and vast. Consider the following:

Bird (Singular): I single bird may speak of a messenger or an angel of the Lord. A wounded bird can symbolize the weak under attack or being harmed (Ecclesiastes 10:22).

Birds (Flock): A flock of birds can symbolize the enemy (Matthew 13:4). Or, on the other hand, speak to a people group flocking to the branches of your ministry (Luke 13:19).

Bird Nest: A bird's nest speaks of nurturing the young or one's house and family (Proverbs 27:8).

Bluebirds, Robins: Can symbolize obedience to God and being a faithful servant (Jeremiah 8:7). Bluebirds or Robins can also speak of Holiness and an invitation to come into His presence.

Cardinals: Cardinals can speak of a mainline denomination of the church, such as God doing a work in the Catholic Church.

Crow, Vulture, Buzzard, Raven: This category often speaks of the enemy, for example a crow mocking, a vulture or buzzard circling the dead or dying, or a raven standing in the road as you travel.

Dove: Doves almost always speak of the Holy Spirit descending to anoint, to be filled (Luke 3:22), or to be called.

Eagle, Hawk, Owl: In general, birds of pray speak of the prophetic, seeing from the heavens (Isaiah 9:11). Of course an Eagle symbolizes Christ (Ezekiel 1:10; Revelation 4:7). Owls speak of the prophetic and how one can peer into the dark places.

Hen: A hen can symbolize God's desire to comfort His children (Luke 13:34).

Hummingbirds: Can symbolize evangelism, pollinating flowers with great speed and urgency.

Parrot: A parrot can symbolize beauty. Or, on the other hand, one who mimics the works and deeds of another.

Pigeon: A pigeon can symbolize folks being feed from the hand of your ministry as in feeding pigeons in a park. A pigeon can also symbolize a messenger or angel delivering a message, as in a homing pigeon.

Roadrunner: A roadrunner can symbolize a warrior, one who fights in the dry places and devours the enemy (snakes). The can also speak to moving fast and staying alert.

Songbird: Songbirds can speak of love or adoration, and is often a call to dive deeper into worship.

Sparrow: Sparrows can symbolize the poor and needy and a call to feed and care for them (Psalm 84:3). It can also speak to loneliness, solitude, or quietness (Psalm 102:7). It can also speak of God's provision (Matthew 10:29).

Stork: A stork can symbolize the birth of something new in your life or finding your home or locking into your destiny (Jeremiah 8:7). It can also speak of angels (Zechariah 5:9).

Swallow: A swallow speaks of peace, rest, and worship, or resting in the house of God (Psalm 84:3). A Swallow can also speak to a need to return to fellowship and the house of worship.

Blood

Blood is a powerful symbol. It points to Christ and the power of the blood of Jesus (Matthew 26:28). Losing blood can speak to the need to put your trust and faith in Christ (Luke 8:43). Walking in blood can symbolize the power of Christ saturating every step that you take. A blood transfusion speaks of regeneration, salivation, and deliverance (Titus 3:5; Romans 12:2).

Body Parts

Symbols that focus on a part of the body are powerful. If it is a vision it may be a word of knowledge for healing or a spiritual condition of a person. On the other hand, they could symbolize faith, weakness, power, strength, or wisdom. Consider the following:

Ankles: Can symbolize weak faith (Ezekiel 47:3) or the need to stabilize your walk with God.

Arms: Can symbolize God's strength (Psalm 89:13; Isaiah 62:8.) Arms can also symbolize giving aid or reaching out, and deliverance (Isaiah 52:10; Psalm 136:12). They can also speak to God having the power to save and meet you need (Numbers 11:23).

Back: Seeing a back can symbolize God desiring you to seek His face (Exodus 34, 34). It may also speak to having feelings of being ignored or someone turning their back against you (Jeremiah 32:33). Seeing a back can also symbolize the need for healing as in by His stripes we were healed (1 Peter 2:24, Isaiah 53:5).

Body: Can symbolize your relationship to fellow members of the church or the equipping of the saints (Romans 12:4; 1 Corinthians 12:12; Ephesians 4:4). It can also symbolize you being the temple of the Holy Spirit and a call to Glorify God in your body and your spirit (1 Corinthians 6:19).

Bones: Can symbolize the lost, being backslidden, or a dead church or member (Matthew 23:27; Ezekiel 37). Bones can also speak to weakness, fear, or a need for God to heal you (Isaiah 58:11; Proverbs 16:24; Proverbs 3:8). It can also symbolize a broken spirit (Proverbs 17:22). Or, it may speak to bringing good news (Proverbs 15:30; 16:24). Bones can also speak of revival and the need to intercede on the behalf of a people group.

Ear: Ears speak to hearing God (Matthew 11:15). They can also speak to His desire to give you a hearing ear as in the prophetic. Being deaf can speak to opening your heart and hearing what the Lord has to say (Acts 28:27).

Feet, Foot: Feet often speak of service and personal ministry (John 13:1, Romans 10:15). Feet can also represent God telling you to "shake of" hurt or rejection (Matthew 10:14). Laying something down at Jesus's feet can speak of worship (Luke 7:38) and giving up your own personal desires (Matthew 18:29; 28:9, Mark 7:25).

Feet can also symbolize the Lord guiding you in your walk (Luke 1:79; Psalm 40:2; 56:14). Feet can symbolize God's protection (1 Samuel 2:9; Psalm 18:33, 36, 38). Feet can speak of the authority you have in Christ (Psalm 8:6). Stand on the power of His Word (Psalm 119:101).

Looking at your feet can speak to examining your walk with God (Proverbs 4:26). I often see the feet of Jesus and the call to walk where He walks, to do what He is doing and to see what He is seeing. Footprints can speak to Christ walking with you even if you don't see Him or recognize He is there (i.e. foot prints in the sand).

Finger: A finger can mean casting out a demon or the power of God (Luke 11:20). A pointing finger can speak of being an accuser or speaking wicked or harmful things (Isaiah 58:9).

Hair: Grey hair or a beard symbolizes old age or wisdom (Proverbs 16:31). Long hair can symbolize a call to the prophetic, like a Nazarite (Numbers 6:2; Judges 13:5). Baldness can symbolize not being covered or not having protection from God (Micah 1:16).

Hand: Hands are powerful. If your hands are lifted it speaks of surrender and worship (Psalm 28:2; 63:4). If your hands are folded it speaks of prayer. Holding hands speak of love and relationship (Psalm 37:24). Washing your hands speaks of being cleansed from sin (Psalm 24:4, 6). Strong hands speak of being made ready to war in the Spirit (Psalm 18:34).

Clapping hands speak of praise (Psalm 47:1). Hands can also speak of angelic protection (Psalm 91:12). A left hand can symbolize wisdom (Proverbs 3:16). An open hand can speak of God's grace (Psalm 123:2). An extended right hand can speak of agreement or a partnership. Trembling hands can speak of fear. Hands that cover your face can speak of shame.

Hands often speak to me about being an extension of Christ's mighty hand in the earth. His hands become my hands. The works of His hands are mighty and call for our adoration, worship, and praise.

Head: A head bowed can speak to humility, shame, or prayer and that God is the lifter of your head (Psalm 3:3; Job 10:15; Zachariah 6:11). A head receiving a crown speaks of your place in the kingdom of God, your royal nature in Him, and the wisdom of God (Psalm 22:7; Proverbs 4:9). A hand under your head speaks of Christ embrace and love for you (Song of Songs 2:6).

The head also speaks of authority. Christ is the head of all things (Ephesians 1:22); He is the head of the Church (Colossians 1:18), and head over all principality and power (Ephesians 2:10). The Husband is the head of the family (Ephesians 5:23). A wounded head is the call to be healed emotionally.

A covered head speaks to covering and relationship to authority. Wrinkles on the forehead can speak to worry or thoughts. A lifted head can speak to seeking the Lord in prayer and supplication or His glory and seeking His face.

Heart: A heart can speak of many things but usually speaks to a heart condition such as a broken heart (Psalm 34:18), joyous heart (Psalm 16:19, Acts 2:26), fools heart (Psalm 14:1), pure heart (Psalm 24:4), wicked heart (Psalm 10:13, Acts 5:3, Acts 7:51), clean heart (Psalm 51:10), sorrowful heart (John 16:6), or a critical heart (Psalm 12:2). Everything starts with the heart (Matthew 5; 12:34, Romans 2:29). Salvation and faith start with the heart (Romans 10:9-10). Doing God's will starts with the heart (Ephesians 6:6).

Your heart is the place of overflowing (John 7:38). Heartstrings can speak of pulling on the heartstrings of Christ. A bleeding heart can mean either be compassion or being mocked because of your service to Christ. You may see a heart darkened (hurt or deceived), a heart beating (the passion of Christ), and blood flowing through a heart (moving out in the power of Christ).

Legs: Legs can speak of strength or weakness (Daniel 2:33) as well as your walk or journey in Christ as in seeing legs walking.

Books, Scrolls, Letters, Writing

Seeing books, scrolls, letters, or writing can be very powerful to your life. As you will see below, their meaning is wide yet pointed.

Books: Books are powerful and their meaning can often be derived by the title, if visible. Often, a book speak of the Word of God, and its power to build you up and guide you in all truth. The Word of God is the revelation of Jesus Christ. The Word speaks to truth (John 17:11, Psalm 33:4). Jesus Himself is the Word incarnate (John 1:1). Seeing the Bible and the wind blowing upon the pages speak to the power of God's word and the authority of Him to bring about what He has spoken.

Often you will see a scripture highlighted. Take note and meditate upon it. Seeing the book of life can speak to the need for salvation (Revelation 20:12). Seeing books can also be a call to study the scriptures (Daniel 9:2). Sometime books can be a graceful admonishment to balance your life between study and living the gospel (Ecclesiastes 12:12). Burning books can symbolize the renunciation of occult practices or witchcraft (Acts 19:19).

Letters: Letters are interesting and involve reading, writing, sending, or receiving a letter. Often what is being written can tell you the meaning of the letter. If you are writing a letter, ask yourself what is the tone of the letter;

Do you have a need to communicate to someone in some way? Letters can be many things, love letters, letters of endorsement, encouragement, admonishment, or a teaching. They can bring good news or speak prophetically. Receiving a letter can be an answer to a prayer or a call to go to a people group or nation. Seeing letters as in the alphabet can speak to words of proclamation or a word of knowledge.

Scrolls: A scroll can carry the same meaning as the Bible (Psalm 40:7). A scroll can also speak of judgment (Isaiah 30:8), proclaiming the prophetic (Isaiah 8:1; Jeremiah 36:1, Ezekiel 2:9, 3:2), or a call to preach and proclaim the Word. A flying scroll can be either a curse (Zechariah 5) or the Word being sent to a nation.

Seeing Jesus reading a scroll in a courtroom or before the throne of God can symbolize His decree over your life and the proclamation of forgiveness. An open scroll extending from heaven to earth can symbolize God's decree being manifest or His Word ushering you into heaven and His presence.

Being Bound

Being bound by handcuffs or any other type of binding speaks of either bondage or to stop a certain behavior, or to release someone from bondage. Binding loosing speaks to doing the works of the Kingdom (Matthew 16:19).

Bugs, Insects

Insects are interesting and typically speak of demonic activity (flies, locusts, cockroaches, spiders, bug bites, maggots, swarming insects, etc.). These types of insects devour, trap, poison, impart diseases, or inhabit a dirty environment.

However, bugs can also speak of good things. For example ants can speak of being industrious, bees can speak of evangelism and pollination, and caterpillars can speak of transformation as into a butterfly, butterflies can speak of a season of transformation and beauty. Grasshoppers can speak of God's promise to restore loss in your life (Joel 2:25) or speak to an impending attack on the harvest of your ministry.

Buildings & Houses

Buildings and houses can speak of many things, for example an abandoned house can speak to barrenness and desolation (Job 15:28). A house can also speak to the state of your life and/or past. A barn can refer to abundance, provision, or great harvest (Proverbs 3:9; Psalm 144:13; Jeremiah 50:26; Luke 12:24). A log cabin or camping in a tent could symbolize the need to find a quiet time or be in a secluded place. A tent or a hotel can also symbolize being in a temporary place (Exodus 14:1).

A castle can symbolize a stronghold in someone's life. A cave can symbolize being trapped (Isaiah 42:2), doing something in secret, or hiding in fear like Elijah.

A house with an exposed foundation, or a house sitting on a rock or in sand refers to the condition of trust in a person's life (Matthew 7:24-27).

A house of cards speaks to folly. A cluttered house speaks of the need to put your house in order. Building a house can symbolize the building of a church or ministry. A house with holes in the roof can speak of areas in your life that are in need of repair.

A shack can speak of self-worth or a need for inner healing or trust. Sometimes seeing building can symbolize the need for shelter, refuge or safety.

A tower can be a refuge (Psalm 61:3) or an attic speaks to your mind. A bedroom speaks of intimacy. A closet can speak of prayer (Luke 8:17) or a place where you bury things or hide things.

Chapter 43

C

Celebration

Celebration can be seen in symbols such as people clapping, watching a parade, a ribbon cutting ceremony, a birthday cake, toasting with a glass of wine, people raising to their feet, or seeing colorful balloons or presents.

Cleaning & Cleaning Agents

Seeing anything related to cleaning such as cleaning agents or cleaning equipment (brooms) can speak to cleaning your life up (Isaiah 14:23; Psalm 26:6; John 13:8).

Colors

Many times colors have significance in dreams or visions. I have seen paint being poured over individuals, or candles with different colored flames signifying a gift or a call on the life of a believer. Below is a brief list of some possible meanings:

Blue, Purple, and Scarlet: These three represent the colors of the Godhead. In Exodus blue, purple and scarlet are mentioned 25 times, all referencing the thread used in weaving the elements of the tabernacle. Blue is symbolic of the Holy Spirit and speaks of the wind of God. Purple speaks to the Father and His royal nature. Scarlet speaks of the Son and the blood of Christ.

Blue: Speaks to holiness, heaven, grace, favor, heavenly activity, anointing. Blue can also speak of being depressed or feeling blue. Blue is often a call to holiness and revelation in the prophetic.

Black: Speaks to the enemy, the atmosphere influenced by the enemy, a dark heart, black eyes, dark shadows, speak to evil influence in a person or place.

Brown: Speaks to things in the natural, earthly things or a condition or change in a region, or natural qualities. Brown often a call to uncharted areas – a mission gift.

Green: Green speaks to life, growth, prosperity, or renewal, for example, a brown and dusty land being transformed into green grassy lands. Green is often a call to evangelism.

Gray: Speaks of wisdom or can speak to a gray area or an infusion of the enemy in a situation. Gray can also speak of an emotional state such fogginess. Gray is often a call to teach as in gray hair.

Orange: Speaks to either caution as in a orange light or the fire of anointing and power in the Spirit. It is often a call to healing.

Purple: Speaks of heavenly royalty and your kingdom identity.

Red: Symbolizes sacrifice, danger, the blood of Christ to over through the enemy, or even anger. Red is often a call to intersession and pleading the blood of Christ over the nations or a call to Apostleship.

Scarlet: Refers to the blood of Christ or possible a sin in someone's life.

White: Speaks of righteousness and holiness before God. Can often speak to a high call of worship.

Yellow: Speaks to the gift of God, something precious and with great value. It carries with it the idea of family, honor, and celebration. On the negative side it can refer to cowardliness or fear and intimidation. Yellow is often a call to service and releasing anointing.

Communication

In today's world methods of communication is everywhere. You might see a phone, cell phone, answering machine, e-mail, antenna, radio, newspaper, or mailbox. At the heart is the essence of listening and often carries the idea of hearing what God is saying, to tune into to Him.

On the other extreme you may see things like a microphone, a platform, or a speaker. This speaks to proclamation and speaking to a people group or a person regarding the Gospel or the prophetic.

Confinement

Confinement can be in a jail, cage, dungeon, pit, or some other place where you or someone else is trapped. This speaks to being either stuck or being in bondage or under oppression, taken prisoner by the enemy (Jeremiah 5:26-27; Isaiah 42:7).

Being bound by chains, locks, or a straightjacket carry the same type of meaning. The latter may speak to mental bondage. Jesus came to set the captives free.

Construction, Building Something

Seeing something being built or constructed often speaks to building God's call in your life, working to fulfill your destiny. Often this involves tearing down (Jeremiah 4:3; Hosea 10:12), establishing a solid foundation, setting up the framework, putting in the infrastructure, and counting the cost (1 Corinthians 3:10-12; Luke 14:28).

On the other hand if you see bricks this can symbolize bondage or slavery (Exodus 5). A carpenter can speak to the office of a pastor, evangelist, or apostle.

Containers (all kinds)

Containers are vast; there are containers that carry things, containers to drink from, containers that hold things, and containers that lock things away. Below is a list of a few examples of containers and their possible meaning:

Containers that carry:

- A basket full of fruit can speak to provision, harvest or blessing being brought to a people group.

- A basket filled with bread can speak to bringing the Word to a people group or feeding the poor and needy.
- A vessel filled with wine speaks to God's desire to pour out His Spirit upon a group and fill them with new wine.
- A briefcase can speak to a call to the business community.
- A suitcase can speak of a journey and being sent out.
- Luggage can speak to carrying around the residue of your past and speak to the need for inner healing.
- A bucket overflowing may speak to renewal and outpouring.

Containers to drink from: Seeing cups, glasses, or bottles filled with water or wine speaks to being filled with the Holy Spirit and the possible need to be refreshed in Him. God's desire is that your cup would overflow and bless many. A broken vessel or a vessel that is leaking, such as a cracked pot can symbolize a crack in your foundation, or running on empty and the need to be filled with His Spirit and repair an aspect of your life. Wineskins speak of your spiritual structure (Luke 5:37).

Containers that hold something: Seeing a treasure chest, a safe, or safe-deposit box speaks of provision, blessing, and favor, but can also mean something that is hidden. Containers that hold something can also speak to storing away for times of famine.

Containers that bind and hold: Containers that secure things away such as a spider in a jar, a snake in a basket, or like Zechariah's basket with a woman in it, spoke of God judging the harlotry of the nation (Zechariah 5) or binding the enemy.

Vessels that are dirty: Speaks to the need to be cleansed so that you can be filled to the fullness of Christ and not be hindered in your walk. Glass, in general speaks to transparency.

Cooking

Cooking is amazing in its symbolism. As a chef by trade the Lord often draws from the well of my life experiences and uses cooking and food to speak to my heart. To get a glimpse of this I encourage you to read my book, "The Eyes of a Chef, Kitchen Tales of Food & Faith" (available on Amazon.com). In addition, throughout this series I share quite a few stories that are drawn from the well of my life experience walking with God.

Cooking is so vast and ranges from savory to sweet, baking to roasting, cold food preparation including working with forcemeats (sausages, pates) to carving ice or making chocolate sculptures. Cooking is about preparation. It starts with raw ingredients and transforms them into something that can be consumed. Thus, the symbolism often speaks to what God is doing in your life or the life of another.

Butchering, filleting, cutting, and carving often speak to things being cut away, works of the flesh, or areas of your life that need to be removed.

Recipes can speak to great truths in scripture, for example a simple preparation of hollandaise sauce points to the sacrifice of Jesus and His redemptive work on the cross; making a consommé speaks to the sanctifying work of the Holy Spirit; making bread often speaks to God building the framework in your life to sustain a filling of the Holy Spirit; Sauce draping a dish can speak to being covered or a covering.

The metaphors are endless. I encourage you to let the Holy Spirit speak to you regarding your own profession, or ask Him to open your eyes when you prepare food for your family and friends, and share with them what He shows you at the table of fellowship.

Simmering, slow roasting, kneading dough, or stewing often speak to that slow sanctifying work of the Holy Spirit in your life.

Tasting, smelling, aroma, fragrance, and seasoning, can speak to the power of His Word in your life to the beauty of His presence.

Covering and Mantles

Mantels speak to the "metron" (sphere of influence and the boundaries of one's authority, Ephesians 4:7) of your anointing, ministry, or office.

Coverings speak to your place under authority and under God. The symbols that speak to coverings include things like feathers, blankets, hats, a roof, sheets, a tent, or umbrella.

Symbols that speak to mantels include things like a robe, cape, jacket, coat, or scarf. When they are combined with a color they can give insight into the meaning. Pay attention of its condition (clean or dirty, whole or torn).

Crime

Seeing crime being committed when it's happening to you or someone else often speaks of an attack by the enemy. The type of crime can indicate what is being done, for example being robed or stealing speaks to the enemy taking away something that God has given you, it can be as simple as stealing your peace to trying to rob you of your destiny; Cheating, rape, or other can symbolize a violation in a relationship; Gangs can symbolize the atmosphere of a region and a stronghold of the enemy; murder can speak to the enemy coming in to rob life and bring despair and hopelessness.

Crushed, Carried, Trapped, Stuck, Smothered

Symbols regarding things that are happening to you, or to someone else, are often about God's desire to release you from a circumstance or an emotional condition. For example, you may see yourself being crushed by a rock or trapped under a log. Situations like this speak to emotional stress over a situation where you feel there is no way out and your hope is dissipating. God desires to release you and set you free. Pay attention to your feelings in a dream. Feelings often accompany images and are part of the context. Visions regarding this type of activity are usually words of knowledge.

Being crushed or smothered: At the heart of this symbol is the sense of being overwhelmed by a situation or crushed by the power of a sin in your life. Powerlessness and panic set in and you feel there is no way out. God's desire is to release you and free you from the situation. Freedom is His heartbeat for you. Emotional distress in your life points to being out of balance and susceptible to the power of fear. No this, perfect love casts out fear!

Being stuck or trapped: The meaning is pretty much the same as above, except for one possible exception. It may speak to your reaction to a season of stagnancy in your life. In seasons like this

God is calling you to a deeper place of trust. He wants the peace of His presence to sustain you. He wants your hope to rest in Him. He is faithful and dry seasons are times to build your trust and ability to stand in any situation.

Being carried: Being carried often symbolizes God's protection, comfort, and ability to carry you through a situation. Think about that simple and profound story of "foot prints in the sand." He is the Good Shepard and He cares for the flock of His inheritance.

Chapter 44

D

Digging

Digging often symbolizes searching out something or digging for a deeper relationship with God. You may be digging for water (His presence or search the Word), for oil (His anointing), or for gold (His provision). The essence of digging is the same as "hunger" or "thirst". It is the cry of ones heart to go deeper in Him.

However, sometimes it's not digging in the sense to find, but to release. I once saw one of our founding fathers digging. I asked the Lord what he was digging for and He said, "*He is not digging, he is releasing the gift of heritage and inheritance upon the land.*" In that case it spoke to inheritance and the releasing of blessing to the nation.

Direction

Seeking direction from the Lord is common to all who love Him and desire to be where He is. There are many ways the Lord speaks to us about direction. Sometimes they involve instruments like a compass, weathervane, road sign, or a map. Other times He uses the road itself, such as a forked road, rocky road, hilly road, a path in a valley, a mountain road, or a freeway.

The context of what you see and the other things going on around you will dictate its meaning. You are looking for things that signify if you are headed in the right direction, wrong direction, or a new uncharted course. Dead ends speak to heading in the wrong direction. Things like road signs, a wall at the end of a road, a closed road, or even the corner of a house or room can symbolize the wrong direction or dead end.

Doors, Gates, Windows

This category of symbols is very powerful and often carries with it the invitation to enter the heavenlies and into the presence of the Lord. One of the most noted open doors in scripture is found in the book of Revelation:

> *"After these things I looked, and behold, a door standing open in heaven. And the first voice which I heard was like a trumpet speaking with me, saying, "Come up here, and I will show you things which must take place after this. Immediately I was in the Spirit; and behold, a throne set in heaven, and One sat on the throne."*
>
> - Revelation 4:1-2

Obviously doors, gates, and windows are either open or closed. Doors typically speak to an entrance into something. In the case above, God was inviting John to enter heaven and see what He was seeing. Just three verses earlier, Jesus, speaking to the Laodicean church says, *"Behold, I stand at the door and knock. If anyone hears My voice and opens the door, I will come in to him and dine with him, and he with Me."* In the latter case, the invitation is to open the door of your heart and let Jesus in. Jesus, in fact, refers to Himself as "the door" (John 10:7-9). One is open the other is closed.

Open doors also speak to the Holy Spirit opening a door to a new area, region, or place of effectiveness (1 Corinthians 16:9; 2 Corinthians 2:12; Colossians 4:3; Revelation 3:8). If an animal or person is blocking a door it speaks to the enemy blocking access and God is calling for intersession.

Gates carry the same thrust of meaning, as seen in Luke 13:24, *"Strive to enter through the narrow gate...."* In Revelation 21:21 we see the New Jerusalem coming down from heaven having twelve gates of pearl. Gates also carry the symbolism of entering the heavenlies with praise and thanksgiving (Psalm 24:7-9, 100:4). We often sing that incredible Jesus Culture song, *"Let it rain... Open the floodgates of heaven and let it rain."* Here, floodgates speak to revival and renewal.

Gates like doors can also speak to the gates of your heart (Psalm 147:13). The difference between gates and doors is that doors, most often, speak to the things Christ is doing or wants to do in your life, gate most often speak of Him wanting to be with you and involves praise and worship. The exceptions in regards to gates are what I call natural gates such as rod iron, gates in a yard, and gates in a jail. These often speak to bondage or oppression of some kind and the call of God to set someone free.

Windows speak to the blessing and anointing of God being poured out from heaven (Malachi 3:10). That wonderful song *"Open the Windows of Heaven"* was first pinned in 1895 by R. G. Staples, and has moved the church for over a century. Since that time many songs have been written that beat to the heart cry of God. That cry is not only for blessing but renewal, where our hearts cry out for the rain of heaven to pour down upon us.

Windows can also speak to the windows of your heart and the Lord peering into the deep places of your soul. Windows can also speak to the eyes of your spirit, or insight (Ecclesiastes 12:3), as in the old English proverb speaking of the eyes being the windows to the soul. The state of a window is also important. Is the window dirty or clean, fogged over or clear, whole or cracked? If, for example, you see yourself driving and the windows are dirty, cracked, or are being pounded by rain, and your vision is impaired, this speaks to something in your life that is hindering you from seeing clearly. The same would apply to seeing the windows of your house. On the other hand, if you see, for example stained glass windows, it speaks to the beauty and glory of God in your life.

Paul, speaking on the revelatory gifts says,

> *"For now we see in a mirror, dimly, but then face to face. Now I know in part, but then I shall know just as I also am known."*
>
> - 1 Corinthians 13:12

This mirror or glass carries the same essence as a window, peering into the revelatory, but seeing dimly, or in part. We also see the same type of thing in 2 Corinthians 3:18:

> *"But we all, with unveiled face, beholding as in a mirror [glass] the glory of the Lord, are being transformed into the same image from glory to glory, just as by the Spirit of the Lord."*

Chapter 45

E-F

Education

Symbolism involving things related to education, learning, or graduating are very powerful and can speak to:

A call (teacher, preacher), Exodus 18:20.

Being called to a campus ministry and to students.

Being tutored in the school of the Holy Spirit (elementary school, or college), Galatians 4:1-3.

Going to the next level (diploma).

Learning something (including apprenticeship, college, library, being a student, etc.).

Passing or taking a test (quiz, test, report card, or grade), James 1:3.

Emotions, Feelings, Reactions

See yourself or someone else getting emotional, displaying feelings, or reacting in an unusual manner often points to possible pain or hurt in one's life. The root of the problem can stem from natural circumstances, past hurts, oppression, or the demonic. They include things like blushing, anger, crying, despair, yelling, hopelessness, or even terror. Pictures such as these can often be a word of knowledge regarding one's emotional state. The Holy Spirit can give you insight.

On the other hand you may see emotions of joy and jubilation. Happiness, peace, and laughing often symbolize the Lord's blessing and favor over a life.

Farming, Planting, Plowing, Harvest

Seeing things relating to farming, plowing, planting and harvest most often speak to what Christ is doing in the earth, releasing waves of grace, salvation, revival, and promise.

Plowing almost always speaks of breaking new ground or turning the soil of your heart. Sometimes God is doing a major work in your life and He may use this symbolism to show the depth of the process. Reaping the harvest speaks to bringing in the lost, however, sometimes it can speak to God's provision.

Grinding wheat speaks to the separation of chaff, and the sanctifying work of the Holy Spirit. On the other hand, seeing farmland that is under a drought or the land is dry, speaks to the spiritual condition of a region or a heart, and is a call to pray for revival rain to soak the land. Notice that the soil can be either a region or the soil of one's heart.

Finance and Provision

Symbols involving finance can speak to a need, provision, warning to save, tithing, or restoration of what was lost. Sometimes the meaning is almost tongue-and-cheek, such as "you can bank on it." Sometimes it speaks to where your real treasure lies (Matthew 6:21, 19:21), or the great heavenly inheritance that is in your life.

At other times it can speak to safety and security. A calculator can speak to counting the cost of something either spiritually or in the natural (Luke 14:28). A check can speak not only of provision, but also of faithfulness and a return on your work for the Lord (Mark 4:8), or the wages of one's life (Romans 6:23). Coins can symbolize service (Matthew 25:14). Things like a creditor or beggar can symbolize a curse on someone's life (Psalm 109:11).

Fire

Symbols involving fire speak to many things and can be either positive or negative. Here are a few examples:

A fire alarm is a warning of impending trouble in one's life.

A house or basement on fire can speak to one heading to the gates of hell.

Ashes speak to memories or residue in a life and the call to heal the brokenness of the past.

Being a fireman, holding a fire extinguisher, or putting out a fire is symbolic of warfare and extinguishing the flames of the enemy.

Breathing fire speaks to words spoken harshly or in anger. They are often hurtful and destructive.

Burning coals symbolize cleansing. Walking across burning coals speaks to trial and testing.

Candles speak to light and the work of the Holy Spirit. Sometimes the color of a candle can speak to gifting's and call. A candlestick can also speak to the church.

Feet set ablaze speak of evangelism and taking the Word of God to the streets.

Fire in the eyes can speak to lust of the flesh and evil desire.

Fire falling speak of the fire of God falling – revival fire.

Fire in general can speak to the presence of God or His Word, but can also speak to the road to hell depending on the context.

Hands on fire speak to healing anointing and a call to heal.

Hearts on fire speaks to hunger for God, hearts set ablaze for Him.

Smoke can speak to hindrance that will soon dissipate. Smoke can also speak to a smoke screen from the enemy.

Fish and Fishing

Fish and fishing almost always speak to saving souls and the harvest. There are a few exceptions, for example a fishhook can speak to an area of one's life where the enemy has snagged them and a possible stronghold has rooted itself. Bait can speak to a trap set by the enemy.

Flying

Seeing yourself flying is often symbolic of soaring into His presence and dreaming your destiny. Flight speaks to freedom in the His Spirit and carries with it a call of passionate union with Him.

> *"So I said, "Oh, that I had wings like a dove! I would fly away and be at rest,*

- Psalms 55:6

Wings have the same connotation, but can also mean a way out of a situation is being given. It is a call to trust and seek His guidance.

> *"Keep me as the apple of Your eye; Hide me under the shadow of Your wings,"*

- Psalms 17:8

Seeing dark shadowy creatures flying speak to the enemy hovering over a situation, person, or place. This is a call to warfare and intersession.

> *'Woe to the land shadowed with buzzing wings,"*

- Isaiah 18:1

Food

Food, as a metaphor, is used throughout the Scriptures. Food in general can speak to many things in the Spirit. For example:

Bread often speaks to the bread of His presence or His body being broken for our salvation.

Bread and butter can also speak of God's provision.

Cheese can speak to a season of development in your life where the Lord is taking the curds and salting, pressing, and aging them for His purpose.

Cinnamon is symbolic of anointing and being set apart (Exodus 30:23-25).

Corn often can speak to the prophetic or having ears to hear.

Cream can speak to the richness of what God is doing in you or a group of people (cream in a sea of milk). **Cream being whipped** can speak to being filled or aerated with the Holy Spirit. **Cream being churned** into butter speaks to being anointed for service, to be spread or smeared upon the hot toast of His body, the church.

Cream of Wheat speaks to a rich and abundant harvest.

Eggs can speak to new things being birthed.

Fruit often speaks to the spiritual fruit in your life (Matthew 3:10, 7:17-19. 12:33).

Grapes speak to the community of believers, the church.

Honey or a honeycomb, often speaks to the sweetness of His words and to proclamation, the comb symbolizing a release of the prophetic, or portals of revelation being poured out upon the church.

Meat speaks to the meat of His Word (1 Corinthians 3:2).

Milk often speaks to the milk of the Word of God (1 Corinthians 3:2, Hebrews 5:12-13, 1 Peter 2:2).

Mustard speaks of faith and the power of small beginnings (Matthew 13:31-31).

Salt speaks to the Life of Christ in you and your character (Matthew 5:13).

Sugar and sweets can point to the sweetness of the Holy Spirit or telling people what they want to hear as opposed to telling the truth in love (2 Timothy 4:3).

CHAPTER 46

G

Garments and Clothing

Clothing and being dressed has powerful symbolism. Pay attention to the type of clothing or what may be out of place, for example:

A run in your stalking or tear in your dress could speak of being violated by a person or, sin, or the demonic.

Jeans with holes in them could speak to poverty and the need for provision.

Pants with no belt could mean the need forth truth in your walk.

Shoes that are too big could speak to how you see yourself in relationship to your call.

The importance of clothing type:

The type of clothing is just as important as what maybe missing. What is the state of the clothing? Are they clean or dirty, new or worn? Color is important. White cloths symbolize righteousness and salvation; dark cloths can mean demonic, bright cloths can speak to your personality, spotted can mean the need to clean up some aspic of your life. Accessories may be important as well. For example:

Apron speaks of service.

Armband speaks of allegiance.

Backpack, baggage, or luggage can symbolize carrying around to many things or worry. Luggage can also symbolize God preparing you to move or take a journey. Or may be a burden you carry from the past.

Being naked can symbolize having your life exposed, or feeling embarrassment, or loss.

Boots are often a symbol of war. Being in camouflage can symbolize being stealth in your service.

Coats and jackets can symbolize helping the needy or being comforted, covered, protected, or even a mantel of ministry.

Coattails can speak of being overly attached to a person.

Cowboy attire can mean you don't work well in a team, you are a cowboy and just rush in.

Diapers can speak to sin and the need to be changed.

Dressed in the opposite gender attire may speak to a sin in your life, gender confusion, or being attacked by the enemy.

Earmuffs can mean you don't want to hear something.

Leisure attire can speak to the need for rest.

Mask, costume, or veil can symbolize putting on a front, not being real, deception, or hiding something.

Military uniform or armor speaks of your call as a soldier of Christ and being equipped to do battle (Ephesians 6).

Pair of overalls can speak to you as an evangelist.

Robes speak of royalty and ministry mantels. The color can be significant, gold, blue, purple, or scarlet is symbolic of holiness, glory, and beauty (Exodus. 28:2).

Vest can symbolize the need for protection, and to walk in righteousness.

Wedding dress can speak to you as the bride of Christ.

Work cloths can speak to a call in your life to a people group for example a suit may be a call to the world of business.

Gems, Jewels, Jewelry

Gems, jewels, and jewelry speak great worth and value of a person to our King. They carry with it the idea of our royal inheritance in heaven. We are priests and kings in the eyes of Christ. We are pearls of great price, diamonds honed from the rock of humanity and stand at the gate of the Kingdom. Jewels speak to our true riches in heaven (1 Corinthians 3:12).

Rings speak to revival and refreshing and point to use as the Bride of Christ. Being given a ring speaks to a revelation of your identity in Christ. A specific ring with a specific gem can speak to a specific call on someone's life.

Geographic, Nations, and Cities

Seeing cities, nations, or geographic locations speak to many things including intersession for a place or people group, a call to missions or evangelism, discernment regarding atmospheric conditions of a region, life in the Spirit, or a personal state of being. Examples include the following.

Cities under siege: If you see a location and it is dark, shadowy, in ruins, or under attack, this often speaks to the spiritual condition and a call to intercede on behalf of the people living there. This is a warfare stance in prayer (Psalm 74:20).

City set on a hill: This is symbolic of being in Christ and the safety and security of His presence. Think of Cities of Refuge.

Golden City: Seeing symbols that point to the Kingdom of Heaven are often revelatory or a call to enter into His presence (Revelation 21:2).

Hustle and bustle of a city: This can speak to being overworks and overwhelmed, and God is calling you to a place of balance and rest.

Maps, Cities, Nations, and Flags: See a physical location and possibly its condition, most often speaks to pray for that part of the world and may include a call to mission life at that local.

Glory of God

Seeing the Glory of God in a dream or vision is an awe-inspiring event. When an event such as that takes place typically there are one of two reasons, either God is embracing you at a deep level to draw you in closer and imparting to you something that will greatly impact your commission in life, or you don't know Him and He is graciously wooing you to Himself. In my case I have experienced both. In book three of this series you can read about my pre-salvation encounter with the Lord Jesus Christ.

Often in visions or a trance one can be caught up to the throne of God and experience the beauty and glory of the kingdom of God. Paul, in 2 Corinthians 12:1-4, describes his own experience of being caught up to the third heaven:

> *"It is doubtless not profitable for me to boast. I will come to visions and revelations of the Lord: I know a man in Christ who fourteen years ago—whether in the body I do not know, or whether out of the body I do not know, God knows—such a one was caught up to the third heaven. And I know such a man—whether in the body or out of the body I do not know, God knows— how he was caught up into Paradise and heard inexpressible words, which it is not lawful for a man to utter."*

From a Seer's gift standpoint, often during ministry one may see the glory of God resting upon people. This activity can either be a word of knowledge calling for an action, or a discerning of the atmosphere that ushers in God's grace for healings, miracles, signs, and wonders.

We are living in a season where God is breaking through in incredible ways. It is not uncommon for individuals not only to experience the glory of God through visions, trances, dreams, and angelic visitations, but through physical signs that make you wonder, all of which are stirring the hearts of this generation to seek His face like never before. This eleventh hour outpouring is only the beginning until we see Him face to face. Press on dear saints and behold the Glory of the Lord.

Chapter 47

H-K

Hell

Experiencing visions or dreams of hell fall into one of two categories. First, it is often a call to the lost and dying in this world or to a people group. Second, it could be a gracious warning to turn to Christ, for the wages of sin is death, and the destiny of such is loss and eternal damnation (Matthew 10:28).

Homelessness

Seeing the homeless situations can range from having a call to the lost and homeless or intersession (James 1:27), to being a symbol of yours or someone else's spiritual condition. Spiritually, being homeless is a state of being lost, without a home in heaven, or a struggle with your old nature that is hindering your true identity in Christ.

Seeing a bum for example, breaking into your house can speak to your old nature (flesh) raising its head and trying to tear down your life in the battlefield of the mind. Context and the tone of compassion will tell the tail.

Hygiene

Seeing symbolism related to one's hygiene often points to a condition in one's life. Symbolism in this category include things like:

Bad breath: Pointing to possibly something you have said that is negative or introspection and self-consciousness.

Bathing or washing: Symbolic of cleansing your life of something (Exodus 30:19-21).

Flushing: Speaks to discarding something in your life, including words aimed at you that may be negative, or getting ride of an attribute or habit. John Wimber used to say, "*I always throw-out the bones when I eat chicken,*" good words to live by. Flushing can also refer to discarding wrong prophetic words in reference to creating a prophetic culture. The body should naturally flush words that miss the mark. This is a sign of a healthy and self-cleaning environment.

Using deodorant: Can symbolize covering up an offence in your life.

Intersession, Watching

Seeing yourself, others, or even angels watching over something is often symbolic of being an intercessor or a prophet, standing in the gap watching and protecting the walls of a person, ministry, community, or region (Isaiah 62:6; Jeremiah 6:17). An example of this might be seeing you standing on a hill, overlooking a valley with binoculars.

Keys

Keys are a very powerful symbol. More often than not they involve binding and loosing, as in Matthew 16:17-19 where the Lord says to Peter:

> *"Jesus answered and said to him, "Blessed are you, Simon Bar-Jonah, for flesh and blood has not revealed this to you, but My Father who is in heaven. And I also say to you that you are Peter, and on this rock I will build My church, and the gates of Hades shall not prevail against it. And I will give you the keys of the kingdom of heaven, and whatever you bind on earth will be bound in heaven, and whatever you loose on earth will be loosed in heaven."*

The context of this message is clear, the keys of heaven bind the enemy, loose the captives, and release the resources of heaven to earth. We also see Jesus holding the keys of hades and death in Revelation 1:18. The context of that passage is Christ's divine authority of all creation, life, and death. The context of your dream or vision will drive its meaning. Keys may mean the following:

Authority: To bind the enemy or loose someone from bondage (a captive or prisoner). You may see a lock on shackles or a prison door, and know it is a word of knowledge to release an individual from bondage.

Access: To a door that is locked. A locked door can mean that a.) The Lord is granting access, or b.) That he is closing the door.

Anointing: You may see golden keys falling from heaven like rain. Here the meaning is a release of fresh grace and anointing to carry out ministry and the opening of new areas of ministry.

Provision: You may see a treasure chest and keys used to unlock provision. Keys that release finance or resources are common.

Simplicity: You may have prayed for something personal like a new home or a car and God is giving you the keys to your quest. You may have simply lost your keys and in His grace He is showing you where they are.

Chapter 48

Ladders, Steps, and Stairs

Often the Lord will use symbols that point to ascension, such as a ladder, a flight of stairs, climbing, taking steps, or ascending up an escalator (modern form of a ladder). I have often seen ladders in visions ascending into Heaven. At the heart of the revelation was God's call to climb higher, to press into His presence and seek that deeper place in Him. He wants us to press in to Him, to ascend to new levels of intimacy. Often this is the meaning of ascension symbols, but not always. In Genesis 28:12-13 we read where Jacob had a dream and in his dream he saw a ladder that stretched from earth to heaven and angels were ascending and descending on it. Listen to God's revelation regarding this dream.

> *"Also your descendants shall be as the dust of the earth; you shall spread abroad to the west and the east, to the north and the south; and in you and in your seed all the families of the earth shall be blessed. Behold, I am with you and will keep you wherever you go, and will bring*

you back to this land; for I will not leave you until I have done what I have spoken to you."

- Genesis 28:14-15

God did not mention angels though it is evident they were engaged in fulfilling the declaration of the Lord regarding Jacob and the nation. His dream was about the promise of inheritance and that his decedents would be vast and cover the earth, and that God would be with him and sustain him on his journey.

Always look at context, ask yourself what activity is happening. Am I climbing or descending? The answer to that will drive the context. Summary, ladders, steps, and stairs could mean the following:

- A call to you, your church, or others to climb higher and press into the presence of the Lord

- A word regarding promotion, that God is taking you to a higher place, spiritually or in your occupation

- A word regarding progression, such as "step out" "take the next step," or "move forward."

Land, Soil, Deserts, Valleys

Seeing the condition of land or some aspect of a landscape can be extremely powerful. Landscapes include deserts, valleys, mountains, remote areas, fields, sands and soils. They can speak to dryness, fruitfulness, kingdom glory, or strongholds. Obviously the context points to its meaning. Here are a few examples:

Cold remote areas: Seeing regions that are cold and remote can symbolize feelings of being isolated and alone.

Islands: These can symbolize rest, isolation, or a temporary season of growth and development.

Fields: Fields typically speak to your sphere of influence and what God is or desire to do in your realm. Fields. Fields point to harvest. Conditions of a field usually have attached to them the solution to that condition. Of course Jesus used the field to illustrate the heart of men and seeds sown in that heart (Matthew 13:31, seeds of faith; 13:38, 13:44, seeds of the enemy; seeds of salivation). Jesus also used the field as a symbol of the world (Matthew 13:36). Plowing a field can point to harvest or plowing the hard places of your heart, breaking up the follow ground.

Hills: Hills often speak of victory, triumph, or progression. Victory and progression call for the spirit of praise and thanksgiving (Psalm 98:8). Green hills speak to the fertilization of Christ's presence in your life and on your journey and walk with Him (Psalm 104:10-13).

Mountain (singular): Can speak to the mountain cut without hands (Daniel 2:45), our Savior and King, Jesus Christ. The mountain of the Lord is mighty and draws us into His presence (Exodus 19:18). The mountain of the Lord speaks not only of our desire to see Him and be with Him, but also speaks to our inheritance in Him as priests and kings of the Lord of Glory (Exodus 15:17). A mountain can also speak to a principality, problem, illness, or obstacle ready to be overtaken through faith and anointing in Christ (Mark 11:23; Psalm 125:1).

Pastures: Speak to the place of comfort, training, and nourishment to your soul. We are the sheep of His pasture, the sheep of His hand (Psalm 79:13, 95:7). We enter His gates and courts with praise and thanksgiving (Psalm 100:3).

Sands: Sands can speak to several things such as a house built on sand (pour foundation). Footprints in the sand (Jesus carrying you through a tough situation). Sands of time (speaking to the hour in which we live or your focus during this hour). Sands can speak to promise and generational blessing as in the case of Abraham. Quicksand can speak to a trap or snare of the enemy.

Tropical locations: Seeing peaceful tropical locations speak to a call to rest and relaxation.

Valley: Are often symbolic of low points in your life or a season of warfare where the Lord is pointing you to rest in the midst of battle (i.e. preparing a table for you in the presence of your enemy Psalm 23).

Wilderness: This includes deserts, dry, remote, or desolate places and often symbolizes a dry season in your life. Often this is a place of training and development. This can also speak to isolation in someone's life.

Light, Electricity, Lightning

Seeing light, lightening, lamps, lasers, and electricity, or the contrasts between light and darkness, can be very powerful, and often carry the message of power, illumination, or enlightenment. Here are a few examples:

Darkness: Darkness including gray scenes, and shadowy places speaks to warfare and the power of Christ to overcome. It can include the word of promise of intercession.

Flashlights or Search Lights: This category of lighting refers to finding one's way in the dark or illuminating a safe harbor for those lost in the dark (Psalm 18:28). It can also symbolize the study of His Word (Psalm 119:105).

Lamps, Lanterns, & Light Bulbs: This category is much like the previous, but may also carry the idea of God's protection and an increase in His anointing (Psalm 132:17). Lamps also speak to your walk with Christ and being filled with the Holy Spirit (Matthew 5:15, 6:22; Luke 11:33).

Lasers: Lasers, like the latter, speak to the power of His Word and the power of proclamation. Lasers cut away and pierce throw the impossible with pointed accuracy.

Light, Highlights, & Illumination: Seeing light, highlights, or illumination on people is often a gift of discerning what God is doing to or about to do on someone. This can come through the gift or prophecy or a word of knowledge. Often the colors associated with light can point to a call or activity that God is doing. Of course Jesus is the light of the world and His presence illuminates our lives and our path. The Holy Spirit will illuminate us with revelation and knowledge in Him.

Lightning & Electricity: Symbolizes the power of the Holy Spirit for renewal, healing, etc. The rain of God coming with power and glory that shakes a region. Lightning also speaks to proclamation and the prophetic (Job 37:3). Impartation of gifting and release of the Holy Spirit can also be symbolized through seeing an electrical current or lightening.

Light Shows: Lightshows in the heavens such as aurora speak to the glory and majesty of Him who sits upon the throne. See the chapter on Aurora in part one.

Chapter 49

M

Medical, Sickness, Healing

Visionary symbols involving sickness are often literal words of knowledge regarding something the Lord want's to heal. Remember what the Lord reveals, He heals. There are two exceptions to this. The first typically takes place in a dream and is symbolic of something in your personal life, either emotional or spiritual. The second is a word of knowledge regarding another person that is metaphorical, a vision that points to a spiritual or emotional condition. Examples include:

Band Aids: Speaks to covering up a wound or hurt in your life that is temporary or hiding and the Lord desires to uncover it and bring real healing to the situation.

Broken Bones: Often broken bones can be symbolic of having a broken place in your life. A broken arm can speak to powerlessness. A broken rib can speak to a broken relationship. A broken foot can speak to something in your life that is affecting your walk with Christ. A broken hip can speak to trial and wrestling with God. A broken finger can symbolize accusation or something spoken that is judgmental.

Bruises: Often speaks to emotional trauma or something from you're past that needs of healing.

Coma: This can speak of depression or spiritual stupor. It may involve spiritual warfare or demonic oppression.

Chocking: This can speak to a spiritual attack or something trying to cut off your voice. This can also speak to an inability to listen, something that is hard to swallow.

Scars: Often speaks to past hurts or curses in one's life and points to a need for healing.

Surgery: Usually points to a work the Holy Spirit is doing in someone's life.

Metal

Seeing metal can be symbolic of an attribute or insight into something. For example, bronze can speak to the strength of the Lord, while Iron on the other hand speaks to the strength of men. Gold speaks to the glory of God and His kingdom or the richness of His ministry in your life.

Fool's gold speaks to a lie or false religion or doctrine. Silver speaks to redemption, or the purity of a ministry and Christ in your life, or the power of His Word. Tin, speaks to worthlessness, cheapness, or something of little value in the kingdom.

Mirrors, Pictures

Looking in a mirror can speak to reflection, identity, self-image, vanity, or a memory of the past. Self-identity is powerful and can launch you into your future or hinder your destiny with false identity. A healthy identity sees one's self in Christ and seated at the right hand of Holy royalty, subservient to the King and His glorious Kingdom.

A poor identity can be linked to past wounds, poor self-esteem, or believing the lies of the enemy. God's desire for you is that of sonship and royalty. You have been bought for a price and have been grafted into the heavenly family. The most cross life is a life of victory and love. It is a life of access and He has opened the windows of heaven over you.

Pictures can speak to your past or to a person in need of prayers and intersession. If God shows you a portrait of yourself and it is glorious he is calling forth your identity in Him and wants you to see how He sees you. If you see a picture of yourself that is distorted, this is symbolic of a poor self-image. Pictures of people can also be a word of knowledge that God is giving you regarding someone.

Music and Worship

David made this proclamation:

> *"Praise the Lord with the harp; Make melody to Him with an instrument of ten strings. Sing to Him a new song; Play skillfully with a shout of joy. For the word of the Lord is right, and all His work is done in truth. He loves righteousness and justice; the earth is full of the goodness of the Lord."*
>
> - Psalm 33:2-5

Experiencing music and worship in a dream or vision often speaks to joy, celebration, thanksgiving, victory, and breakthrough.

Worldly music, on the other hand, can point to being in a situation or atmosphere that is unhealthy or a bad environment. Individual instruments or melodies can speak to a worship or prophetic call. Here are a few examples:

Bell: Bells often speak to a call to missions or to power evangelism. A mission bell is a good example of this.

Flutes: A flute can speak to your walk with God. The melody can speak to a wooing, a loving call to follow.

Stringed Instruments: Melodies on stringed instruments such as a guitar can be a call to the ministry of worship. This can include prophetic proclamation through song.

Trumpets and Horns: Carry a sense of urgency, a call to attention, or a call to proclaim a prophetic word from the Lord. Many times the Lord will alter the focus or direction of a ministry or person, giving a declarative call to do something. Horns also speak to power and strength in Christ. Trumpets can speak to a call to warfare or taking a warfare stance.

Melodies: Depending on the song can speak to the Holy Spirit or Christ's tender embrace and a healing work of love He is doing in your life.

CHAPTER 50

N

Numbers

Numbers, like colors, often carry meaning. The Scriptures are full of numeric patterns that speak to various truths. Numbers can be literal, but also carry a meaning that is personally significant to you. E.W. Bullinger in his classic work "Numbers in Scripture" (first published in 1894) writes on this topic extensively. Here are a few examples:

One: the number one represents unity, oneness, and God (Deuteronomy 6:4).

Two: Is the symbol of witness (Mark 6:7), testimony (Matthew 18:19), unity (Matthew 19:5), or choice (as in choose between two – Matthew 6:24).

Three: Speaks to the Godhead, Father, Son, and Holy Spirit. It can also represent completeness, fullness, or perfection (Ephesians 3:19, 4:13; Colossians 2:9).

Four: Speaks to things created Genesis 1:14-19), established boundaries, or realms of authority (4 seasons; 4 regions of the earth – north, south, east, and west; 4 corners; 4 sides; a cube being 4 x 4; 4 elements – earth, air, fire, and water). Four living creatures surround His throne (Revelation 4:6-8). The bride of Christ symbolized as the New Jerusalem is symbolized as a square or cube coming out of heaven (Revelation 21:9-21).

Five: Is symbolic of favor, blessing, and grace. The five smooth stones of David, speak of God's grace to defeat Goliath. This is also seen in Leviticus 26:8 where five will chase a hundred. Five also speaks to the hand of God, as in the last two examples. Other examples of five speaking to grace include anointing oil which had have parts (Exodus 30:23-25) and incense, representing the prayers of the saints, was made of five parts (Exodus 30:34). The Hebrew word for "gift" appears five times in the Old Testament. The Greek word "Parakleetos" translated "comforter" (speaking of the Holy Spirit) appears five times in the New Testament (4 in John – 14:16, 26, 15:26, 16:7 and once in 1 John 2:1). There are five office gifts of Christ listed in Ephesians 4:7-16.

Six: Is symbolic of man or humanity. Man was created on the sixth day (Genesis 1:31). Six also speaks to human labor or the work of one's hands (Exodus 6:22). Six can also symbolizes man's imperfection and lost dominion. The sixth commandment relates to the worst sin – murder. Six can symbolize false accusation – Christ was accused of having a demon six times in the gospels (Mark 3:22; John 7:20; 8:48, 52; 10:20; Luke 11:15). This act confirms man's enmity with the person of Jesus Christ. In the book of Nehemiah we see six-fold opposition to the work of God (2:10; 2:19; 4:1-4, 7, 8; 6:1, 2, 7, 9-14). Words that appear only six times in scripture include: destruction (Hebrew: avaddohn), yoke (Hebrew: moht), shame (Greek: aischunee), to change (Greek: allatte), ungodliness (Greek: asebeia), or abomination (Greek: bdelugma). The first miracle in the book of John was changing water to wine in six earthen vessels, speaking to the healing and redemption of man and filling the earthly vessel with the Spirit of the living God (John 2).

Seven: In scripture seven is symbolic of spiritual perfection or completion. In Isaiah 11:2 we see the seven Spirits of God marking Christ. In Joel 2:28, 29, we see the Holy Spirit poured out on seven people groups. The golden candlestick had six branches and one steam making seven points of light. The armor of God in Ephesians 6:14-18 consists of seven parts, the latter being prayer. In Hebrew, the root word for seven is "savah" meaning to be full or satisfied, to have enough of. Of course, on the seventh day of creation God rested, giving us the Sabbath.

Abraham receive a seven-fold blessing from God in Genesis 7:2, 3. In Judges 6, there are seven attributes listed as qualifications for service. Jesus preformed seven miracles in the book of John. He spoke seven words to the woman of Samaria. During His life on earth He had seven appearances of angels. Of course there are seven letters to seven churches in the book of Revelation. We also see seven seals and seven trumpets. In Matthew 13 Jesus gave seven parables. There are seven "gifts" in Romans 7, "unities" in Ephesians 4, "characteristics of wisdom" in James 3, "gifts of Christ" in John's gospel, "better things" in Hebrews, "titles of Christ" in Hebrews. Clean beasts were taken into the ark by sevens. Finely, the mystery of God is completed in the seventh vial of the seventh trumpet of the seventh seal in the book of Revelation. The number seven is stamped throughout the scripture.

Eight: The number eight in Hebrew is the word "Sh'moneh" from the root "Shah'meyn" meaning to "to make fat", "cover with fat", "to super-abound". It carries the meaning of a "superabundant" life or "fertile". Eight is also the number of "new beginnings". It is the number of resurrection and regeneration.

Other than the Lord and the saints there are eight resurrection in scriptures (3 in the Old Testament, 3 in the Gospels, 2 in the book of Acts). The feast of Tabernacles lasted 8 days (John 1:14). The transfiguration of Jesus took place on the 8th day. There are 8 songs in the Old Testament outside the Psalms. Elijah preformed 8 miracles in Kings. Elisha preformed double that number (14). There are 8 references to the Old Testament in Revelation 1.

In my own life 8 symbolizes "new beginnings." My daughter was born at 8:08 in 88. Every time I see the number 808 I am reminded of His complete control to fulfill all of His promises and dreams in my life. It is established like bookends (808). When I see 818, the Lord speaks to my heart about being one step closer and His continued hand on my life.

Nine: The number nine in Scripture is the number of judgment. There were 27 sieges of Jerusalem (3 x 9), 3 symbolizing God's completeness, and 9 being the number of judgment. The judgments of God in Haggai contain 9 components (Haggai 1:11). Words that occur 9 times in the New Testament include: bottomless pit, or deep; ungodly, lasciviousness, and lightning. From a redemptive standpoint, there are 9 gifts of the Holy Spirit in 1 Corinthians 12:8-10. These gifts are given to produce life and bring redemption, a model of the churches role in judging: under the New Convenient we bless and curse not!

Ten: This is the number of completeness and represents law and divine order, or nations. It can also represent God's portion, i.e. tithe. We see completeness in Noah as being the 10th generation from Adam; the 10 commandments; the tithe; the 10 plagues of Egypt in Exodus; the 10 worldly kingdoms of antichrist; the 10 nations of Genesis 15:19; the ten trials of Abraham's faith; and the 10 rebellions of Israel in the wilderness (Numbers 14:22).

Ten times in the Old Testament fire fell from heaven, six of which were judgments. We also see shouts of Joy mentioned ten times in the Old Testament. We have the parable of the ten virgins. Ten times the phrase, "I have sinned" mentioned in scripture. There are ten parables of the kingdom in the gospel of Matthew. Ten times Jesus uses the phrase "I AM" in the book of John, pointing to the voice in the burning bush, "tell them I AM has sent you" and for this they tried to stone Him.

Eleven: This number is marked by disorder, disorganization, or imperfection. This is seen in the 11 sons of Jacob and the lives of Jehoiakim and Zedekiah who both reigned for 11 years. Of course we have the phrase "11th hour" in Matthew 20: 6, 9, speaking to the time of the end and an accounting of one's work and wages.

Twelve: This number symbolizes Divine government as seen in the 12 tribes of Israel; the 12 Apostles; and the 24 elders before the throne in the book of Revelation (12 x 2). We also see 12 foundations in the heavenly Jerusalem with 12 gates, 12 pearls, and 12 angels. Its measurement was 12,000 furlongs square (144 or 12 x 12 cubits). 12 people were anointed in the Old Testament. Jesus was 12 years old when He first appeared in public. 12 legions of angels are mentioned in Matthew 26:53. The day is divided into 2 – 12 hour parts (night 12 hours, day 12 hours). There are 12 months in a year.

Numeric perfection

Numeric perfection is everywhere. We not only see it in scripture but also in the mater created by the author of scripture, God. In his 1894 in his Christian classic "Numbers in Scripture," E. W. Bullinger points out some fascinating facts. Consider nature, with numeric stamps marked throughout. Take the rows of kernel-corn on a cob of Indian corn. Wither straight or spiral they are always arranged in even numbers, never odd.

When we look at the leaves on a plant we notice that they always grow in a spiral and as they spiral, after a certain number of leaves, one leaf will always line up with the first leaf, creating a numeric pattern. In the case of the apple it lines up at the fifth leaf; the oak is the forth, the peach is the sixth; and the holly it is the eighth, and in the case of the holly, it takes two turns before lining up.

This numeric pattern is woven into to everything. In physiology, there are seven divisions of age: Infancy, childhood, youth, adolescence, manhood, decline, and senility. We also see this numeric thumb print of the Holy Spirit on the development of life. Consider gestation periods, which are often marked by the number seven, wither days or weeks. The mouse is 21 days (3 x 7), hare and rat is 28 days (4 x 7), cat is 56 days (8 x 7), dog is 63 days (9 x 7), lion is 98 days (14 x 7), sheep is 147 days (21 x 7), a hen is 21 days (3 x 7), a duck is 28 days (4 x 7) and the human is 280 days (40 x 7).

This numeric perfection extends to every created being as well. Take the bee for example. The number 3 marks the bee. In 3 days the egg is hatched. It is fed for 9 days and reaches maturity in 15 days. The worker bee reaches maturity in 21 days and it works for 3 days after leaving its cell. The bee is composed of three parts, the head and two stomachs. The eyes are made up of 3,000 small eyes. The bee has 6 legs composed of three parts. The foot has 3 sections and the antennae consist of nine sections. Is this by chance? I don't think so. It is the beauty of design by an incredibly loving creator.

In music and sound we see the same perfection as seen in the seven notes or tones in a music scale. Light, or electromagnetic radiation, is classified into eight classes, seven not visible and one visible to the human eye:

- Gamma radiation
- X-ray radiation
- Ultraviolet radiation
- Visible radiation (Color)
- Infrared radiation
- Terahertz radiation
- Microwave radiation
- Radio waves

The visible spectrum of light (color), according to Newton, consists of seven primary colors, as seen in the color spectrum of a rainbow or in the breaking of white light through a prism. Color (vibration of light) and sound (vibration of air) both are divided into two groups: three primary and four secondary, from which all others proceed.

For the purpose of this section of the book regarding numeric symbolism, it is very clear that the Lord uses numeric symbols when speaking to us through the language of visions and dreams.

There are many other examples of numeric symbolism in scripture than those listed. Here are a few more with brief explanations.

Twenty Four: an elder in the Church or elderly wisdom (Revelation 4:10)

Forty: judgment (Genesis 7:4); wilderness experience or a season of wondering (Exodus 16:35, Deuteronomy 2:7, Joshua 5:6); season of rest (Judges 3:11. 5:31, 8:28); or a time of warfare perpetration (Matthew 4:2).

Fifty: Grace, Jubilee or free from debt (Leviticus 25:10)

Seventy: Elders (Exodus 24:9); A full life (Psalm 23:15); Season of judgment or set seasonal framework (Jeremiah 25:11-12; Daniel 9:24); Grace as seen in forgiveness (Matthew 18:22). Being sent or ministry expansion (Luke 10:1-2).

Eighty: Extended grace (Psalm 90:10)

One Hundred: Blessings and the fruit of ministry or one's life (Mark 4:8).

One Hundred Fifty Three: Revival and great harvest (John 21:11).

Six Hundred Sixty Six: End times and the beast, the man of sin, the antichrist (666).

CHAPTER 51

O-P

Occult and Witchcraft

Any symbolism involving the occult speaks to demonic activity and influences. This includes tarot cards, palm reading, Ouija boards, fortune telling, witchcraft, zodiac signs, séances, etc. If an animal, person, or supernatural being manifests it and speaks to you and the essence of the dialog relates to a spirit guide, this is demonic. Often a demon will pose as guide, and even can come at times as a relative.

The scripture is very clear in this matter (Deuteronomy 18:10; Leviticus 20:6; 2 Kings 9:22; Acts 16:16; Ezekiel 21:21). If you are harassed by the demonic, resist the devil and he will flee. Seek spirit-filled counsel and prayer. If you have been involved in the occult repentance and reconciliation is essential.

Oil

Oil most always symbolizes an outpouring of the Holy Spirit, renewal, or anointing including not just anointing for service but also healing. Oil often is seen as golden but may well include crude black oil speaking to the heritage of the saints and release of rich blessing that fuels and energizes the body of Christ.

Oil may appear in many types of vessels including lamps, buckets, falling as in rain, or bubbling up like crude from the ground. The vessel and quantity of oil may have meaning as well. Is God pouring out the oil? Are you personally carrying a lamp with oil? Are you anointing someone with oil? Each of these will carry their tone of meaning. Context will determine what God is saying. See Matthew 25:1-10, Psalm 23:5, 45:7.

Plant Life

Plants speak of life, wither vibrant and growing or withered, dry and dying. Plants are dependent; they need three things to grow and thrive: water, sunlight, and healthy soil. The energy of the sun transforms air (carbon dioxide) into sugar. We call this photosynthesis. Water brings life and structure to the plants, and soil imparts nutrients for healthy cell function.

Symbolically, this is pretty evident, we have the life changing power and radiant light of the Son of God transforming the very air we breathe, giving us the Holy Spirit like wind from heaven, and pouring in us living water, that we may thrive and grow into His image and nature. He transforms the very soil of our hearts so that we can draw upon the nutrients of heaven. Without basting in His presence and being watered by His Word, we wither. Without good soil (Matthew 13:8) the Word cannot take root and growth, life and fruitfulness is hindered.

All plants have some type of root system. Visually seeing a root system most always points to a symptom of something. Jesus explained this very clearly in the parable of the sower.

> *"Then He spoke many things to them in parables, saying: 'Behold, a sower went out to sow. And as he sowed, some seed fell by the wayside; and the birds came and devoured them. Some fell on stony places, where they did not have much earth; and they immediately sprang up because they had no depth of earth. But when the sun was up they were scorched, and because they had no root they withered away. And some fell among thorns, and the thorns sprang up and choked them. But others fell on good ground and yielded a crop: some a hundredfold, some sixty, some thirty. He who has ears to hear, let him hear.'"*
>
> - Matthew 13:3-9

He goes on to explain the meaning in verses 18 to 23:

> *"Therefore hear the parable of the sower: When anyone hears the word of the kingdom, and does not understand it, then the wicked one comes and snatches away what was sown in his heart. This is he who received seed by the wayside. But he who received the seed on stony places, this is he who hears the word and immediately receives it with joy; yet he has no root in himself, but endures only for a while. For when tribulation or persecution arises because of the word, immediately he stumbles. Now he who received seed among the thorns is he who hears the word, and the cares of this world and the deceitfulness of riches choke the word, and he becomes unfruitful. But he who received seed on the good ground is he who hears the word and understands it, who indeed bears fruit and produces: some a hundredfold, some sixty, some thirty."*

Root systems are powerful. They point to things that hinder us in our walk with Christ. We see roots of bitterness (Hebrews 12:5), roots of lust or greed (1 Timothy 6:10), roots of rebellion (Isaiah 5:24), roots of promise (Isaiah 37:31), or roots of inheritance and blessing (Romans 11:16-18; 15:12). When God shows us a root system, it is often a word of knowledge pointing to His desire to heal an area of one's life. Sometimes that means laying an ax to the root of the tree or uprooting something in the heart or mind. Sometimes healing comes through saturating our hearts with living water by soaking in His presence.

Plant symbolism takes many forms and not only includes the plant type and its condition, but also may include the landscape, scene, season, or action (i.e. farming, planting, surveying, and watering). Here are a few examples of plants and their meaning (for symbolism relating to fruit – see fruit; trees – see trees).

Flowers: Flowers speak to love, harmony, and fruitfulness. They call out the glory of what God is doing or bringing forth in one's life. They carry the aroma of Heaven and draw people into His presence.

Gardens: Gardens speak to the work of God in your life relating to your walk, mind, or ministry. A garden is about fertility and expansion. Gardens are kept and pruned by the master gardener, the Holy Spirit.

Grass: Speaks to green pastures, comfort, and grazing. Grass carries in it peace and tranquility, or being called to a place of rest.

Herbs: Speak to the love gifts of the Father, those natural gifting He pours into the life of all people. They are not only fragrant but also edible and are used to round out the make-up of a person or group. When one honors the gifting of the Father in one's life it spawns wholeness to the individual and the culture.

Leaves: Speak to growth, transition, or change. Green leaves blowing in the wind can speak to a season of growth in the Holy Spirit. Autumn leaves speak of transition between the seasons of your life. Withered leaves speak to dry areas of one's life and the need for living water.

Lily Pads: The water lily speaks to navigation, or how to navigate the waters of life in Christ. As a water plant, their source of life comes from the water. Typically you will see lily pads scattered across a pound or stream like steppingstones.

Reeds: Reeds or water-grass speak to wading in the presence of God. They speak to the understanding of your metron and line the boundaries of your life. Reeds gain their life substance from the river and thrive at the water's edge.

Seeds: Speak to planting and birthing. Seed in the Greek is "sperma," meaning that which is sown. It is the germ of life. It speaks to heritage, linage, family, offspring, or ministry. Sometimes it speaks residue or remnant, that which is left, and out of a few many shall grow. Seeds can also speak to faith and promise.

Sprouts or Shoots: Sprouts speak to that which is shooting forth, growth, springing up or budding. This is an action word pointing to something that springs up or is brought forth. Sprouts also speak to the "newness" of something, its tenderness and fragility. Sprouts need care to become strong.

Thorns: A thorn bush speaks to danger either in life-style choices or actions.

> *"By their fruit you will recognize them. Do people pick grapes from thorn bushes, or figs from thistles?"*
>
> – Matthew 7:16.

They gave Jesus a crown of thorns. Jesus spoke of seed sown amongst thorns (Matthew 13:7).

Vines: A vine is symbolic of Christ and His church. A vine can also speak of a person's life or their relationship to the church. A grape vine or vineyard speaks to the fruit of God's grace upon His people, the nectar of heaven released into the earth.

Weeds: Weeds speak of falsehood or lies. They grow up to choke out the truth. They hinder the growth of harvest. Weeds can also speak to the lost or the sons of the evil one. At the end of the ages the reapers will gather the weeds and cast them into the fire. Thorns and weeds often grow together. Weeds take over the fruit of labor and choke out provision.

Chapter 52

Q-R

Roads, Trails & Potholes

Roads, trails, or paths often speak to our walk with Christ in this life. Sometimes the road involves a decision we have to make, other times it points to our progress or regress. Are their obstacles in the road? Is the road straight and smooth or rugged, rocky, and full of potholes? Is the path progressing down a hill or up a mountain? Can you see the distance or is there a bind up ahead? Life choices often are symbolized on a road. If it is bumpy and hard it could symbolize a rough season in life. If it is smooth it may be highlighting God's favor upon your life and walk.

Pay attention to the condition of the road or the way the road engages the landscape. Things like roadside signage, bridges, tunnels, rocks, potholes, fallen trees, and such each carry a meaning. God may be igniting hope or faith in your life or He may be bringing a warning or showing you a change in direction.

Rocks, Walls

A rock in general is symbolic of Christ and can speak of Christ as your refuge and strength. At the same time a rock can speak to the condition or your heart i.e. a stony heart. Context will always tell the story. Stony walls on the other hand speak of an obstacle. If a stone wall is incomplete or falling down it could speak of something that needs to be rebuilt or it might point to rebuilding the defenses in your life and putting on the full armor of God.

Walls are interesting. On the one hand they can symbolize a boundary embossed by God, or a hindrance put up by the enemy, such as barbed wire. God also puts up a hedge of protection around us; we can see this as an actual hedge or a wall as in a fortress. Hiding behind a wall can mean finding protection, being in a state of fear, or being bound by a past hurt.

Royalty

God so desires you to understand your place in the kingdom. As a child of God you are of the royal line of heaven. You are kings and priests of the Lord. Having a healthy understanding of your identity in Christ produce fruit and a mindset that is able to flow with His Spirit in your life and ministry. Peter tells us in 1 Peter 2:9, 10 that,

> *"... You are a chosen generation, a royal priesthood, a holy nation, His own special people, that you may proclaim the praises of Him who called you out of darkness into His marvelous light; who once were not a people but are now the people of God, who had not obtained mercy but now have obtained mercy."*

Symbolisms of royalty include crowns, scepters, the throne room, signet rings, a staff, a royal garment, or being a prince in a kingdom. Embrace you position in Christ and move out as an ambassador of heaven.

Running

Running in a dream can symbolize a few things. If you are running in a race it speak to your walk of ministry in Christ and God is encouraging you to press on and run the race as if to win (Philippians 2:16). He longs for you to obtain the victor's crown and cheers you on, pointing you into the way to go. Jogging can speak to a healthy pace in your walk with Christ.

Running away from something speaks to fear and being chased by the enemy or by a stumbling block. Supernatural running like outrunning a car or motorcycle speaks to divine acceleration and progression in your ministry life. God is showing you your progression and success and is encouraging you press on in His power and might.

Chapter 53

S

Seas, Lakes, Rivers, and Streams

There is probably no other symbol greater in scripture regarding the grace, peace, and presence of Christ and the Holy Spirit than rivers, streams, waterfalls, fountains, and water. We see the power of the river symbol in Ezekiel's famous vision in chapter 47 verses 1-12, where the river of God flows out of the temple in all directions, and on its banks grow fruit whose leaves bring healing.

> *"Then he brought me back to the door of the temple; and there was water, flowing from under the threshold of the temple toward the east, for the front of the temple faced east; the water was flowing from under the right side of the temple, south of the altar. He brought me out by way of the north gate, and led me around on the outside to the outer gateway that faces east; and there was water, running out on the right side.*
>
> *And when the man went out to the east with the line in his hand, he measured one thousand cubits, and he brought me through the waters; the water came up to my ankles. Again he measured one thousand and brought me through the waters; the*

> water came up to my knees. Again he measured one thousand and brought me through; the water came up to my waist. Again he measured one thousand, and it was a river that I could not cross; for the water was too deep, water in which one must swim, a river that could not be crossed. He said to me, "Son of man, have you seen this?" Then he brought me and returned me to the bank of the river.
>
> When I returned, there, along the bank of the river, were very many trees on one side and the other. Then he said to me: "This water flows toward the eastern region, goes down into the valley, and enters the sea. When it reaches the sea, its waters are healed. And it shall be that every living thing that moves, wherever the rivers go, will live. There will be a very great multitude of fish, because these waters go there; for they will be healed, and everything will live wherever the river goes. It shall be that fishermen will stand by it from En Gedi to En Eglaim; they will be places for spreading their nets. Their fish will be of the same kinds as the fish of the Great Sea, exceedingly many. But its swamps and marshes will not be healed; they will be given over to salt. Along the bank of the river, on this side and that, will grow all kinds of trees used for food; their leaves will not wither, and their fruit will not fail. They will bear fruit every month, because their water flows from the sanctuary. Their fruit will be for food, and their leaves for medicine."

Zechariah tells us that on the day Christ returns, His feet will land on the Mount of Olives and split it from east to west and out of the mouth of that split will flow a river of living-water. John sees the river of the water of life in Revelation 22, and like Ezekiel, the leaves of the fruit trees bring healing to the nations. Jeremiah refers to God as the fountain of living water. Jesus said:

> *"If you knew the gift of God and who it is that asks you for a drink, you would have asked him and he would have given you living water.*
>
> *Sir, the woman said, you have nothing to draw with and the well is deep. Where can you get this living water? Are you greater than our father Jacob, who gave us the well and drank from it himself, as did also his sons and his livestock?*
>
> *Jesus answered, Everyone who drinks this water will be thirsty again, but whoever drinks the water I give them will never thirst. Indeed, the water I give them will become in them a spring of water welling up to eternal life."*
>
> - John 4:10-14

And again:

> *"On the last and greatest day of the festival, Jesus stood and said in a loud voice, let anyone who is thirsty come to me and drink. Whoever believes in me, as Scripture has said, rivers of living water will flow from within them."*
>
> - John 7:37, 38

The mood, tone, scene, and action, taking place while seeing rivers, streams, waterfalls, and such help determine the voice of Christ. If the river is raging it may speak to turmoil blocking your ability to press into Him. If a river is full of life and you can see fish swimming about it speaks to abundance and revival. If you are peering into the water and you see it bubbling it is symbolic of the prophetic and wisdom being released. If you find yourself stepping into the water and you are moving from shallow to deep, it is symbolic of your progressing and God's call to bring you deeper in Him.

Oceans are often symbolic of the nations. Calming stormy seas is symbolic of intersession. Seeing Christ calming the seas is symbolic for His deep love for the nations or for you. A tidal wave can be symbolic of revival coming or it may be impending disaster. If you are in a boat on the ocean it can refer to your life, walk, or ministry in Christ.

Seasons

Seasons almost always symbolize times, epochs, periods, stages, or chapters in your life or the life of the church or people group. In the ancient times of the Hebrew people, seasons spoke of and centered on the harvest. The very lives of the people, as an agrarian society, were dependent upon the harvest. In life we move through periods that reflect the nature of the seasons. There is a time for everything under the sun and seasons speak to those times. Here are a few examples:

> *"And it shall be that if you earnestly obey My commandments which I command you today, to love the Lord your God and serve Him with all your heart and with all your soul, then I will give you the rain for your land in its season, the early rain and the latter rain, that you may gather in your grain, your new wine, and your oil. And I will send grass in your fields for your livestock that you may eat and be filled."*
>
> - Deuteronomy 11:13-15

> *"Preach the word! Be ready in season and out of season."*
>
> - 2 Timothy 4:2

Autumn: Speaks of transition, the end of a season, completion, change, harvest, reflection, rejoicing, or time of preparation.

Spring: Speaks to the newness of life, ne beginnings, life, harvest, renewal, refreshing, regeneration and salvation.

Summer: Speaks to opportunity, trial, community, fellowship, vacation, service, heat of affliction, or preparation.

Winter: Speaks to rest, tranquility, going deeper in Christ, strength, heritage, remembering the accomplishments of God in your life, dormant, or waiting on God.

Sight, Eyes, and Lens

Symbols relating to your ability to see most always speak to your ability to see as God sees or from His perspective. For example, if you are wearing glasses, God is giving you wisdom to see clearly and go deeper. If your lenses are colored it could mean that you are filtering what you are seeing and God is calling you to look from a different perspective. If you lens are dirty there is something hindering you from seeing clearly. This could be sin or a belief system. Likewise, windows carry the same meaning a lens.

If you are blindfolded it is symbolic of having a blockage to see the truth. If you are blind, it is symbolic of the need for salvation or repentance that you may see and know the truth, Christ Jesus.

If you see your eyes, God is showing you that you have the eyes of a Seer. Wide eyes mean He is expanding your ability to see. Binoculars speak to seeing beyond you current situation, gaining understanding or being prophetic.

Signs, Banners, and Billboards

Signs, banners, and billboards always carry a message God is trying to get across to you. Here are a few examples and their possible meaning:

Banners: Almost always speak to victory in your life and God's favor over you. Banners are a call to celebrate.

Billboards: Are important messages to get your attention. They are large and typically on the side of the road speaking to the direction you are heading.

Bumper Stickers: Speak to a belief or life message that is important to you in your life.

Direction Signs: Speak to point you in the right direction. They are markers to guide you. Street signs speak to the same thing.

Exit Sign: Speaks to a way out of a situation.

Hazard Sign: Is a warning to be cautious and avert an upcoming hazard.

Mile Markers: Speak to progression and your growth in your life.

Stop Signs: Are symbolic to stop, reflect, look in all directions, and only proceed when you have the right of way or a green light from the Lord.

Yield Sign: Is symbolic of submitting to authority or your need to be humble.

Sounds

Sounds often have meaning in dreams or visions. They can symbolize warnings, proclamations, messages, or worship. Here are a few examples:

Amplifier: Is symbolic of a message going out and the call to speak and proclaim.

Barking: Is symbolic of a spiritual enemy coming against you trying to intimidate you.

Chatter: Is symbolic of the cares of a people group and the call to intersession. On the negative side, it could symbolize confusion and a call to be still and listen in a season of rest.

Crying: Is symbolic of the crying of a people and God calling you to act on their behalf.

Echo: Is symbolic of the sound of salvation going across the land, His word not returning void.

Music: The call to worship and go deep into the love of Christ.

Sirens and Alarms: Are symbolic of warning, a call to be alert or awaken to do something.

Soft Stringed Instrument: A call to rest in the love of God or to soak in His presence.

Trumpets: The call to proclaim a message from the Lord, to herald, or gather the people of God.

Whispers: Hearing the secret thing of Christ or on the negative side, gossip.

Space

Symbolism relating to things in space such as planets, stars, and space speak to the glory of God and His bigness. He uses symbols like this to call you into your destiny. He is pointing to things bigger than yourself. He is expanding your vision and giving you promise. Seeing the sun points to Christ and His power and burning love for you.

Speaking

Symbolism relating to speech speak either to the conduct of your actions or the call to speak and proclaim. Belching or burping speaks to wrong things coming out of your mouth. A bridle speaks to the same thing but also speaks to a lack of self-control. Biting someone is symbolic of strife or fighting with someone.

On the other hand, speaking through a microphone is a call to proclaim to a people group. Whistling speaks to calling someone to Christ or to come along side in support. Speaking in a foreign language is a call to a people group or speaking so that others understand what you are saying.

Sports & Games

Sports and games are powerful symbolic language of God, the former speaking to position and destiny, the later speaking to strategies for victory. In sports related symbols the position you play is just as important as the game itself. In games it's all about making the right move. Most often the thrust of sport symbolism is a call to participate and win. Sport metaphors are loaded with promise and hope for your future. They reach out and call you to get with the program and take it to the finish line. Games are solo; sports are about your importance on the team. Here are a few examples:

Baseball: It's the ninth inning, bases are loaded, and you're up at bat. It's not too late for you. You were made for this hour. The team is depending on you and it's your time, you are not too old to get back in the game. It's not too late. If you step up and swing... the team wins. Now is your time. Seize the day and take your place in His story. Think "the Natural", or "Field of Dreams." Are you on the bench or in the game?

Basketball: All sports are about teamwork, but I think basketball illustrates the beauty of teamwork and precision like no other. There is finesse in basketball. In basketball, everyone has to learn to dribble, shoot, and maneuver. Without the team fully engaged there is no win. The big question is: Are you a team player, fully equipped to take the shot at any given moment?

Cards: Many people live their lives from a position of stagnancy. They view their situation as if they were stuck and must live their life with the cards they were dealt, not knowing that God can win with any hand. When we walk through life with the eyes of faith we believe in destiny. We dream the impossible and those impossible dreams become our future.

Cheerleading: Cheerleading is all about the gift of encouragement. Like Barnabas was to Paul, this gift lifts up those around them with a voice of victory. Their ministry is that of enablement. They are partners in ministry holding up the right hand and the left. They are like the cloud of witnesses that cheer on the saints to victory.

Chess: Chess is a game of strategy. Seeing yourself playing chess is God's promise to give you clarity and wisdom in dealing with a situation. He wants to show you how to navigate your steps in such a way as if to win.

Football: Football is about taking ground across enemy lines and brings the ball to the end zone. Football is warfare. George Carlen said it well: "In football the object is for the quarterback, also known as the field general, to be on target with his aerial assault, riddling the defense by hitting his receivers with deadly accuracy in spite of the blitz, even if he has to use shotgun. With short bullet passes and long bombs, he marches his troops into enemy territory, balancing this aerial assault with a sustained ground attack that punches holes in the forward wall of the enemy's defensive line. In baseball the object is to go home! And to be safe!, I hope I'll be safe at home!"

The metaphor is obvious, the question is: Are you in the game? God is a God of promise and destiny and He speaks to draw you into the game. He wants to throw you the long bomb. He wants you to run, block, kick, and fight your way into the enemy lines and win. What position are you playing?

Gambling: In Christ there is no gamble. Seeing yourself gambling points to things in your life that erode your faith. In essence you are gambling with your future. God's desire for you is to hear the voice of heaven and to run the race through faith. Life in Christ is not a game of chance.

Gymnastics, Ballet: When I think of gymnastics and ballet I think of beauty and grace comingled with strength. I call this symbolism the dance of the Bride where the grace of God shines forth in power and beauty. This is a picture of the end times Bride in all her glory.

Hiking & Rock Climbing: This type of symbolism is about staying the course. It is about ascension and God is calling you to press onward and upward and to obtain the high calling of your Lord.

Hockey: When I think of hockey I usually think of a goalkeeper. He is the one guy on the ice that is constantly under assault. He is protecting the goal and stopping the other team from scoring. He is the prayer warrior – the intercessor, the watchmen on the wall, determined, no matter the cost, to stop the opposing team from scoring.

Locker room: Seeing yourself or someone else waiting in a locker room speaks to release in to ministry or a work God has called you to. This could be pregame preparation or half-time encouragement. In either case it is a call to get ready and prepare to fulfill your calling.

Monopoly: The game of Monopoly speaks to growth and expansion where God is giving you the gift of favor and expanding your sphere of influence. Monopoly is about taking territory and increasing your footprint in life.

Track: Track is a game of endurance. Paul speaks of running in a race four times in the New Testament and in each case he is using the symbolism of a race to encourage the saints to press on and run the race of faith as if to win (Acts 20:24; 1 Corinthians 9:24; 2 Timothy 4:7; Hebrews 4:7). The key elements are to run with endurance, to finish the course, and to win.

Stage, Platforms

Seeing a stage, platform, auditorium, audience, curtain call, or podium points to preparation for the next season in your life. God is setting the stage and getting ready to release you into a new area of ministry. He is orchestrating things in such a way to release you into new measures of favor. When the stage is set and you hear the curtain call, it's time to enter into your destiny and calling in the Lord.

CHAPTER 54

T-Z

Tickets

Tickets are interesting symbols. There are so many types of tickets: Winning tickets, "two tickets to paradise" (Eddie Money), "Ticket to Ride" (the Beatles), Golden ticket (Charlie and the Chocolate Factory), speeding ticket, tickets of admission, ticket book, and so on. Like always, context will tell the tale. The following demonstrate the possible meaning of various tickets:

Golden Ticket: Financial provision. God is restoring all the years the locusts have eaten and bringing you to a place of prosperity.

Tickets to paradise and ticket books: If you see yourself handing out free tickets this can often mean the gift of evangelism, and God if give you anointed grace to give the free gift of salvation to the lost.

Ticket to ride and tickets of admission: This is all about transition and destiny. A ticket to access a train, for example, may mean the God is opening doors and taking you into a new place in Him or new areas of ministry. If the destiny is to a specific location, say, "China," the Lord is opening doors for work or intersession for that nation. A ticket to ride a Farris wheel, for example, can mean God is calling you to relaxation and life balance. If wants you to enjoy the ride with Him, and learn to live with Joy in your heart.

Tickets of warning: If you receive a ticket from a police officer for a traffic violation this is a godly warning regarding your walk with Him. You are violating His will in some aspect of your life. A speeding ticket is a call to slow down and access your direction. Running a stop sign can mean that you're doing something and God wants you to stop. Failing to yield in traffic could be attitudinal, and God is calling you to love and yield to your neighbor, to be cognizant of your fellow man and give precedence to others before yourself. In all cases there is a call to change, either your heart or direction.

Winning tickets: At the heart of a winning ticket is the fulfillment of a dream, it carries the weight of surprise. Dreams, visions, quests that may appear to have dissipated, and the Lord is saying, "You win, this dream is for you." Winning tickets can also me prayers of provision answered. God cares about your provisional needs.

Time

Symbolism involving time include calendars, clocks, hour-glass, seasons, sunsets, sunrise, high noon, and night. Each speaking to change, wither it's in the current season or its pointing to the next season of your life. God is always on time. He is never late and is always calling us to that next level in our walk with Him. Sometimes we are under time constraints.

Other times God is setting up a divine appointment and is using this symbolism to point the way. In either case, time is on our side and God is the one who opens and no man can shut and who closes, and no man can open. Sometimes He is restoring hope and reminding you of your destiny in Him. Remember, in Christ, it is always your time.

Tools

> *"Therefore whoever hears these sayings of Mine, and does them, I will liken him to a wise man who built his house on the rock: and the rain descended, the floods came, and the winds blew and beat on that house; and it did not fall, for it was founded on the rock.*
>
> *But everyone who hears these sayings of Mine, and does not do them, will be like a foolish man who built his house on the sand: and the rain descended, the floods came, and the winds blew and beat on that house; and it fell. And great was its fall."*
>
> *- Matthew 7:24-28*

Scenes involving tools or construction are very interesting.

Tools are used to fix or repair something and secondly, to build or construct something. The Holy Spirit is so vested in your life and destiny in Christ that He is constantly working to hone your life into the image of Christ. This honing process involves not just your character, but your mind, will, and emotions. He is vested in renewing the whole person, body, soul, and spirit of a person. The symbolism of tools (various kinds) can point to this type of work in your life, for example:

Ax: An ax is used to clear a path, to create fuel for fire (wood), or to chip away at a root system. The cutting way of brush or trees can speak to expansion of your territory or clearing a path in the direction the Lord is taking you. Chopping wood speaks to being filled with the Holy Spirit and gathering the fuel needed to sustain you in your life. An ax laid to the root of a tree speaks to areas of healing and removing negative root systems in your life. Many times situations, sins, and mindsets of our past can create a root system. Unless the ax is laid to the root of that tree, a stronghold in that area of our lives will drive us. The ax becomes a sozo moment where the Holy Spirit moves us in the process of setting us free from bondage or ways of thinking.

Chisel: A chisel is symbolic of one of two things. The first is that of chipping away as in sculpting or carving. This is the process of transformation and being conformed into the image of Christ. The second is engraving, where God is chiseling His word for you into your heart. This can be a life mission or a truth of scripture embedded in your spirit.

Hammer: Jeremiah (23:29) compares the Word of God to a hammer. A hammer has the power to construct areas in our life together. This nailing together is symbolized in the nailing of Himself to the cross. It is here, in that place, that all of our sins have been covered and dealt with. When you see, for example, a carpenter securing the framework of a house to a foundation, this may refer to God building your core belief system with the power and truth of His word. Kingdom infrastructure is what will sustain you in your life-walk with Christ.

Monkey Wrench: Seeing imagery such as a leaky faucet being repaired may point areas in your life that are stopping the flow of the Holy Spirit and the need to be refreshed or filled. This can be a call to rest or it may point to areas of a lack of trust. When we get tired or worn we loose our ability to function in the Spirit. We constantly need the sweet presence of the Lord to fill us, and to rest in His nature and love for us. Dependency on Him and in Him will keep the water flowing.

Plane: Scenes such as a carpenter planning a piece of wood often speaks to striping away an area of your life. This is about preparation. God is smoothing out the surface of your life and preparing you for the next level.

Saw: Saws speak to a cutting away of something. This again is construction. The care and vestment of the carpenter creates the measure of a man. There is an old carpenter saying, Measure twice – cut once. God is in the business of constructing you. He is all about precision.

Transportation

Vehicles such as bikes, cars, trucks, boats, planes, and trains often speak of your ministry. The vehicle type can, at times, speak to the size, scope, or condition of your ministry. The Holy Spirit is very creative in this regard. I remember the Lord showing me farmers ridding wave-runners on the ocean. They were in formation riding the wave of His presence. I was struck by the parallelism of the wave runners to the fore runners of evangelism (i.e. John the Baptist).

This generation of believers was revivalists bringing the power of the Spirit to a new generation and ushering in renewal as they road the wave of His presence. This was a harvest move in the power of the Holy Spirit.

Other areas of transportation involve the condition of the vehicle or how the vehicle is stored. Here are a few examples.

Car Crash: This is symbolic of a warning regarding your walk in ministry. This can also refer to something that hurt you in this regard. Did you hit someone due to driving too fast? If so, it's time to slow down and regain your bearings. Where you rear-ended? If so, this can be as a result of warfare or being hurt by someone.

Cracked Windshield: A cracked windshield also speaks to impaired vision, however, often this refers to something that hurt you in your past and the residue of that wound is hindering how you view thing. Like seeing through rose-colored glasses your vision is filtered and God wants to bring healing to that area of your life.

Flat Tire: Symbolic of being stuck or the inability to get where you are trying to go. A flat tire is a tire with a leak. All the air that enabled it to move is gone. Air is symbolic of the Holy Spirit and the loss of air speaks to the need to be filled and refreshed.

Garage or Carport: Seeing a car parked in a garage or under a carport speaks two one of two things: 1. Covering – this symbolizes the order of the kingdom and the power of being in the right relationship in the body and under authority. 2. Rest and being hidden in Christ – this symbolizes a season of rest and rejuvenation where God hides you in the palm of His hand and uses this season to speak life under the safety and shelter of His wings. This is a season of reflection and honoring who God is for you, to remember all the wondrous things He has done. It is a time of strengthening your inner man to run the next leg of the race.

Out of Gas: Running out of gas is symbolic of running out of energy and the need to be refreshed and filled with the Holy Spirit. This is a call to rest. A balanced life and continuous filling of the Holy Spirit is the only thing that will sustain your ministry.

Stolen Vehicle: Experiencing a robbery where your vehicle is stolen or someone is trying to take it from you symbolizes an act of warfare where the enemy of your soul is trying to rob you of your destiny. This is a demonic assault to stop you from attaining all that God has giving to you. God uses this symbolism to awaken you to a warfare stance and to stand firm and use your authority in Christ to rebuke the enemy and press in.

Vehicle Fishtailing: Fishtailing is symbolic of being out of control or feeling out of control.

Vehicle Restoration: Seeing a vehicle being restored or seeing a restored antique car can speak to two things:

1. Revitalized call late in life. When the promises of God seem to tarry and you find yourself thinking of dreams that have never been fulfilled, God is igniting dreams from your past and calling you into your destiny. He is restoring the years the locusts have eaten and bringing your life mission or dream to reality. Remember you are never too old to dream and walk in your destiny.

2. Restoration of a past anointing or an incomplete work from the past. The ministry of the past is our heritage and they become our floor so we can take it to the next level.

Windshield Wipers: Dirty windows or a windshield that is being hammered by rain speaks to an inability to see clearly. This can be a result of an issue in your life or the result of warfare being waged against you. Wipers washing away the debris speak to the Holy Spirit bringing clarity of vision and guiding you in the midst of the storm.

Trees

Trees are amazing. The Lord's use of trees as symbols of His Word a will are so abundant it's mind-boggling. Genesis opens with the story of two trees: the "tree of life" and the "tree of the knowledge of good and evil." The book of Revelation closes with the "tree of life" as an emblem of the joys of the celestial paradise. Moses was drawn to his destiny by seeing the manifestation of God's presence in a burning Acacia tree that was not consumed.

Peter refers to Christ on the cross as "who Himself bore our sins in His own body on the tree, that we, having died to sins, might live for righteousness—by whose stripes you were healed (1 Peter 2:24; see Acts 5:30, 10:39, 13:29)."

Of course Jesus utilizes trees as a metaphor throughout the gospels. We see the character of man defined by a tree and it's fruit:

> "Even so, every good tree bears good fruit, but a bad tree bears bad fruit. A good tree cannot bear bad fruit, nor can a bad tree bear good fruit. Every tree that does not bear good fruit is cut down and thrown into the fire. Therefore by their fruits you will know them."
>
> - Matthew 7:17-20

The Kingdom of Heaven and its influence upon the planet is described as a tree:

> "The kingdom of heaven is like a mustard seed, which a man took and sowed in his field, which indeed is the least of all the seeds; but when it is grown it is greater than the herbs and becomes a tree, so that the birds of the air come and nest in its branches
>
> - Matthew 13:31-32

The fruit of Israel is re-erred to as a withering fig tree (Matthew 21:18-21). The timetable of Christ's return is hidden in the parable of the fig tree (Matthew 24:32).

Paul uses the symbol of a wild olive tree to explain how gentile believers were grafted into the body of Christ. Jesus, himself is referred to as the Branch (Isaiah 11:1, Zechariah 3:6-8). In John 15, Jesus referred to us as branches and He as the vine, when speaking about our necessity to abide in Him. We also see in Zechariah 4, two "olive trees" flowing with the oil of anointing continually to the lampstand (His body the Church). Finely, David refers to God's children as "Trees of the Lord" Psalm 104:16, a fruitful tree in Psalm 1:3, a "green olive tree" Psalm 52:8, and a "palm tree" in Psalm 92:12.

The Lord has used trees to speak to me in so many ways it's amazing. In a dream He called me to the high place of His presence as I watched myself scaling a might pine tree. I saw the wind of the Spirit blowing between the leaves of a weeping willow during a season of transition. I heard the Lord speak of healing as I watched the bark of a birch tree peel away exposing the white inner wood. I saw the angels of God standing at attention as mighty red woods I ascended to the top of a mountain. I watched creation groan for the revealing of the Sons of God as I saw trees weeping tears of sap. Trees are powerful in the language of God. Let's look at a few trees and their possible meaning.

Acacia Tree: There are a number of acacia trees mentioned in the scripture, the most notable being Moses's burning bush. A common variety of acacia is the thorny acacia tree. This was probably the tree that Moses saw. It's interesting to note that some scholars believe that the crown of thorns that was placed on the head of Jesus was made from the thorny acacia.

Many of the articles in the tabernacle were made of acacia wood. Acacia wood was also used to make incense (henna). Seeing a thorny acacia tree may point to worship and redemption, pointing you to praise Him and His redemptive work in your life.

Almond Tree: Almond trees are often a symbol of God's promise to perform His word (Jeremiah 1:11, Genesis 43:11). They can also speak to anointing and confirmation as in Aaron's rod. Sometimes it can mean watchfulness and to be awake (Jeremiah 1:12). Other times it may refer to your place in the body and His anointing over your life as in the Candlestick of Exodus 25:31-39.

Apple Tree: Apple trees often speak of God's love for you (Psalm 17:8) or the love of a married couple (Song of Solomon 2:5, 7:8). It's interesting the David's "*Apple of the Eye*" latterly means the "Gate of the Eye" which may speak to a release of the prophetic and the seer's gift (Zechariah 2:8).

Bark: Bark can speak of several things. First, it can symbolize the flesh and a striping away of those things that are not pleasing to the Lord. Secondly, it may symbolize strength as in the shield of faith that protects your spiritual vital organs.

Branch: Speaks to abiding in Christ and your place in the body or network of believers.

Eucalyptus Tree: As a native Californian Eucalyptus trees were a major part of the landscape in my life. Whenever I travel back to California I am drawn into memories of my childhood sparked by the aroma and beauty of these smooth majestic trees. One of the byproducts of this tree is its oil, steam distilled to create sweets, cough drops, decongestants, and toothpaste. Seeing this tree may peak to the promise of healing or the fragrance of His life in you to touch others and bring refreshing and healing to others.

Fig Tree: The fig tree is the third tree mentioned by name in the Bible, after the Tree of the knowledge of good and evil, and the Tree of Life. In Deuteronomy, the Promised Land is describe as,

> "*A land of wheat and barley, of vines and fig trees and pomegranates, a land of olive oil and honey; a land in which you will eat bread without scarcity, in which you will lack nothing; a land whose stones are iron and out of whose hills you can dig copper*"

- Deuteronomy 8:8-10

Proverbs uses the tending of the fig tree as a symbol of caring of the Master's needs (Proverbs 27:18). Ironically, the fig is the only tree pollinated by the wasp speaking to the reward obtained after seasons of struggle and adversity. The fruit is sweet, rich, and costly. Its aroma is inescapable.

As a child I lived next to a fig orchard surrounded by eucalyptus trees and the combined aroma was amazing. When figs are ripe the skin often bursts weeping out sweet nectar. Seeing figs speaks to rich fruitfulness in your life and the favor and blessings of God upon your life. The fig is a sign of honor and your place in the Kingdom (Proverbs 27:18).

Forest: Seeing a forest often speaks to the nations or navigation the public sphere. If the focus is on a trail in the woods it may symbolize a current season in your life and point to navigation during this time of walking with God. Seeing a forest fire can symbolize trouble or calamity coming upon the nations. Seeing a forest ranger symbolizes the Holy Spirit as the helper in times of need.

Log: Logs can symbolize a couple things. If the context is gathering firewood, then the meaning may point to the need to refuel with the in filling of the Holy Spirit in seasons of isolation. If a log is being plucked from a fire this points to the glory of redemption and the saving grace of Christ. If the log is stripped down and transformed into usable wood for construction, this symbolizes the work of God in your life to transform you into His image.

Oak Tree: Oaks often speak to strength but more specifically your ability to endure and persevere during extreme seasons in your life (Isaiah 6:3; Ezekiel 6:13).

Olive Tree: Olive trees are wonderful. They often speak to the endless supply of the anointing oil of God (Zechariah 4). The also speak to the fruitfulness in your life and symbolize your union with Christ in the Kingdom of God (Romans 11:17). An olive tree may also symbolize end times evangelism and power in the Holy Spirit (Revelation 11:4). A green olive tree speaks to a prosperous Christian (Psalm 52:8).

Palm Tree: A palm tree is symbolic of the peace of Christ in your life (Song of Solomon 7:8), or prosperity and blessing in your life (Psalm 92:12; Exodus 15:27). They can also symbolize worship and honor of Christ the King (John 12:13; Revelation 7:9).

Pine Trees: I love pine trees. The evergreen aroma calls me to press in to the wonders of God. Their tall majestic nature adorns mountainous regions around the world. Pine trees are strong and armored with thick scaly bark. Their buds shoot out at the tips and their fruit (the pine cone) produces both male and female cones. The seeds of the pine are small and flavorful (pine nuts and pesto).

However, the seeds are only released when a bird breaks open the cone with its beak. However, some cones may release their seeds on their own, but only after a number of years. Pine trees grow in acidic soil and, like us, need fire to regenerate. This is symbolic of the fire of the Holy Spirit. Their leaves are needle like, strong, and piercing. Their aroma can transform the atmosphere of a room (potpourri). Pine trees point to Christ's birth as seen in the living room of every Christian at Christmas. Pines speak to you in your full strength and destiny in the Lord. They call out to you and point to your potential. Pine trees are an invention to climb higher and speak to the power of endurance and legacy. Pines speak to the glory of God in your life.

Sap: Sap is the lifeblood of all plants. The water-based fluid brings nutrients from the root system to all extremities. Seeing trees weeping sap can symbolize many things from the blood of Christ to the tears of creation calling all Saints to fulfill their destiny. Psalm 104:16 proclaim, *"The trees of the Lord are full of sap...."* The fullness speaks to the life-blood of our Savior and calls for the abundance of His saving grace.

Stump: Seeing a stump speaks of judgment (Daniel 4:15-26), but with the judgment is the promise of redemption. In Nebuchadnezzar's pride, judgment was pronounced, but only for a season. After repentance is sanity returned and freedom was realized. Job 14:8,

> *"Though its root may grow old in the earth, and its stump may die in the ground, yet at the scent of water it will bud and bring forth branches like a plant."*

Repentance always brings forth life; sin on the other hand brings forth death.

Sycamore: Seeing a sycamore tree typically speaks to being called out for service by the Lord. The prophet Amos said, *"I was no prophet, nor was I a son of a prophet, but I was a sheep breeder and a tender of sycamore fruit. Then the Lord took me as I followed the flock, and the Lord said to me, go, prophesy to My people Israel."* The most famous story of one being called out is Zacchaeus in the book of Luke. In this story Zacchaeus is so eager to see Jesus that he climbs a sycamore tree to get a better view. When Jesus saw him He said, (Luke 19:5)

> *"Zacchaeus, make haste and come down, for today I must stay at your house."*

With eagerness and joy he came down from that tree and went to Jesus and offered to give half his goods to the poor. Jesus response was (Luke 19:8),

> *"Today salvation has come to this house, because he also is a son of Abraham; 10 for the Son of Man has come to seek and to save that which was lost."*

The symbol of the sycamore can either be a call to salvation or a call to witness to the lost or to the prophetic ministry.

Weeping Willow: Weeping willows speak of a season of sorrow and the promise of hope and comfort. The promise of God found in Psalms 23:4-5 is this,

"Yea, though I walk through the valley of the shadow of death, I will fear no evil; for You are with me; Your rod and Your staff, they comfort me. You prepare a table before me in the presence of my enemies; You anoint my head with oil; My cup runs over."

BIBLIOGRAPHY

Doug Addison, Prophecy, Dreams, and Evangelism, 2005, Streams Books, 1st Ed.

James W. and Michal Goll,

> Dream Language, 2006, Destiny Image Publishing, 1st Ed.
>
> Angelic Encounters, 2007, Strang Communications/Chrisma House, 1st Ed.

John Crowder, The New Mystics, 2006, Destiny Image, 1st Ed.

Jim Driscoll, The Modern Seer, 2010, Orbital Book Group, 1st Ed.

Gary Oates, Open My eyes Lord, 2008, Open Heaven Publications, 1st Ed.

John Wimber, Keven Springer, Power Healing, 1987, Harper Collins, 1st Ed.

Kris Vallotton, Developing a Supernatural Lifestyle, 2007, Destiny Image, 1st Ed.

Jonathan Welton, The School of the Seer, 2009, Destiny Image, 1st Ed.

Dennis Cramer, Breaking Curses, 1997, Arrow Publications, 1st Ed.

Bill Johnson,

> Release the Power of Jesus, 2009, Destiny Image, 1st Ed.
>
> When Heaven Invades Earth, 2003, Treasure House, 1st Ed.

Randy Clark, Ministry Training Manual, 2004, Global Awakening, 1st Ed.

Dr. Bill Hamon, Apostles, Prophets, and the Coming Moves of God, 1997, Destiny Image, 1st Ed.

Graham Cooke, Approaching the Heart of Prophecy, 2009, Brilliant Books, 1st Ed.; Developing Your Prophetic Gifting, 1994, Chosen Books, 1st Ed.

Randy Clark, Ministry Training Manual, 2004, Global Awakening, 1st Ed.

About the Author

From Chef to Author... Fred L. Raynaud, a third generation restaurateur and founder of the Culinary Executive Leadership Institute—CELI, now writes to inspire and makes his home in Anna Maria, Florida, with his amazing wife Jan. Learn more at www.fredraynaud.us

www.ingramcontent.com/pod-product-compliance
Lightning Source LLC
Chambersburg PA
CBHW070745230426
43665CB00017B/2258